We Care

A Curriculum for
Preschool Through Kindergarten

Bertie Kingore & Glenda Higbee

 GOOD YEAR BOOKS

Dedication

Wonderful husband and friend who encouraged us to be all we can be;

Enthusiastic daughter and sons who knew we could do it.

Caring parents who nurtured us as children and adults;

All the teachers and children at the schools and centers who participated in the field testing;

Rewarding feelings that result from creating;

Educators of young children everywhere who honor children as the promise of a fulfilling future.

The following people have contributed to the development of this product:
Art & Design: M. Jane Heelan
Editorial: Constance Shrier, Monica Glina
Illustrator: Chris Knowles
Manufacturing: Mark Cirillo, Thomas Dunne
Production: Karen Edmonds, Jennifer Murphy
Publishing Operations: Carolyn Coyle

ISBN: 978-1-59647-300-3
Printed in the United States of America

TABLE OF CONTENTS

Preface   vii

Introduction   vii
   The Authors' Educational Philosophy   vii
   Features of the Units   viii
   Activities Using Unit Topic Pictures   ix
   Planning the Sequence for Using the Units   x
   Connecting the Topics: Alphabet Time   xi
   Literacy Learning Goals and Content
      for Pre-K and Kindergarten   xii
   High-Frequency Words   xiii
   Creating a Word Wall   xiv
   Nursery Rhymes   xiv
   Mathematics Learning Goals and Content
      for Pre-K and Kindergarten   xv
   A Calendar for Communication and
      Organization   xv
   Portfolios for Young Children   xvi
   References   xviii

September Curriculum   1

Marvelous Me   **2**
   Concepts   2
   Continuing Concepts   2
   Portfolio Products   2
   Art   3
   Blocks   5
   Bulletin Board   6
   Cooking   6
   Language Arts   7
   Math   10
   Movement   11
   Music   12
   Role Play   12
   Science   13
   Transition Activity   13
   Children's Books   13
   Teacher Resource Book   14

Our Families and Where We Live   **15**
   Concepts   15
   Continuing Concepts   15
   Portfolio Products   16
   Art   16
   Blocks   19
   Bulletin Board   19

   Cooking   19
   Language Arts   20
   Math   22
   Movement   24
   Music   25
   Role Play   26
   Science   26
   Transition Activity   27
   Children's Books   27

October Curriculum   29

Fall Changes   **30**
   Concepts   30
   Continuing Concepts   30
   Portfolio Products   30
   Art   31
   Blocks   33
   Bulletin Board   33
   Cooking   34
   Language Arts   34
   Math   36
   Movement   38
   Music   38
   Role Play   39
   Science   39
   Transition Activity   40
   Children's Books   40
   "The Riddle of the Star"   41

Hands and Feet   **43**
   Concepts   43
   Continuing Concepts   43
   Portfolio Products   43
   Art   43
   Blocks   46
   Bulletin Board   46
   Cooking   46
   Language Arts   47
   Math   50
   Movement   51
   Music   52
   Role Play   53
   Science   53
   Transition Activity   54
   Children's Books   54

November Curriculum   55

Tools and Simple Machines   **56**

Concepts	56
Continuing Concepts	56
Portfolio Products	56
Background Information	57
Art	57
Blocks	59
Bulletin Board	60
Cooking	60
Language Arts	61
Math	63
Movement	64
Music	65
Role Play	66
Science	67
Transition Activities	68
Children's Books	68

Thanksgiving and Life in Early America   **70**

Concepts	70
Continuing Concepts	70
Portfolio Products	71
Background Information	71
Art	71
Blocks	72
Bulletin Board	73
Cooking	73
Language Arts	74
Math	79
Movement	80
Music	81
Role Play	82
Science	82
Transition Activities	83
Children's Books	83

December Curriculum   85

Toys   **86**

Concepts	86
Continuing Concepts	86
Portfolio Products	86
Art	87
Blocks	88
Bulletin Board	88
Cooking	89

Language Arts	89
Math	93
Movement	94
Music	95
Role Play	95
Science	96
Transition Activity	96
Children's Books	97

Holiday Season   **98**

Concepts	98
Continuing Concepts	98
Portfolio Products	98
Art	99
Blocks	102
Bulletin Board	102
Cooking	103
Language Arts	104
Math	106
Movement	107
Music	108
Role Play	108
Science	109
Transition Activity	109
Children's Books	110

January Curriculum   111

Life in Winter   **112**

Concepts	112
Continuing Concepts	112
Portfolio Products	112
Art	113
Blocks	115
Bulletin Board	115
Cooking	116
Language Arts	116
Math	119
Movement	120
Music	121
Role Play	121
Science	122
Transition Activity	123
Children's Books	123

Imaginary Friends and Monsters   **125**

Concepts	125
Continuing Concepts	125
Portfolio Products	125

Art	126
Blocks	127
Bulletin Board	128
Cooking	128
Language Arts	129
Math	132
Movement	133
Music	134
Role Play	135
Science	136
Transition Activities	136
Children's Books	137

February Curriculum 139

Valentines and Friendship 140
Concepts	140
Continuing Concepts	140
Portfolio Products	140
Art	141
Blocks	143
Bulletin Board	143
Cooking	144
Language Arts	145
Math	148
Movement	149
Music	150
Role Play	150
Science	151
Transition Activity	152
Children's Books	152

Dinosaurs 153
Concepts	153
Continuing Concepts	153
Portfolio Products	153
Art	154
Blocks	155
Bulletin Board	155
Cooking	156
Language Arts	157
Math	161
Movement	162
Music	163
Role Play	164
Science	164
Transition Activity	165
Children's Books	165

March Curriculum 167

The Animal Kingdom 168
Concepts	168
Continuing Concepts	168
Portfolio Products	168
Background Information	168
Art	169
Blocks	171
Bulletin Board	171
Cooking	172
Language Arts	173
Math	176
Movement	178
Music	178
Role Play	179
Science	179
Transition Activities	180
Children's Books	180

Birds—Real and Imaginary 182
Concepts	182
Continuing Concepts	182
Portfolio Products	182
Art	183
Blocks	185
Bulletin Board	185
Cooking	186
Language Arts	187
Math	190
Movement	192
Music	193
Role Play	193
Science	194
Transition Activity	195
Children's Books	195

April Curriculum 197

Spring and Growing Things 198
Concepts	198
Continuing Concepts	198
Portfolio Products	198
Art	199
Blocks	202
Bulletin Board	202
Cooking	202
Language Arts	203
Math	206

Movement	207
Music	207
Role Play	208
Science	208
Transition Activities	210
Children's Books	210

Insects and Spiders **212**

Concepts	212
Continuing Concepts	212
Portfolio Products	212
Art	213
Blocks	215
Bulletin Board	215
Cooking	216
Language Arts	216
Math	220
Movement	221
Music	222
Role Play	223
Science	223
Transition Activity	225
Children's Books	225

May Curriculum 227

People Work **228**

Concepts	228
Continuing Concepts	228
Portfolio Products	228
Art	229
Blocks	231
Bulletin Board	231
Cooking	231
Language Arts	232
Math	235
Movement	237
Music	238
Role Play	238
Science	239
Transition Activity	240
Children's Books	240

Water and Rainbows **241**

Concepts	241
Continuing Concepts	241
Portfolio Products	241
Art	242
Blocks	244

Bulletin Board	244
Cooking	245
Language Arts	246
Math	249
Movement	250
Music	251
Role Play	252
Science	252
Transition Activity	254
Children's Books	254

June Curriculum 255

Summertime and the Sun **256**

Concepts	256
Continuing Concepts	256
Portfolio Products	256
Art	257
Blocks	259
Bulletin Board	259
Cooking	260
Language Arts	261
Math	264
Movement	266
Music	266
Role Play	267
Science	267
Transition Activities	268
Children's Books	269

Appendices 270

I Free, Inexpensive, or Simple-to-Make Teaching Aids	270
II Art Recipes and Concoctions	273
III Activity Masters	277

PREFACE

Why We Care

Parents trust us to care for and nurture a most cherished part of themselves — their children. They know that children of preschool and kindergarten age are capable of more than mere playtime and naptime. Children three through six can learn a great deal and begin to function in group situations. This book is dedicated to helping teachers create a delightful learning environment for all preschool through kindergarten children.

We Care provides a well-balanced curriculum in an easy-to-follow organizational format. Written in a simple, clear style, the text allows teachers to readily use the hundreds of ideas and activities within the book.

All of the fingerplays and songs are adaptations created by the authors. You are encouraged to adapt these and other traditional fingerplays and songs to meet the unique needs of the children in your class.

We encourage teachers to be creative. Modify the activities to add your personal touch. In your hands, this book can be a means of enriching each child's educational opportunities.

INTRODUCTION

The Authors' Educational Philosophy

All activities and instructional ideas are based on the following assumptions.

All children are capable of learning and are equally valuable.

We assume that all children have the potential to learn more than we thought possible in the past. This assumption requires us to realistically expand our expectations and establish rich learning environments that promote and extend children's learning. The goal is not to push children faster but to provide a nurturing and stimulating environment and the guidance of an educator who responds to children's leads and needs.

Since children differ in their background opportunities and experiences, they demonstrate different needs, interests, and levels of readiness. But these differences do not make one child more or less important than another. By nature of being human, every child has the same high value.

Process is often as important as the product.

For young children, the ultimate value of an activity lies in the experience of doing the activity rather than in just the quality of the end product.

Children learn through active involvement and mental engagement.

Young children need to have their bodies and minds actively involved in learning experiences. They benefit from experiences and activities that allow them to experiment and discover on their own. They need open-ended learning tasks that encourage them to unravel real problems and construct their own meaning. We should encourage children to proceed at their level of readiness and avoid doing for them anything that they can do for themselves. As much as possible, we should allow children to do their own drawing, cutting, experimenting, buttoning, cleaning, and so forth.

Developing creative and productive thinking is paramount.

The end result of an activity should not be a group of products that all look the same or a set of ideas that all sound the same. Ask children, "What else could you do?, What could you change?" and "How can you make yours different?" The question "What do you think?" may be as important as "What do you know?" Accordingly, prompts that encourage children's language development and higher-order thinking are incorporated in most activities.

The majority of the activities in the Art section of each unit are creative experiences that invite children to experiment and explore. Other experiences involving typical arts and crafts activities, such as cutting and pasting, do not encourage the creativity of children, but are considered to be skill developers. Many children enjoy arts and crafts activities, but such activities should be presented in addition to, not instead of, creative experiences.

Valuable learning experiences can be repeated.

Children benefit from doing some high-quality activities more than once. Repeating these activities allows children to gain experience and expertise. An activity demonstrated by the teacher can be continued later by pairs or small groups of children working independently and then placed in a center.

We also suggest that you use some books in more than one unit. These books have connections to multiple topics. Do not hesitate to reread them, as children love hearing familiar books read more than once.

All activities and learning experiences are opportunities to help children develop responsibility.

Consider arranging supplies, such as paper, scissors, and pencils so that children can get their materials as needed without relying on an adult. Collecting supplies requires children to independently count the number of items needed and permits them to stay more actively involved. Involving children in preparation also limits waiting time and reduces the potential for behavioral problems.

Clean-up should also be planned and organized so that children can do it themselves. Prevent unnecessary messes by having children cover work areas. Regularly ask them to check the floor around their work area, pick up scraps, and put them in the wastebasket. When appropriate, have available a small tub or bucket with two or three inches of water, a small amount of soap, and sponges cut in half so little hands can manage them effectively. Some children enjoy clean-up time as much as they enjoy the original activity!

Activities do not have to be expensive.

A myriad of activities can be done using free or inexpensive materials. The equipment and materials needed to implement the *We Care* curriculum are minimal because we recognize that excellent facilities can and frequently do operate on limited budgets.

Planning should be thorough but flexible.

Your plans need to be specific and clearly formulated, but they must be flexible in implementation. Good teachers are sensitive to the needs of individual children and flexible enough to take advantage of learning opportunities that develop unexpectedly.

Planning evolves from the needs of children.

Curriculum plans for children evolve from the concepts teachers need to teach, the experiences they want children to have, and the overall objectives for children of a specific age. However, planning is always done with the needs of individual children in mind as well.

A teacher's avocation is to encourage and facilitate learning.

A teacher is a powerful influence and encourager. A teacher has the power to facilitate the learning of each child.

Features of the Units

We Care consists of nineteen units that are each based on a main topic, such as the animal kingdom. There are one or two topical units for each month of the school year, from September through June. The following features are incorporated within each unit to enhance learning opportunities for young children.

• With young children, several concepts require continual revisiting rather than a one-time only presentation. Accordingly, concepts related to color, geometric shapes, health, the senses, and traditional rhymes and tales are integrated into every unit. Specific connections to the topic are described for each of these concepts in Continuing Concepts and developed throughout the unit.

Many specific ideas are offered to help you develop children's awareness of their senses. Of course, reading fiction and non-fiction books to children and playing recorded music to provide soft background sound as they complete activities are two excellent methods you can use frequently to stimulate children's senses.

• Activities and teaching ideas that relate to the unit topic are described for the following curriculum areas: art, block play, cooking, language arts, math, movement, music, role play, and science.

• One or more bulletin board ideas appropriate to the topic are described in each unit. Each bulletin board serves as an interactive learning task that stimulates rich discussions, provides challenging problem-solving opportunities, and promotes skill development.

• One or more transition activities are included at the end of each unit. These transition activities can be used to help children remain positively focused when moving from one activity to another. They are designed so that a few children may be involved initially and additional children may join in as they finish a previous task.

• Multiple ideas and activities are easily adaptable to large groups, small groups, individual instruction, or centers.

• An annotated bibliography of recommended books that relate to the topic is included at the end of each unit. Some of the books are classic favorites, while others are newer publications you can use to expand your instructional choices. Annotations can help you select books that serve the needs and interests of your class. Skill connections are often listed.

• Discussion prompts are included in most activities, so you can continually develop children's language and thinking skills.

• Open-ended learning experiences are emphasized because they allow for different levels of readiness and encourage different levels of

response. The term *open-ended* does not imply that all answers are correct; it means that more than one correct response is possible. Open-ended activities encourage students to express their individuality.

• Opportunities for small-muscle development and fine-motor skills are incorporated in each unit. Multiple experiences with cutting, pasting, play dough, shaving cream, finger painting, and manipulatives help children develop the control needed for handwriting and other school-related tasks.

• Portfolio product ideas and authentic assessment tasks are incorporated into each unit. You can use these ideas and tasks to document learning, substantiate growth, record change over time, celebrate the unique strengths and needs of each child, and provide concrete examples of children's abilities during conferences with children, parents and caregivers, or other educators.

• Activity masters for duplicating material needed for some activities are in an appendix at the end of this book.

Activities Using Unit Topic Pictures

Each of the ten monthly sections within this book (September through June) is introduced with four pictures that represent the unit topics in the section. They can be used for calendar, math, and language arts activities. Some suggestions follow to prompt your creative applications.

• Make copies of pictures in three to four sizes and have children use the pictures to complete math seriation tasks.

• Enlarge and laminate pictures and then punch holes around their outlines to create lacing activities that can be used to develop children's fine-motor coordination.

• Use a picture to prompt descriptive words. Work with children to brainstorm and list all the words that could describe the picture. Then incorporate those words in oral language and writing activities.

• Have children explore their senses by asking, "What could we see, hear, taste, feel, or smell if this picture were real?"

• Enlarge pictures and cut them into three or more pieces to create topic-related puzzles.

• Use the pictures as stencils for felt board figures. Then use the figures to create math sets and patterns.

• Duplicate and color the pictures to create matching pairs of pictures for matching games. Use the pictures to create other kinds of matching cards, such as cards that use objects to show numbers and matching numeral cards, letter cards and cards that show pictures that begin with those letter sounds, and picture cards that show colors and matching word cards for those colors.

• Enlarge pictures to create topic-related books in various shapes. Have children use the books to write and/or illustrate stories.

• Use the pictures to decorate your monthly calendar, letters to parents, announcements, and bulletin board borders.

• Create appealing paper for the children to write on when recording information or working in a writing center.

• Enlarge and color pictures. Then place them on the classroom door with a caption that informs the children and other interested people of the topic currently being studied.

• To introduce a unit, have children list as many words as they can that relate to a picture that represents the unit topic.

Planning the Sequence for Using the Units

The order of the units in this book is based upon three key guidelines: 1. allowing the concepts within one unit topic to lead to those in another; 2. achieving a balance between the development of imagination through fantasy and the acquisition of factual information about real-life topics; and 3. placing date-specific topics at the appropriate time of the year. However, teachers should implement the units in the sequence that best meets the unique needs of the children in their class. Although some unit topics relate to a specific time of the year, such as the seasons and holidays, most may be used in any sequence. Teachers may also prefer to change the sequence of the units to better fit their schedule or area. For example, if you live in a geographic area in which migrating birds return later than March, you can use the unit on birds later in the school year.

The learning needs, background experiences, and interests of the children should determine the amount of time spent on any of the units. Some units can effectively be explored in one week of instruction. Others, with more complex concepts to develop and expand upon, may require two or three weeks.

Whatever the preferred order of the units, teachers should create transitions from one to another by highlighting the relationships between unit topics. Reminding children of concepts and experiences from previous units encourages recall of prior learning and helps children build upon prior experiences. Connecting ideas enables children to make sense of them, understand the bigger picture, and retain more information.

The following are some examples of ways teachers might explore relationships among the unit topics.

Fall / Winter / Spring / Summer
• Brainstorm and list five or more ways in which the seasons are similar and five ways in which they are different.
• Use words and pictures to complete a senses chart like the one below to compare the seasons.

Senses Chart for the Seasons

	See?	Hear?	Feel or Touch?	Taste?	Smell?
Spring	baby animals	birds singing	soft grass	honeysuckle	flowers
Summer	baseball	kids playing	hot sun	ice cream	ripe tomatoes
Fall	colored leaves	wind	hard, dry grass	Halloween candy	turkey cooking
Winter	snowballs	bells; singing	ice	hot apple cider	Christmas tree

Dinosaurs / The Animal Kingdom / Birds

• Discuss how dinosaurs are similar to and different from other animals, especially birds.

• Compare living and extinct animals. For example, display pictures of Stegosaurus and a present-day reptile. Discuss how they are similar and different and list the children's ideas in a Venn Diagram.

Water and Rainbows / Birds / Animal Kingdom / Insects and Spiders

• Discuss the fact that birds, animals, and insects all need water to live and that this need is one way in which these animals are similar to each other. List as many other similarities among birds, animals, and insects as possible.

Our Families and Where We Live / Tools and Simple Machines / People Work

• Discuss what kinds of tools might be used in our homes and at work.

• Discuss ways people work at home and away from home to help the family.

Thanksgiving / Holiday Season / Valentines and Friendship

• Develop the understanding that holidays occur throughout the year.

• Compare holiday traditions and celebrations.

Connecting the Topics: Alphabet Time

Alphabet Time is a vocabulary and information organizer for any topic (Kingore, 2001). Children think of the most significant things they know about a stated topic, and the teacher or adult organizes those ideas by listing each word or fact under its beginning alphabet letter. Alphabet Time connects topics throughout the year by providing a familiar and predictable activity that can be repeated in every unit topic. It serves as a literacy model as it stores the topic-related words that children know and may want to write. A partial example for the topic of dinosaurs follows.

• To make an Alphabet Time chart, print Alphabet Time at the top of a large sheet of paper or poster board, leave a place at the top to write the topic, and then write the alphabet in alphabetical order down the left-hand margin of the paper. Laminate this paper if you wish to use it multiple times. However, some teachers prefer to make a new Alphabet Time chart for each unit topic. They then use previous charts to refresh

---

Alphabet Time

Topic <u>Dinosaurs</u>

A   animals (JS); Apatasaurus (BK)

B   bones (IM); Brachiosaurus (RN)

C   claws (OY); carnivores (WH)

D

E   eggs (PL); excavations (ED)

children's memories about earlier topics, to help integrate one topic with another, and as a word source for children when writing stories.

• Introduce an Alphabet Time chart to the class. Model the process by adding one or two words to the chart. Then ask the children to share the most important ideas and words they can think of about the topic. Do not try to complete the chart in alphabetical order as that frequently blocks ideas. As each word is offered, determine together which letter of the alphabet that word begins with and where to position the word in the chart.

• Record the initials of the child who offers each idea. Giving children credit often encourages more participation. It also develops the grapheme-phoneme relationship as children can later look at the initials and try to figure out which child shared that idea.

• Alphabet Time is most effective when you complete only a few letters each day. Completing the chart over several days encourages children to continue thinking about the topic. Frequently, children talk about the chart with family members and ask them to think of ideas to include.

• The chart may be completed with single words, phrases, or sentences. Single words or phrases are effective when beginning the process with young learners.

• It is not necessary to fill in words and ideas for every letter of the alphabet for each topic. However, some children like to have all the letters completed and are motivated to keep searching for content connections that fit "blank" letters.

• Make the process more challenging by inviting children to think of more than one response for as many letters as possible.

• After several experiences, some children demonstrating advanced skills may be able to use the Alphabet Time format individually or in small groups to organize the results of their reading or independent studies.

• Alphabet Time activity masters (Activity Masters 1–2, pp. 278–279) are provided. These activity masters are useful for making transparencies when you want to model the Alphabet Time process on the overhead. You may also wish to use them with individuals or small groups of children who are ready to do an independent Alphabet Time activity.

Literacy Learning Goals and Content for Pre-K and Kindergarten

Listening and Speaking
• Listening to learn
• Listening to literature and music for enjoyment
• Participating in rhymes, songs, conversations, and discussions
• Asking and answering relevant questions
• Participating in dramatic interpretations and role playing
• Increasing control of grammar when speaking
• Increasing ability to speak in sentences
• Producing rhyming words

Reading and Print Awareness
• Learning the directionality of print, from left to right and from top to bottom
• Recognizing the parts of a book such as the cover, the title, and a page
• Recognizing the role of the author and illustrator
• Recognizing one's own name in print
• Learning the difference between individual letters and words
• Participating in voice printing (pointing at words as someone reads them)
• Using environmental print such as "Exit" and "Stop"
• Interpreting illustrations in a story
• Retelling events in stories in sequence
• Predicting events in a story
• Acting out and interpreting stories
• Retelling the beginning, middle, and end of a story
• Distinguishing fact from fantasy
• Developing alphabetic knowledge; identifying letters in sequence and out of sequence
• Clapping syllables in words
• Identifying initial and final sounds of spoken words
• Blending phonemes into words
• Learning letter-sound correspondence to begin to read

- Using some word recognition strategies, such as picture clues and initial letter sounds
- Recognizing some high-frequency words in print
- Conducting simple research to learn about topics of study

Developing Writing

- Dictating messages and observing as others write them
- Using print forms such as pictures, scribbles, letterlike shapes, and letters to convey messages
- Writing one's name
- Writing each letter of the alphabet
- Using directionality in writing, from left to right and from top to bottom
- Generating ideas before writing
- Writing messages by using phonological knowledge to match sounds to letters
- Writing labels and captions
- Writing to express ideas; writing sentences
- Leaving spaces between words
- Developing awareness of and beginning to use capital letters and simple punctuation, such as periods and question marks
- Writing some high-frequency words
- Increasing fine-motor control of letter formation
- Using available technology to compose text

Vocabulary

- Using positional words and directions
- Using vocabulary to describe feelings and experiences
- Using color words
- Developing vocabulary through meaningful experiences

Applications

- Talking about reading and writing daily
- Observing adults and other children reading and writing daily
- Incorporating authentic reasons to read and write daily, such as reading or writing an invitation or thank-you note

High-Frequency Words

Certain words are particularly useful because they occur repeatedly in oral and written work. These words are referred to as high-frequency words. Recognizing these words is beneficial to beginning readers and writers. While instructional emphasis should not be on a controlled vocabulary, it is obvious that knowing these words facilitates fluency in reading and writing. They also provide a useful schema for decoding unfamiliar words. Hence, knowing high-frequency words helps children develop pride in what they have learned and greater confidence as beginning readers and writers. (Refer to Fountas & Pinnell, 1996, and Snowball, 1996, for further information about the relationship between high-frequency words and literacy development.)

The following chart contains an alphabetized list of high-frequency words that are appropriate for emerging readers and writers. Select a few of these high-frequency words to model when writing with the class. Over time, add those words to a

a	because	don't	her	keep	my	people	them	well
about	been	down	here	kind	no	play	then	went
after	before	first	him	know	not	put	there	were
all	big	for	his	like	now	ran	they	what
am	boy	from	house	little	of	run	this	when
an	but	get	how	long	off	said	three	where
and	by	go	I	look	old	saw	to	which
are	came	going	if	looked	on	see	too	who
as	can	good	I'm	made	one	she	two	will
asked	come	got	in	make	only	so	up	with
at	could	had	into	man	or	some	us	would
away	day	has	is	me	our	that	very	you
back	did	have	it	more	out	the	was	your
be	do	he	just	mother	over	their	we	

Word Wall (see below). Also place short lists of high-frequency words on tables or desks at which children are seated when writing.

Creating a Word Wall

A Word Wall is a wall display of topic words and high-frequency words that are organized alphabetically. The teacher and the children cooperatively create this wall throughout the year, and the children use it as a resource. An example of a portion of a Word Wall is shown below.

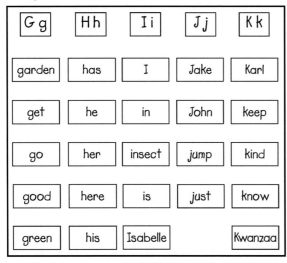

G g	H h	I i	J j	K k
garden	has	I	Jake	Karl
get	he	in	John	keep
go	her	insect	jump	kind
good	here	is	just	know
green	his	Isabelle		Kwanzaa

Designate an area of the room where you can set up a Word Wall that can be expanded throughout the year as the wall is constructed and refined by the class. Begin by placing the name of each child in the class on the Word Wall. Including names creates an opportunity to recognize each child and promote emerging phonic awareness skills.

The Word Wall should contain very useful words that children need and want to use in their writing. It should also incorporate words that children have found to be similar in various ways, such as words that begin with the same letters or have similar endings.

Guidelines for Developing an Effective Word Wall

1. To organize the wall, post both uppercase and lowercase letters of the alphabet.
2. Arrange each word alphabetically to facilitate locating words and to emphasize phonic connections.
3. Print each word on a separate word card

for more flexibility in use.
4. Make the words large enough to be clearly seen and copied by children in different areas of the room.
5. Do not laminate the word cards because laminating causes glare and may prevent children from clearly seeing the words.

Activities and Skill Development Opportunities With a Word Wall

1. Have children identify the names of other children in the class.
2. Have children use a pointer to locate and read words.
3. Have children write words and have other children read them.
4. Have children classify words that are similar.
5. Point out or have children identify rhyming words.
6. Identify or have children identify initial consonants and ending consonants

Nursery Rhymes

Nursery Rhymes as Fingerplays and Action Rhymes

Adding gestures and actions to nursery rhymes as children recite them actively involves children with nursery rhymes in a way that is fun and increases their understanding of the content. Let the children help you decide which fingerplay or whole-body actions to add to the nursery rhymes as you recite them together.

Vocabulary Concepts

Nursery rhymes offer valuable opportunities to reinforce children's understanding of words that denote position. These are especially important words because they are frequently used when adults are giving directions to children. Examples of some of the position words you can reinforce through nursery rhymes are listed below.

• Little Miss Muffet: on, beside, away

• Peter, Peter Pumpkin Eater: in

• Hey Diddle, Diddle: over, away

• Jack and Jill: up, down, after

- Wee Willie Winkie: through, upstairs, downstairs
- Little Boy Blue: in, under
- Little Bo-Peep: alone, behind
- Hickory Dickory Dock: up, down

Mathematics Learning Goals and Content for Pre-K and Kindergarten

Number Concepts
- Counting, one-to-one correspondence, for the numbers 1 to 20 or more
- Making sets
- Counting backwards, from 10 to 0
- Comparing two sets using the terms *greater than, less than,* or *same as*
- Recognizing the numerals 0 to 20 or more
- Writing the numerals 0 through 9 or more
- Learning about fractions: whole and half
- Using ordinal numbers, such as first, second, and third
- Estimating how many
- Recognizing coins and a dollar
- Using a number line
- Skip counting by 2s, 5s, and 10s
- Beginning to combine and separate sets (addition and subtraction)

Patterns
- Recognizing, continuing, and creating simple patterns with two to three elements, such as AB, AAB, and ABC

Geometry
- Identifying simple geometric figures, such as circles, squares, and rectangles

Measurement
- Using a calendar
- Comparing:
  Longer or shorter
  Taller or shorter
  Largest or smallest
  Heavier or lighter
  Big, bigger, or biggest
  Near or far
- Using simple measurement tools
- Recognizing time to the hour

Vocabulary
- Using the language of mathematics
- Using positional words

Graphs
- Organizing and discussing simple graphs
- Graphing everyday things, such as favorite fruits and numbers of people in families

Applications
- Using mathematics daily by counting items, telling time, measuring for a recipe, and so forth

A Calendar for Communication and Organization

Mother: "What did you do in school today?"
Young child: "Nothing."
The above response is typical! It's not that

September						
Sunday	Monday	Tuesday	Wednesday	Thursday	Friday	Saturday
1	2 LABOR DAY	3 Every person is unique and special. Measure heights and weights.	4 Identify the first letter of each child's name.	5 Read M. Bang's <u>When Sophie Gets Angry–Really, Really Angry.</u>	6 Parents: Ask your child about our feelings experiment.	7
8	9 Recognize our names in print. Play name games.	10 Read: K. Henkes's <u>Chrysanthemum.</u> Make thumbprint cookies.	11 Write poems about Marvelous Me. Make cut paper people.	12 Make Look What I Can Do books. Students: bring one piece of fruit for class fruit salad.	13 Celebration of Marvelous Me party. Students bring baby pictures to show.	14

children don't want to share their day. They just need more concrete prompts to help them remember. To provide these prompts use the blank calendar (Activity Master 3, p. 280) to fill in and highlight some main activities and plans for each month, as shown in the sample on p. xv. Post the completed calendar on your door or duplicate a copy for each family. A parent can refer to the calendar and ask questions such as, "What's this about making a mask today?" The child, who now has something concrete to remember, can respond with detailed information.

Thus the calendar subtly encourages both parent-child communication and better teacher organization. It can also serve as an effective tool for teacher-parent communication, as the teacher can note on the calendar any special help needed from parents, such as donations of items needed for an upcoming art project.

Each month's calendar may be decorated with one of the topic cards on the first page of the section for each month or with symbols appropriate for that time of year. If the calendar is displayed on a wall or door, it can be surrounded with the children's artwork. Whether plain or fancy, the calendar works! It provides teachers, parents, and children with important information and an overview of the exciting plans for the month.

Portfolios for Young Children

Portfolios are a vital assessment tool for young children. They provide more accurate and concrete information about children's achievements and needs than any test alone could ever provide. The objective in creating portfolios for preschool and kindergarten children is to have students save and file work to celebrate and document their learning.

The benefits of portfolios for young children are numerous and significant. (See Kingore, *Assessment: Time-Saving Procedures for Busy Teachers,* 1999.)

• Portfolios enable children to experience high self-esteem because they illustrate children's efforts and progress in addition to their achievements. Children often voice great pride in

their work as they look back at what they have accomplished. As one excited four-year-old exclaimed to her friend at the end of the year, "I know a lot!" Then she showed a product from the beginning of the year and explained, "Look at this baby stuff. I did this when I was little."

• Portfolios motivate children to want to learn. Children try harder because they see concrete evidence of how much they are learning.

• Portfolios encourage the talents of all children regardless of their current levels of development. After two or three months, children can look at the earlier work in their portfolios and see growth. Thus, even if they are not performing on grade level, the portfolio confirms that they are learning and making progress.

• Portfolios increase the effectiveness of teacher and parent communication by providing parents with evidence of their child's development and progress. After discussing a child's portfolio in a conference with the teacher, parents leave thinking, "You really know my child," instead of "You like (or do not like) my child."

• Portfolios for this age group can be relatively small and yet serve as a tremendous source of pride for children and families. Plan a one-fourth to one-half-inch thickness as the total size of each portfolio at the end of the year. Preschool and kindergarten children produce fewer products than older children do, since much of the learning completed by very young children is process oriented. Thus, to build portfolios for very young children, you need to select only one product every two to four weeks.

Introducing the Process to Children

Make the portfolio process as concrete as possible to enable children to understand what portfolios are and become excited about creating their own. Show them a portfolio book from last year, or put together a collection of children's work to create a mock-up of what their portfolios will look like. Explain to the children that they will take many papers home to show their family but will keep a few products at school that will be placed into a wonderful book that will surprise and please their family at the end of the year.

Have an adult visitor such as a parent or the principal talk with the class about how wonderful it will be to have this portfolio book at the end of the year. Talk about how the children can look through their portfolios when they are older and remember this school year and the great things they learned.

After you have selected a product to save in the portfolio, write the date on it and have the children write their names. Any stage of scribbling or creative spelling can communicate that child's name as long as it is recognizable to the child. The children's ability to write their names can serve as a repeated assessment task since their writing growth will be obvious as the year progresses.

Teaching Children to Manage Their Portfolios

Preschoolers and kindergartners can successfully file their own products if teachers organize portfolios in a developmentally-appropriate manner. A plastic crate with hanging files is a great storage choice for portfolios and one that young children can manage. On each hanging file, write a child's name and staple that child's photograph to the file so that it extends above the top of the file and can be easily seen. Young children can use the photographs to find their own portfolios even if they cannot recognize their names.

Demonstrate how to file papers in a portfolio so that children see how it is done. Simply teach children to file their work in the back of their portfolio each time. When products are filed in the back, the portfolio tends to remain in chronological order. Furthermore, each time children file a product they see their earlier work. This becomes a concrete reminder that they are learning.

Later in the kindergarten year, many teachers recommend increasing children's involvement in the portfolio process by allowing them to select some products for their portfolios. (For a complete discussion of this selection process and examples of forms to use, refer to Kingore, 1999.)

Inviting children to talk about their products is an important language arts activity. For example, a teacher can work with one group of children each day while taking their dictation. The teacher can prompt children's thinking with reflective statements such as the ones that follow.

"Tell me about your work."

"Tell me more so I understand your ideas."
"What was your favorite part?"
"What did you think was easy to do?"
"What was the hardest thing to do?"

Choosing Products That Document Children's Achievements

A portfolio should be an integral reflection of what children learn rather than evidence of rote activities and isolated skills. Attention to real and meaningful tasks is a crucial consideration in selecting products. The information below describes ideas for generating and selecting recommended products and the kind of information that can be gleaned from them. Specific suggestions are also described in each unit, but you should base your selection on what you think best reflects the growth of the children in your class.

Recommended Portfolio Products

Art Collect natural, creative explorations (rather than crafts) that reflect developmental levels and interests.

Photographs Represent three-dimensional products by taking photographs of children's math manipulatives and patterns, group work, sculptures, role playing, models, dioramas, and block constructions.

Videotape Have each child bring a tape that can be used to film the child's activities throughout the year or over several years. Limit each tape segment to two or four minutes. These videos can become a significant visual celebration of academic or personal achievements.

Audiotape Tape children as they tell story problems using math concepts, retell stories, and share ideas and problem solutions. Audiotapes can demonstrate oral language development, fluency, and concept mastery.

Dictation Take or have an adult volunteer take a child's dictation or process response. Adults can prompt these dictations with statements such as, "Tell me about your picture" and "Tell me how you did that." Dictation increases the adults' understanding of why and how children do something. It indicates children's oral language development, fluency, and concept mastery.

Writings Have children use lined or unlined paper to writes numerals, shapes, letters, words, or sentences. Emphasize the children's ability to express themselves meaningfully rather than their ability to form exact letters. Children's written products are a measure of their awareness of print concepts, emergent literacy, and fine-motor skills.

Graphs or Charts Have children produce graphs or charts to show the results of simple investigations. For example, a child folds a piece of paper in half and then surveys classmates to determine how many children are wearing velcro or tied shoes and tallies the results. Graphs or charts demonstrate acquisition of specific skills or concepts applied in the task, data-recording strategies, and organizational skills.

Computer Products Have children use a computer to create products. For example, children type and print out stories using simple computer software. Computer-generated products indicate computer literacy, emergent literacy, and the topic-related academic skills or concepts applied in the task.

What To Do With Portfolios at the End of the Year

At the end of the year, a few products may be selected from each portfolio to be passed on to next year's teacher. The rest of the products can be put together and bound in a book to take home as a keepsake for the family. Children and parents are very enthusiastic and positive about the portfolio books! *Assessment: Time-Saving Procedures for Busy Teachers* (Kingore, 1999) details options for making this bound portfolio book attractive and special.

References

Fountas, I. C., and G.S. Pinnell. *Guided Reading: Good First Teaching for All Children.* Portsmouth, NH: Heinemann, 1996.

Kingore, B. *Assessment: Time-Saving Procedures for Busy Teachers,* 2nd ed. Austin, TX: Professional Associates Publishing, 1999.

Kingore, B. *Kingore Observation Inventory,* 2nd ed. Austin, TX: Professional Associates Publishing, 2001.

Snowball, D. "Learning High-Frequency Words." *Instructor,* September 1996, 42–43.

September Curriculum

Marvelous Me

Our Families and Where We Live

Marvelous Me

CONCEPTS

- Every person is unique and special.
- Everyone can do some things well. We can learn to do many new things.
- Everyone has feelings. We feel happy, sad, scared, angry, tired, and surprised.
- Everyone has a body with many parts. Children's bodies grow bigger and bigger until they are adults.
- Everyone can be a friend and have a friend.

CONTINUING CONCEPTS

- **Colors** Have children wear their favorite color and explain why it is their favorite.
- **Geometric Shapes** Relate the shape of a circle to the shape of a face.
- **Health and Nutrition** Have children make a graph to show which fruit is liked most by the greatest number of children. Make fruit salad.
  Discuss the importance of cleanliness.
  Identify parts of the body.
- **Senses** Have children close their eyes and identify pieces of fruit, first using only smell and then only taste.
  Discuss the parts of the body we use to identify objects through our sense of touch.
- **Traditional Rhymes and Tales** Recite "The Old Woman Who Lived in a Shoe" with the children.

PORTFOLIO PRODUCTS

Refer to Portfolios for Young Children, page xvi, for an overview of the purpose and value of this important assessment tool. During the first month of school, many teachers recommend selecting two to four products to establish benchmarks of each child's readiness and skill levels. While the teacher or children must always determine the most appropriate products for the portfolio, some suggestions follow to guide selection.

- Look What I Can Do books (see p. 8) are useful for assessing children's concept and skill development at the beginning of the year. Plan to repeat the same tasks in another Look What I Can Do book in the middle of the year and at the end of the year to document growth.
- Include each child's completed Cut-Paper Person (see p. 4) and Marvelous Me poem (see p. 7) in the portfolio to celebrate the uniqueness of the child and to assess emergent literacy skills, oral language skills, and fine-motor development.

ART

✳ Friendship Tree

Materials: tree branch; coffee can; plaster of Paris; construction paper; marking pen

"Plant" a real tree branch in a coffee can filled with plaster of Paris that is still wet. Place a label that reads "Friendship Tree" on the coffee can or on a wall above the tree. After the plaster of Paris has dried, use the friendship tree to display children's completed artwork. When finished using the tree for this purpose, consider storing it until you are ready to use it to display a new art project.

✳ Handy Me Booklets

Materials: construction paper; crayons; scissors; yardstick; tempera paints; paper plates; paintbrushes (optional)

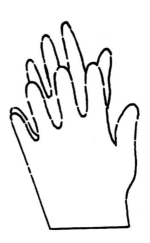

Trace each child's left hand on a folded piece of construction paper, positioning the hand so that the left side is against the fold line. Cut out the paper hand, leaving the fold uncut, so that you end up with a hand-shaped booklet that opens, as shown.

Have children print their name in large letters on the outside. Weigh and measure the height of each child and then record these measurements on the inside of his or her booklet.

Provide small amounts of tempera paint on paper plates. Encourage children to decorate their hand booklet by dipping one thumb in the paint or painting their fingertip with a paintbrush and then making thumb prints all over the outside of the booklet.

✳ Celebration of Marvelous Me Place Mats and Artistic Cups

Materials: 12" × 18" construction paper; scissors; white paper or Styrofoam® cups; crayons or markers

Have each child make a special place mat and cup for the Celebration of Marvelous Me party discussed on page 9.

Place mats: Give each child a piece of construction paper and scissors. Have the children make a fringe around the paper by making 1-inch cuts on each side. Then have them draw a picture in the center of the paper. Print each child's name in large letters under his/her picture.

Artistic cups: Give each child a cup. Use a marker to print each child's name near the top edge of the cup. Have children decorate their cup using a crayon or marker in their favorite color. (Pretest the markers to ensure that the ink does not come off the cups and stain children's hands.)

✳ Cut-Paper People: Marvelous Me Poem

Materials: mirrors; construction paper; scissors; glue

Talk about similarities and differences in children's appearances. For example, discuss the fact that we all have two hands, two eyes, and one head, but we are different heights and have different hair colors. Provide mirrors so that children may study and talk about their own features.

Have children complete the Marvelous Me poems described on pages 7–8. Then have them use their poems to complete a cut-paper person. The paper on which the poem is displayed is used as the trunk of the body. Have the children cut a circle for a head and glue it on the top edge of the poem paper. Then have them cut out facial features and hair that resemble their own to add to the head. Model how to cut strips for arms and legs or jeans. Encourage the children to add hands, shoes, jewelry, hats, and so forth, so that each cut-paper person looks like the child making it. The completed cut-paper people celebrate the uniqueness of each child.

✳ Shaving Cream Faces

Materials: shaving cream

Put a small amount of shaving cream on a tabletop. Show the children how to spread out the cream to make a smooth area. Draw a circle in the cream. Discuss how a head is shaped like a circle. Add eyes, a nose, a mouth, ears, hair, and other details as children suggest them. Lightly rub over the area to erase the picture and then draw it again. Then put a small amount of shaving cream on the tabletop for each child, and let them spread the cream and draw faces.

To record the activity, take a picture of each child standing by his or her shaving cream face. You may wish to display the pictures on a wall or door, at the children's eye level, with their names under the pictures.

✳ Something I Do Well; Something I Do Not Do Well

Share with the children things you do well and do not do well. Discuss different things the children think they do well and do not do well. Point out that everyone does some things well but no one does everything well. Explain that we are all here to learn to do some things better. Have children fold a large piece of paper in half and draw what they do well on one half and what they don't do well on the other.

✳ Hanging Soap Creations

Materials: ingredients for Soap Creations (see Appendix II, p. 275); electric mixer; wax paper; 24-inch pieces of wide yarn, in the children's favorite colors

Knot together the two ends of each piece of yarn. Let each child select a piece of yarn in a favorite color. Have the children measure the soap flakes and water, pour them into a large mixing bowl, and take turns helping you to hold the electric mixer. The mixture should have a thick, clay-like consistency.

Give about $\frac{1}{2}$ cup of the mixture on a piece of wax paper to each child. Have children knead, squeeze, and explore the mixture for a minute or so. Talk about how it looks, feels, and smells.

Show children how to mold the soap into a desired shape around the knot of one piece of yarn, and then have them mold their own shapes. Set the shapes aside to dry.

Suggest that children wear their soap creation at bath time. Talk about how a clean body helps contribute to a healthy, "marvelous me."

✳ Everyone Has Feelings (A Class Collage)

Materials: 24" × 24" butcher paper; permanent ink marker; old magazines and newspapers; scissors; glue

Use a marker to divide the butcher paper into four or six sections. Label each section with a word that conveys a common emotion or feeling such as: happy, sad, surprised, excited, scared, or angry. At the top of the paper, add the caption *Everyone Has Feelings*.

Provide magazine and newspaper pages that have pictures of people's faces. Have children cut out each face, decide which emotion it shows, and then glue it in a section of the butcher paper that matches the emotion expressed in the picture.

✳ Traceable Me

Materials: white butcher paper; crayons or markers; full-length (preferable) or hand-held mirrors

Begin the activity by reviewing the different parts of the body. For example, ask children, "What body parts do we have on our faces? How many legs do we have?" Provide mirrors, so that children can study their own features. Discuss the individual features of each child. Then have children take turns lying on a large sheet of paper while you or another child draws around each child's body. Have children add their features to these body-shape drawings. Encourage them to color their drawings to reflect the clothes they are wearing. You may wish to do this activity over two days, since coloring an entire drawing in one day may be too fatiguing.

BLOCKS

During the first week of school, introduce the block area. Establish any rules concerning how much time children can spend in the block area, how many children can participate at one time, and safe and courteous conduct. Stress that the block area is a place for sharing, and explain that children need to resolve conflicts by talking.

Encourage children to manipulate the blocks and block buildings. You may want to suggest that children work together to build a block structure. Encourage children to talk to one another when they need blocks they cannot reach. Model naming the blocks by their shapes (cube, rectangular prism, cylinder, triangular prism, and so forth).

BULLETIN BOARD

✳ The Old Woman Who Lived in a Shoe

Draw a large, old-fashioned high-top shoe or a contemporary knee-high boot. To make windows for the shoe, cut out a small square of paper for each child in the class. Glue the top edge of each square to the shoe or boot drawing so that the paper forms a flap that may be raised. Glue a picture of each child behind each flap and print the child's name on the back of the flap. Have children open each window to discover who is behind it.

Recite the nursery rhyme "The Old Woman Who Lived in a Shoe." Then recite a new rhyme, like the one below, that is based on the original pattern.

There was a nice teacher with children like you.
She/he had so many children who knew just what to do.
She/he smiled and laughed and nodded her head.
"Hello and good morning, dear children," she said.

After reciting the new rhyme, open each flap and have everyone say "Good morning, (child's name)," as the photograph is revealed.

COOKING

✳ Fruit Salad

Several different fruits, such as   *Wax paper*
bananas, apples, pineapple, and grapes *Nondairy whipped topping*
Round toothpicks   *Paper cups*
Plastic spoons and plastic serrated knives *Cutting board*

Supply the fruit or have the children each bring in one piece. As you and the children wash your hands, explain why this is important before one prepares food. Discuss the names, shapes, sizes, and colors of the fruit. Cut each fruit into small pieces and insert a toothpick into each piece. Have children take turns closing their eyes and identifying the kind of fruit they are asked to smell. Then have children identify a fruit by tasting a piece. Discuss which fruits are easiest to detect by smell and which by taste.

Have children select a small amount of each fruit they like to eat. Allow them to work on wax paper and cut the fruit into smaller pieces, using the plastic knives. They can then mix their pieces in a cup with a small amount of whipped topping if desired.

As children eat, discuss how the class is like the fruit salad. Help children realize that just as different pieces of fruit work together to make a great salad, different children can work together as a great class, just as they do!

LANGUAGE ARTS

✳ Fingerplay – I Have Two Little Hands

I have two little hands.
    (Hold up both hands.)
They both belong to me.
    (Point to self.)
And they can help me do many things.
Watch me and you will see!
    (Hold out hands.)
They can pat me on the back.
    (Perform appropriate action for each line.)
They can pet a kitten.
They can wiggle high up in the air.
They can wear a mitten.
They can help me eat and work.
They help me have some fun.
Then I can fold them together
To rest when their job's done.
    (Quietly fold hands and place in lap.)

✳ Most Special Person Box

Put a small mirror inside a little box with a lid. Tell the children to take turns opening the box and looking inside to see who is "a most special person!"

✳ Our Initials Word Wall

Display the alphabet where children can clearly see it. This can serve as the beginning of a Word Wall (see p. xiv) that can be expanded all year to aid in literacy development.

Discuss names and help each child identify the letter with which his or her name begins. Write each name on a card to post under the appropriate letter in the Word Wall. Add the word *me* or the words *marvelous me* to the Word Wall. Add other words that children suggest.

✳ Marvelous Me Poem

Talk about similarities and differences among the children. Make a chart by dividing the chalkboard or a large piece of paper into five columns. Add these headings: *adjectives, I am, I like, I want,* and *favorite place.* Write each heading in a different color to visually guide the children as they use the chart.

adjectives	I am	I like	I want	favorite place
funny brave	a good friend	my new puppy	to go swimming	the zoo

With the children, brainstorm words and ideas about individual children and list them in each column, using the column's designated color. When the chart contains a substantial number of words and ideas, model how to write a Marvelous Me poem by using the template below and writing one about yourself. A completed example is also shown below. Then have each child compose an original poem and dictate it to you, or if children are writing, have them use the template to write a poem. Have younger or less-experienced writers complete one verse. Other children may complete two or more verses.

_____(adjective)_____ me,
_____(adjective)_____ me,
I am _____ .
I like _____ .
I want _____ .
_____ is my favorite place to be,
Marvelous, marvelous me.

Example:

Funny me,
Helpful me,
I am good at drawing pictures.
I like kids to ride bikes with me.
I want to learn to read.
The park is my favorite place to be,
Marvelous, marvelous me.

Children may be able to work more independently when writing or composing their own poem if you show them how to use markers to color code each line of the poem so that it matches the color of the appropriate column. This may help them to recall ideas and find spellings of needed words that fit each line.

To frame the finished poem, glue it to a piece of construction paper. You can use these poems to complete the Cut-Paper People activity described on page 4.

✳ Feelings

Read Judith Viorst's *Alexander and the Terrible, Horrible, No Good, Very Bad Day.* Talk about feeling happy, sad, angry, or surprised. Help children know that everyone has these feelings sometimes.

✳ Look What I Can Do!

Duplicate the Look What I Can Do book pages (Activity Masters 4–6, pp. 281–283), and staple the pages together to make a book for each child. (Alternately, make booklets by dividing three sheets of $8\frac{1}{2}$" × 11" paper in half, adding captions like those on Activity Masters 4–6, and duplicating the pages. Each caption should be a concept or skill you want to assess. Have the children fold the three pieces in half to make a $5\frac{1}{2}$" × $8\frac{1}{2}$" booklet.) On each page, have children write and draw their response to the caption.

The completed books can serve as a useful tool for assessing children's skills and knowledge of concepts at the beginning of the year. To document each child's growth, you may wish to have each child make another Look What I Can Do book later in the year. Date each book and have the children file them in their portfolios for comparison with the earlier books.

✳ Body Rhymes

Brainstorm with the children various parts of the body that are important for children to know. You might prompt their responses by asking:

"What parts of your body can you see outside of your clothes?"

"What parts would you find inside your shoes?"

"What parts would you find inside a mitten"?

List their ideas on the chalkboard or a chart. Then brainstorm and list two or three rhyming words for each body part. Use each body part and the matching rhyming words to complete sentences like "Say bed. Touch your head." You may wish to write the sentences on a chalkboard or large piece of paper. (You can use some of the examples to point out to the children that all rhyming words do not have the same spelling pattern.) Write multiple rhymes using different parts of the body. Have children chant the rhymes and act out each one. Later, you could invite children to make a class book by collecting rhymes they have created, written, and illustrated.

✳ Celebration of Marvelous Me!

Plan a party to celebrate the special uniqueness of each child and encourage positive self-concepts. Make the place mats and cups described on page 3. Have children display their artistic cups and talk about their favorite colors.

Ask the children to wear one article of clothing to the party that shows their favorite color. Children can play a guessing game at the party that involves identifying each child's favorite color. Have each child ask, "What do you think is my favorite color?" Allow each child three guesses per turn and have children use their fingers to keep track of the number of guesses.

Ask each child to bring a baby picture to show at the party. Discuss how people change as they grow.

Serve fruit salad (see p. 6) and talk about which fruit each child likes best. Remind children that "We all are similar, but no one is exactly like you. You are special, and you are marvelous!"

Sing the "I Am Special" song (see p. 12). Ask children to tell something they like about themselves.

Take several photographs of the party. Be sure to include each child in at least one photo. Use the developed photographs to help children recall and talk about the party. Place the photographs in sequence and have children dictate a caption that describes each one. Use the words *first, second, third,* and *last* to talk about events that took place during the party.

✳ Recorded Interviews

Tape record a short interview of only two to three questions with each child. Possible questions include, "Are you a boy or a girl? What color hair do you have? Who is in your family? and What do you like to do after school?" Make "What is your name?" your last question.

After you've interviewed all the children, play back the tape for the entire class. Stop the tape just before each child says his or her name so that the class can guess who is speaking.

✳ My Name Is Important to Me!

Read *Chrysanthemum* by K. Henkes. Discuss our feelings about our names and how important our names are to us. Ask, "How did Chrysanthemum feel when others made fun of her name? What else do you think she could have done when that happened?" Have children list all the things Chrysanthemum could have said to her classmates.

✳ Name Card Activities

Carefully print the first name of each child on a 3" × 6" card and then laminate the cards. The cards will last a long time and provide a correct model for children to look at and copy. Use the cards to play some of these games.

1. **Play Dough** – Have children roll play-dough snakes and then form the letters of their name by laying the snakes over the letters on the name card.

2. **Name Hunt** – Place the name cards on chalkboard rails, on chairs, along baseboards, and so forth. Have the children tiptoe around the room to find their own name. Later, make duplicate name cards and hold up one at a time while the children silently tiptoe around to find the name card that matches the one you are holding.

3. **Fishing** – Put a large paper clip on each name card. Lay the cards on the floor. Have children take turns "catching" their name, using a pole and a string with an attached magnet.

4. **Silent Lineup** – After children have had a lot of practice with the name cards, use the cards to have them line up silently at the front of the class. Hold up each card and have children walk to the line when they see their name.

✳ "I Can" Classification

Read aloud Curtis' *When I Was Little: A Four-Year-Old's Memoir of Her Youth.* Discuss what the character can do now that she could not do when she was little.

Staple three pockets on a sheet folded in thirds, as shown. Make a set of cards to fit in the pockets. Glue pictures of some common tasks children learn to do around age 4–5 on the cards. Have children take turns classifying each card as a task they can either do with help, do alone, or learn to do in the future.

MATH

✳ Calendar

Provide the children who can write numerals with their own copy of a blank calendar (Activity Master 3, p. 280). Help them to write the name of the month and fill the date in the appropriate place each day. Some children like to record a symbol for the weather, write a favorite word, draw a face to show how they feel, or cut out and paste a small picture in each day's space. You may wish to repeat this activity each month to increase children's fine-motor coordination, mathematical skills, and organizational skills.

✳ How Many Hops?

Use a stopwatch to time each of these activities.

1. Children hop up and down in place 10 times.

2. Children hop in place as everyone counts how many hops they can make in one minute. Repeat the task daily and record and discuss the results.

Height and Weight

Weigh and measure the height of each child. Since many children enjoy seeing their name and measurements and "reading" each other's, you may wish to display the measurements on a wall chart, poster, or door decoration. A drawing of a dachshund standing on his hind legs or a giraffe with a very long neck is an attractive way to display children's heights. If you are concerned that some children may be sensitive about their measurements, you can simply record children's measurements in the Handy Me Booklets described on page 3.

Natural Counting Opportunities

As a class, children look for natural opportunities to count real things in the room. For example, they count the number of shoes with shoelaces or Velcro® buckles, or they count the number of buttons on one child's clothes.

Children in a Shoe

Provide a collection of old shoes and photocopies of the children's pictures that were used in the bulletin board display. Tape a numeral (up to 9) on each shoe. Have the children read the numeral aloud and then put the matching number of photos inside each shoe.

Circles

Children search for objects that have the shape of a circle. Examples they may find include a wall clock, a button, and the round lid of a cylindrical container.

MOVEMENT

Name Game

The class sits in a circle. The teacher says one child's name and rolls a large, soft ball to that child. (An inflatable beach ball works especially well.) The child catches the ball, says another child's name, and rolls it to that child. The game continues until all children have had a turn.

Body Rhymes

Act out the body rhymes the children created in the Body Rhymes activity (see p. 9).

Simon Says

Play Simon Says using body parts. For example, tell the children, "Simon says touch your knee." Or, "Simon says wiggle your arm."

✳ Tangle Up

Begin by describing one simple body movement. Ask the children to perform that movement. For example, say, "Put one hand on your knee." Tell the class to continue to hold that position as you give them new directions about how to move, such as "Now put your elbow on your hip." Continue adding one more movement until someone becomes too "tangled up." Then say, "Tangle up!" and tell everyone to all fall down.

Children love to play this game. You can repeat it several time using different directions. End with a soothing sequence, such as "Lay down; curl your body; rock gently; close your eyes; and pretend to rest."

MUSIC

✳ Song Fest

Ask children to name their favorite songs. Sing as many together as appropriate. Teach the children these new songs that are based on familiar tunes.

✳ No One Like Marvelous Me

(Tune: "Row, Row, Row Your Boat")

Nobody's just like me,
I am marvelous me.
There never was and never will
Be someone one just like me.
Look, look, look at me,
I'm glad that I am me!
I'll be the best that I can be,
Marvelous, marvelous me.

✳ I Am Special

(Tune: "Are You Sleeping?")

I am special, I am special
So are you, so are you.
We can play together. We can work together.
While we're at school. While we're at school.

ROLE PLAY

✳ Interviews

Begin by brainstorming a list of questions children can use to interview one another. Then have pairs of children take turns playing a TV reporter and the interview subject. Provide a toy microphone, or have children use a cylindrical block or an empty toilet paper roll as a microphone. Or, if you prefer, use a real microphone and cassette tape recorder. Provide dress-up clothes so that children can dress like adult reporters.

✳ Getting Ready for School

Provide dolls and personal care products, such as washcloths and combs. Suggest that the children pretend that they are parents getting their children clean and ready for school.

✳ I Used To Be a Baby

Provide baby dolls and a plastic tub with 1 to 2 inches of water. Let the children add a little soap to the water and then bathe the babies. Have lots of towels available.

SCIENCE

✳ Marvelous Me

1. Look at skin, hair, and fingernails with a magnifying glass.
2. Use a stethoscope to listen to heartbeats.
3. Have children make fingerprints with a stamp pad and paper and examine them with a magnifying glass. Talk about how the prints look when they are viewed with a magnifying glass.

✳ Feelings Experiment

Explain that scientists conduct experiments, watch or observe what happens, and record the results. Then have the class conduct a "feelings" experiment. In the hallway, children smile at each person they meet and observe the person's reaction. Then they frown at each person and observe the reaction. As a class, discuss and compare the results of smiling and frowning. Discuss how our feelings influence others.

TRANSITION ACTIVITY

Identify and discuss different parts of the body. Move your body slowly and carefully and point out how joints such as elbows and ankles help us move. Then play music quietly and ask children to listen very carefully. Have children move their bodies in rhythm to the music and freeze when the music stops. Start and stop the music frequently to maintain their interest.

CHILDREN'S BOOKS

Bang, M. *When Sophie Gets Angry—Really, Really Angry*. New York: Blue Sky Press, 1999. People handle anger in different ways. When Sophie gets angry, she runs out and climbs her favorite tree.

Carlson, N. *ABC I Like Me.* New York: Viking Penguin, 1997. An alphabet book that celebrates feeling good about yourself.

Charlip, R., and L. Moore. *Hooray for Me!* Berkeley, CA: Tricycle Press, 1996. This story celebrates a child's relationships to family, friends, and pets.

Curtis, J. *When I Was Little: A Four-Year-Old's Memoir of Her Youth.* New York: HarperCollins, 1993. The story cleverly contrasts what a four-year-old can do now with what she was able to do when she was very little.

Fregmann, S., and J. Elffers, J. *How Are You Peeling? Foods With Moods.* New York: Arthur A. Levine Books, 1999. Great illustrations of real-life vegetables, with faces added to convey feelings that a child can relate to.

Henkes, K. *Chrysanthemum.* New York: Greenwillow, 1991. Classmates tease Chrysanthemum about her name, but her parents and teacher provide love and support. Then Chrysanthemum's teacher provides the ultimate validation of her name.

Hobbie, H. *Toot & Puddle.* Boston: Little, Brown and Company, 2000. Puddle teaches Otto the alphabet and how to write his name. Provides many opportunities to talk about the alphabet and learning to write.

Hoffman, M. *Amazing Grace.* New York: Dial, 1991. Because her family believes in her, a girl is able to be the best Peter Pan.

Jones, R. C. *Matthew and Tilly.* New York: Dutton, 1991. A boy and a girl are best friends. As they play and have fun, however, they argue and then feel sad about it.

Lester, H. *Tacky the Penguin.* New York: Houghton Mifflin, 1988. Being different sometimes saves the day and lets you be a hero!

McCully, E. *Mirette on the High Wire.* New York: Scholastic, 1992. An award-winning book about working to be what you want to be.

McPhail, D. *Drawing Lessons From a Bear.* Boston: Little, Brown and Company, 2000. "Be all you can be" lessons from a bear. It takes practice and perseverance.

Most, B. *The Cow That Went Oink.* New York: Harcourt Brace, 1990. A cow oinks, and animals make fun of her until a new friend helps. This story could prompt positive discussions of the value of being bilingual.

Ross, T. Eggbert *The Slightly Cracked Egg.* New York: Putnam's Sons, 1994. Eggbert has many humorous adventures trying to fit in and be accepted.

Shannon, D. *No, David!* New York: Blue Sky Press, 1998. Based on a book the author wrote as a child. Children can easily relate to all of the nos in this book and most especially to the yes on the final page!

Viorst, J. *Alexander and the Terrible, Horrible, No Good, Very Bad Day.* New York: Antheneum, 1981. A humorous story of a boy's "bad" day. Children relate well to the daily events.

TEACHER RESOURCE BOOK

Gainer, C. *A Leader's Guide to I'm Like You, You're Like Me: A Child's Book About Understanding and Celebrating Each Other.* Minneapolis, MN: Free Spirit, 1998.

Our Families and Where We Live

CONCEPTS

- A family is generally made up of one or more adults and children who live together, care for each other, and do many things together.
- Each member of a family is important and special.
- Family members are alike in some ways and different in some ways.
- Some families are large, some are small.
- Every family member has responsibilities that help the family function successfully.
- A home is a place where a family lives together.
- People live in different kinds of homes, such as single houses of one, two, or three stories; mobile homes; apartments and condominiums; and houseboats.
- Some people live in the city; others live in the suburbs; still others live in rural areas.
- Each house or apartment has an address.

CONTINUING CONCEPTS

- **Colors** Have children count and graph the colors of the houses, apartment buildings, and mobile homes in their neighborhoods.
- **Geometric Shapes** Continue to focus on the circle and relate it to the shape of faces. Focus on squares and rectangles and relate them to the shapes of windows and doors.
- **Health and Nutrition** Discuss what family members do to exercise. Discuss car safety, including the importance of wearing a seatbelt. Identify parts of the body.
- **Senses** Talk about the children's favorite smells, especially mealtime smells. Have children use a feely box (see p. 270) to match pairs of items related to families and homes. Record sounds typical of the sounds a family or individual family members make at home, such as the sound of someone laughing or calling another family member. Have the children identify and discuss each sound as it is replayed.
- **Traditional Rhymes and Tales** Recite "The Old Woman Who Lived in a Shoe" with the children. Discuss who might really live in a shoe. Possible examples include hermit crabs, insects, and mice. Discuss and list the reasons why a shoe might make a good home for these animals. Read or recite "The Three Little Pigs," "Wee Willie Winkie," and "Little Boy Blue" with the children.

PORTFOLIO PRODUCTS

While the teacher or children should determine the most appropriate products to place in portfolios, you may wish to use the following products in order to further document each child's readiness and skill levels.

- Have the children draw a picture of their family. Notice whom each child includes and how she or he shows the position and size of each family member. Since some children will include extended family members or even their pets, you may wish to discuss their importance in the children's lives.
- Have children paint a picture of where they live. Notice how much detail children include in their drawings. Most children will draw a house but some may draw an entire scene.

ART

✳ Easel or Tabletop Painting

Materials: tempera paints; paintbrushes; art paper

1. Invite children to paint a picture of their family and/or where they live. To encourage children to show details in the paintings, name and talk about parts of the body and building details, such as doors, doorknobs, windows, sidewalks, steps, and chimneys. Have children describe their home and record each response on their finished painting.
2. Have children paint a picture, using the same number of colors as the number of people in their family. When the paintings are dry, have each child hold up the painting while the rest of the class counts the number of different colors and then tells how many people are in the child's family.

✳ Family Collage (A Group Project)

Materials: magazine and newspaper pictures of families; scissors; glue; butcher paper

As a whole class or in small groups, children make a collage by cutting out pictures of families and gluing them on a large piece of butcher paper. Display the collage on a wall, setting it low enough for the children to see and talk about the family members. Add the caption *Everyone in a family is important.*

✳ Light-Up Pictures

Materials: cotton swabs; tempera paints; recycled meat trays; Manila paper; paint or basting brushes; salad oil

Provide cotton swabs and small amounts of tempera paints on meat trays. Have the children use the cotton swabs to paint pictures of their family or where they live. After the paint is dry, have children use a paintbrush or basting brush to quickly spread salad oil over their entire picture. Light will show through the pictures when they are hung in a window.

Encourage the children to talk about who or what they painted. Some children may like to have you write a caption at the bottom of the painting as they talk. Others may want just a name or label under each person in the picture.

✳ Paper Plate Family Masks

Materials: large and small paper plates; construction paper shapes for noses, mouths, and ears; yarn; craft sticks; glue; mirror

Discuss how heads and faces are shaped like circles. Ask children to identify the shape of the paper plates and tell how they are like the shape of our heads. Discuss the parts of a face. Have children touch and feel each part of their face as you discuss it. Provide a mirror for children to look into.

Provide each child with the same number of paper plates as the number of family members he or she has. Have an adult cut out eye shapes from the plates so that children can see out of their completed masks.

Before giving the children glue, show them how to lay a nose, ears, and mouth in the appropriate places on a paper plate to make it look like a face. Have the children practice laying the facial features on the paper plate before they begin to glue them on their plates. Provide cut lengths of yarn so that the children can add hair to their masks. Some children may want to add construction paper hats, jewelry, or other details. Make a handle for each mask by gluing a craft stick at the bottom.

Encourage children to use their masks to role play. They could use two masks to play two family members having a conversation about the jobs they do to help the family.

✳ Heart Necklaces

Materials: ceramic dough (see Appendix II, p. 273); heart-shaped cookie cutter (optional); red tempera paint; brushes; yarn or string

Give each child a $1\frac{1}{2}$-inch ball of ceramic dough. Have the children roll the dough and experiment with it. Then show them how to mold the dough into a heart shape. Alternately, have the children use heart-shaped cookie cutters to mold the heart shapes. Although this method is less creative for the children, it does work well. Scratch the child's initials on each heart and poke a hole in the top of the heart with a pencil. Let the hearts dry for one to two days.

Next, have the children paint the hearts using tempera paints and brushes. Once the paint has dried, pull a piece of yarn or string through the heart to make a necklace.

Consider allowing the children to each make two heart necklaces so that they can keep one and give one to a family member.

✳ Paper Box Town or Farm (A Whole-Class Project)

Materials: paper boxes and cups; empty spools of thread; wooden beads; construction paper in a variety of colors; scissors; glue; markers or crayons; large piece of butcher paper; tempera paints; old newspaper

Children create houses, apartment buildings, and stores for a town by decorating boxes and cups to make them look like buildings. Have the children cut out construction paper squares and rectangles for windows and doors or, if possible, have an adult volunteer carefully cut out needed doors or windows. Have the children make people by decorating the spools and gluing a bead on

the top to represent the head. If time permits, they can also make trees by wrapping cups in brown paper and attaching leafy treetops made from green paper.

When the buildings and people are finished, attach the butcher paper to a table top with tape. Protect the floor with newspaper or plastic drop cloths. Children take turns painting a ground or surface mural of roads or streets, sidewalks, grass, a pond, and so forth. When dry, the children glue or place their box stores and homes on the mural. The name and address of the child who created each building may be printed on the roof or front of the building. During creative play, the children may drive small matchbox-sized cars, trucks, and buses through their pretend town.

You may wish to vary this activity by having children create a paper box farm. If desired, let the children complete both a town and a farm and then compare and contrast them.

✳ Apartment Buildings

Materials: pictures of apartment buildings; 12" × 18" construction paper; 1-inch yellow squares; glue; magazines; 4" × 6" index cards

Show pictures of apartment buildings and discuss how apartment buildings are similar to and different from other homes in which people live. Talk about the large number of windows that is typical of an apartment building. Point out the square-shaped windows in the pictures.

Before giving the children glue, explore the square pieces of paper with the children, using the term *square* frequently. Give each child several squares to count and arrange in a row. Help children to explore the concept that four squares can be placed in two rows of two to make a larger square and the concept that two or three squares can be lined up together to make a rectangle.

✳ House Book

Materials: cardboard; wallpaper book; scissors; magazines or catalog

Using a cardboard template, children cut out simple house shapes that are as large as possible from pages of a wallpaper book. Children staple at least four house-shaped pages together to make a book. With your assistance, they label each page with the name of one kind of room. Their books should contain a kitchen page, a bathroom page, a living room page, and a bedroom page. Then they cut out catalog and magazine pictures of objects that could be found in a house. The children then categorize each object and glue it on the page where it is most likely to be found or used in a house.

BLOCKS

Encourage the children to build block neighborhoods similar to their own neighborhoods. For example, children could put blocks side by side as if they were attached row houses, apart as if single-family houses in the suburbs, or in rows like trailers in a mobile-home park. Provide small cars and other props to enhance their play. Talk about car safety, including how important it is for children and adults to wear seatbelts and to keep their arms and heads inside a moving car. Ask the children to tell you about where they live, where they play or buy groceries, and so forth.

BULLETIN BOARD

✳ We Help Our Families

Each child uses markers or crayons to draw a picture of himself or herself. The children then cut out small pictures in magazines and catalogs to represent ways they can help their family. They glue their helping picture on an index card, and an adult writes a sentence on the card to explain how the child helps the family. For example, the caption "I can put away the silverware" could be added to a picture of silverware, and the caption "I can put away my toys" could be added to a picture of children's toys. Display the completed cards near each child's picture on the board.

COOKING

✳ Cinnamon Mes

Refrigerated biscuit dough
Cinnamon sugar
($\frac{1}{2}$ cup sugar + $\frac{1}{2}$ teaspoon cinnamon)

Melted butter or soft butter
Wax paper
Pastry brush

Wash hands. Provide a piece of wax paper for each child to use as a clean work surface.

Talk together about family names. Encourage children to say their last name. Help them identify the letter with which their last name begins.

Let the children roll one or two biscuits into long snakes and then shape them into the initial of their last name. Give each child a card with his or her initial on it so that they have an accurate model.

Lay the initials on a baking sheet. Then let each child brush the initial with melted or soft butter and generously sprinkle cinnamon sugar over it. Bake as directed on the biscuit can.

✳ S'mores

Individual recipe:

2 graham crackers
1 teaspoon chocolate frosting

1 teaspoon marshmallow cream
Plastic knives

Wash hands. The children make s'mores by spreading frosting on one cracker and marshmallow cream on the other and putting the crackers together. As the children eat their s'mores, ask if anyone has ever gone camping or been at a cookout with a campfire. Talk about how families sometimes make s'mores by roasting marshmallows over a campfire rather than using marshmallow cream.

✳ House Sandwiches

House-shaped cookie cutter
Slices of bread
Low-fat cream cheese, softened

Jelly
Plastic knives

Wash hands. Have the children use the cookie cutter to cut two houses out of bread slices. Then have the children spread the cream cheese on one piece of bread and the jelly on the other and put the two pieces together to make a house sandwich.

LANGUAGE ARTS

✳ Action Play – Where I Live

Some people live in big houses.
(Stretch arms out as wide as possible.)
But some people's houses are small.
(Bring arms in close together.)
People live in mobile homes.
(Arms move in round wheel motions.)
Or in apartments so tall!
(Stretch up on tiptoes.)
But I think the place where I live
(Point to self.)
Is the very best place of all!
(Smile broadly, thumbs pointed up confidently.)

✳ Talking About My Family and Where I Live

Encourage the children to make up sentences using words such as *house, home, parents, family, street, road, name of city,* and so forth. Print the sentences on chart paper to "read" during the day. For children who are ready and interested, print their sentence on poster board also. Then cut the sentences in half and have the child arrange the parts in a sentence by matching each part to the sentence on the chart.

✳ Word Wall

Add the words *family* and *house* to the word wall. Add other topic-related words that children suggest. Also add a high-frequency word you want children to incorporate in their writing.

✳ What Mommies Do Best/What Daddies Do Best

Read aloud Numeroff's *What Mommies Do Best/What Daddies Do Best.* Children are surprised and delighted when the book has to be turned over midway through the story to finish the tale. Have the children use the format to create a class book entitled *What Adults Do Best/What Children Do Best.* The book could show that adults and children can do many of the same things at home. Let each child dictate or write an entry and illustrate a page of the book.

✳ Pajama Day

Arrange a special day for all to enjoy. Have the children (and teachers) wear pajamas to school and bring a favorite book from home or select one in school to read at the pajama party. (The pajamas may, of course, be worn over regular clothes.)

Talk about evening activities at home, including reading bedtime stories.

✳ Country Life/City Life Folder Game

Show several pictures or a video that portrays living in the country and living in the city. Talk about things that are found in the country and things that are found in the city.

Tape a piece of paper to each side of a folder to make two pockets. Label the pockets *Country* and *City*. Provide several small pictures of typical things found in the country and in the city, such as a tractor, fire hydrant, barn, store, apartment building, and so forth. Let the children place each picture in the appropriate pocket of the folder. If possible, ask them to explain why they think each picture belongs on one side or the other.

To make this activity more complex, provide some pictures that could belong in either pocket. Discuss the idea that while some things are different in the different places we live, other things remain the same.

✳ Matchups

Assemble an assortment of pairs of related objects that are often used by a family in or around the home. Some examples include: broom and dustpan, paper and pencil, spoon and fork, cup and saucer, shoe and sock, salt and pepper.

Discuss how members of a family use each object. Encourage the children to handle the objects. Then mix up all the objects, and have the children match the objects that go together.

You may wish to use a feely box (see p. 270) during this activity. A child feels one item in the box, identifies it, and then matches it to an object that is openly displayed nearby. For example, "I feel a sock. It goes with that shoe."

✳ Lacing Shapes

Lacing cards are an appealing left-to-right sequencing activity. Refer to the directions for making Lacing Cards in Appendix I, p. 271. Make topic-related lacing cards by making simple line drawings of several different houses and family members on pieces of poster board.

✳ The Three Little Pigs

Materials: piece of straw; stick; brick

Read or tell the story "The Three Little Pigs." Talk about why the house built of bricks was the strongest. Have the children try to break a piece of straw, a stick, and a brick in half.

Ask the children to think of all the things that are used to build houses today. Ask, "Do we use straw or sticks or bricks to build houses today?" If possible, take a field trip to a construction site where a house is being built.

✳ Family Talk

Allow the children to tell what their family does together to have fun. Have the children tell what jobs and/or chores each family member does to keep the household running smoothly.

Some children may enjoy making up one sentence about their family. Print their sentences on chart paper with children's names beside them.

✳ Picture Security

It helps reassure some children to have a picture of mom, dad, or the family in school. It helps them relate the familiarity of home with the newness of school. It also gives them something to show others and to talk about.

✳ Are You My Mother?

Adapt the popular book *Are You My Mother?* as a flannel-board story. Make characters from nonfabric interfacing by tracing the book's illustrations onto the interfacing and then coloring them. Let the children take turns placing the characters on the board as the story progresses.

Consider adding a special sound effect to each event in the story. For example, when the car appears in the story, have all the children make a car sound as one child puts the car on the flannel board. Adding sound effects increases the children's involvement and enjoyment.

✳ Which One Is Missing?

Provide a group of pictures of different family members cut from magazines or real photographs. Include a variety of ages, cultures, and clothing styles. Show each picture to the children and discuss who the family member might be and what that person might do in a family.

Place three or more of the pictures in a row on the table or floor where all the children can see them. (Vary the number according to the ability of the children.) Ask the children to close their eyes while you take away one picture. Have the whole group or individual children tell which picture is missing.

MATH

✳ Different Kinds of Homes – Graph Making

Talk with each child to determine the kind of home in which he or she lives (apartment, one-story house, and so forth). Find or draw a simple picture of each kind of home mentioned. Make a two-column chart by placing the pictures of the different homes along the left side of a piece of posterboard. Put the name and/or photograph of each child in the class in the row to the right of the kind of home in which the child lives.

Talk with the children about the ways in which the homes are different and the ways in which they are the same. Count together the number of different kinds of homes; the number of children living in each kind of home; and the number of girls or boys living in each kind of home.

✳ Flannel Board – Categorizing and Counting

Children cut out pictures of objects associated with fathers, mothers, children, babies, and pets from catalogs and magazines. Laminate each picture if desired and glue a small piece of sandpaper or Velcro® to the back so that it adheres to a flannel board.

Depending on the children's readiness, put some or all of the pictures on the flannel board. Have the children take turns identifying the objects. Then work together to make a set of objects associated with one of the family members. Have everyone count the objects as you point to or remove them. Continue making sets of objects for different family members and counting them.

✳ Family Puzzles

Find or draw pictures that show family groups of two, three, four, five, or more people. If desired, glue each picture on construction paper or poster board to make it sturdier. Cut each picture into the same number of puzzle pieces as the number of people in the picture. Provide matching numeral cards that indicate the number of people in each family group. Have children put together the pieces of each family puzzle and then place the card with the numeral that matches the number of family members next to the puzzle.

✳ Kerplunk

Materials: tin can; buttons or dried beans

Let each child take a turn telling the names of all the people in his or her family. As each name is said, the child is given a button or bean to hold. Then the child drops a button or bean into the tin can for each person in his family. As an item drops, the children count the "kerplunk."

To vary this activity, have two children stand together. Say, "Let's see how many people are in (child's name) and (child's name) families if we count them together." Have each child in turn drop his or her buttons or beans into the can, as the rest of the class counts.

✳ Three Little Pigs – Sets of Three

Make sets of three objects that are the same or similar: three blocks, three paper squares, three cups, and so forth. Mix up the sets and have the children put the objects back into sets. Then have the children take turns finding or creating sets of three classroom objects, for example, three crayons or three books.

✳ Puzzles of Three

Provide 6-inch to 8-inch cardboard or poster board cutouts of the numeral 3. Let the children trace around the pattern. Then have them cut their numeral 3 into three pieces to make a puzzle that they can put together again and again.

✳ Large and Small

Talk about making our bodies as large as possible and as small as possible. Then have all the children stretch their arms high above their heads to make themselves as large as possible. Next, have the children huddle in a ball on the floor to become as small as they can. Do this activity several times as you say "large" or "small."

✳ Large and Small Riddles

Play the following game allowing children to complete the riddle sentence.

Moms and dads are large; children are _____ .
Elephants are large; kittens are _____ .
Dogs are small; cows are _____ .

✳ Large and Small With Play Dough

Have the children use play dough to make large and small objects they can compare. For example, they can roll out large sheets and small sheets, make large balls and small balls, and pat out large house shapes and small house shapes.

✳ Squares and Rectangles

Children search for naturally occurring examples of squares and rectangles, such as windows, doors, picture frames, and ceiling tiles, in the classroom or school.

✳ "Wee Willie Winkie"

Recite the nursery rhyme "Wee Willie Winkie" together. Use a clock face to show eight o'clock and talk about how this is the bedtime of the children in the rhyme. Discuss the bedtimes of the children in the class and show each time on the clock face.

MOVEMENT

✳ Where Do I Live?

Where are you going Red Bird, Blue Bird?
We're flying to our homes in the tree.
    (Flap arms like a bird flying.)
Where are you going Mr. Horse, Mrs. Horse?
We're trotting to the barn don't you see?
    (Trot in place.)
Where are you going Little Fish, Big Fish?
We're swimming in the pond, let us be.
    (Lying on the floor, move arms and legs in swimming motions.)
Where are you going little girl, little boy?
We're skipping to my home, come with me!
    (Skip around the room.)

✳ Number Toss

Materials: opened cans; black marker; masking tape or foil

Use three to five clean, opened cans. Use a black marker to print a numeral from 1 through 5 or 9 on each can. Make a small ball about the size of a large walnut by wadding up pieces of masking tape or foil.

Set the cans on the floor against the wall and out of a busy area. Have the children play a ball toss game by tossing the tape or foil ball into a can. They then read the numeral on the can and complete a movement suggested by the teacher: hop on one foot that many times, do that number of jumping jacks, touch your toes that many times, and so forth.

✳ Family Fitness

Talk about families exercising to stay healthy. Model different exercises and have the children do them with you. Model jogging in place; log rolling by lying on the floor with arms stretched over head and then rolling over and over; opening or closing (one-half of jumping jacks movement); and twisting at the waist from side to side with arms extended.

✳ Walk the Line

Put an 8- to 10-foot strip of masking tape on the floor. Have the children walk the line in suggested ways, such as walk like a tall dad; walk the line like an old grandfather; walk the line like a child going to school; and crawl the line like a baby.

MUSIC

✳ Rock-a-Bye Baby

Sing the song through once to remind everyone of its familiar melody and lyrics. Have all the children sit on the floor and rock from side to side while they sing. You could also have them lie on their backs and rock from side to side while singing.

✳ Coming Round the Mountain

Using the familiar song "She'll Be Coming Round the Mountain," make up verses about families going places. Sample verses: *We'll all go see a real cool movie in the theater. We'll all go grocery shopping at the store. We'll all go hiking and camping in the woods.*

✳ At Our Home

(Tune: "London Bridge")

Have the children talk about the activities they do at home, suggest movements that show these activities, and then perform these movements as they sing a song based on "London Bridge." For example, children could sing:

This is how we play with our toys, play with our toys, play with our toys,
This is how we play with our toys, with our families.

Additional verses could include:

This is how we read a story . . . . . .
This is how we make our beds . . . . . .
This is how we eat our breakfast . . . . . .

ROLE PLAY

✳ Three Little Pigs

Have the children act out "The Three Little Pigs." Let them make their own props and spontaneously create dialogue. You might wish to have them use small chairs to create an area for each of the three houses.

✳ Keeping Clean Where I Live

Provide simple cleaning supplies such as broom and dustpan, cleaning rag, soapy water, and sponge. Encourage the children to clean and organize the home living area of the room.

✳ Family Activities

Encourage the children to role play going to the store or out to eat with their families. Props from the home living center could be used.

Role play going on a vacation or a trip. Use the chairs to make the bus, train, or airplane, or make a family car. Talk about the importance of wearing seatbelts when riding in a car. Decide which family member will drive, read the map, describe the scenery, and so forth.

SCIENCE

✳ Classification – Natural and Man-Made

Invite the children to bring objects for the science table that they have collected on family outings. Pine cones from a camping trip or shells from the beach are great to share. Talk about the similarities and differences among the treasures the children bring. Talk about the differences between natural and man-made objects. Invite children to separate the objects into two sets by classifying them as *natural* or *man-made.*

✳ Nature Observation

Go for a science walk outside. Collect interesting items such as leaves, bark, twigs, rocks, insects, and nests to display on a low table. Provide a good magnifying glass so that the children can closely examine their treasures.

Remove a weed from the ground, keeping the root system intact. Gently knock off the excess soil to expose all of the roots. Put the weed on the science table with the magnifying glass. Encourage the children to examine the root structure closely.

✳ Straw, Sticks, Bricks

Materials: straw; stick; bricks

After retelling "The Three Little Pigs," provide samples of straw, sticks, and bricks for the children to feel and discuss. Place three to six samples of each material on a tabletop. Help the children conduct several experiments with the materials and record the results of each. You could have the children:

1. Weigh each sample.
2. Measure the length of each sample.
3. Try to blow each sample to make it move.
4. Try to stack each sample as if building a structure.

Encourage the children to observe and discuss what happens. Talk together about what it would be like to live in a house made of sticks or straw. List as many advantages and disadvantages as the children can think of.

TRANSITION ACTIVITY

Children take turns role-playing an activity that a family member does. The rest of the children try to guess the activity. Encourage children to repeat the following pattern each time they begin to role play: " I am a (kinds of family member). Guess what I am doing." For example, "I am a baby. Guess what I am doing." (The child acts out crawling.) "I am a mommy. Guess what I am doing." (The child acts out driving a car.)

As appropriate, encourage children to model nonstereotypical gender roles. For example, both a dad and a mom could cook or vacuum.

CHILDREN'S BOOKS

Beil, K. *Grandma According to Me.* New York: Dell, 1992. This story portrays the special bond between a grandmother and her granddaughter.

Blume, J. *The Pain and the Great One.* Scarsdale, NY: Bradbury, 1974. The first half of this book deals with an older sister's view of her younger brother; the second half deals with the brother's view of his sister.

Brown, M. *D. W., Go to Your Room!* Boston: Little, Brown, 1999. D.W. is sent to her room for being mean to her baby sister. Her sister makes her feel better, and they end up playing together.

Eastman, P. D. *Are You My Mother?* Random House, 1996. A newly hatched bird travels to find her mother and considers the most unlikely and humorous possibilities.

Finchler, J. *Miss Malarkey Doesn't Live in Room 10.* New York: Walker & Co., 1995. A first-grade boy is sure his teacher lives at school. He's very surprised when she moves into his apartment building.

Flournoy, V. *The Patchwork Quilt.* New York: Dial, 1985. Making a quilt brings a family together.

Fox, M. *Wilfrid Gordon McDonald Partridge*. New York: Kane/Miller, 1985. A warm-hearted story of a small boy who lives next door to a home for the elderly and tries to help the residents recover their memories.

Joosse, B. *I Love You the Purplest*. San Francisco: Chronicle Books, 1996. A clever, loving mother of two brothers answers the question "Who do you love the most?"

McCutcheon, J. *Happy Adoption Day*. New York: Little, Brown, 1996. A sweet story about parents and child celebrating the anniversary of the child's adoption.

Numeroff, L. *What Mommies Do Best/What Daddies Do Best*. New York: Simon & Schuster, 1998. Read half of the book and then turn it over to read the other half from a different family member's point of view. Shows everyday family tasks while avoiding stereotypical gender roles.

Penn, A.. *The Kissing Hand*. Washington, D.C.: Child Welfare League of America, 1993. Chester the raccoon does not want to go to kindergarten, but Mother comes up with a loving secret to help him.

Polacco, P. *My Rotten Redheaded Older Brother*. New York: Simon & Schuster. 1994. Autobiographical. Sibling rivalry with a pleasant surprise.

Sruve-boden, S. *We'll Paint the Octopus Red*. Bethesda, MD: Woodbine House. 1998. The baby is born with Down's syndrome. Daddy is sad, but Emma figures they'll do a million things together, as long everyone is patient.

Viorst, J. Alexander, *Who's Not (Do you hear me? I mean it!) Going To Move*. New York: Simon & Schuster, 1995. A kid's perspective on the difficulties of moving, told with humor.

Wood, S. *What Dads Can't Do*. New York: Simon & Schuster, 2000. This book has a great message, alligator characters, and a story that appeals to children. Your class can imagine also what moms, sisters, and brothers can't do..

Yolen, J. *Off We Go!* Boston: Little, Brown, 2000. A rhyming, progressive story about a variety of animals going to their Grandma's house.

October Curriculum

Fall Changes

Hands and Feet

Fall Changes

CONCEPTS

- Fall is a season that comes after summer and before winter.
- Autumn is another name for fall.
- Leaves on many trees change color, die, and fall to the ground.
- Many foods ripen and are harvested in the fall. Some of these foods are apples, pumpkins, nuts, and potatoes.
- The weather becomes cooler in the fall, and people begin wearing sweaters and jackets.
- Days become shorter, and nights become longer.
- Halloween is a holiday celebrated on October 31 each year.
- Some symbols used to celebrate Halloween are scarecrows, pumpkins, corn stalks, black cats, witches, and ghosts.
- Orange and black are Halloween colors.
- It is important to practice safety on Halloween and throughout the year.

CONTINUING CONCEPTS

- **Colors** Have children count, identify, and graph the different colors of fallen leaves they collect around school and where they live.
  Have children identify fall colors and talk about why those colors are associated with fall.
  Have children identify orange and black as Halloween colors.
- **Geometric Shapes** Focus on a square and help children recognize that a square has four sides.
  Focus on a rectangle and help children recognize that a rectangle has two long sides and two short sides.
- **Health and Nutrition** Discuss why it is important to wear sweaters and jackets on cool days.
  Talk about washing fruits and vegetables before eating them.
  Discuss safe behavior on Halloween.
- **Senses** Talk about the sights and smells of fall. Ask: "What can we see in fall that we can't see at other times? What can we smell?"
  Have children listen as you crunch a dried leaf. List together words to describe the sound.
  Have children touch a dried leaf and a fresh leaf and compare how they feel.
- **Traditional Rhymes and Tales** Recite "Peter, Peter, Pumpkin Eater" and "The Old Woman Who Lived in a Shoe" with the children.

PORTFOLIO PRODUCTS

The teacher or children can consider the following suggestion as they select at least one product from this unit to place in each portfolio.

- To assess fine-motor coordination and knowledge of geometric figures, have children fold a large sheet paper into four sections and then draw a different shape in each box, for example, a circle, a square, a triangle, and rectangle. Drawing a circle, square, and triangle involves the same strokes required in letter formation. Children who experience difficulty completing those geometric figures, therefore, may have a lower readiness for handwriting, especially in respect to their ability to control letter formation between lines.

ART

✳ Easel or Tabletop Painting: Fall Colors

Materials: tempera paints in fall and Halloween colors; brushes; sponges; corncobs; paper

1. **Free Exploration** – Provide children with fall colors of paint and encourage them to freely explore as they use and blend the colors. Talk about where children might see each color.
2. **Leaf Shape Painting** – Have the children paint large leaf shapes in fall colors using a brush or sponge.
3. **Corncob Painting** – Give the children orange and black paint and corncobs. Explain that orange and black are Halloween colors. Talk about where corncobs come from and how scarecrows are made to scare the birds away from eating the corn. Discuss how the cob feels when touched. Children dip a cob in the tempera and gently brush it across the paper. Encourage the children to use gentle strokes so that they see the patterns the cob makes as it lightly brushes across the paper. Have them paint with different parts of a corncob and compare the different patterns they produce.

✳ Fall Tree Door or Wall Decoration

Materials: brown butcher paper; tempera paints in fall colors; art paper; tissue paper in fall colors or real leaves; paper towels; watercolor paints

Cut a tree shape from brown butcher paper or twist lengths of butcher paper. Use it to make a three-dimensional tree trunk and branches. Choose one or more of the following ways for the children to make fall leaves for the tree.

1. Children make their handprints using tempera paints in fall colors. They cut out the prints and place them on the tree as leaves.
2. Provide fall colors of tissue paper cut in squares. Have children twist squares and glue them on the tree to produce the effect of leaves.
3. Have children collect fall-colored leaves. Dry the leaves by pressing them in heavy books between sheets of waxed paper before placing them on the tree.
4. Cut leaf shapes from paper towels. Have children use watercolors to paint the towel leaves. The colors will run and create different color tones.

✳ Nature Collages

Materials: natural objects gathered on a nature walk; construction paper; glue

Children make collages using the objects they collect on a nature walk (see p. 40). Talk about the colors of fall. Use descriptive words about fall as you encourage the children to talk about how the natural objects feel.

✳ Apple Printing

Materials: one apple cut in half vertically and one apple cut in half horizontally; 3 plastic foam trays or paper plates; red, yellow, and green tempera; Manila paper; paper towels

Talk about the colors of apples. Pour a small amount of one color on each of the trays or plates. Demonstrate how to press an apple half in the paint and then press it on a paper to create an apple print. Call attention to the different prints made by apples that are cut in different ways. Have children change colors and continue printing and overlapping the colors. Ask children what they notice about how the colors change when they overlap. Show children how to gently wipe off an apple by pressing it on a paper towel when they finish using it.

✳ Leaf Mobile

Materials: fall leaves; clear contact paper; string or yarn; small branches found on the ground or wooden dowels

Cut squares of clear contact paper. Have children press one leaf between two squares of contact paper. They then cut around the leaf, leaving a $\frac{1}{4}$-inch edge of contact paper all around the edge of the leaf to prevent the contact paper from peeling off. Make several contact-covered leaves and tape a string to each. Tie each leaf to a small branch or dowel so that it will dangle as if from a mobile. Hang the mobile from the ceiling.

✳ Pumpkin Puppets

Materials: 5-inch squares of orange construction paper, two for each child; black and green construction paper; glue; stapler

Talk about a square and a rectangle with the children. Point out that the orange paper is cut into squares. Cut a small rectangle from a piece of green paper. Count together the number of sides both shapes have.

Give the children black construction paper and have them cut out triangles, circles, or free shapes to make jack-o-lantern features. They then glue the features on one of the orange squares. Then have them cut out a green rectangle and glue it on the top for the stem. Finally, help them glue or staple a second square to the first square on three sides to make a simple hand puppet, as shown.

✳ Halloween Turn-around Drawing

Materials: child pattern cut from cardboard; paper; crayons or markers

Use this activity the day after Halloween so that children can draw what they looked like in their Halloween costumes.

Children draw an outline of their bodies or trace around a simple pattern of a child that is similar to a paper doll pattern. They cut out the figure and use crayons or markers on the front to draw their facial features and usual, everyday clothing. Then they turn the figure over and draw themselves in Halloween costume. The final product is a turn-around drawing that shows the child as he or she is usually dressed and as he or she was dressed for Halloween.

Encourage children to show both sides of their drawing and tell about their Halloween.

BLOCKS

✳ Raking Fall Leaves

Add one or two plastic toy rakes and a small pile of leaves to the block area. Encourage children to use blocks to build a fence area into which they can rake the leaves.

✳ Forming Geometric Shapes

Ask two children to find four short blocks that are the same length. Model how to use the blocks to make a square. With the children, count the number of blocks that were used. Encourage the children to make additional squares using four different blocks.

Continue the activity by asking one child to find two long blocks that are the same length and another child to find two short blocks that are the same length. Model how to use the blocks to make a rectangle. Count the blocks that were used and then encourage children to make more rectangles with different combinations of blocks.

BULLETIN BOARD

✳ Apple-picking Time

Prepare 45 laminated cutouts of apples and 9 felt bushel baskets with one numeral, 1 through 9, on each. Cut a tree shape from brown butcher paper or use twisted lengths of butcher paper to make a three-dimensional tree trunk and branches. Staple the tree to the bulletin board and use Velcro® to attach the apples on the branches and around the base of the tree. Arrange the felt baskets in the remaining space on the board. You may also wish to add a border of apples or fall leaves in different sizes or colors.

Have the children pick the apples and place the appropriate number in each numbered basket. (The Velcro® on each apple allows it to stick to a felt basket.) When the activity is completed, have the children return the apples to the tree and ground so that the board is ready for another child. Children may want to repeat the activity several times.

To vary the activity, place the baskets on the board in numbered sequence from left to right. Have the children pick the apples and put the corresponding number of apples in each basket. When the children are familiar with this activity, place the baskets in random order to encourage recognition of the numerals out of sequence. For children who display the appropriate level of readiness, you can increase the total number of apples and baskets.

COOKING

✳ Cinnamon Applesauce

Apples, ½ apple for each child   Wax paper
10-oz package Cinnamon Red Hot Candies   Plastic knives
1 cup water   Electric pan

Wash hands and then wash the apples together. Talk about the importance of washing fruit to remove the chemicals used when the apples are growing. Read or tell the story "The Riddle of the Star" (see p. 41). As you finish the story, cut an apple in half horizontally through the middle and show the children the star pattern formed by the seeds inside. Cut and slice the rest of the apples. Give each child a few slices to cut into smaller pieces on wax paper.

Combine the apple pieces in the electric pan. Measure and add the water and candy. Bring it to a boil in a location that is off limits to the children. Reduce the heat and let the mixture simmer for 20 to 30 minutes. Stir it occasionally and call children's attention to the yummy smell in the air. Point out the change in the color of the cooked apples.

Ask the children to help you retell "Riddle of the Star" as you share the cinnamon applesauce.

LANGUAGE ARTS

✳ Action Play – Fall Tree

I am a large fall tree.
(Raise arms overhead.)
Winds blow and blow at me.
(Sway back and forth.)
My leaves come tumbling down.
(Swirl hands in downward movement.)
And make a blanket on the ground.
(Lay down on the floor.)

✳ Jack-O'-Lantern

There's a scary jack-o'-lantern.
(Circle shape with two arms.)
It's staring straight your way!
(Open eyes wide and extend head forward.)
Don't be scared! Don't be afraid!
(Hide eyes with hands.)
It probably just wants to play!
(Spread arms open wide and smile.)

☀ Word Wall

Add the word *fall* to the word wall. Brainstorm a short list of words that rhyme with *fall* and add them to the word wall. Also add other topic-related words that children suggest and a high-frequency word you want the children to incorporate in their writing.

☀ Nutty Classification

Provide a bowl with several different kinds of unshelled nuts. Ask the children to sort the nuts, grouping them by size, color, or type.

☀ Our Fall Story

Write a class story about the nature walk the class went on to collect objects for their Nature Collages (see p. 40). Ask leading questions to elicit statements about the walk from the children and guide them through a retelling of events in sequence. Encourage the children to use sentences rather than one-or two-word phrases. Write their statements on chart paper. When the story is complete, ask the class to decide on a good title; write the title at the top of the paper. Finally, invite each child to glue a leaf from the nature walk around the border of the story.

Copy and duplicate the story for children to read and take home. You may wish to take a picture of the original story to include in a parent newsletter or to add to the parent calendar.

☀ Feely Box

For directions for making a feely box, see Appendix I, p. 270. Out of sight of the children, put one fall object, such as a nut, leaf, pine cone, or apple, into the feely box. Have children take turns reaching inside to feel the object and guess what it is.

☀ Carve a Jack-O'-Lantern

If possible, go on a class trip to a pumpkin patch, vegetable stand, or grocery store and buy a pumpkin. Decide in advance on a maximum amount of money to spend so that the children can discuss which pumpkins are too expensive and which are within their price limit. Talk about the different sizes and shapes of the pumpkins you see.

After the trip, work together to design a face for the pumpkin. Have the children suggest different shapes and sizes of shapes for the design. Draw their suggestions on chart paper. Use the terms *circle, square, triangle,* and *rectangle* as you work. Sketch several different faces and have the class vote on which one to use.

Cut an opening at the top of the pumpkin. Have the children take turns peeking inside. Discuss how the pumpkin and seeds look. Have children pull out some seeds and feel them. Have the children brainstorm all the words they can think of to describe how the seeds feel when they handle them. Write their ideas on chart paper.

Talk about how seeds grow inside the pumpkin. Ask, "What is all that fiber inside the pumpkin?" Take turns pulling out the seeds and fiber. Save the seeds.

Use a marker to draw the face design on the pumpkin. Cut the face using a small, sharp knife. This is best done with the children's assistance.

✳ Safety Rules

As a class, talk about Halloween safety rules. Discuss what children will wear and where they will go on Halloween evening. Talk about carrying a flashlight on Halloween evening in order to be easily seen. During the discussion, encourage children to take turns speaking, to speak in complete sentences, and to listen to others.

Invite a police officer to visit the class and talk to the children about safety at Halloween and all year through. Discuss safety when walking, crossing streets, playing near a street, riding a bike, wearing a seatbelt when riding in a car, carrying a light while trick-or-treating, and not eating any treats until an adult at home has checked them.

✳ Leaf Game

Provide cutout pairs of leaves in several fall colors. This activity works best in small groups so that children don't have to wait long for a turn.

1. **Colors** – Mix up the color pairs and let children match them again. Talk about the color names.
2. **Position Directions** – Provide a small, real tree branch, or use the Friendship Tree made previously (see p. 3). Ask children to take turns listening and following directions that include position words, such as "Put the yellow leaf on top of the branch" and "Put the red leaf beside the branch."

✳ Frog and Toad in the Fall

Read Lobel's *Frog and Toad All Year* to the class. Have the children retell the story in sequence. Provide prompts by asking them about what happens first, next, and so forth. Write their statements on sentence strips and place them in a pocket chart. Reread the sentence strip story several times. A few days later, when children know the story well, arrange the strips out of sequence and ask children to help you put them in order.

Discuss what Frog and Toad did in the fall and how they dressed. Provide Manila paper and markers. Write or have the children write *Frog and Toad in the Fall* at the top of their paper and then draw a picture of what Frog and Toad looked like and what they did.

MATH

✳ Calendar

Give copies of a blank calendar (Activity Master 3, p. 280) to the children who can write numerals. Help them write the name of the month and then add the date in the appropriate space each day. Have children compare their calendar from last month with this month's calendar.

✳ Counting

1. **Nuts, Leaves, Apples** – Provide groups of real nuts, leaves, or apples and have the children count each group. Change the number of objects and have the children count again.

Put together mixed groups of the objects. Make a pattern with some or all of them and discuss your pattern with the children. Later, give each child a mixed group of the objects. Ask them to make a pattern with their objects and then describe their pattern to you.

2. **Fall Leaves**

One fall leaf, two fall leaves,
   (Hold up another finger for each additional leaf.)
Three fall leaves, Hooray!
Four fall leaves, five fall leaves,
The wind blows them away!
   (Blow on fingers and let the fingers wiggle and swirl away.)
Six fall leaves, seven fall leaves,
   (Continue to hold another finger for each additional leaf.)
Eight fall leaves, Hooray!
Nine fall leaves, ten fall leaves,
The wind blows them away!
   (Blow on fingers and let the fingers wiggle and swirl away.)

✳ Scarecrow Match

Duplicate Activity Master 7, p. 284; you will need one copy for each child. Cut out the scarecrow parts on each. Show pictures of scarecrows to the children and discuss why farmers use them in their fields and why we use them as Halloween decorations. Give each child a set of cutout scarecrow parts. Have them match the numerals on the parts and then use paper fasteners or glue to put the parts together. They may add a face to the scarecrow if they wish.

✳ Squirrels and Nuts

Cut out several squirrels using the pattern shown. Staple each squirrel to a small paper cup so that it will stand up by itself. Then print a numeral on each cup. Use numerals that are appropriate to the children's level of readiness. Some preschoolers may need to concentrate on numerals 1 to 5 or 6, while other children may be ready for numerals up to 9 or higher.

Discuss how squirrels collect nuts in the fall. Ask children why they think squirrels do that? Provide a bowl of small nuts, such as acorns. If possible, use nuts gathered outside. Have the children count out the correct number of nuts to put in each cup.

✳ Apple, Apple

1. Provide two or three apples of as many different varieties and sizes as possible. Place them all in a large bowl. Have the children sort and categorize them in as many ways as possible, for example, by color, kind, and size. Ask children to tell you how they categorized the apples each time.

2. Count the apples as a total group and by variety. This is a good opportunity to talk about groups and combining and separating groups. Discuss and demonstrate adding small

groups of apples and then subtracting by taking one or more apples from a group. If children are ready, show them how to write a number sentence, such as 2 + 1 = 3 and draw an illustration that shows each number sentence. Explain the meaning of the plus, minus, and equals signs. Encourage children who demonstrate readiness to write and illustrate their own addition and subtraction number sentences.

MOVEMENT

✳ Falling Leaves

Lay a long rope on the floor in a spiral pattern. Have children walk barefooted on the rope as they imitate the motion of a falling leaf.

✳ Little Squirrel

Little squirrel, little squirrel,
Swish your bushy tail.
   (Children wiggle bottoms as if swishing tails.)
Little squirrel, little squirrel
Swish your bushy tail.
   (Wiggle bottoms.)
Hold a nut way up tall,
   (Pretend to lift a nut overhead between two hands.)
Wrinkle up your nose so small,
   (Wrinkle and wiggle noses.)
Little squirrel, little squirrel,
Swish your bushy tail.
   (Wiggle bottoms.)
1-2-3-4-5-6-7-8-9-10.
   (Count out loud from 1 to 10 as the children swish that many times.)

MUSIC

✳ Seed Shakers

Make rhythm instruments by stapling large seeds or small nuts between two small paper plates. Children shake the instruments in rhythm and dance as music is played.

✳ Falling Leaves

Play short excerpts of music with three different tempos. Ask the children to decide which is best for pretending to be falling leaves. Talk about what children have observed about real falling leaves. Discuss if leaves fall fast or more slowly. Use the word *gently* as you discuss the leaves.

Play slow, graceful music. Have the children envision leaves *gently* swirling and falling to the ground. Play the music again and have the children move to the music as they pretend to be falling leaves.

✳ Flapping Scarecrow

(Tune: "Did You Ever See a Lassie?")

Did you ever see a scarecrow, a scarecrow, a scarecrow,
Did you ever see a scarecrow flap this way and that?
With his loose arms and wobbly head and straw hands and long legs,
Did you ever see a scarecrow flap this way and that?

Have the children move their bodies like scarecrows, waving and wobbling each body part as it is mentioned in the song. Then have everyone hum the tune while moving like scarecrows and parading in a circle.

ROLE PLAY

✳ Harvesting

Place a pumpkin and an assortment of apples and nuts in a variety of places in the classroom. Supply small baskets. Have the children pretend to harvest apples and nuts by picking apples from trees and collecting nuts from the ground.

✳ Costumes

Provide old Halloween costumes and a mirror. Have the children try on the costumes and look at themselves in the mirror. Encourage them to talk about the costumes.

✳ Halloween Parade

Have each child choose a Halloween character (jack-o'-lantern, bat, scarecrow, witch) and act out the character while parading around the room. You don't need props or costumes for this parade. The children have to figure out how to act like a character, rather than simply dress as one. Continue the activity by having each child choose a different character. Play a marching song during each parade.

SCIENCE

✳ Signs of Fall Display

Ask children to bring objects to school that show that fall is here. Use a large, empty picture frame to create an effective visual display for the objects. Make a stand-up sign by folding a piece of heavyweight paper in half and writing the caption *Signs of Fall* on one half.

You may wish to prepare an insect "house" in case some children bring in insects. Provide a magnifying glass and encourage children to closely inspect the fall items.

Note: Do not leave the magnifying glass in a sunny spot for an extended period of time.

✳ Nature Walk

Take the children on a walk around the area or through a park. Give each child a paper sack for collecting signs of fall, such as fallen leaves, nuts, pine cones, weeds. Observe changes in nature and in the color of natural things. Carefully observe trees. Have children find and touch roots, bark, and leaves. Use and encourage children to use descriptive words as they examine the parts of trees. Ask, "Are all the trees losing their leaves?" Point out evergreens and talk about them.

Back at school, examine and count the collected objects. Challenge children to classify the objects in as many ways as possible.

✳ Growing Pumpkins

After making a jack-o'-lantern, save some of the pumpkin seeds for planting. Soak a few seeds overnight. Plant them in a large pan and water them as needed. (Use a clear plastic pan so that children can see root growth. Large but inexpensive plastic pans, meant to collect water under plants, are available in most discount stores.) Make an illustrated chart that shows when the seeds were planted, when they sprouted, and the heights of the growing plant. Supply a magnifying glass so that children can examine the plant closely.

TRANSITION ACTIVITY

✳ Pumpkin Jack-O'-Lantern

Use the pumpkin puppets created in art. One side has a jack-o'-lantern face. The other side is plain, like an uncut pumpkin.

1. Hold out the pumpkin side and say, "Pumpkin, pumpkin, round and fat." Quickly turn your hand around to show the jack-o'-lantern side. Hold that side out and say, "Turn into a jack-o-lantern just like that!" Repeat the rhyme a few times. Then encourage children to use their puppets and say the simple verse with you.

2. As children wear their puppets, have children follow simple directions that use position words. Some suggestions follow:

    Put your puppet over your head.
    Put your puppet under your arm.
    Put your puppet upside down.
    Walk your puppet down your leg

CHILDREN'S BOOKS

Adoff, A. *Touch the Poem.* New York: Blue Sky Press, 2000. Throughout the seasons, children can explore their senses through kid-friendly poetry. Includes photographs and computer graphics.

Arnosky, J. *Every Autumn Comes the Bear.* New York: Putnam, 1996. Follow a bear as he prepares for winter hibernation. Simple text and great illustrations.

Buck, N. *Creepy Crawly Critters and Other Halloween Tongue Twisters.* New York: HarperCollins, 1995. Children laugh as they try to say these Halloween tongue twisters.

De Groat, D. *Trick or Treat, Smell My Feet.* New York: Morrow, 1998. Gilbert mistakenly takes his sister's ballerina costume to school instead of his. What will he do now?

Ehlert, L. *Red Leaf, Yellow Leaf.* San Diego: Harcourt Brace Jovanovich, 1991. Die cuts and beautiful color are used to show how a tree grows. Some children will be interested in the instructional information at the end.

Fowler, A. *How Do You Know It's Fall?* Chicago: Children's Press, 1994. Photos of traditional signs of fall, including people playing football!

Huck, C. *A Creepy Countdown.* New York: Greenwillow, 1998. A counting book with a Halloween theme.

Hunter, A. *Possum's Harvest Moon.* New York: Houghton Mifflin, 1998. Possum wants to throw a party for his friends and enjoy the harvest moon. But they are all preparing to hibernate.

Lionni, L. *A Busy Year.* New York: Scholastic, 1992. Willie and Winnie love their tree through all the seasons.

Lobel, *Frog and Toad All Year.* New York: Harper & Row, 1976. Frog and Toad share funny adventures throughout the seasons.

Lotz, K. *Snowsong Whistling.* New York: Puffin, 1997. Simple rhyming verse takes us through many fall activities and concludes with the first snowfall.

Martin, Jr., B. *The Turning of the Year.* San Diego: Harcourt Brace, 1998. The months of the year told in rhyme and traditional illustrations.

Plourde, L. *Wild Child.* New York: Simon & Schuster, 1999. The story presents beautiful art and rich vocabulary to relate the problems Mother Earth encounters as she attempts to put her wild child, Autumn, to bed.

Rathmann, P. *Officer Buckle and Gloria.* New York: Putnam's Sons, 1995. An award-winning book with a warm and humorous safety message. Use this book after having a guest speaker on safety.

Ray, M. Pumpkins: *A Story for a Field.* San Diego: Harcourt Brace, 1996. A man doesn't have the money to buy the field to save it from developers. He talks to the field and they decide to grow pumpkins. An introduction to conservation.

Rylant, C. *Henry and Mudge Under the Yellow Moon.* New York: Simon and Schuster, 1998. Best friends, a boy and a dog, enjoy the fall season from Halloween to Thanksgiving.

Schnur, S. *Autumn: An Alphabet Acrostic.* New York: Clarion, 1997. Brief acrostic poems for words associated with fall. Appealing illustrations.

The Riddle of the Star

Retold by Bertie Kingore

Once upon a time a little girl was bored and asked her mother to help her think of something fun to do. Her mother said, "Be a detective. See if you can answer this riddle:

"I'm a little, round house, colored yellow, green, or red.
I have no doors or windows, but a chimney is on my head."

"You'll know when you find the right house," said her mother. "Because when you open it up there's a star inside." So the little girl skipped off to figure out the riddle. She skipped a short distance and saw a police car and her police friend, Miss Owens.

The little girl called out, "Miss Owens, can you help me solve this riddle?"

"I'm a little, round house, colored yellow, green, or red.
I have no doors or windows, but a chimney is on my head."

"I'll know when I find the right house," said the little girl, "because there's star inside."

"I'm sorry," said Miss Owens. "I've been assigned to patrol this area for eight months now. But I don't remember a house like the one you've described. You might ask Mr. Matthews, the mailman. He surely knows every house in this area."

So again the little girl skipped off. She soon found Mr. Matthews delivering mail to a neighbor's mailbox.

"Mr. Matthews! Mr. Matthews!" yelled the little girl as she ran up to the mailbox. "Can you help me solve this riddle?"

"I'm a little, round house, colored yellow, green, or red.
I have no doors or windows, but a chimney is on my head."

"I'll know when I find the right house," said the little girl, "because there's a star inside."

"Dear me," said Mr. Matthews. "I've been delivering mail to this area for nine years now. But I don't remember a house like the one you've described. Say, you might ask Granny Smith. She's lived here longer than anyone else has. She surely knows every house in this area."

So once again the little girl skipped a short distance and found Granny Smith working in the orchard beside her house.

"Granny Smith," called the little girl as she ran up to her. "Can you help me solve this riddle?"

"I'm a little, round house, colored yellow, green, or red.
I have no doors or windows, but a chimney is on my head."

"I'll know when I find the right house," said the little girl, "because there's a star inside."

Granny Smith just laughed and laughed. She picked an apple from one of her trees and then sat down on the ground to talk with the little girl. "When I was just a little girl like you," Granny said, "I planted some apple seeds in this rich ground. I watered the seeds and cared for them, and they grew into these lovely trees. Now I have an apple orchard." Then she said,

"My apples are little and round, they are yellow, green, or red.
They have no doors or windows, but a chimney is on each head."

And Granny pointed to the stem on the top of the apple. "Oh," said the little girl. "The stem *is* like a chimney, and your apples are like little round houses. But I've eaten lots of apples and I've never seen a star inside."

Granny smiled and said, "Take this apple home and ask your mother to help you open it to find the star inside."

"Thank you, Granny Smith!" called the little girl as she skipped back to her house. She quickly ran inside and showed her mother the apple. "Look, Mom," said the little girl. And she said,

"An apple is a little, round house, colored yellow, green, or red.
It has no doors or windows, but a chimney is on its head."

"You are a clever detective," laughed her mother.

"But you have to show me if there's a star inside!" pleaded the little girl.

Her mother took the apple and got a knife. She cut the apple in half. But she did not cut it in half from the stem down to the bottom. She cut it in half through the middle of the round part of the apple. And, when the little girl lifted the pieces apart, there was a star. The beautiful seeds made a star, a star inside an apple!

Hands and Feet

CONCEPTS

- Hands are important parts of our body. They enable us to pick up and carry things, write, and draw. They also help us communicate.
- Feet are an important part of our body. They help us balance and move.
- It's fun to do silly things with our hands and feet.
- Everyone's fingerprints and toe prints are different.
- Hands and feet enable us to identify objects through our sense of touch.

CONTINUING CONCEPTS

- **Colors** Sort mittens and shoes by color.
- **Geometric Shapes** Compare a square and a rectangle. Talk about the similarities and differences between these two shapes.
- **Health and Nutrition** Discuss when and why some people wear mittens or gloves. Discuss why most people wear shoes. Why do people wear shoes more often than they wear mittens or gloves?
- **Senses** Compare the sense of touch using hands versus feet.
  Discuss why feet sometimes smell.
  Explore sounds that can be made using our hands.
  Visually investigate fingerprints and compare them.
- **Traditional Rhymes and Tales** Read or tell the story "The Gingerbread Man."

PORTFOLIO PRODUCTS

The teacher or children select at least one product from this unit to place in each portfolio. Two suggestions follow.
- Include each child's Hand and Shoe Flower (see p. 44), or have children trace around their own hands on construction paper and cut them out as an initial assessment of fine-motor coordination.
- Include each child's completed monthly calendar in the portfolio as evidence of his or her ability to write and organize numerals.

ART

✳ Easel or Tabletop Painting: Sponge Painting

Materials: tempera paints; art paper; small sponges cut into simple hand and foot shapes; plastic foam trays or paper plates; clothespins

Cut flat sponges into simple hand and foot shapes. Put small amounts of tempera paint on trays or plates. The children dip the sponge shapes into the paint and press them on their paper. To limit the messiness, pinch a clothespin on each sponge before it is used. The children can use the clothespin as a handle when they dip the sponge in paint.

Ask children to name the colors they are using. Ask them to notice what happens when they print one wet color over another. Ask, "How does the color change?"

✳ Hand and Shoe Flowers

Materials: butcher paper; multiple colors of construction paper

Create a funny hand and shoe flower garden "planted" along a wall. You may wish to have children work in pairs and help each other during this activity.

On one color of construction paper, children trace one hand with their fingers spread out as far as possible and cut out the hand shape. They then trace two or more shoes on green paper and cut out these shapes. The hand cutout becomes the blossom and the shoe cutouts become the leaves of a flower. Children cut out a green stem and glue their flower together on a piece of construction paper. Display the flowers along the wall. Cut the butcher paper in strips to create a fence in front of the flowers.

Later, encourage children to find their flower among the others in the garden and match their hand to the blossom. Talk about right and left as the children match their hands to the blooms.

✳ Monster Feet

Materials: large piece of cardboard; 12" x 18" construction paper; cotton swabs; tempera paints; comic sections of newspapers, cut or torn in small sections; hole punch; glue

Complete this activity over a two-day period.

Day 1: Cut one or more monster foot patterns from a large piece of cardboard, making each as large as possible but no larger than 12" × 18" sheet of construction paper. Invite children to compare the size of their feet with the monster foot. Use the words *large* and *small*.

Have children trace around the pattern on a piece of construction paper and cut out the foot shape. Then have them use cotton swabs and tempera to paint designs on their monster foot.

Day 2: Provide one or more one-hole paper punches. Have the children take turns punching out circles from the comic sections of the newspaper to produce brightly colored confetti. Children enjoy this activity, and it is very good for small-muscle development. Then children decorate their monster foot by gluing on the circles in a random design. Children can put a touch of glue on each circle and place it on the foot or can use a cotton swab to draw glue patterns on the foot and then sprinkle confetti circles over the glue.

Display the feet along the walls so that it looks like a monster left footprints as it walked through the room.

✳ Finger Painting

Materials: finger paint (see Appendix II, p. 274); paper

Demonstrate the finger painting process. (You can purchase prepared finger paint, but having the children mix their own paint increases the value of the activity.) Encourage exploration and spontaneous finger and hand movements rather than drawing a picture. Point out what happens if you add a second color of tempera powder on top of the first.

As children begin work independently, remind them to squeeze much of the water out of the clean sponge before they use it to wet the paper. Ask each child to name the color of tempera powder that he or she sprinkles on the paper. If children's paper begins to dry out, simply sprinkle a few drops of water over the paper and encourage them to continue.

Consider providing soft music for the children to listen to and move to as they paint.

✳ Feet Butterflies

Materials: construction paper; pipe cleaners; glue; torn tissue paper scraps in a wide range of colors

Have each child put both feet close together, but not touching, on one piece of construction paper while another person traces around the feet. Children cut out each foot and a strip of construction paper to form the parts of the body of a butterfly. They then glue one foot on each side of the body, as shown.

Provide short lengths of pipe cleaners for each child to curl and glue on as antenna. Children then use glue and torn tissue paper scraps to decorate the butterflies.

✳ Handprint Class Mural

Materials: white shelf or butcher paper; tempera paints in three colors; three plastic foam trays or paper plates; pan of soapy water; towel

Lay a large sheet of paper on a tabletop. Put a small amount of paint on each of the trays or plates. Children take turns naming the color they want to use, put their hands in the paint, and press both hands on the paper to make their left- and right-hand prints. As children finish, they rinse their hands in the pan of soapy water and dry them with the towel. Print each child's name in bold letters under his or her handprints.

To make the mural more interesting and show a variety of hand sizes, invite adult guests to add their hand prints to the mural and write their names underneath.

When the mural is dry, tape it on the wall at children's eye level. Ask them to match their hands to their handprints and use the words *left hand* and *right hand* to describe their prints. You can use the mural when talking about the concepts left /right and large/small.

✳ Feet Printing

Materials: white shelf or butcher paper; tempera paint; plastic foam tray or large paper plate; pan of soapy water and towel

Tape a very long sheet of paper to the floor. Put a small amount of tempera paint in a tray or plate. Provide a second tray of paint, if you wish, so children can make prints with two colors or color blends.

One at a time, children name their choice of color, put their bare feet in the paint, and immediately walk up and down on the paper to make footprints. Provide a chair, a small pan of soapy water, and a towel at the edge of the paper, so children can sit down as soon as they've finished the printing process and wash the excess paint off. After awhile, have children start at the other end of the paper to ensure that the entire paper is printed.

The finished print is strikingly different. Display it near the Handprint mural to encourage verbal comparisons of size and color. Children tend to talk about this activity for a long time! They like to identify their footprints and tell others how they made them.

BLOCKS

✳ Legos®

Add Legos® or other connecting blocks to the block area. Discuss the different ways we use our hands. Compare the way we use our hands when putting small blocks together with the way we use them when handling large blocks.

✳ Squares and Rectangles

Encourage children to use blocks to make both squares and rectangles and then compare the two shapes.

BULLETIN BOARD

✳ We Use Our Hands and Feet

Use wide yarn to divide the board in half from top to bottom. Add a border of hands around the edges of the left side of the board and a border of feet around the edges of the right side. Add the caption *We Use Our Hands and Feet.* Have children draw pictures or cut them out of magazines and catalogs to produce an assortment of pictures that show different ways we use our hands and feet and various objects associated with hands or feet. Some possible examples follow:

Hands: scissors; mittens; rings; a child drawing, holding a book, or carrying a bowl

Feet: shoes; socks; a balance beam; a person dancing, running, or climbing stairs

As a class, look at all of the pictures and decide whether to pin them on the left (hands) side of the board or the right (feet) side. Use pushpins to attach the pictures as decisions are made.

You can remove the pictures and place them in a pocket folder so that children can take turns categorizing them and attaching them to the board during center or free time.

COOKING

✳ Handwiches or Feetwiches

Hand-shaped or foot-shaped cookie cutters
Bread
Sandwich fillings: marshmallow cream and
peanut butter; jelly and peanut butter;
honey and peanut butter

Small paper cups
Craft sticks

Wash hands. Make bread cutouts. Give each child a paper cup and a craft stick. In each cup, put a small amount of the two ingredients for the sandwich filler that each child chooses. Children stir the ingredients with a craft stick until they are well mixed and then use the stick to spread the filling on the bread cutout.

✳ Toes in a Biscuit

Refrigerator biscuits   *Wax paper*
Small smoky sausage links

Wash hands. Each child flattens a biscuit as much as possible. Then, they lay the sausage in the center of the biscuit, fold the sides over, and pinch them together. Write the children's names on strips of aluminum foil, place the foil on a cookie sheet, and lay the biscuits on top of the foil. Bake them according to package directions.

LANGUAGE ARTS

✳ Action Play – These Feet Are Made For Walking

(Act out each action.)
These feet are made for walking,
These feet are made to run.
These feet like to be tickled,
And play and have some fun.

✳ Fingerplay - I Have Two Little Hands

Have children do the "I Have Two Little Hands" fingerplay from the Marvelous Me unit, p. 7.

✳ Action Play - Left and Right

Have children act out each action.

We stamp, stamp, stamp with our left foot.
We stamp, stamp, stamp with our right.
Then we turn ourselves around and around
And clap with all our might.

✳ Special Days

1. **Barefoot Day** – Have a barefoot day on which no one wears shoes for a certain period of time. The children are especially delighted if their teacher is barefoot also. Have children use their feet to explore as many different surfaces as possible and discuss how each surface feels, for example, soft, bumpy, smooth, slick, hard, and cold.

2. **Mitten or Glove Day** – Everyone wears mittens or gloves for a certain period of time. Explore together which things are easy to do when wearing mittens and which things are harder to do while wearing mittens. Use the term *pair* frequently.

   Ask children to wear one mitten or glove and put the other on the tabletop. Mix up the mittens and randomly hand out one to each child. Have each child find another child wearing a matching mitten.

   Provide sets of mittens of many styles and sizes such as leather work gloves, baby mittens, children's mittens, driving gloves, gloves without fingers, and so forth. Discover several similarities and differences. Discuss who is most likely to wear each kind of glove or mitten and why they would wear that kind.

3. **Crazy Socks Day** – Have a day on which everyone wears socks that do not match—the wilder the socks, the greater the fun. Invite children to talk about where they got their socks or why they decided to wear that pair. Have children march in a shoeless socks parade.

✳ Word Wall

Add the words *hands* and *feet* to the word wall. Brainstorm and write a list of a few rhyming words for both *hands* and *feet*. Add other topic-related words and one high-frequency word you want children to incorporate in their writing.

✳ The Sense of Touch Game

Provide objects with a variety of textures, for example, sandpaper, carpeting, satin, velvet, corduroy, Velcro® tape, tile, a prickly door mat, a sponge, and a scrub brush. Show the objects to the children, and have the children feel them, discuss them, and name them. Then have children take turns closing their eyes or being blindfolded and rubbing a bare foot over one of the samples. Remove the blindfold and ask the children to point to the sample they think they felt. After each child has had a turn, conduct the same experiment but have children use their fingers instead of a bare foot to feel an object. Discuss whether children could identify the object more readily using their fingers or their feet.

✳ Color Categorization

Have children place their mittens or shoes on a tabletop. Help them to sort the mittens and shoes by color. Select the word card for each color category and use the card to label the mittens or shoes in that category.

Mix up the mittens or shoes and allow children to repeat the activity independently. Some children may be able to mix up the word cards and correctly place them again.

✳ Similarities and Differences

Discuss all the ways that hands and feet are similar and different. Show similarities and differences in a Venn Diagram like the one below. If necessary, complete the activity in two or more sessions to allow the children to think about the similarities and differences over time. Help children understand how the diagram shows how hands and feet are similar and different. You may wish to have children draw or cut out small hands and feet to place on the appropriate sides of the diagram.

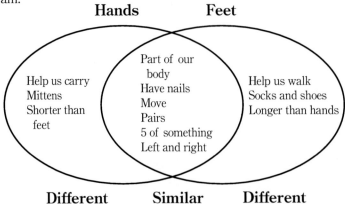

Hands   **Feet**

Help us carry
Mittens
Shorter than
feet

Part of our
body
Have nails
Move
Pairs
5 of something
Left and right

Help us walk
Socks and shoes
Longer than hands

Different   **Similar**   **Different**

✳ Toe Puppets

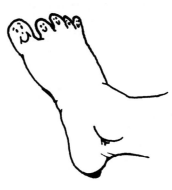

Materials: nonpermanent ink markers

Use non-permanent ink markers to make puppet faces on each toe of the children's feet. Wiggle toes to make the puppets move and talk. Encourage the puppet toes to talk with others about how they feel and what they like to do.

✳ Vocabulary Discussion: Plurals

Elicit children's responses to complete the following sentences. Hold up your hands for the first sentence and extend your feet for the second.

1. Here is one hand. Now I have two _____.
2. Here is one foot. Now I have two _____.

Explain that most of the time we add an *s* to the word when we have more than one of something, for example, *hand* becomes *hands*. But some words require special new words to show there is more than one, for example, *foot* becomes *feet*. If appropriate, continue with additional examples of words children probably know with special plural forms, such as *child* and *children*, *mouse* and *mice, man* and *men*, and *woman* and *women*. Use the words in sentences, such as, "Here is one mouse" and "Here are lots of mice."

✳ Going for a Walk

Prepare for the activity by using Circle Map 1 (Activity Master 8, p. 285) to make an overhead transparency. Read *Rosie's Walk* by Pat Hutchins to the children. Then read the story again, asking children to say the position word each time. As you reread the story, illustrate the events that take place by using colored overhead marking pens to make a simple drawing in each of the numbered sections of the circle map. Then have children retell the story. Point to each section of the illustrated circle map to help them recall events.

Use Circle Map 2 (Activity Master 9, p. 286) to create a new story about the children. Include where they might go and what they would walk across, around, over, past, through, and under. An example follows.

> *Ms. Walter's class went for a walk...*
> *across the playground,*
> *around the flag pole,*
> *over the flower bed,*
> *past the parking lot,*
> *through the front door of the school,*
> *under the Exit sign,*
> *and got back in time for a popcorn snack.*

✳ Guess the Feet Contest

Hang up or hold up a blanket just off the floor. Small groups of children take turns hiding behind the blanket, with only their bare feet showing. The rest of the children guess the owner of each pair of feet.

After everyone has had a turn, provide pictures of many different animals, birds, and people. Cover each picture with a blank sheet of construction paper so that just the feet show. Have the children figure out which feet belong to which animal, bird, or person.

✳ Pick It Up!

Collect several common objects, such as a pencil, a crayon, a cotton ball, and a piece of paper. Have barefoot children take turns sitting in a chair and trying to pick up one of the objects placed in front of them with just their toes! Ask the children to think about why fingers can pick up objects more easily than toes.

✳ Parts of a Foot/Parts of a Hand

Discuss and name the parts of a foot: heel, toe, ankle, and toenail. Ask the children to point to each part on their feet as you name it. Discuss and name the parts of a hand: palm, finger, knuckle, and fingernail. Ask the children to point to each part on their hand as you name it. Later, reverse roles by pointing to a part of your foot or hand and asking children to name it.

✳ Feet Begins With F (A Whole-Class Project)

Cut a large square of butcher paper in a shape of a very large foot. Write *Feet Begins With F* at the top of the paper. Children cut pictures out of magazines and draw pictures of things that begin with *f.* Discuss each picture and then have children glue each on the paper. Children continue the activity at center and free time until the paper is filled with pictures.

MATH

✳ Counting Fun

1. Count the number of shoes with ties. Then count those with buckles (or Velcro® closures). Ask, "Are there more shoes with ties or more shoes with buckles?"
2. Count the number of red shoes, white shoes, and so forth. Record the number of each.
3. Count the number of people wearing rings. Count how many rings there are in all.
4. Count how many toes are on one foot. Ask, "How many are on both feet if we add them together?"
5. Count how many fingers are on one hand. Ask, "How many fingers are on both hands if we add them together?"
6. Count the number of steps it takes to walk across the room, to the door, around the table, and so forth. Count the giant steps, regular-size steps, and tiptoe steps needed to walk the same distance, and compare the numbers.

✳ Numeral and Number Match

Materials: poster board; multiple cutouts of the foot; markers; yarn; Velcro® tape

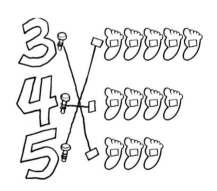

As the illustration shows, make a matching game with feet cutouts and numerals. Show numbers that are appropriate for the children in your class. Have the children work from left to right to attach the yarn for each numeral to the Velcro® strip that is next to the matching group of feet.

✳ Using a Ruler

Show the class how to use a ruler to measure length to the nearest inch. Use the terms *ruler* and *inch*. Be sure children understand that the ruler must be lined up with one end of the object being measured. Have the children measure one of their feet. Talk about the measurements. Then ask them to try to find something else in the room that is about the same length. Discuss what they find.

Discuss going shopping for new shoes. Ask if any child has ever had a foot measured by someone at the shoe store. Ask, "What did that person use to measure your foot size?"

✳ Size Relationships

Provide several pairs of shoes of different sizes. Children arrange the pairs from smallest to largest size, then arrange them from largest to smallest size.

✳ Pairs

Challenge children to find as many pairs as they can on their bodies and clothing, for example, hands, elbows, thumbs, eyes, buttons, shoelaces. Have the children take turns finding or creating pairs of objects in the room.

✳ Squares and Rectangles

1. Show several examples of different sizes and colors of squares and rectangles. Ask the children to try to think of ways that squares and rectangles are similar and ways that they are different.
2. Have children search for naturally occurring examples of squares and rectangles in the room or school, such as a window, door, picture frame, or ceiling tile.
3. Play "Is it a square or a rectangle?" Point to an object in the room and ask children to answer when you ask, "Is it a square or a rectangle?" You could also have children take turns pointing to an object and asking the question.

MOVEMENT

✳ Step Right Up

Direct children to take giant steps, baby steps, side steps, backward steps, run leaps, skipping steps, skating steps, and so forth.

✳ Finger and Feet Wiggles

Have the children sit in a large circle on the floor with shoes and socks off. Ask them to wiggle their fingers and toes, wiggle their hands and feet, stretch their fingers and toes apart, and lift their hands and feet up. Let the children think of hand and feet exercises for all of them to try.

While everyone is sitting in the circle barefoot, ask, "How could we all get in line so that we are in order from the person with the biggest foot to the person with the smallest foot?" Have the children share their ideas and choose one method, and then have the children use that method to arrange themselves in size order according to foot size. Be sure to include yourself! Consider taking a photo of everyone in line so that the children can see and discuss the results of their method.

✳ Jumping Feet

Have the children jump over a rope or a broom handle that's lying on the ground or floor. Gradually move it up as the children jump each height.

✳ Stilts

Materials: two empty coffee or large juice cans; two pieces of twine or heavy string; hammer and nail

Using a hammer and nail, punch a hole on each side of each can near the top. Thread the twine through the holes to make a loop long enough to hold. Knot the twine securely. Children take turns trying to walk on the stilts. Ask children to think about why it is harder to walk with stilts than in just shoes.

✳ Rope Walk

Lay a rope in a random pattern on the floor in an open area of the room. With shoes off and eyes closed, children walk on the rope and follow where it leads by feeling with their feet. Be sure there are no objects that children may bump into or fall over. Change the rope pattern and continue the activity. If a very large space is available, you may wish to use multiple ropes so that more children can be involved.

MUSIC

✳ Feet and Hands Can Move to Music

Use different tempos and styles of music to show how our hands and feet can move to music. Play tapes or CDs, and ask the children to determine ways to move their feet and hands in rhythm to the music. Encourage children to clap, sway, march, walk, hop, skate, and tiptoe.

✳ Loopy Loo

Use a tape of the song "Loopy Loo" or sing the words together as the class acts out the song. As a variation, try "Barefoot Loopy Loo." Everyone takes off shoes and socks. Tie a piece of red yarn around each child's right big toe and right thumb. As the children sing and dance, they can use the yarn to distinguish left and right.

✳ Kazoo

Children make a kazoo that they use to make music as they march. Give each child a cardboard tube from an empty toilet paper roll. Cover one end with wax paper and fasten it tightly with a rubber band. Punch three holes in a line near the open end. If preferred, children can use markers to decorate their tubes while waiting turns for an adult to punch the holes in the tube or attach the wax paper.

The child makes music by humming on the open end of the tube. Children love the sound. To keep germs from spreading, tell children not to use other children's kazoos. Invite them to take the kazoos home at the end of the day.

ROLE PLAY

✳ Work Shoes

Bring in pairs of adult-size boots, work shoes, high heels, and others. Have the children try them on and "walk to work" in them.

✳ The Gingerbread Man

Tell children the folk tale of the Gingerbread Man. Discuss the actions the children could use for each character. Then act out the tale, using the character actions. Have the children run in place when they act out the line "Run, run, run as fast as you can. You can't catch me, I'm the Gingerbread Man."

SCIENCE

✳ Magnifying Prints

Materials: Play dough (see Appendix II, p. 275); magnifying glasses

This activity works best in small groups or centers so that children don't have to wait long for a turn. Children roll or pat out a circle of play dough and press a little finger in the dough to make a print. Then they press a thumb in the dough and compare the two prints by talking about shape and size. Point out the lines in the fingerprint. Ask children to highlight the lines by tracing over them with a pencil. Repeat the process with a toeprint and compare toe and fingerprints. Explain that everyone's fingerprints are different. Provide magnifying glasses so that children can closely study the fingerprints and toeprints and compare them.

✳ Tracks

Examine footprints or pictures of footprints of a dog, class pet, chicken, bird, cat, and child. Match each print to a picture of the animal or child.

Give interested children a small ball of play dough to take home. The children make a print of their pet at home by gently pressing a foot or paw into a flattened circle of play dough. When they bring the print back to school, the group tries to figure out what animal made the print. If possible, encourage children to bring a picture of the animal to show the other children.

✳ Fingernails and Toenails

Prompt children to think about and talk about their fingernails and toenails through questions such as the following:

What are fingernail and toenails?

Why do we have them?

How are fingernails and toenails different?

Do they grow? How do you know?

Talk about why it hurts if you cut your hand but it usually does not hurt when someone trims your fingernail.

TRANSITION ACTIVITY

✳ Rhythmastics

1. Clap a rhythmic pattern. The children softly clap to repeat the pattern. Then a new leader claps a different pattern for the group to repeat.
2. Use your toe to tap a rhythmic pattern. The children softly tap to repeat the pattern. Then a new leader taps a different pattern for the group to repeat.

CHILDREN'S BOOKS

Brett, J. *The Mitten.* New York: Scholastic, 1989. A boy loses his mitten in the snow and several woodland animals try to make it their home.

DeRegniers, B. S. *What Can You Do with a Shoe?* New York: Harper & Row, 1955. A simple rhyming tale about the usefulness of shoes.

Fain, K. *Handsigns: A Sign Language Alphabet.* New York: Scholastic, 1993. This animal alphabet book models the sign for each letter and provides brief background information helpful to teachers.

Fox, M. *Shoes from Grandpa.* New York: Trumpet, 1989. A cumulative tale that begins with shoes from grandpa. Helps to develop sequencing and storytelling skills.

Hutchins, P. *Rosie's Walk.* New York: Macmillan, 1968. Rosie the hen goes for a walk over, under, around, and through the barnyard. Someone is following her! Position words and sequence skills.

Jonas, A. *Watch William Walk.* New York: Greenwillow Books, 1997. William, Wilma, Wally the dog, and Wanda the duck take a walk. Good vocabulary and alliteration.

Martin, B. and Archambault, J. *Here Are My Hands.* New York: Scholastic, 1985. A simple book about body parts and their functions.

Paul, A. *Hello Toes! Hello Feet!* DK Publishing, 1998. A delightful story that follows a girl through her day as she goes wherever her feet take her.

Perkins, A. *Hand, Hand, Fingers, Thumb.* New York: Random House, 1969. This classic favorite is a rhythmic adventure using hands. Read it at a fast pace. Repeating patterns.

Rankin, L. *The Handmade Alphabet.* New York: Dial, 1991. The author was inspired by a hearing-impaired family member to create this intriguing alphabet book. Children are fascinated with this book and begin trying to make the sign letters on each page.

Rankin, L. *The Handmade Counting Book.* New York: Dial, 1990. The American Sign Language signs for 1–20 and beyond, with numerals and corresponding numbers of objects.

Reser, L. *Beach Feet.* New York: Greenwillow, 1996. Rhyming text and grand illustrations of many kinds of feet found at the beach.

Seuss, Dr. *The Foot Book.* New York: Random House, 1965. A whimsical, rhyming book that is fun to share.

November Curriculum

Tools and Simple Machines

Thanksgiving and Life in Early America

Tools and Simple Machines

CONCEPTS

- We use tools and machines to do a job or task; tools make work easier.
- Most tools and machines help us to do specific things and are used in specific ways.
- We use tools or simple machines everyday to complete many tasks.
- Safety gear must be worn when using some tools or machines.
- Children need adult permission and/or supervision to touch or use many tools or machines.
- Animals use parts of their bodies in ways that are similar to the ways we use tools.

CONTINUING CONCEPTS

- **Colors** Identify the colors (for example, silver, gray, black) of the simple tools frequently used at home.
  Discuss why bright colors are used on construction hard hats.
- **Geometric Shapes** Focus on the triangle and emphasize that a triangle has three sides.
- **Health and Nutrition** Discuss the importance of safety and supervision when using tools.
- **Senses** Talk about the sounds and smell produced when wood is sawed or drilled.
  Post pictures of people using tools and encourage children to discuss them.
  Compare the texture of different fabrics, yarns, and tiles.
  Lift various tools and machines. Compare their weight using the terms *heavier* and *lighter.*
- **Traditional Rhymes and Tales** Recite "Hickory Dickory Dock" with the children.

PORTFOLIO PRODUCTS

The teacher or children can consider the following suggestion as they select one or more products each month to place in the portfolios.

- Ask a child to tell you about a completed art project and write what the child says about it. This product celebrates the child's art and documents oral language development, fluency, and concept mastery.

BACKGROUND INFORMATION

There are six simple machines:

1. **Lever:** A lever is a rigid bar, pole, or board that rests on a fixed point called a *fulcrum*. A lever can be used to lift heavy items a short distance. The distance between the fulcrum and the load determines the ease of lifting or if the load can be lifted at all! Crowbars, claw hammers, scissors, nutcrackers, and seesaws are all types of levers.

2. **Wheel and Axle:** The children are most familiar with this simple machine because of their wheeled vehicles. A simple wheel and axle machine has a large wheel connected to a smaller wheel or shaft called an *axle*. When either the wheel or the axle turns, the other part also turns. Other examples of a wheel and axle are found in a pencil sharpener and an eggbeater.

3. **Pulley:** A pulley is a wheel that turns around an axle. Usually there is a groove in the rim of the pulley so that a rope around the pulley does not slip off. The rope is attached to the load at one end. A person pulls down on the rope to lift the weight up. Cranes and window blinds use a pulley.

4. **Inclined Plane:** An inclined plane is a slanting surface that connects one level to a higher level. It gives us a gain in force because it is easier to move up a gradual slope than to lift straight up. The height of the inclined plane determines the ease of moving an object. A plank, ramp, and the sloping floor of a theater are examples of an inclined plane.

5. **Wedge:** A wedge is a form of an inclined plane that moves into or under the object to either spread an object apart or raise an object. With an inclined plane, the object moves up the incline. An ax, a knife blade, and a chisel are examples of a wedge.

6. **Screw:** A screw is an inclined plane wrapped in a spiral around a rod. It can be used to lift (car jack), press together, or force things apart. A wood screw, caps on jars and bottles, and the base of a light bulb are examples of a screw.

ART

✳ Easel or Tabletop Painting: Tools

Materials: paper; tempera paints; brushes used for many different tasks, in a variety of sizes (house-painting brush, scrub brush, toothbrush, and so forth)

Talk with the children about the fact that artists use brushes as tools to paint pictures. Explore the many other tasks that people do using brushes as tools. Display brushes and talk about what each brush might be used for. Quickly demonstrate how brushes can make wider or narrower strokes or even dots.

Encourage the children to experiment with brushes as they paint at the easel. See how many different brushes they can use. Ask, "What kinds of different strokes or shapes can you make?" Also, talk about what other tools besides brushes artists might use to paint a picture (for example, rags, knives, sponges).

✳ Papier-Mâché Hard Hat (Group Project)

Materials: *medium- and large-sized heavyweight balloons; newspaper strips; paste; tempera paints*

This activity is an effective way to introduce children to the papier-mâché process; later you may wish to have them complete individual projects. Inflate one to three balloons and tie them off. Children tear or cut the newspaper into approximately 2" × 6" strips. Demonstrate dipping one entire paper strip into the paste, wiping off the drips, and then smoothing it out on a balloon. Encourage the children to repeat the process and apply the strips until the top half of the balloons are covered with one layer. Allow the balloons to dry overnight.

Repeat the procedure the next day and continue adding layers over four or five days. When completed and dry, pop each balloon and pull it out. Use scissors to cut and even the bottom edges. Provide pictures of workers wearing hard hats. Talk about the colors of the hats. Discuss why the hats are usually bright colors. Then children paint the hard hats with tempera paints. When dry, add the hard hats to the role-play or workbench area. (Note: for a more detailed description of papier-mache shape making, see Appendix II, p. 275.)

As the children work, talk about why people must wear hard hats when working on certain kinds of jobs and with certain tools. Read Byron Barton's *Machines at Work* to show examples of the need for hard hats.

✳ Play-Dough Tools

Materials: *play dough (see Appendix II, p. 275); an assortment of real tools*

With the children, talk about and, as appropriate, handle each real tool. Name the tools and talk about their parts and how each part helps make the tool useful. Have the children make play-dough tools by combining play-dough balls and snakelike shapes. Encourage them to use the real tools as models.

✳ Splatter Painting

Materials: *an assortment of tools; cutout of tool shapes (see Activity Master 10, p. 287); tempera paints in two or three colors; a toothbrush for each color of paint; newspaper; dress or shirt boxes; one or more pieces of window screen in wooden frames or with edges covered with duct tape; Manila paper*

Provide an assortment of real tools and cutout tool shapes. Help children to match each tool with its cutout and then discuss the similarities and differences between the tool and its matching cutout. Next, spread out newspaper, place the screened frames on top of the newspaper, and let the children explore splatter painting. Show them how to dip a toothbrush in paint and then move it across the screen so that the paint splatters on the newsprint.

After exploring the procedure, put Manila paper in the bottom of a box. Children choose one or more of the tool cutouts to lay on the paper. Then they dip a toothbrush in one color and brush paint over the screen to splatter paint on the paper in the box. Next, they remove that tool cutout, put another one in its place, and repeat the process. Use the names for the real tools as children handle the cutouts. Talk with the children about where real tools like these might be found in people's homes. Ask, "How would someone use each tool?"

✳ Cut-Paper Design Collages

Materials: construction paper in a dark color; construction-paper scraps in light and bright colors; glue; scissors

Explain that scissors are also a tool. Talk about all the ways people use scissors to help them do a task, such as cutting out fabric patterns to make clothes. Encourage the children to experiment with you to find many ways scissors can be used to cut paper to create interesting collages. Demonstrate how to cut fringes; how to cut strips and curl them by wrapping them around a pencil; and how to make an interesting shape by folding a piece of paper and cutting around the fold line. Then let the children experiment with cutting and folding paper. Have them glue each cutout on a dark piece of construction paper to make a collage. Encourage them to make their collage three-dimensional by not gluing down all the edges.

With older or interested children, explain that a pair of scissors is really a lever. Compare it to other levers discussed in the Science section of this unit. Ask children to figure out which part of the scissors is the fulcrum.

✳ The Mechanical Kid

Materials: a variety of hardware and household items, including springs (for example, springs from old ballpoint pens), nails, screws, bolts, nuts, washers, foil, gears, parts of watches and appliances, straws, pipe cleaners, buttons, old silverware, and craft wire; cardboard tubes or white drinking cups; glue or cool glue gun; paint (optional)

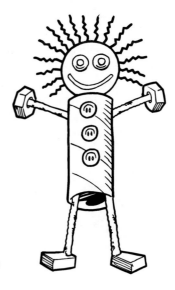

Discuss the term *mechanical*. The children choose various items to create a mechanical kid using a cardboard tube or cup as the body. Begin by brainstorming with children about what kind of mechanical person they want to make. Then guide their selections of materials to help them produce that result. The children should first assemble their mechanical kid without glue to determine how best to arrange all the pieces.

BLOCKS

✳ Measurement Tools

Add a yardstick, a metal retractable tape, and a folding extension ruler to the block area. Discuss how builders use measurement tools in their construction projects.

✳ Inclined Plane

Add 4" × 8" and 2" × 8" pieces of heavy-duty cardboard to the block area and show the children how to use them as inclined planes. Use a block to demonstrate a fulcrum. Add small cars and trucks and encourage children to build structures with inclined planes that the vehicles can go through.

✳ Forming Geometric Shapes

Ask for three long blocks and model how to use the blocks to make a triangle shape. With the children, count the number of blocks used to form this shape. Ask the children to choose other blocks and use them to form a triangle. Encourage them to continue to explore by making triangles in different ways.

BULLETIN BOARD

✳ What Tool Do I Need?

Draw or cut pictures from magazines of people doing a wide variety of jobs that use basic tools. For example, the pictures might include people painting a house, sweeping, hammering a nail, fighting a fire, repairing a car, sawing a board, typing a letter, or painting a picture. Ensure that both men and women are equally represented without stereotyping. Glue each picture on a piece of construction paper and laminate it. Arrange these pictures randomly on the left side of the bulletin board. Add a caption such as *What Tool Do I Need?* Cut out a picture or silhouette of the appropriate tool for each job and arrange the tools randomly on the right side of the bulletin board. Make a set of cards with the name of one of the tools carefully printed on each card. Store these cards in an envelope that is stapled to the lower left-hand corner of the board.

Staple a length of yarn securely to each picture of people working. Staple a piece of Velcro® beside each tool. Have children take turns working from left to right to match the picture to a tool being used in the picture. Older or interested children may also want to a match the word card to each tool and use a pushpin to pin the card in place beside the tool.

COOKING

✳ Fruit Cooler

1 cup strawberries	*1 tablespoon honey*
1 small banana	*2 cups crushed ice*
2 cups milk	*Blender*

Wash hands. Have the children cut the banana and strawberries into small pieces and measure the rest of the ingredients. Blend the first four ingredients for thirty seconds in a blender. Add crushed ice and blend until smooth. Serve immediately. Discuss all of the tools used to make the fruit cooler. Review the sequence of steps in the process.

Other fruit combinations produce yummy coolers as well. Try orange juice with strawberries or bananas. Grape juice is another good substitute.

LANGUAGE ARTS

✳ Fingerplay – Tools

(Act out appropriate actions as suggested by words).

Let's pretend to get some tools and see what we can do.
I can use the tools to work, and you can do it too.
Here's a hammer, 1, 2 ,3; pound with the hammer just like me.
Here's a wood saw, 1, 2, 3; saw the log, just like me.
Here's a ruler, 1, 2, 3; measure the board, just like me.
Here are some pliers, 1, 2, 3; hold the bolt, just like me.

Vary the fingerplay by using school tools such as books, paper clips, paper, and crayons.

✳ Word Wall

Add the word *tool* to the word wall. Add other topic-related words that children suggest. Add or emphasize a high-frequency word you want children to incorporate in their writing. Cut pieces from a colored, see-through plastic report cover and place the pieces over cards with words you wish to highlight and encourage children to use in their writing.

✳ Picture That!

Post pictures of workers using tools in centers that are appropriate for those tools. For example, place pictures of adults cleaning or fixing food in the role-play area, pictures of office workers or typists in the writing area, and pictures of construction workers at work in the block area. Encourage children to check the pictures to identify simple machines and to look for safety goggles and hard hats.

✳ Tool-in-the-Box

Use a real toolbox and tools for this activity, if possible. Have several tools hidden in the box. Give clues to the identity of one of the tools. When the children guess correctly, pop the tool out from the box like a jack-in-the-box. Repeat several times. An example follows: *This tool has a long handle and a very heavy part at one end. A carpenter uses it to pound nails into a board.* A saw, screwdriver, pencil, ruler, paintbrush, and scissors are other tools that may be used.

To vary this activity, have individual children describe a tool for others to identify. You could also put one tool at a time in a feely box (see p. 270) and allow the children to feel and guess the name of the tool without seeing it.

✳ Guest Speaker

Invite parents or people from the community to do a show-and-tell presentation on the tools they use. Explain to each speaker that an interactive presentation, rather than a lecture, would be most effective with young children because they enjoy touching and handling new objects. When appropriate, let the children hold the tools and pass them around.

✳ Similar and Different

Bring in a carpenter extension ruler, a retractable metal tape measure, and a conventional yardstick or meter stick. Let the children examine each measuring tool by looking, feeling, pushing, and moving them. Discuss the similarities and differences among the tools. Show a tool belt or a picture of a carpenter wearing a tool belt. Ask, "Which of these tools would a carpenter want to carry in a tool belt? Why?"

Duplicate Activity Master 11, p. 288, and use it to help children think about ways the three measuring devices are similar and different. Write the name of each tool in one of the rectangles. Act as a facilitator and ask leading questions that encourage the children to think about the differences. List one or more differences on the lines under the name of the tool. Possible ideas include: *folds; does not fold; is long; is not long; made of wood; made of metal.*

Then, in the center circle, list ways in which the tools are similar. Possible similarities include: all have numbers; all measure things; none are heavy.

Try substituting other tools for comparison using this form.

✳ Take-Apart Clock

Provide an old wind-up clock for the children to assist in taking apart. Ask, "What tools might we use to safely take this clock apart?" Examine the gear assembly. A gear is a wheel with teeth. Turn the gears slowly and have the children observe what happens. Help the children see that the small gear goes faster and moves around more times than the larger gear. Also, help them realize that the two gears travel in opposite directions. Then, look at the face and see that the gears are turning the hands of the clock.

End the activity by reciting "Hickory Dickory Dock" together.

✳ Other Tool Users

Talk about how people use their hands as tools sometimes, like when they pick up something or push open a door. Explain that some birds use their beaks like tools also. For example, a parrot uses its beak like a nutcracker when cracking seeds to eat; a woodpecker uses its beak like a hammer when hunting for insects in a tree; a robin uses its beak like tweezers when picking up food from the ground. Show and model these tools: a nutcracker, a hammer, and tweezers. Read and discuss together *Animals That Use Tools* by Barbara Ford.

✳ Tool Inventions

Discuss the concept of a tool as something that makes a job possible and/or easier or faster. Ask, "What tool do we use to pick up toys?"

Brainstorm a new invention that picks up toys or makes a bed! Discuss what attributes this machine would need. On a piece of chart paper or on the chalkboard, list the ideas offered by the children as well as your own ideas. Review what has been written.

Then ask for ideas about what this machine looks like and how it is operated. Make a sketch according to the ideas that are listed. Write a class-dictated story about this invention. Make a copy for each child, if possible. Some children may wish to write and illustrate their own stories.

MATH

✳ Calendar

On the first school day of the month, provide the children who can write numerals with their own copy of a blank calendar (Activity Master 3, p. 280). Have them write the name of the month and fill in the date in the appropriate place each day. (See p. 10 for more about this activity). Ask children what similarities and differences they notice between their calendar from last month and this month's calendar.

✳ Dig for Marbles

Fill a small dishpan halfway with sand. Bury 12 marbles or small rocks in the sand. Tell the children that 12 things are called a dozen, like a dozen eggs. Provide an empty egg carton and count together the 12 cups.

Have children use a small tool (spoon, scoop, shovel, or hand) to find the marbles and place each in an egg-carton cup. The children hunt until there is one marble in each eggcup. Later, the children can hide the marbles for others to find.

✳ Classifying

Metal nuts and bolts come in a variety of sizes. Most hardware stores have bins from which you can select a few of each style. Select six matching pairs of nuts and bolts. Separate the nut and bolt in each pair, and mix all the hardware together in a box. Have the children separate the nuts and bolts, sort by size, and then screw the matching sizes together. Then have them count the matched pairs.

To challenge children, provide on extra bolt. When the rest are matched, talk about one bolt being left. Ask, "Are there more nuts or more bolts? Can I take this one bolt away? Now, is there the same number of nuts and bolts?

✳ Golf Tee Nails

Allow younger children to hammer golf tees into a thick piece of foam block with a wooden or plastic hammer. Later, draw one or two large shapes on the foam block with a marker. Give directions such as, "Hammer the nail inside the circle." Or, "Hammer the nail outside the square."

With more experienced children, divide the foam block into six to ten sections with a marker. Write a numeral in each section. Have children take turns nailing the number of tees in each section that matches its numeral.

✳ Larger and Smaller

Gather several tools in larger and smaller sizes, such as a larger and smaller spoon, a larger and smaller pair of scissors, a larger and smaller shovel, and so on. Have one child act as the teacher, ask for a certain size tool, and choose another child to get it. Children then switch roles and continue the game.

Some children may enjoy the challenge of a blindfold. Let them feel the pair of items to determine which is larger or smaller.

✳ Triangles

Children search for naturally occurring examples of triangles in the classroom or school, such as a block or pennant.

MOVEMENT

✳ Wheelbarrow

Show a real wheelbarrow or a picture of a wheelbarrow. Discuss how it is used and how it helps people. Ask if any children have seen a wheelbarrow and discuss how it was used.

Explain that a *pair* is two. Group the children in pairs. One child in each pair lies on his or her stomach on the floor. The other child picks the first child up by the ankles. The first child then walks on his or her hands as the other child carries the feet, making a human wheelbarrow. The children switch positions and repeat the movement. You may wish to use masking tape to mark a starting and ending place in the room and have children try to wheelbarrow-walk that distance.

✳ Inclined Plane

Lean one edge of a wide board on a floor block to create a ramp. Hold children's hands as they walk up and down the ramp. Ask, "What piece of playground equipment is an inclined plane? How could we use inclined planes in our block center?"

✳ Listen and Jump

Make a tape of the sounds of familiar tools and machines in operation. Play the tape and identify each tool with the children. Give each child a picture card of a tool on the tape. Replay the tape. When children hear the sound of their tool, they jump up and show the card. Sample sounds could include: a hammer, saw, drill, electric mixer, hair dryer, can opener, typewriter, truck or car, jackhammer, and vacuum cleaner. Modify the number and types of tools involved according to the age of the children.

To vary the activity, change the way in which children respond when they identify the sound of their tool.

✳ Golf

Have children help organize and lay out a miniature golf course with inclined planes, unit blocks, and/or hollow blocks. Use a drink cup or empty can taped to the floor as the hole, a ruler or yardstick as the club, and a plastic golf ball or Ping-Pong® ball as the ball. To ensure the children's safety, remind them to just putt. Explain that no long swinging movements are allowed.

MUSIC

✳ Old McDonald

Old McDonald had some tools, E I E I O.
With his hammer he fixed the barn, E I E I O.
With a pound, pound here, a pound, pound there,
Here a pound, there a pound, Everywhere a pound, pound.
Old McDonald had some tools, E I E I O.

Other verses:

With his saw he cut the boards . . ., With a saw-saw here . . .
With his drill he made some holes . . ., With a brr-brr here . . .
With his pliers he tightened a bolt . . ., With an ugh-ugh here . . .
With his brush he painted the barn . . ., With a swish, swish here . . .

✳ Clap Rhythms

With the children, clap the rhythm of their names: Sa–ra, Gab–ri–elle, Matt. Then clap the rhythm of several tool names that the children suggest, such as ham–mer. After several tool claps, some children may be able to match rhythms of several of the words you've done. Ask, "Can you think of another tool that has the same rhythm as ham–mer?"

✳ Rhythm Instruments

Discuss how rhythm instruments are tools used to make music. Play an instrumental recording and let children decide which rhythm instruments they want to use to play along. Replay the recording and let children accompany it with the rhythm instruments.

✳ Tool Tune

(Tune: "If You're Happy and You Know It")

1. *If you need to weed the garden use a hoe.*
   If you need to weed the garden use a hoe.
   If you really use a hoe,
   You get rid of weeds just so.
   If you need to weed the garden use a hoe.

Other verses:

2. *If you need to sweep the floor use a broom.*
   If you need to sweep the floor use a broom.
   Just sweep across the floor.
   Sweep the dust right out the door.
   If you need to sweep the floor use a broom.

3. *If you need to paint a picture use a brush.*
   If you need to paint a picture use a brush.
   Brush the paint around and around.
   Paint a sky, a house, the ground.
   If you need to paint a picture use a brush.

ROLE PLAY

✳ Workers and Tools

Add some safe tools and clothing items worn by workers on their jobs to the dramatic play area. Examples of clothing might include: a straw hat, plastic hoe, and rake for gardener's or farmer's tools; hard hat, carpenter's apron, plastic hammer, saw, wrench, pliers, and work boots for construction workers or repair people; an old typewriter, a mechanical pencil, eraser, ruler, paper clips, and paper for office workers.

✳ Building a Box House

Read aloud Alice McLerran's *Roxaboxen*. Discuss any similar experiences the children might have. Suggest that the class work together to construct a box house.

1. **Construction**

   Get a large refrigerator box from a local appliance dealer. Plan with the children where to cut several windows and a door for the house. Have them draw the windows and door on the box. Discuss what tools are needed to do the cutting. Talk about tools real carpenters use to build houses.

2. **Painting**

   Provide tempera paints and large house-painting brushes or a roller. Encourage the children to work together to paint the outside of the box house. Discuss why house painters use bigger brushes than artists usually use to paint pictures at an easel.

3. **Wallpapering**

   Provide mixed flour or wallpaper paste, paste brushes, and a book of wallpaper samples. Have the children take turns choosing pages from the book, turning the pages over on newspapers to spread paste on the underside, and then pasting the pages in collage fashion on the inside of the box house to wallpaper and decorate the house. For fun, provide a roller and wallpaper brush for children to run over the wallpaper to smooth it. Ask, "What tools do people use to help them wallpaper?"

4. **Landscaping**

   Provide sand, plastic flowers, and small cups or cans. Have the children use garden tools to plant flowers to landscape around the house. Discuss how gardening tools are similar to and different from farm tools.

   Leave the box house in the dramatic play area for several days for the children to incorporate into their role-playing.

✳ Tool Charades

As some of the children pretend to be using a tool or machine, the rest of the class tries to guess the tool being used.

SCIENCE

✳ Simple Machines

Help children identify simple machines in their environment. Some possibilities include:

1. Wheel: rolling pin, wheelchair, pizza cutter
2. Lever/Fulcrum: spatula, bottle opener, seesaw
3. Inclined Plane: screw, ramp, slide at the park
4. Pulley: window blinds, flagpole
5. Gears: can opener, bicycle, clocks
6. Screw: jar lid, light bulb, corkscrew

✳ Experiments With Tools

Read *Mike Mulligan and His Steam Shovel* by Virginia L. Burton. Discuss how machines help us do work by making the task easier. To demonstrate this concept, conduct two experiments with the children.

1. Have a child sharpen a pencil by twisting a small hand-held pencil sharpener. Then have the same child use a wall-mounted or electric pencil sharpener. Ask the child to compare the two tasks. Discuss which tool made the task easier and/or faster and which did the better job.
2. Give the children play dough and a piece of paper with a six-inch circle drawn on it. Challenge them to mash the play dough with their hands and spread it to cover the circle as quickly as possible. Then gather the play dough and have them do the same task, but give them a cylinder block, dowel rod, or rolling pin to spread the dough. Ask, "Which way is faster? Why?"

✳ Lever

Use a long, wide board and a unit block or broomstick to demonstrate a lever and fulcrum. On one end of the board set a box with books too heavy for one child to pick up. Put the block or broomstick under the board. Adjust the position of the fulcrum as the child carefully tries to lift the books by pushing down on the opposite end of the board. Ask, "Where does the fulcrum end up as the job gets easier, close to the box or far from the box? How is this like a seesaw at a playground"?

✳ Simple to Complex Machines

Challenge older children or those who are ready to find and discuss the simple machine that is the basis for each more complex machine shown in many picture books, such as Robert Crowther's *Most Amazing Pop-Up Book of Machines*.

TRANSITION ACTIVITIES

✳ Memory

Place three or more common tools on a table or tray. Cover and remove one tool. Ask the children to guess which one is missing. Challenge older children by removing more than one tool at a time and by using similar tools such as a mechanical pencil, ballpoint pen, wooden pencil, ruler, staple remover, and a marker.

✳ Who Uses This Tool?

Hold up a tool and ask the children to guess who uses it. Possible examples could be a hammer, broom, pencil, shovel, hose, or wrench. Each tool might have several answers.

CHILDREN'S BOOKS

Barton, B. *Building a House*. New York: William Morrow, 1990. Clear text, bright and bold illustrations. Follow a house being built from pouring the cement to the putting in electricity and plumbing.

Barton, B. *Machines at Work*. New York: Crowell, 1987. Large, colorful illustrations showing construction equipment.

Burton, V. L. *Mike Mulligan and His Steam Shovel*. New York: Houghton Mifflin, 1939. A children's classic that deserves to be shared. Compare the steam shovel in the story to construction tools used today.

Cameron, P. *"I Can't," Said the Ant*. New York: Scholastic, 1961. An ant is challenged to help a fallen teapot. Each line rhymes with the pictured object that is speaking. A good rhyming model. You can ask the children to look for a pulley and other simple machines in the book.

Flanagan, A. *Call Mr. Vasquez, He'll Fix It!* Chicago: Children's Press, 1996. Mr. Vasquez is a maintenance worker. He keeps things in the apartment building in good repair for the residents. Multicultural photos.

Ford, B. *Animals That Use Tools*. New York: Messner, 1978. An interesting exploration of how animals use their body parts as tools.

Macaulay, D. *The Way Things Work*. New York: Houghton Mifflin, 1988. Excellent nonfiction information for children who seek more in-depth answers.

Mazer, A. *The Fixits*. New York: Hyperion, 1999. A whimsical tale of the Fixits who use the wrong tools to fix a broken plate.

McLerran, A. *Roxaboxen*. New York: Scholastic, 1991. Children's imaginations go to work as they construct a town out of stones and old boxes.

Neitzel, S. *The House I'll Build for the Wrens*. New York: Greenwillow, 1997. A young boy has his plans and tools in hand and is ready to build a birdhouse. His mom is so proud when she sees his creation and his ability to use tools.

Schultz, C. M. *Charlie Brown's Fifth Super Book of Question and Answers About All Kinds of Things and How They Work.* New York: Random House, 1981. Appealing illustrations of familiar characters effectively add to the question-and-answer format.

Spier, P. *Oh, Were They Ever Happy!* New York: Doubleday, 1978. A humorous story about children who decide to paint their house.

Steig, W. *Dr. DeSoto.* New York: Farrar, Straus & Giroux, 1982. An award-winning book in which a mouse dentist must figure out how to help a fox in pain without getting eaten.

Trumbauer, L. *Balance and Motion.* New York: Newbridge Educational Publishing, 1997. Investigates gravity, movement, and balance.

Trumbauer, L. *Simple Machines.* New York: Newbridge Educational Publishing. 1995. Examples of simple machines children use indoors and outside.

Thanksgiving and Life in Early America

CONCEPTS

- Thanksgiving is a time to give thanks and to share with others.
- Pilgrims and Native Americans celebrated the first Thanksgiving.
- The Native Americans and Pilgrims taught each other many useful and helpful things.
- Many people serve turkey, cranberries, vegetables, cornbread stuffing, and pumpkin pie for Thanksgiving dinner to remember and celebrate the foods that the Pilgrims and Native Americans grew and ate together at the first Thanksgiving feast.
- Native Americans today dress and act differently from the way they did in early America. Descendants of the Pilgrims also dress and act differently from the way the Pilgrims did.

CONTINUING CONCEPTS

- **Colors** Have children do research to learn the colors of real turkeys.
  Have children identify the colors of fruits and vegetables.
- **Geometric Shapes** Continue to encourage children to develop their ability to recognize circles, triangles, and rectangles.
- **Health and Nutrition** Discuss the value of vegetables in our diets.
  Discuss the importance of washing foods thoroughly.
  Help children identify different kinds of fruits and vegetables.
  Talk about foods that are cooked before we eat them.
- **Senses** Have children listen to rhythms played on a drum and repeat the patterns.
  Discuss the smells of the stone soup as it cooks and the taste of the soup.
  View and discuss pictures of the clothing and lifestyle of people in early America.
- **Traditional Rhymes and Tales** Tell the tale "Stone Soup" to the children.

PORTFOLIO PRODUCTS

- The teacher or children selects at least one product every month to place in each portfolio. You may wish to provide an inexpensive blank audiotape for each child, and use it throughout the year to make an oral portfolio product. Each child's tape can document oral language development, fluency, and mastery of concepts. State the child's name and the date at the beginning of each tape segment. To document the ability to structure a story, tape-record each child as he or she tells a story. To document understanding of number concepts, record each child as he or she tells an original math story problem, while using small Thanksgiving items as math manipulatives. For example, a child may say, "Two turkeys were walking. They met a scarecrow, and the three of them played together." At the same time, the child places two felt turkey shapes and a felt scarecrow together.

BACKGROUND INFORMATION

Be alert to children's statements that contain misinformation or stereotypes about Native Americans. Avoid stereotypic terms such as *how, chief, squaw, papoose,* and *savage.* Avoid the phrase *sit like an Indian* to describe sitting cross-legged at circle time, since that phrase suggests to children that present-day Native Americans do not sit in chairs. Emphasize the idea that during Thanksgiving we celebrate the way our early American ancestors cooperated with one another.

ART

✳ Easel or Tabletop Painting: The Colors of a Turkey

Materials: tempera paints in colors selected by the children; art paper; paintbrushes

Show the children a drawing of a turkey with feathers in multiple colors. Challenge them to find out the colors of real turkeys. Discuss the difference between what is real and what is imaginary. Discuss the difference between photographs and drawings. Have interested children research the colors of turkeys by searching for photographs in books, using the Internet, or talking to people who have seen real turkeys. Each time a child documents a realistic color for a turkey, add that color of paint to the painting area. When all the colors have been identified, have the children paint large turkeys.

✳ Mosaic Turkey

Materials: poster board or cardboard stencil of a turkey; brown construction paper; scissors; glue; collage materials, including beans, rice, macaroni, seeds, corn kernels; pieces of pinecones (optional)

Children trace the turkey stencil on brown construction paper and cut out a turkey shape. They make a mosaic turkey by gluing pieces of the foods listed above on the turkey shape. Alternatively, they can make feathers on the turkey shape by gluing on pinecone pieces.

✳ Sand/Salt/Cornmeal Painting

Materials: sand, salt, or cornmeal, depending on what is least expensive and most readily available; dry tempera paint powder; plastic zippered bags; funnels; shakers; glue in small glue bottles; paper

Talk about sand pictures made by Native Americans. If possible, show examples from books.

Children help color the sand/salt/cornmeal by measuring one cup, pouring it into a zippered plastic bag, and adding one teaspoon of dry tempera powder. Close the bag securely and have the children shake it to mix the color well. Observe and talk about how the color spreads throughout the mixture. Mix several colors. Next, use funnels and help children funnel the mixture into shakers. (Empty spice containers with perforated tops work well. Or, you can make shakers by taping wax or foil paper over the opening of a paper cup filled with a mixture and then carefully poking small holes in the covering with a round toothpick.)

Let the children squirt designs with the glue, then shake the colored mixture over the glue. Carefully shake off the excess on a sheet of wax paper so that it can be recycled.

✳ Handy Turkey Puppets

Materials: brown construction paper; construction paper scraps; glue; crayons or markers; hole punch

Help children trace around their hands without tracing their thumbs. They then cut out the shape and cut holes near the bottom of the shape. The children will later make the legs of the turkey puppet by putting two fingers through these holes. To create a hole large enough for small fingers, children can use a hole punch to make three or four overlapping punch in the same area.

Children use construction paper scraps to make circles for the turkey head and eyes, a triangle for the beak, and a red wattle. Discuss the shapes and colors as children glue the shapes on their hand turkey to complete their puppet. Have the children use the puppets during story time and in movement, role play, and transition activities.

✳ Thanksgiving Table Covers

Materials: butcher paper; crayons; markers; paint; sponges; cotton swabs

Cut the paper the length of the tables and tape it down. If children decorate more than one table cover, have them use a different method to decorate each, for example, sponge paint on one, paint applied with cotton swabs on another, and crayons and/or markers on another.

If desired, the children's names can be written next to their designs so that they can sit at their own design during the celebration.

BLOCKS

✳ Logs

Add pictures of log cabins and toy building logs to the block area. Talk about how early settlers often used logs to build houses. Encourage children to make log constructions.

✳ Forming and Comparing Geometric Figures

Display drawings of squares, triangles, and rectangles made by tracing blocks. Be sure that the drawings show shapes in different sizes and positions. Encourage children to try to draw these geometric shapes by tracing blocks. You may wish to have children post each of their drawings beside the model drawing it matches. Take dictation from the children to gradually develop a record of all the things they notice about the squares, triangles, and rectangles. Post this record beside their geometric figure drawings.

BULLETIN BOARD

✳ We Are Thankful

Display the caption *We are thankful* on the board. Pin up a large cornucopia. Provide stencils or cutouts of different kinds of fruits and vegetables. Give each child a cutout or let each child use construction paper scraps and a stencil to make one fruit or vegetable. Have each child name something for which he or she is thankful. Print children's names and ideas on their fruit or vegetable. Then pin or staple each fruit and vegetable on the board as if they are pouring out of the cornucopia.

During group time, point to each fruit or vegetable on the board and ask the children to name it. Ask the children to tell its color. Then, ask the child whose name is in on that cutout to tell the group what she or he is thankful for. Later, you may wish to have the children take turns using a pointer to point out a fruit or vegetable that the class then identifies.

COOKING

✳ Maple-Flavored Popcorn

Individual recipe:

$\frac{1}{2}$ *cup of popped corn*   *Paper cup*
1 teaspoon maple-flavored syrup   *Spoon or craft stick*

Wash hands. The children measure and mix the syrup and the popped corn in a paper cup until the corn is well coated. It's sticky, but good!

Talk about how early Americans made maple syrup from the sap of maple trees, and explain that maple syrup is still made in the same way today. Explain that most sources suggest that Native Americans popped corn in clay pots set in a campfire. Some sources, however, suggest that they tossed corn kernels on the hot rocks of their fire and then caught the popped kernels as they flew out in all directions.

As the children eat their popcorn, read Tomie DePaola's *The Popcorn Book*.

✳ No-Bake Pumpkin Pie

Individual recipe:

2 tablespoons canned pumpkin
1 tablespoon marshmallow creme
1 tablespoon prepared whipped topping
Sprinkle of cinnamon

Individual-size pie crust
Paper cup
Spoon

Wash hands. The children mix the ingredients together in a paper cup and carefully pour the mixture onto the crusts. The recipe is ready to eat immediately, but it may be refrigerated or frozen for later use.

LANGUAGE ARTS

✳ Fingerplay – Ten Native Americans

Ten Native Americans dance around.
(Extend ten fingers and wiggle them.)
Ten Native Americans plant corn in the ground.
(Close one hand; push index finger of the other hand into the hole in the first hand.)
Ten Native Americans crawl into a tepee.
(Bring fingertips together to make a point over head.)
Ten Native Americans as quiet as can be!
(Fold hands and lay head on hands.)

Later, complete the same chant using whole-body movements. Children can dance around, bend to plant corn, crawl, and curl up to rest.

✳ Fingerplay – Ten Little Pilgrims

Ten little Pilgrim children are we.
(Hold both hands up with fingers extended.)
1–2–3–4–5 Pilgrim boys.
(Wiggle each finger in turn.)
1–2–3–4–5 Pilgrim girls.
(Wiggle each finger in turn.)
Working together so carefully,
(Use appropriate actions.)
Playing together so fancy-free!
(Use appropriate actions.)
Happy to live in a land that's free!
(Hold hands together as if praying.)

✳ Word Wall

Add the word *Thanksgiving* to the word wall. Add other topic-related words that children suggest. Add or emphasize a high-frequency word you want children to incorporate in their writing. Cut pieces from a colored, see-through plastic report cover and place the pieces over cards with words you wish to highlight and encourage children to use in their writing.

✳ Thanksgiving Past and Present

Read Jean Craighead George's *The First Thanksgiving* or Gail Gibbons' *Thanksgiving Day* to the children. Discuss the first Thanksgiving celebration and the way Thanksgiving is celebrated today; talk about how these celebrations are similar and different. Draw a large turkey on butcher paper as shown. Use the turkey drawing to create a Venn Diagram. In the left wing, write the caption *The First Thanksgiving,* and list things that describe the first Thanksgiving but not Thanksgiving today. In the right wing write the caption *Our Thanksgiving,* and list things that describe Thanksgiving today but not the first Thanksgiving. On the body of the turkey, list similarities between the two celebrations, for example, *getting together with people we care about, eating some of the same foods,* and *playing games.* Use the diagram to discuss the similarities and differences with the children.

✳ Thanksgiving Feast Costumes and Props

Many children enjoy dressing up and acting out the first Thanksgiving feast. The feast could take place in the cafeteria or in the classroom, with a long piece of butcher paper spread on the floor to serve as a table.

You can serve traditional Thanksgiving dishes, or have each child bring a piece of fruit to share. Recipes may be prepared in the classroom starting a day or so in advance, or you may wish to invite other classes to share in the feast, with each class producing one dish to share. The emphasis should be on celebrating and sharing, rather than on serving a complete meal.

Props and costumes add to the spirit of the occasion. See below and on page 76 for directions for making Pilgrim collars, Pilgrim hats, and Native American vests. The children might enjoy displaying their costumes and props by parading down a hallway. Keep the event child oriented and stress free by choosing activities the children can largely do themselves, rather than having adults prepare costumes and food. Have a camera available to take photographs that will help the children retell the event later. Consider inviting family members to enjoy the feast with the children. See page 76 for more information on invitations.

✳ Pilgrim Collar

Materials: 12-inch white paper squares; small paper plates; scissors

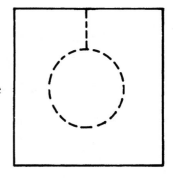

Provide squares of construction paper or butcher paper. Children place a paper plate in the center of the square and trace around it to make a circle. They cut from the one edge of the square to the circle, and then they cut out the circle, as shown, to make a neck opening for the Pilgrim collar.

✳ Pilgrim Hats

Materials: aluminum foil; black 12" × 15" construction paper; scissors

Have each child use scissors to round off the corners of a rectangular piece of construction paper. Then have an adult cut a three-sided opening that is large enough for the child's head to fit through. Children fold up the cutout area so that it stands up to make the top of the hat. To make a hatband, children glue a rectangular piece of black construction paper across the front of the hat. To make a buckle on the front of the hat, they cut a square of aluminum foil and glue it on the hatband.

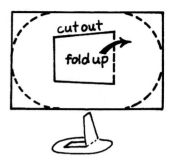

✳ Vests or Ponchos

Materials: brown paper grocery bags; markers, crayons, or tempera paints; cotton swabs; scissors; copies of Activity Master 12, p. 289

Make paper-bag vests by cutting large grocery bags, as shown. If children are given a cardboard pattern for a half circle, they can mark the three cutting lines and then cut along them. (If cutting the vests is too difficult for children, an adult can quickly make ponchos that slip over the head by using a paper cutter to cut off each side of the bag and cutting out a hole for the head.) Have children use markers, crayons, or tempera paint and cotton swabs to decorate the vests. They can draw pictographs (see Activity Master 12) or designs of their own.

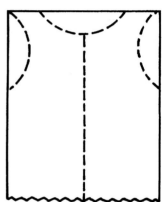

Demonstrate how to make short, parallel cuts to fringe the bottom edges of a vest and encourage children make a fringe.

✳ Family Invitations

Talk about the purpose of an invitation. As a class, decide what information needs to be included on the family invitations, for example, a description of the event, the date, the time, and the location. Then, help the children compose the Thanksgiving feast invitation. Print the final wording on a piece of chart paper.

Have each child design the outside of a card and then copy the invitation from the chart paper or glue a copy you provide to the inside of the card. Children take the invitations home to present to their families. Some children may enjoy making additional invitations for people in the school, such as the principal.

✳ Stone Soup

Read Ann McGovern's *Stone Soup* to the children. Talk about how enough food to feed many people can be created if many individuals each add a small amount of food to the pot. Use pieces of felt to make a simple cooking pot and each ingredient mentioned in the story. Reread the story and have children "make" the soup by adding each ingredient to the felt pot in the order in which it is used in the story. As each ingredient is added, have the children repeat the chant: *Soup from a stone. Fancy that.*

Tape record yourself reading the story with the children. Place the tape and the felt pieces in the reading center so that children can listen to it independently and add each ingredient to the pot as the story progresses.

✳ Colored Feather Match

Use permanent ink markers to color the edges of feathers. Prepare two feathers of each color you wish to use. Put all the feathers together in a box or bag and have the children match the two feathers in each pair. Give cards that show color words to children who are ready to read these words, and have the children match the color words to each matching pair of feathers.

To make a device that can help children form matching pairs, staple one half of a heavy-duty paper plate to a whole paper plate to form a storage pocket. Cut an even number of slits along the top edge of the whole paper plate. Store the colored feather pairs in the pocket. Have the children remove the feathers from the pocket and then place the feathers in each matching pair beside one another in the notches along the top of the plate.

✳ Feather Headdresses

Explain that some Native Americans earned feathers to wear in a headband by accomplishing difficult tasks. Ask, "What difficult task could each of you do to earn a feather?" Work together to set realistic and specific goals to work toward. Emphasize social goals, such as helping one another clean up after snacks, and learning goals, such as learning to write three words. On a chart, list each child's name and beside it print one or two goals that the child dictates. Later, recognize children with a feather when they achieve a goal. Write the achievement on the feather if possible. Send a note to parents about the achievement so that they appreciate what a feather means when a child brings one home.

✳ Storytelling

Storytelling was an important part of early American culture. Children learned the ways and beliefs of their people through stories. Stories were also important because people had very few, if any, books.

Choose a story that includes interesting and accurate information about life in early America. Use facial expressions and different voices as you tell the story to the children. Children are fascinated by the intimate nature of storytelling and often ask to hear a story again and again.

Learning to tell stories is an excellent way to develop oral-language skills and self-esteem. Encourage children to become storytellers by learning to tell a story they love. Have children tell stories to audiences of family members or children in other classes. If possible, videotape the storytellers in action and replay the tape at parent meetings and open houses.

✳ A Turkey for Thanksgiving

Show the cover of Eve Bunting's book *A Turkey for Thanksgiving.* Discuss the picture and title. Ask children to predict what the story is about. Write their predictions on a chalkboard or chart paper. Then read the story aloud. Return to the list of predictions and compare them to the what the children now know about story. Talk about how the endings of stories sometimes surprise us.

✳ Guest Speaker

Invite a Boy Scout leader or YMCA Indian Guide leader to talk to your class about early Native Americans. Many of these leaders have complete, authentic costumes that they could wear or bring to show the class. They might also be willing to teach the children an early American craft or game.

✳ Native American Sign Language

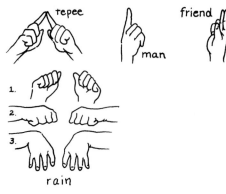

Native Americans sometimes used sign language to communicate with other tribes that spoke different languages. Talk about how we use our hands to tell people *come here, good-bye,* and *OK.* Teach the children a few simple signs, such as those shown.

✳ Early America

Display pictures or real items that represent life in early America. Some examples include: a pestle for grinding seeds, models of log cabins and/or tepees, jewelry, pottery, and clothing. Parents and other community members may have items they are willing to share. Discuss how and why each item was used.

Explain that life in early America was sometimes difficult because people had to make most things they needed, instead of buying them as we do. Show a small amount of cornmeal. Explain the importance of corn to Native Americans of long ago, and tell children that they taught the Pilgrims how to grow and use corn. Explain that they used a pestle and grinding stone to turn dried corn kernels into cornmeal. If possible, demonstrate this process. Grind several corn kernels so that they are broken into coarse pieces and then let children take turns using the pestle to grind the pieces into cornmeal. Children are usually amazed at how hard it is. Have children feel the finely ground cornmeal you brought and compare the texture to the texture of the meal they helped grind.

Place the pestle, grinding stone, whole corn kernels, and the partially ground kernels in the science center so that children can continue to experiment with the process of grinding cornmeal.

✳ Classification: Today or Early America

Prepare a folder game in which children classify pictures as pictures that show life today or pictures that show life in early America. Begin by labeling one pocket of a two-pocket folder *Today* and one pocket *Early America.* Collect pictures of homes, clothing, vehicles, and other items that were typical of life in early America and pictures of items that are typical of life today. At the bottom of the folder, tape or glue an envelope in which to store the set of pictures. Have the children classify all the pictures by placing them in one folder pocket or the other.

For children who are ready, provide pictures of some items that are used similarly today as in the past, such as a canoe or a horse. Talk about how many things change over time but some things remain the same.

MATH

☀ Home or Away for Thanksgiving? – A Math Graph

Children draw a picture to show where they will be on Thanksgiving. Categorize the pictures as *At Home or Away*. Tape up the pictures under each category to make a graph. Count the pictures in each category with the children and write the total for each. Discuss which category has the *most* and how many pictures there are in all.

☀ Corn Count

Provide an egg carton and a small bowl of corn kernels. Write a numeral in each cup and then have the children count out the appropriate number of kernels to place in each cup.

☀ Pretzel Math

Give ten pretzel sticks to each child. Have the children use the pretzel sticks to complete the following activities:

1. Count out three sticks; then arrange them to make a triangle.
2. Count out four sticks; then arrange them to make a square.
3. Count out three sticks. Carefully break one pretzel stick in half. Then arrange the remaining two whole sticks and the two half-sticks to make a rectangle.
4. Mix together all the sticks and make another triangle, square, and rectangle.
5. As appropriate to children's readiness, formulate math problems that involve addition and subtraction. Have the children use pretzels to solve the problems. Write number sentences that show the solution.

   Start with 5 pretzels. Now take one more. How many pretzels do you have now?
   (6 pretzels; 5 + 1 = 6)
   Show 5 pretzels. Take 2 away. How many pretzels do you have now?
   (3 pretzels; 5 – 2 = 3)

☀ Fruits and Vegetables Bulletin Board

As a class, count the fruits and vegetables on the bulletin board. Count to figure out if there are more fruits or vegetables.

☀ Triangles, Squares, and Rectangles

Have children continue to search for naturally occurring examples of triangles, squares, and rectangles in the classroom or school. Play I Spy using one of the shapes and have the children figure out your object. For example, when referring to a switchplate on the wall, say, "I spy a rectangle next to the door."

✳ One Half Cup and One Whole Cup

Measure one half cup of large potato pieces and then one full cup of large potato pieces. Dump the contents of each measuring cup onto a paper plate and have the children count to determine which holds more pieces. Combine the two amounts. Ask, "How many pieces are there altogether?" Have the class count all the pieces to find the answer.

MOVEMENT

✳ The Little Pilgrim Hunter: An Action Story

Read the story and have the children perform each underlined action as the story progresses. Before starting the story, you may wish to model the movements you want the children to use.

Once upon a time a little Pilgrim hunter went hunting for a turkey. He <u>bent over</u> to pick up his trusty gun, but oops, he lost his balance and <u>fell down.</u> He <u>jumped</u> back, brushed off his clothes, <u>bent over</u> again, and picked up his gun. Then he went <u>walking</u> toward the woods to find a turkey.

He <u>walked</u> a little way until he <u>saw</u> a squirrel in a tree. He <u>looked</u> up at the squirrel. But he didn't want a squirrel, so he <u>walked</u> on.

He <u>walked</u> a little further, and he came to a big hole. He <u>looked</u> in the hole. No turkey. So he backed up, <u>ran</u> fast, (pause) faster, (pause) faster, and <u>jummmmmmmmmped</u> over the hole. Then he <u>walked</u> on.

He <u>walked</u> a little further, and he saw a rabbit hopping through the grass. He <u>looked</u> at the rabbit. He laughed and tried to <u>hop</u> like the rabbit. <u>Hop, hop, hop.</u> But he didn't want a rabbit, so he walked on.

The little Pilgrim hunter <u>walked</u> a little further until he came to a cave. He <u>looked</u> into the cave. But it was too dark to see. So he got down on his knees and crawled into the cave. He <u>crawled</u> until he bumped into something! It was soft and warm. Was it a turkey? No, it was a big bear!

He <u>yelled</u> and quickly <u>crawled</u> back out of the cave. (The following should be read and acted out quickly.) He <u>ran</u> back toward home. He <u>hopped</u> by the rabbit. He ran toward the hole and <u>jummmmmmmmmped</u> across. He <u>ran</u> by the squirrel, out of the woods, and back to his log cabin. He was out of breath and so worn out that he never went hunting for a turkey again until he was grown up!

The End

The following are possible movements the children could use.

> <u>Bent over</u> – With legs straight, touch hands to floor.
> <u>Fell down</u> – Drop to floor.
> <u>Jumped</u> – With hands raised over head, jump in place.
> <u>Walked</u> – Pat legs and walk in place
> <u>See/looked/saw</u> – With hands over eyes to shade them, look in both directions.
> <u>Ran</u> – Pat legs quickly and run in place.
> <u>Hopped</u> – Hop in place like a rabbit.
> <u>Crawled</u> – Move in place on all fours.
> <u>Yelled</u> – Call out "Oh!"

☀ Indian Toss Game

Materials: foam cubes or scraps; 2–4 small baskets

The Crow Indians played a game in which they tossed stones into the air to catch them in a basket. Have two to four children at a time each use a basket to try to catch pieces of foam that other children gently toss toward them.

To vary the activity, have children toss a foam piece into the air with one hand and try catching it in a basket held in the other hand.

MUSIC

☀ Paddle Your Canoe

(Tune "Row, Row, Row Your Boat")
Children sit in pairs facing one another with their feet together and holding hands. They rock back and forth as they sing, "Paddle, paddle, paddle your canoe . . ." With each repetition of the song, have them change the tempo. Have them progress from very slow to very fast, but encourage them to maintain a consistent tempo throughout each verse.

☀ Thanksgiving Ways

(Tune: "Mulberry Bush")
This is the way to paddle canoes,
Paddle canoes, paddle canoes.
This is the way to paddle canoes
On Thanksgiving morning.

Other verses:

This is the way the Pilgrims work. . .
This is the way the turkey struts. . .
This is the way the popcorn pops. . .
This is the way to eat the feast. . .

☀ Drum Rhythms

Practice typical $\frac{4}{4}$ drum-beat rhythms, varying the beat that is accented, as shown.

   1–2–3–4   1–**2**–3–4   1–2–**3**–4   1–2–3–**4**

Have the children use knees or tabletops as drums, or provide drums, such as those made from coffee cans and oatmeal containers. Begin clapping a rhythm and invite the children to join in, following your model. Beat the same rhythm together several times before changing the beat that is accented. Have the children take turns beating the rhythm while other children walk, dance, hop, or jump to the beat.

ROLE PLAY

✳ Grocery Store

Set up a grocery store so that children can role play buying groceries for the family's Thanksgiving dinner. By pretending to buy and sell groceries, children can gain organizational skills and a sense of responsibility.

You may wish to ask parents to donate items for the store by writing a note one or two weeks in advance. Include a list of suggested items and invite them to add others. The most important items are empty food containers, boxes, and cans. (Ask for cans that have been opened from the bottom so that they will look unopened. Be sure that the cans are clean and have no sharp edges that can cut fingers.) Other useful items include blocks or bricks and boards for building shelves; paper, stickers, and markers for making signs and price tags; baskets with carrying handles or toy shopping baskets; a small table for a creating a checkout area; and a cash register or box for collecting money.

Involve children in setting up the store. Place the materials in the role-play area and let children decide how to arrange them. When children set up the store themselves, they tend to engage in higher-level reasoning, communication, and problem solving.

Challenge children to determine the price of each item by choosing a price from 1¢ through 10¢. Have them write the price on a tag and attach it to the item.

Some children may be ready to learn about the value of coins. Provide play coins (pennies, nickels, and dimes). When these children are "buying," have them read the price of each item and select the coin or coins they need to purchase it.

SCIENCE

✳ Raw and Cooked Foods

Have children try to pierce pieces of raw carrot and potato with a fork. Then have them try to pierce cooked carrots and potatoes. Talk about whether it is easier to pierce raw or cooked food. Explain that we sometimes cook our food to make it easier to chew. Also explain that we cook some foods to kill germs and make the food healthier to eat. With input from the children, develop a list of foods we eat raw. (You may find that some children do not realize that certain foods, such as bread, crackers, and doughnuts, have been cooked.) Also make a list of foods that we can eat cooked or uncooked.

✳ Seeds

Provide a variety of seeds, such as pumpkin seeds, apple seeds, corn kernels, and pine-cone kernels. Let the children examine the seeds. Show the children pictures of mature plants that grow from these seeds. Then have the children match the seeds to the pictures of the mature plants.

✳ Shelling Corn

Display an ear of dried corn. (You can obtain dried corn from farms and stores that sell it as a seasonal decoration.) Have the children shell the corn. Encourage them to use a magnifying glass to examine the place where a kernel came off the cob and to examine a single kernel. Cut a kernel in half and have the children examine one half.

✳ Apple Faces

Explain that the Iroquois Indians made apple dolls. Demonstrate how to make a head and face for an apple doll by peeling a firm apple and carving large features, as shown. (As the apple dries, it will shrink to one-quarter its size, so don't cut away too much.) Insert cloves in the apple to make eyes.

Dry the apple head by leaving it on a plate, away from drafts, so it does not mildew. It takes about four weeks for the apple to shrink and harden. Explain to the children that since the apple will become more and more distorted as it dries, they will not know what it will look like for a whole month! Take a photograph of the fresh apple and the newly carved apple. Then take one photograph of the apple each week until it has dried. Display the pictures and discuss what happened to the apple. Then mix up the pictures and ask the children to arrange them in the correct sequence.

TRANSITION ACTIVITIES

✳ Thanksgiving Feast Game

The children sit in a circle. The first child says, "At my Thanksgiving feast I ate turkey." The second child repeats the sentence and adds another food. Continue around the circle, with each child adding a food, until someone gets mixed up. Then let all the children say "Gobble-gobble-gobble," and start the game over with the child who is next in the circle.

✳ Where Is the Turkey?

Children listen as you make statements like these: "The turkey is sitting on your head; The turkey is walking up your leg" and "The turkey is pecking at your elbow." Have the children use their turkey puppets (see "Handy Turkey Puppets, p. 72) to act out each situation. Each statement should include a verb that describes something the turkey is doing, a position word, and a part of the body.

After children are accustomed to the activity, have them describe new situations for others to act out. Encourage them to speak in complete sentences.

CHILDREN'S BOOKS

Accorsi, W. *Friendship's First Thanksgiving.* New York: Scholastic, 1992. The events leading to the first Thanksgiving are told from the perspective of Friendship, a Pilgrim dog.

Bunting, E. *A Turkey for Thanksgiving.* New York: Clarion, 1995. Mrs. Moose wants a turkey for Thanksgiving, so Mr. Moose goes on a hunt. The surprise ending invites children to make predictions.

Cohen, M. *Don't Eat Too Much Turkey.* New York: Bantam Doubleday Dell Publishers, 1996. The first-grade class prepares for Thanksgiving. Anna Maria is her bossy self and the rest of the class has to cope.

Cowley, J. *Gracias, the Thanksgiving Turkey.* New York: Scholastic, 1998. Papa sends Miguel a turkey to raise for Thanksgiving. His multiethnic community supports the boy and his bird. Spanish words are included in the text, and there is a glossary at the end.

DePaola, T. *The Popcorn Book.* New York: Holiday House, 1978. A lot of nonfiction information about popcorn is conveyed through a funny dialogue between two fictional characters.

Devlin, W. and H. Devlin. *Cranberry Thanksgiving.* New York: Aladdin, 1990. Grandmother always makes cranberry bread for Thanksgiving dinner, using a secret recipe. A mystery develops when the secret recipe is missing.

George, J. C. *The First Thanksgiving.* New York: Putnam, 1996. Thoroughly researched, written with sensitivity, and illustrated with great art, this book depicts the plight of the pilgrims and the valuable aid given by the native people.

Gibbons, G. *Thanksgiving Day.* Holiday House, 1983. A picture information book about Thanksgiving in the past and today. Offers opportunities for children to compare and contrast.

Kroll, S. *The Squirrel's Thanksgiving.* New York: Scholastic, 1997. Brother and Sister squirrel learn sibling tolerance after cousins come to visit.

McGovern, A. *Stone Soup.* New York: Scholastic, 1996. A retelling of the classic folk tale of a wandering young man who tricks a woman into making soup from a stone.

Rader, L. *A Child's Story of Thanksgiving.* Nashville, TN: Ideals Children's Books, 1998. Recounts the first Thanksgiving and describes present-day celebratory customs in language that children can understand.

Spinelli, E. *Thanksgiving at the Tappleton's.* New York: HarperCollins, 1992. The story concerns the importance of a family's being together during the holiday. What can go wrong does, but humor prevails.

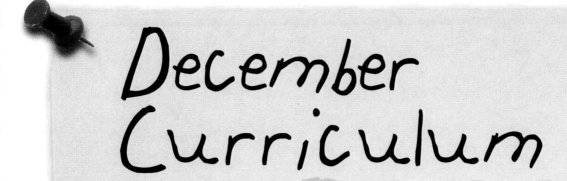

December Curriculum

Toys

Holiday Season

Toys

CONCEPTS

- Toys are objects that people play with and learn from.
- Children play with some of the same toys that their parents and grandparents enjoyed when they were children.
- Creative toys enable children to invent, to discover, and to solve problems.
- Toys can help children to actively use their imaginations.
- Toys may be commercially made or homemade.
- Authors and illustrators create books using toys as characters because children know and love toy characters.
- Children need to play with safe toys.

CONTINUING CONCEPTS

- **Colors** Emphasize the primary colors red, yellow, and blue. Discuss why many toys are brightly colored.
  Investigate as many shades of purple as possible.
- **Geometric Shapes** Review circle, triangle, square, and rectangle.
- **Health and Nutrition** Talk about safe toys and dangerous toys. Stress the importance of wearing helmets when biking and helmets and pads when skating or skateboarding.
- **Senses** Children close eyes and identify toys by the sounds they make.
  Children view a toy and describe as many of its attributes as possible.
  Discuss the surfaces and textures of various toys.
- **Traditional Rhymes and Tales** Recite "Baa, Baa, Black Sheep," "Mary Had A Little Lamb," and "Three Blind Mice" with the children.

PORTFOLIO PRODUCTS

The teacher or children select at least one product from this unit to place in each portfolio. A suggestion follows.
- Duplicate a recent entry from each child's journal. This product can celebrate the child's art, emergent literacy, and fine-motor skills.

ART

✳ Easel or Tabletop Painting: Primary Colors

Materials: red, yellow, and blue tempera paints; art paper; paintbrushes

1. Talk about the bright colors often used on toys. Explain that toy manufacturers use bright colors because they make people feel happy. Have the children explore using bright paints at the easel.
2. Invite children to use primary colors to paint a picture of their favorite toy or a toy they would like to share with someone else.

✳ Marble Painting

Materials: shallow box; Manila paper; tempera paints in primary colors; marbles; golf ball

Show the children marbles. Explain that their parents and grandparents might have enjoyed playing with marbles when they were children. Invite children to ask an adult in their family if he or she had marbles as a child. If so, suggest that the children ask, "Can you teach me a marble game?" Have the children share what they learn with the rest of the class. Then have the children play some of their marble games.

Cut Manila paper to fit in the bottom of the box. Pour tempera paints in primary colors into bowls. Put a marble into each bowl. Using a plastic spoon, children remove one marble and place it into the box. Then they tilt the box first one way, then another so that the marble rolls over the paper. The children dip the marble in the paint again as necessary. Encourage the children to use all of the primary colors to produce a rainbow of designs.

To vary the activity, dip golf balls in the paints to obtain a different effect. After the paintings are dry, ask children to identify which lines were made by the marbles and which lines were made by the golf balls.

✳ Blue Balloon Art

Materials: blue balloons; string; crayons or markers; glue or tape; Manila paper

Read Mick Inkpen's book *The Blue Balloon*. Talk about the strange and wonderful powers of the balloon. Discuss what children would do if they had a balloon like that. Give each child an inflated blue balloon with a string attached. Next, have children draw pictures showing what they would do with the blue balloon. When their drawings are complete, glue or tape a blue balloon that has not been inflated on each drawing.

✳ Create a Toy

Materials: copies of Activity Master 13, p. 290; scissors; attribute blocks or building blocks with square, rectangular, and triangular faces (optional); construction paper; glue; crayons or markers; collage materials including, buttons, metal washers, rickrack, yarn, and sequins

Duplicate one or two copies of the activity master for each child. Cut out or have the children cut out the toy parts on the activity masters. You could also have children make additional toy parts with geometric shapes by tracing around blocks and cutting out these shapes. Show children how the toy parts can be combined in a variety of ways to create different toys. Also show children that parts can be connected along an edge and/or can partially overlap one another.

Children then create a toy by arranging toy parts so that they are connected. When they are satisfied with the assembled toy, they glue the parts on construction paper, color the toy, and decorate it with collage materials. You may also wish to have them write or dictate a story about their toy and what it can do.

✳ Toy Stick Horses

Materials: a 1-inch dowel rod 36 inches long or a yardstick for each child; socks; felt, fabric or construction paper; wide yarn or ribbon; buttons; sequins; beads; fabric glue; old newspapers

Tell children that a stick horse is a toy that children and adults used to make themselves. Tell children that they are going to have fun making their own stick horse.

Have the children decorate a sock to make a horse's head. They cut out eyes and a nose from felt, fabric, or construction paper and glue these features on the sock. They make a mane by gluing yarn, ribbon, or construction paper strips on the sock. They could also add buttons and other collage materials to enhance the horse's features. Then they stuff the socks with crumpled newspapers to form the head. With adult help, they use a rubber band to tightly attach the head to the stick. Finally, they make reins using yarn.

Create opportunities for the children to use their toy stick horses. For example, play recorded music and have the children gallop around in time with the rhythm, or have the children use the horses to ride back and forth to the playground.

BLOCKS

1. Add stuffed animals to the block area, and have the children use blocks to build fences or cages for the animals.
2. Add dolls to the area and suggest the children use blocks to build small beds for the dolls.
3. Add an assortment of small toy vehicles to the area and encourage children to construct roads that are the appropriate width for the vehicles.

BULLETIN BOARD

✳ Toys on Parade

Use a die cut to make three small toy shapes in the three primary colors. Alternate the shapes along the edges of the board to create a border that shows a repeating pattern.

Use simple cutouts of a variety of brightly colored toys to show different number sets, such as two skates, four dolls, and seven balls. Put a piece of Velcro® tape at the bottom of each toy set. Make a set of numeral cards for the numbers 1 through 5 or 9, depending on the readiness of children, and attach small pieces of Velcro® tape to the back of each card. Have children take turns placing the correct numeral card under each set of toys.

Print one-digit numbers up to 5 or 9 on cards. Have children match each number card to a set that shows that number. To extend the activity, print one-digit equations, such as 3 + 1 = 4, on cards. Children who are ready to explore addition can use the toy shapes to show a group of 3 plus a group of 1.

COOKING

✳ Pudding Pops

2 three-ounce boxes of instant pudding
4 cups cold milk
Small paper cups

Craft sticks
Hand mixer

Wash hands. The children help measure and prepare the pudding according to the directions. Let children take turns mixing with a hand mixer. Pour the pudding into small paper cups and insert a craft stick in each. Place the cups in a freezer and serve the next day.

LANGUAGE ARTS

✳ Fingerplay – Toys on Parade

One teddy bear, I love him so.
(Hold up one finger; hug arms around self.)
Two roller blades, they help me go!
(Hold up two fingers; rub two hands together to show skating motion.)
A ball, bat, and glove are here to play.
(Hold up three fingers; act out hitting ball with bat.)
Toys on parade for me today.
(March as soldiers.)

✳ Word Wall

Add the word *toys* to the word wall. Brainstorm a few rhyming words for toy and add these words to the word wall. Add other topic-related words that children suggest. Cut pieces from a colored, see-through plastic report cover and place the pieces over cards with words you wish to highlight and encourage children to use in their writing.

✳ A Famous Bear

A. A. Milne wrote *Winnie-the-Pooh* after creating bedtime stories for his son, Christopher Robin, that featured his son's favorite toys. Read this classic story about Christopher Robin's toys to the children. Ask children which character is their favorite and graph the results by having children write their name in a space under the character's name and picture. You may wish to have children draw pictures of their favorite character and display them around the graph.

✳ Toy Matching Game

Materials: Manila folder; colored pictures of several kinds of toys cut from catalogs or coloring books; yarn; sandpaper or Velcro® tape

Cut several pictures of toys from the catalogs or coloring books. Then cut each toy in half; cut some vertically and some horizontally. Glue one half of the toy on the left side of the folder and the other half on the right side of the folder. Arrange the matching halves in random order on the two sides so that the children must look and think carefully to make a match. Cut a 14-inch piece of yarn for each toy. Under each toy on the left side of the folder, glue, tape, or staple one end of a piece of yarn. Glue or staple a small piece of sandpaper or Velcro® tape under each toy on the right side. Demonstrate how to match the halves by attaching the loose end of the yarn to the sandpaper or Velcro® tape under the matching half. Then have children complete the game.

✳ Toy Safety

Discuss toy safety with children. Ask the children to consider what things about toys make them unsafe. Talk about toys that are safe and most appropriate for different age groups. For example, discuss what would make a toy less safe for a toddler and have children suggest safe toys for toddlers.

✳ A Favorite Toy

Read Margery Williams' *The Velveteen Rabbit*. Have each child take a turn telling about a favorite toy. Explain that the toy can be one a child has or one he or she would like to have. Next, have children draw pictures of themselves playing with a favorite toy. When finished, the child or an adult writes the child's name and a sentence about the toy on each drawing. Use the drawings to create a class book.

You could also read Leo Lionni's *Alexander and the Wind-up Mouse* and help the children compare this book to *The Velveteen Rabbit*. Discuss the difference between what is real and what is imaginary.

✳ Toy Classification

Children love to handle small things. Collect a set of inexpensive miniature toys and objects by shopping at either a carnival supply shop or in the birthday favors area of a discount store. Let the children handle the miniatures and describe them. Talk about several different ways the objects might be classified, for example, by color, whether or not they have wheels, and whether or not they make noise.

Provide two to six 24-inch pieces of wide yarn. Children make a ring from each piece of yarn on a tabletop or on the floor. They then use the rings to separate the miniatures into different categories. Ask the children to explain and talk about the categories they create. For example, ask, "Why did you put those objects in the blue ring?"

Note: You can do the same activity using pictures of toys cut from catalogs. However, miniatures motivate children more than pictures.

✳ Attribute Analysis

Cut a large piece of chart paper or butcher paper in the shape of a simple toy, such as a doll or teddy bear. Discuss words that could describe the toy. On the toy shape, print all the words the children suggest. Then have children select some of the words to complete a sentence frame like the following. Help the children form several different sentences using the words.

The _____, _____ doll is _____.
      adjective   adjective   feeling word

Examples:

The soft, brown doll is sleepy.
The torn, old doll is sad.

✳ Teddy Bear Day

Encourage everyone to bring a teddy bear to school. (If necessary, other kinds of stuffed animals can be substituted. Label each animal, using a piece of masking tape with the child's name on it.) Supply some extra toy animals for children to borrow for the day if they forget or are unable to bring a toy. Plan the day's activities around the teddy bears. For example,

1. Have each child show and tell about his or her animal.
2. Have a teddy bear picnic at snack time.
3. Conduct a parade around the school or play music and have a parade in the room.
4. Have children hold the toys and gently rock them to sleep during story time. *The Velveteen Rabbit* and *Winnie-the-Pooh* are particularly good books to choose for this activity.
5. Perform the Teddy Bear Stretch, p. 94.
6. Have the children make Teddy Bear Flap Stories. See next activity.

✳ Teddy Bear Flap Stories

Materials: cardboard teddy bear stencils; construction paper in light colors; scissors; markers; buttons; glitter; sequins; construction-paper scraps; glue

Give children stencils and have them trace teddy bears on light-colored construction paper. Adults or children then write words or sentences about each child's stuffed bear (or other animal) on the tummy of the bear cutout. Next, children cut out a circle that is large enough to cover the bear's tummy. Write *My Teddy Bear* on the circle. Help the children glue the top edge of the circle to the top of the bear's tummy to make a flap that covers the words or sentences on the bear's tummy. Children love to lift the flaps to read what's underneath. Supply buttons, markers, glitter, sequins, construction-paper scraps, and glue so that children can decorate their bears.

✳ Holiday Greeting Card Puppets

Materials: used or unwanted holiday cards; scissors; craft sticks; glue

Ask parents to donate any Christmas or other holiday cards that are used or unwanted. Also ask the owners of local card shops for cards they plan to discard. When you have a sufficient

supply of cards, have children choose cards they like. Children cut out the main figure and glue it to a stick to make a stick puppet.

Children may move the puppets as they recite a favorite rhyme, poem, or song. Or, invite them to use the puppets to retell stories you told them. Explain that puppets are another kind of toy that children have enjoyed for generations. Show examples of puppets that are commercially made and homemade.

✳ Blowing Bubbles

Materials: Bubbles Solution (see Appendix II, p. 273); plastic-coated craft wire

Blowing bubbles is an activity that has been enjoyed by children for many years. Read Tomie DePaola's *The Bubble Factory*. Instead of inventing a wish-making bubble formula as the twins did in the story, challenge children to invent a new shape for bubbles. Make the bubble solution with the children. Then give them pieces of wire to bend and twist into shapes. Have them dip each shape into the bubble solution and gently blow bubbles. Ask the children to notice and compare which shapes work best. Ask, "What other shapes can we make that might work well?"

After blowing bubbles, the children can work together to tell a story about the bubble-blowing activity. Encourage them to describe the sequence of tasks involved in the activity. As the children recall events, emphasize words that show their order (*first, second, third, then,* and *next*). Take notes on chart paper as children work on the story and write the complete story when children are ready to dictate the completed version.

Note: If weather permits complete this activity outside. Avoid blowing bubbles on a tile floor, as it will become slippery.

✳ Feely Box

Secretly place a toy in a feely box (see p. 270). Have the children feel inside and try to guess what the toy is. Ask children to describe what they feel.

✳ Toy Riddle Match

Think of a toy that the all children are familiar with. Give clues about the toy without naming it, and have the children take turns guessing its name.

I am often red. I have four wheels and a tongue to pull. What am I? (wagon)

I am worn on your feet. I have four wheels and like to run on the sidewalk. What am I? (skates)

I am large. I have two wheels, handlebars, and a seat. What am I? (bike)

Have the children help you create toy riddles like the ones above. Begin by having children choose pictures of familiar toys from catalogs or advertising supplements. Talk together about the characteristics of each toy. Then work with the children to create a riddle for each toy. Print each riddle on an index card, and glue each picture on another index card. You may wish to print the name of each toy under its picture.

Display the picture cards along the chalk rail, on a table, or on the floor. Mix up the riddle cards. Have the children take turns drawing a riddle card looking at it while you read it to the class, and then placing the riddle card next to the picture it matches.

✳ The Yellow Ball

Read *Yellow Ball* by Molly Bang to the children. As a class, have the children retell the story of the ball's adventures and travels. Discuss what else could happen to a ball. Involve the class in writing and illustrating books about the adventures of the yellow ball. This is an excellent opportunity to concentrate on several important concepts, such as opposites and rhymes. For example, you could have children make books entitled *Our Yellow Ball Book of Opposites* and *Our Yellow Ball Book of Rhymes*. A book about opposites could include sentences such as, "The yellow ball rolled up the hill and down the hill." A rhyming version could include sentences such as, "The yellow ball hit a cat and knocked off his hat."

MATH

✳ Calendar

Provide the children who can write numerals with their own copy of a blank calendar (Activity Master 3, p. 280). Help them write the name of the month and fill in the dates in the appropriate spaces. Invite children to write alternating dates in red and green to form a repeating pattern on their calendar. (See Marvelous Me, p. 10, for more about this task.) Ask children to compare their calendar from last month with this month's calendar. Give children Christmas stickers, and show them how to place a sticker on the calendar space that shows December 25.

✳ Count-a-Toy

Provide real toys.

1. Have the children identify and name the parts of the toys that are circles, squares, triangles, or rectangles. Count how many of each shape is found on the toys.
2. Have children count the toys with specific colors or color combinations. For example, ask, "How many red and white balls do we have?"
3. Have the children count the toys of the same type. For example, ask, "How many balloons do we have?"

✳ Whole and Half

Remind children of the pictures of toys that were cut in half for the Toy Matching Game (p. 90). Demonstrate the concept of whole and half by showing children several whole objects, such as a sheet of construction paper and an apple, and then folding or cutting each in half. Be sure to cut or fold objects vertically and horizontally.

✳ Heavier and Lighter

Collect toys of various weights. You could use toys the children bring from home or classroom toys. Be sure to include some heavy toys, such as a metal truck, skates, or a riding toy. Then divide a table top in half with masking tape. Label one side *heavier* and the other *lighter*. Have each child pick two toys and classify them by putting the heavier toy on the side of the table labeled *heavier* and the lighter toys on the other side. When all the toys have been classified, have the children count the number of toys in each category and the total number of toys.

Note: Some children may be ready to classify three toys as heavy, heavier, and heaviest, or light, lighter, and lightest.

✳ Toy Windups

Children pretend to be windup toys that you have wound up. They move their arms, legs, and heads like mechanical dolls or robots.

✳ Teddy Bear Stretch

Repeat the lines below in a singsong chant and have the children act out the suggested movements.

1. *Teddy bear, teddy bear, stretch up tall.*
2. *Teddy bear, teddy bear, make a big ball.*
3. *Teddy bear, teddy bear, lean to the right.*
4. *Teddy bear, teddy bear, jump up with all your might!*
5. *Teddy bear, teddy bear, walk around.*
6. *Teddy bear, teddy bear, curl up on the ground.*
7. *Teddy bear, teddy bear, pat your head.*
8. *Teddy bear, teddy bear, go quietly to bed.*

✳ The Toy Store

Look in the window of the toy store.
    (Fingers make glasses for eyes to look through.)
See the jack-in-the-box and a whole lot more!
    (Crouch down and then leap up with arms over head.)
Here's a telephone that really can ring,
    (Hold receiver to ear and move arm in an exaggerated dialing motion.)
And a little bird that can chirp and sing.
    (Tuck hands under arms like wings. Point head up and tweet.)
Over there's a top to spin around,
    (Spin in a circle.)
And here's a ball to bounce on the ground.
    (Move arms as if bouncing and catching a ball.)
They have a robot you can program to walk,
    (Walk with stiff legs and arms.)
And a baby doll that can wave and talk.
    (Wave and say "Ma-Ma.")
Oh, it's fun to look at all the toys,
Such wonderful things for girls and boys!

✳ Balloon Walk

Blow up several balloons and tie each end in a knot. Demonstrate how to gently bat a balloon to keep it in the air, and then have children gently bat the balloons to keep them aloft. After children have practiced for a while, mark off a starting and ending line. Have the children try to walk that distance while batting a balloon to keep it in the air.

MUSIC

✳ Here's a Toy

(Tune: "London Bridge")

Here's a toy, so let's all play,
Let's all play, let's all play!
Here's a toy, so let's all play,
All play together.

Children take turns naming a toy before a verse is sung. Then, one child leads the rest of the group in acting out that toy while all are singing.

ROLE PLAY

✳ Toy Store

Open a classroom toy store so that children can pretend to buy and sell toys. This is an excellent way for children to develop organizational skills and a sense of responsibility. Refer to the Grocery Store activity on p. 82 for information on gathering materials for the store, involving children in setting up the store, and math concepts and skills that children can practice while playing in the store.

Be sure to provide a variety of toys that appeal to children with different interests. Notice how children organize and categorize the toys when they put them on the display shelves. Encourage older or more interested children to design an advertisement for one or more of the toys.

✳ Box Playhouse

Materials: empty furniture or appliance boxes; heavy-duty tape; clothespins; box-cutting knife; paints or markers; wallpaper books; glue

Children place several boxes next to each other to create rooms in a box playhouse. An adult cuts openings on the sides of the boxes that touch and securely tapes the edges of these openings together to create doorways between rooms that children can crawl through.

Tape a smaller box on top of one or two of the large boxes. Cut openings so that the children can stand up and peek out the top of the stacked boxes. Cut openings for windows.

Have interested children help paint designs on the house or decorate it using markers. Children can cut and tear pages from a wallpaper book to create a wallpaper collage on the inside walls of the playhouse.

Provide small props that will add to the fun of playing in the box playhouse. Small tea sets for tea parties and books and pillows for reading time are nice additions. Allow two or three children to play together in the house at one time. The structure can easily last a week or two if children use it gently.

SCIENCE

✳ The Sounds of Toys

Provide an assortment of toys, such as a ball, push toy, drum, small car, and marbles. Ask the children to predict which ones they can and cannot identify from only the sound each makes. List their predictions. Then have children turn their backs and close their eyes. Use each toy to produce a sound. Ask children to tell which toy it is. Next to each prediction, write the outcome. Discuss the results. Repeat the sound experiment if interest continues; children often want to try it again.

✳ Bell Sounds

Provide bells in several different sizes. Ring each bell and talk about the sound it makes. Then have the children turn their backs and ring the bells one at a time. Have the children raise their hands high over their heads when a sound is higher than the one before it and crouch down to the floor if the sound is lower. At first, produce sounds that are very obviously different, and later produce sounds that are closer in pitch. After the children have explored the different sounds of the bells, have them help you sort the bells into three sets: those that make high sounds, those that make low sounds, and those that make middle sounds that are between high and low. Then ask the children what they notice about the bells in each group. For example, ask, "Do all big bells make sounds that are low?" Or, "Are all the bells that make high sounds made from the metal?"

✳ Water Glass Sounds

Provide three or four glasses and one stick. Pour different amounts of water into each glass and demonstrate how to make different musical notes by gently tapping each glass with the stick. Mark each glass with a piece of colored tape to show the level of the water.

Give the children a small plastic pitcher of water. Have them refill the glasses to each marked line and then produce musical sounds by gently tapping each glass. Ask more advanced children to arrange the glasses by pitch, from highest to lowest. Then ask them what they notice about the amount of water in each glass. When they are finished, have them carefully pour the water back into the pitcher so that others can conduct the experiment.

✳ Jar Noise

Provide an empty glass jar. Hold the jar near each child's ear. Talk about the noise they hear in the jar and ask what they think makes the noise. Explain that there are sound waves all around us. The sound waves make the air in the jar move or vibrate. When the sound waves reach our ear, we hear them.

Fill the same jar with water. Have children put an ear down close to the jar and listen. Now what do they hear? They will hear nothing because the water pushed the air out of the jar.

TRANSITION ACTIVITY

1. Repeat the Toy Windups activity, p. 94.

2. Have the children sit in a circle. If possible, use a yellow ball and remind the children of the book *Yellow Ball* that you read to them. Say, "When I roll you the ball, tell me your favorite toy." Slowly roll the ball to one child so that he or she can successfully catch it. After the child names a favorite toy, he or she rolls the ball back to you or to another child to continue the game.

CHILDREN'S BOOKS

Bang, M. *Yellow Ball*. New York: Morrow, 1991. A boy's lost ball causes an adventure that is seen from lots of different perspectives.

Blake, Q. *Clown*. New York: Henry Holt, 1998. A wordless book follows the adventures of a rag clown and his friends as they make their way into the arms of the right family.

Bunting, E. *Ducky*. New York: Clarion, 1997. When Ducky falls out of a crate, he has an adventure getting safely back. Based on a true incident.

Burns, M. *The Greedy Triangle*. New York: Scholastic, 1994. A triangle is dissatisfied with its shape and asks the local shape-shifter to help him change into other shapes.

Crockett, J. *Harold and the Purple Crayon*. New York: Harper & Row, 1955. A young boy with a purple crayon goes on a walk and draws himself in and out of many adventures.

DePaola, T. *The Bubble Factory*. New York: Scholastic, 1996. Twins visit a bubble factory and invent a wish-making bubble formula.

Inkpen, M. *The Blue Balloon*. Boston: Little, Brown, 1989. A boy and his dog find a blue balloon with strange and wonderful powers. Pages open and change to surprise the reader.

King, S. *A Special Kind of Love*. New York: Scholastic, 1995. A father builds toys for his son from boxes.

Lionni, L. *Alexander and the Wind-up Mouse*. New York: Pantheon, 1969. A real mouse learns it's better to be real than to be a toy.

Milne, A. A. *Winnie-the-Pooh*. New York: Dutton, 1957. The classic story of Christopher Robin's toys.

O'Malley, K. *Leo Cockroach. . .Toy Tester*. New York: Walker & Co, 1999. A cockroach that tests toys keeps having close calls with the bottom of his owner's shoe! Bold illustrations.

Spier, P. *The Toy Shop*. New York: Doubleday, 1981. Intricate drawings reveal the details of a toy store.

Van Leeuwen. J. *Emma Bean*. New York: Dial, 1993. Follow Molly and her stuffed bunny, Emma Bean, from babyhood through the first day of school.

Viorst, J. "Teddy Bear Poem," *If I Were in Charge of the World and Other Worries*. New York: Aladdin, 1981. A child has mixed feelings about throwing away an old teddy bear.

Williams, K. *Galimoto*. New York: Lothrop, Lee & Shepard, 1990. A boy in Africa finds scrap materials to construct his own toy truck. Shows everyday activities in the life of a child in a distant country.

Williams, M. *The Velveteen Rabbit*. New York: Doubleday, 1958. The classic story of a toy rabbit that is given life because he is loved by a child.

Zolotow, C. *William's Doll*. New York: Harper & Row, 1972. Family members respond in a variety of ways to a boy's wish for a doll.

Holiday Season

CONCEPTS

- The winter holiday season is a time for sharing. People like to give and receive gifts.
- Many children visit friends and family during the winter holiday season.
- Christmas, Chanukah, and Kwanzaa are holidays celebrated in December.
- Children in other countries celebrate the holiday season in many ways.
- Symbols are used to represent important holiday traditions and principles. Christmas symbols include angels, stars, wreaths, evergreen trees, bells, Santa Claus, and reindeer. Chanukah symbols include the menorah, candles, and a dreidel. Kwanzaa symbols include a straw mat, a candleholder, candles, an ear of corn, and a unity cup.
- The colors of Kwanzaa are black, red, and green. The main colors of Christmas are red and green, but gold, silver, and white are also important Christmas colors. Chanukah colors include white and blue, but other colors may also be used.

CONTINUING CONCEPTS

- **Colors** Emphasize the use of red and green as Christmas colors.
  Discuss the meaning of red, green, and black in the celebration of Kwanzaa. Relate the Chanukah colors white and blue to the colors of the Israeli flag.
- **Geometric Shapes** Identify geometric figures in holiday symbols. For example, help children realize that a picture of a Christmas tree is shaped like a triangle, and a wreath has a circular shape.
- **Health and Nutrition** Discuss the importance of eating a healthy diet and getting exercise during the busy holiday season.
  Discuss the different foods served at family holiday celebrations.
- **Senses** Talk about the sounds of the holidays, such as bells ringing, special songs, and families telling stories about past holidays.
  Display pictures of people enjoying winter holiday traditions and different celebrations.
  Have children compare how play dough, ceramic dough, and gingerbread dough feel when they are rolled and shaped into figures.
  Have children smell fresh evergreens, freshly baked gingerbread cookies, potato pancakes (latkes), and sweet potato pie.
- **Traditional Rhymes and Tales** Recite "Little Jack Horner" with the children and tell them the story of the Gingerbread Man.

PORTFOLIO PRODUCTS

The teacher or children select at least one product from this unit to place in each portfolio. One suggestion follows:
- Tape record each child singing a favorite holiday song. The recording can be used to celebrate the child's knowledge of music and to document his or her individual preferences.

ART

✴ Easel or Tabletop Painting

1. Red and Green

Materials: tempera paints; paper

Talk about how often we see red and green decorations at Christmas time. Provide children with red and green paint and encourage them to freely explore these colors at the easel.

2. Evergreen Painting

Materials: small cuttings from evergreen trees; tempera paints; paper

Children explore using evergreen branches as paintbrushes. Encourage children to make gentle movements in order to produce delicate lines. Have children compare paint strokes made with the evergreen with those made with a brush. Ask, "How do they look different?"

3. Hebrew Letters

Materials: dreidel; tempera paints; paper; small brushes

Provide a dreidel or pictures of the four Hebrew letters on the sides of a dreidel. Encourage children to paint designs and patterns using the letters.

✴ Class Christmas Tree (A Whole-Class Project)

Materials: tempera paints in green, red, and a variety of other colors; large cutout of a Christmas-tree shape; glitter; cotton swabs; glue; small pieces of plastic packing material or colored, circle-shaped cereal; large, plastic needles; thread

Have children work together over two or three days to paint a class Christmas tree to hang on the wall. Provide a large cutout of a Christmas tree and green tempera paint. Children should begin by taking turns painting the entire tree green. When the tree is dry, supply several colors of tempera paint and have the children paint ornaments on it. Then have the children use cotton swabs to paint glue designs on the ornaments and sprinkle glitter over the glue. Recycle the glitter that does not stick by tapping the tree so that the glitter falls onto a piece of paper. Finally, under the supervision of an adult, have children make garlands for the tree by using a large plastic needle to string packing material or circle-shaped cereal. (Stringing popcorn is too frustrating for most young children because many kernels break apart as children try to string them.) Tape the garlands to the tree and put the completed tree on a wall in a prominent place in the room. You can use the Christmas tree throughout the holiday celebrations.

1. Sit around the tree while reading holiday stories.
2. Play Christmas music and have a sing-along around the tree.
3. Write stories on paper shaped like presents and put under the tree.

✳ Gingerbread People

Materials: play dough and ceramic dough (see Appendix II, p. 273 and p. 275); tempera paints

Tell the story of the Gingerbread Man to the children. Encourage them to recite the repeating verse with you:

Run, run, run as fast as you can.
You can't catch me, I'm the Gingerbread Man.

Provide lots of play dough and have children practice making gingerbread people. They can make a simple gingerbread-man shape by rolling two strips and one ball. Show them how to roll strips and balls. Then show them how to curve one strip up to form the arms and upper part of the body and the second strip down to form the bottom portion of the body and the legs. Show them how to gently pat the two parts of the body together, place the ball at the top to form the head and pat the head flat. After children have made their own gingerbread people, have them use play dough in a different color to make small balls. They can use the balls to add buttons and facial features to the gingerbread people.

✳ Fish Pinata (A Whole-Class Project)

Materials: large brown paper bag (not a heavyweight bag); newspaper; wrapped candy; a piece of string or yarn; crepe-paper strips; glue or tape; tissue paper or construction-paper scraps

Explain what a pinata is and tell children that they are used in celebrations in Mexico. Encourage children to talk about their experiences with pinatas. Tell children that they are going to make a pinata that is shaped like a fish.

Put the wrapped candy in the paper bag and have children fill the bag with small balls of wadded-up newspaper. Tie the end of the bag shut with the string. Fan the opening out so that it looks like the tail of the fish.

Have the children glue a strip of crepe paper around the sack, starting at the tied end. Children should take turns gluing on each strip, each time overlapping the strip with the last one applied. They continue putting on strips until the bag is covered. Have some children use the tissue paper or construction paper to make cutout eyes and decorative spots and glue them on the fish. Have other children cut 8-inch crepe paper strips and glue these on to make fins.

Hang the pinata in the room. Later, use the pinata during a holiday celebration (see p. 105).

✳ Rudolph Reindeer

Materials: 9-inch brown construction paper triangles; construction paper scraps; packages of 9" × 12" construction paper; glue; red glitter (optional)

Display and discuss pictures of reindeer and Rudolph the Red-Nosed Reindeer. Look at the brown triangles together and talk about how a reindeer's head is shaped a little like a triangle. Ask children to tell you what else you could do to make the triangle look more like a reindeer. As they suggest adding details such as eyes and a nose, use construction-paper scraps to make those details. When possible, make the details in familiar geometric shapes, for example, make circle-shaped eyes and nose and discuss the shapes with the children. Next, trace around both hands and cut out the shapes. Show children how the shapes look like antlers when placed at the top edge of the triangular face.

Children then take a triangle and begin to make their reindeer face. Encourage them to help each other trace around their hand to make the reindeer's antlers. Provide different shades of brown construction paper, but allow children to use a bright color for the antlers if they wish. If children want to make Rudolph the Red-Nosed Reindeer, supply red scraps or red glitter so that they can make a red nose.

❋ Holiday Art Experiences

Materials: 9" × 12" paper; old newspaper; one or more of the following: tempera paints in holiday colors; crayon or markers; small sponges cut in holiday shapes; cotton swabs; string; tissue paper in holiday colors

Note: The projects below can be completed using one of several art techniques, including sponge painting, handprints, cotton swabs to paint delicate or small designs, string painting, and making a collage with tissue-paper scraps. String painting involves dipping string in paint and pulling it through sheets of folded paper. Provide materials that match the holiday or holidays on which the project is focused.

Talk about the custom of giving gifts to people we care about as part of our celebration of Kwanzaa, Chanukah, or Christmas. Explain that creativity is one of the seven principles of Kwanzaa. Discuss with the children how satisfying it is to create holiday gifts, cards, and wrapping paper for our friends and family members, instead of buying everything that we give others.

1. **Holiday Cards –** Talk about the custom of sending cards to others during the holidays. Have children fold construction paper in fourths to make a card shape and decorate the outside of the cards by using one of the art techniques listed above. When the outside is dry, children can copy or write a simple greeting or message inside.
2. **Holiday Picture Gifts –** Encourage children to create a picture to give as a present to someone special.
3. **Wrapping Paper –** Children design their own wrapping paper to add a special touch to a gift. Children decorate a sheet of newspaper using one of the art techniques described above.

❋ Bearded Santas

Materials: small paper plates, 1½ plates for each child; construction paper and construction-paper scraps; scissors; glue; cotton puffs; plastic foam packing material or elbow macaroni; plastic foam food trays; triangle stencil

Show children a paper plate and discuss how it is shaped like a person's face. Explain that they are going to make Santa's face and ask what they could add to make the plate look more like Santa. As children suggest various facial features, show them items they could use to make those features. For example, show them how to cut circles from construction paper or use macaroni to make eyes. Also demonstrate how to make eyebrows and a moustache from paper, packing material, or pieces of cotton.

Display one-half of a paper plate and talk about whole and half. Compare the half plate to a whole plate by laying the half inside the

whole. Then, staple a half plate on a whole plate to make a beard form, as shown in the illustration. Pour a small amount of glue onto a food tray. Show children how to dip the packing material, macaroni, or cotton into the glue and then glue it on to create a beard. Finally, add a red triangle on the top of Santa's head to make a cap and decorate the cap with cotton.

Give each child one whole plate for a Santa face and a half plate for a beard. Staple the two pieces together for each child. Then have children follow the procedures you demonstrated to make their own bearded Santas.

BLOCKS

✳ Block Patterns

Cut long, narrow strips of poster board. On each one, trace different block shapes in a repeating pattern, for example, a pattern that shows the repeating sequence *one long block, one short block*. Have children use blocks to reproduce the patterns on the floor.

✳ Building Chimneys

Add pictures of chimneys and brick walls to the block area. Help the children experiment with several ways to stack the blocks safely when building tall structures, such as a chimney. Have them look at pictures of a brick wall to see how the bricks are stacked. Talk about which stacking method is the strongest and safest.

BULLETIN BOARD

✳ A Present (or Stocking) Full of Wishes

Discuss what children want to receive as a holiday gift and what they would like to give someone. Then talk about wishes that could help other people and make the world a good place for everyone to live.

Provide a stencil for a large gift package or a stocking and have children trace the stencil and cut out the package or stocking shape. Print each child's name along the top of his or her package or stocking shape. Along the bottom of each shape, print a sentence dictated by the child about a holiday wish. Have children decorate their packages or socks as they desire, using crayons, markers, and construction-paper scraps. Then, give children magazines and catalogs that show toys and have them cut out pictures of toys and other things they wish to receive or give. They then glue the cutouts inside the package or along the top edge of their stocking, as if the gifts were in the stocking.

Add the caption *A Present (or Stocking)* Full of Wishes to the board. As children complete their products, staple them to the board. Provide 2" × 9" strips of red and green construction paper and glue. Have children glue together alternate strips of red and green to make a paper chain as a border for the bulletin board. Count the number of links in the finished paper chain. Ask, "How many links did it take to make a chain to go all around our bulletin board?"

Use the bulletin board during circle time in the following ways.

1. Review the wishes of each child. One child can use a pointer to touch a present or stocking, and the child who made it can tell the class about her or his wish.

2. State a certain number. Say, "Let's count the links on our paper chain and stand up when we come to this number." Repeat the activity, varying the number each time. Later, display a numeral but do not name it. Count slowly and have children stand up when you reach that number.

COOKING

✳ Potato Latkes – A Chanukah Tradition

6–8 potatoes
1 egg
1 teaspoon salt
$\frac{1}{4}$ cup bread crumbs or matzo meal

$\frac{1}{2}$ teaspoon baking soda
$\frac{1}{2}$ cup finely chopped onion (optional)
Vegetable oil for frying
Applesauce

Wash hands. Children scrub the potatoes and, if appropriate and with adult supervision, help grate the potatoes and onion. Mix the potatoes with the baking soda and allow the mixture to sit for a few minutes. Invite the children to notice what happens to the mixture. Then squeeze the liquid out of the potatoes and mix all the ingredients together.

With children at a safe distance, carefully drop the mixture by spoonfuls into a frying pan that contains a thin layer of hot oil. Turn each pancake when golden brown. Drain the pancakes on paper towels, and serve them warm with applesauce. Read L. Glaser's *The Borrowed Hanukkah Latkes* as the children eat.

✳ Peanut Butter for Kwanzaa – A Celebration of the African Harvest

Package of peanuts in the shell, enough to
   produce $1\frac{1}{2}$ cups of shelled peanuts
$1\frac{1}{2}$ tablespoons peanut oil

Plastic knives
$\frac{1}{2}$ teaspoon salt
Bread or crackers

Wash hands. Discuss where peanuts are grown in the United States and Africa. Ask children to shake a peanut shell and listen to what they hear. Have them smell a peanut shell and then smell a shelled peanut. Talk about how the shell protects the peanut. Demonstrate how to shell peanuts. As children shell all the peanuts, ask them to predict each time how many peanuts they think will be in each shell. Discuss what they notice about the number.

Put the shelled peanuts in a food processor or blender. Blend for one minute or until the peanuts are crushed into a paste. Stir in oil and salt. Have the children use plastic knives to spread the peanut butter on half slices of bread or crackers.

✳ Gingerbread People – A European Favorite

No cookie cutter is needed!
5 cups flour
$1\frac{1}{2}$ teaspoons soda
$\frac{1}{2}$ teaspoon salt
2 teaspoons ginger
1 teaspoon cinnamon
1 teaspoon ground cloves

1 cup shortening
1 cup sugar
1 egg
1 cup molasses
2 tablespoons vinegar
Raisins

Sift the first six dry ingredients together. Cream together the shortening and sugar. Stir the egg, molasses, and vinegar into the shortening and butter mixture. Beat well. Stir in the sifted dry ingredients and mix well. Chill.

Wash hands. Have children help roll the dough in pecan-sized balls. Use three balls for each cookie. Place one ball on a greased baking sheet and flatten it with thumb to make the head. Roll one ball into a fat rope for the arms. Roll one into a rope and curve it for legs. Put the three pieces together and pat the edges to connect them. Add raisins for eyes and buttons. Scratch children initials on the cookies. Bake at 350° F for 10–12 minutes.

LANGUAGE ARTS

✳ Fingerplay – Chanukah Lights

One light, two lights, three lights, four,
    (Hold up four fingers, one at a time.)
Five lights, six lights, then light three more.
    (Hold up five more fingers.)

For Chanukah watch the nine pretty lights
On the Menorah burning bright.
    (Wiggle fingers to show flickering flames.)

✳ Fingerplay – Santa's Helper Elves

Santa's little helper elves are standing in a row.
    (Hold up five fingers.)
Santa comes in and they bow just so.
    (Wave; bend fingers as if they are taking a bow.)
They stack toys to the left,
    (Move hand to the left.)
They stack toys to the right.
    (Move hand to the right.)
Then Santa's little helper elves sleep all night.
    (Curl fingers; hide hand behind back.)

✳ Word Wall

Add the words *holiday, Christmas, Kwanzaa,* and *Chanukah* to the word wall. Add other topic-related words that children suggest. Add a high-frequency word that you want children to use. Place a piece of colored plastic (cut from a plastic report cover) over cards with words you wish to highlight and encourage children to use in their writing.

✳ Red and Green

Explain that red and green are the colors most associated with Christmas. Make a list of all the red and green things, such as poinsettias, children can think of. Add to the list whenever possible. Invite children to draw a picture of each red and green object and display the drawings next to the list.

✳ Chanukah

Invite a class parent or community member to visit the class and share the traditions and symbols of Chanukah (also spelled Hanukkah). Show a menorah and let children count the candles. Demonstrate how to spin a dreidel (also spelled *draydel*) and teach children the dreidel song. Point out the Hebrew letters on the sides of the dreidel and compare the letters with the letters of the English alphabet.

✳ Kwanzaa

Explain that Kwanzaa is an American holiday inspired by African traditions. It is a seven-day festival that lasts from December 26 through January 1. During this time people of African descent rejoice in their ancestral values. The dates correspond to the days of African harvest celebrations. Show and discuss the foods we know and use that are part of African harvests, such as yams and peanuts. Read together J. G. Ford's *K is for Kwanzaa: A Kwanzaa Alphabet Book*.

✳ Holiday Celebrations Around the World

Show the class a globe or world map. Locate the United States. Talk about how people around the world celebrate the winter holiday season differently from the way we do. Locate each country as you talk about it.

Great Britain – British people call Santa Claus Saint Nicholas. The day after Christmas is Boxing Day, because churches have traditionally opened their poor boxes after Christmas to distribute the money. Today Boxing Day is the day that mail-carriers, newspaper carriers, and other public servants go from house to house to receive their Christmas gifts.

France – French people exchange presents on New Year's Day instead of at Christmas.

Denmark – Gingerbread is very popular in Denmark. Many vendors sell it during the Christmas season. Many people hang it on their Christmas trees as decorations.

Switzerland – The Swiss also call Santa Claus Saint Nicholas. Saint Nicholas does not come to Switzerland on Christmas Eve. He visits Swiss homes on December 6, which is the anniversary of the first Saint Nicholas, a fourth-century saint who gave secret presents to the poor and was known for his kindness to children.

Mexico – Mexican celebrations often include breaking a pinata full of candy and fruits. End the discussion with a pinata celebration. Use the fish pinata that the class made (see p. 100). Hang it up in a safe area. One at a time, the children put on a blindfolded and try to hit the pinata with a dowel rod or yardstick. When the pinata breaks open, children collect the candy. Count the candy together and determine how many pieces each child gets. Stress the value of equal sharing so that all can enjoy the fun.

✳ Sharing

Encourage children to bring in holiday objects made in other countries to show. Enlist the help of parents who are from other countries or have lived or visited other countries. Ask them to tell the class about holiday celebrations in those countries.

✳ A Classic Poem

Read or recite to the children Clement Moore's classic poem *The Night Before Christmas*. Have the children act out the parts in the poem while you repeat the poem. Remind the children that people in Great Britain, Switzerland, and other European countries call Santa Claus *Saint Nicholas*.

✳ Polar Express

Read Chris Van Allsburg's *Polar Express* to the children. Discuss the story. Invite children to describe their favorite parts. Then reread the book. Supply a small bell for each child to hold and ring at the appropriate place in the story. (Do not use real bells if the children are very young and likely to put the bells in their mouths. Instead, have them pretend to ring a bell as they say "ding-dong.")

✳ Recipes for Holiday Dinners

Discuss special foods that are served for different holidays. Have each child dictate a recipe for a favorite holiday dish to you. Children often have some rather fantastic versions to share! Invite the children to illustrate their recipes and put them together in a class book. Consider making a copy of the book for each child so that children can give their families the book as a holiday present.

MATH

✳ How Many Days Until Christmas?

Materials: 2" × 9" strips of red and green construction paper; glue

Count together on a calendar the number of days until Christmas Day. Have the children help you glue together alternate strips of red and green to make a paper chain with that number of strips. Print or staple a numeral on each strip of the chain. Hang the chain under the sign *Christmas is December 25. How many days are there until December 25?* Each day, children take turns tearing off one numbered strip of the chain and then counting together the remaining strips to keep track of how many days remain before Christmas.

Additional "countdown" activities:

1. Use a wreath made from construction paper and poster board. Cut twenty-five windows in it. Number each window. Put a Christmas picture cut from magazines and cards behind each window. Take turns opening a window each day until Christmas.

2. Start with a December calendar that is blank except for one special sticker that marks Christmas Day. Have the children take turns adding a sticker to the calendar each day.

3. Draw or make a large Santa head. On his beard, draw 25 quarter-sized circles. Write a numeral (1–25) in each circle. Each day, a child glues a cotton ball on a circle to cover up one of the numerals.

✳ Counting With Santa's Bag

Fill a large bag or pillowcase with stuffed animals and toys from the classroom. Have the children count each item as you remove it from the bag. You can also call out items for the children to find and put in the bag. For example, say, "Find three red things (or two heavy things or one rectangle) that can fit in Santa's bag."

✳ Heavier-Lighter Packages

Wrap several boxes of different sizes in holiday gift wrap. Put something in each box. Make one of the smaller boxes noticeably heavier than some other boxes and one of the larger boxes noticeably lighter. Have them predict which boxes might be heavier or lighter. After they guess, let the children lift each box to test its weight. Ask the children to think of things that are small but heavy, as well as things that are large but light.

✳ Geometric Figure Trees

Give children precut felt Christmas trees and small, felt circles, squares, rectangles, and triangles. Have children use the geometric shapes to decorate their trees. Have them identify and categorize the geometric shapes.

✳ Triangle Stars

Provide triangles of equal sizes or provide a triangle pattern for tracing. Show the children how two triangles can be overlapped to make a Jewish star.

MOVEMENT

✳ Stick the Star on the Tree

Pin up a paper Christmas tree at the children's eye level. Put a ring of tape on the back of a paper star. Blindfold each child in turn and have the child try to place the star on the top of the tree. Be sure there are no obstacles in the child's path. You may wish to have the class help the child by giving directions such as "higher" or "lower."

✳ Obstacle Course for Delivering Presents

Set up an obstacle course within the classroom and provide one or more empty, wrapped packages. Have children pretend to travel along the obstacle course in order to deliver presents. Instruct children to move through the course in different ways, for example, by crawling and by walking backwards.

MUSIC

✳ Kwanzaa Drum Rhythms

Demonstrate simple African drum rhythms for the children and have them repeat the rhythms. Invite interested children to make up a dance to the drum rhythms and perform it. Explain that the dance is a way of expressing creativity, one of the principles of Kwanzaa.

✳ The Nutcracker

Play selected parts of a tape or CD of Tchaikovsky's *The Nutcracker.* Have the children move freely in rhythm to the music. Provide scarves or crepe-paper streamers for children to wave in rhythm as they move.

✳ S-A-N-T-A

(Tune: "Bingo")

*There is a fat and bearded man
And Santa is his name-o
S-A-N-T-A, S-A-N-T-A, S-A-N-T-A,
And Santa is his name-o*

✳ It's a Small, Small World

Sing along to a tape or CD of "It's a Small, Small World." Remind the children of the different holiday celebrations you have discussed.

ROLE PLAY

✳ People Around the World

Share Peter Spier's *People* book. As you talk about holiday celebrations, look at the pages that show people from the different areas you have discussed. Pin up pictures of the way people dress in some other countries. If possible, provide articles of clothing that suggest the costumes worn by the people in the pictures. Have the children dress up and talk about what country they represent. Take photographs of the children to display alongside the original pictures.

✳ One Horse Open Sleigh

Provide a cardboard box, large enough for a child to stand in. Reinforce the box by tucking the flaps down on the inside. Cut a large rectangle from the bottom of the box, leaving three to four inches as a frame. From another box, cut out two sleigh runners. Attach the runners to the sleigh box along the bottom of each side.

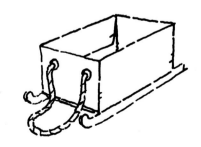

Punch two holes in the sleigh's front and add a rope harness. You may wish to have children paint the sleigh before they use it in role play. A child carefully steps inside the box and holds it up around his or her waist. Another child pretends to be a horse that pulls the sleigh. The children walk slowly, pretending to pull and ride in the sleigh.

SCIENCE

✳ Ice

Talk about how cold it is in many places at holiday times. Ask children if there is sometimes ice outside when it is cold. Encourage the children to share any experiences they have had with ice.

Fold a piece of chart paper in half vertically. Write *Ice* at the top of the left side and *Water* at the top of the right side. Place ice cubes in a zippered freezer bag. Have the children feel the bag of ice cubes. Brainstorm and list words that describe the ice, such as *cold* and *hard,* in the *Ice* column.

Put the bag on a table. Ask, "What will happen next? Why?" From time to time during the day, have the children check the bag to observe what is happening. When the cubes melt, talk about how the ice has changed, using the terms *solid, melted,* and *liquid.* Have the children feel the bag again. In the *Water* column of the chart, list the words they use to describe how the bag feels.

Finally, put the bag of water in a freezer. Ask, "What will happen next? Why?" Examine the bag the next day and talk about how the water changed. A child may mention that the ice is not in cubes. Talk about how water freezes in the shape of the container it is in. Have the children add water to small containers and put the containers in the freezer. You may wish to purchase containers that make ice in different shapes. If the containers are clean, the children can have ice water to drink, using the "special" ice cubes.

✳ Evergreens

Provide different kinds of evergreen branches. Have the children smell and feel each kind. Also have the children compare the needles of different evergreens and classify them according to length.

Pull off one needle from a branch and have the children use a magnifying glass to examine the cut end of the needle and the point where the needle was attached to the branch. Talk about the sap, and have the children feel its stickiness.

✳ Reindeer

Show photographs of real reindeer. Tell the children about reindeer, including information about where they live and what they eat.

TRANSITION ACTIVITY

✳ Gift Toss

Provide a small, empty, wrapped box. Have the children stand in a circle and gently toss the box to one another until everyone has caught the box once. As children catch the box, have them tell what they would like to receive as a present. Later, repeat the activity and have children say what they would like to give someone else.

Brett, J. *The Wild Christmas Reindeer.* New York: Putnam, 1990. While getting the reindeer ready to fly on Christmas Eve, Teeka learns the importance of teaching with kindness. Children study the margins on each page that show daily preparations for Christmas for the days from December 1 through 25.

Edens, C. *Santa Cows.* New York: Simon & Schuster, 1991. In the spirit of "'Twas the night before Christmas," this rhyming verse tells about the arrival of the Santa Cows and the presents they bring.

Fishman, C. G. *On Hanukkah.* New York: Atheneum, 1998. Warm watercolor illustrations add richness to this retelling of the Hanukkah celebration. Includes a glossary.

Ford, J. G. *K is for Kwanzaa: A Kwanzaa Alphabet Book.* New York: Scholastic, 1997. This book celebrates Kwanzaa by introducing related words from A to Z.

Glaser, L. *The Borrowed Hanukkah Latkes.* Morton Grove, IL: Albert Whitman & Co, 1997. A young girl figures out how to involve her lonely neighbor in her family's Hanukkah celebration.

Kimmel, E. *The Chanukah Guest.* New York: Holiday House, 1990. A funny story in which a bear is mistaken for a rabbi and given the latkes.

Kimmelman, L. *Hanukkah Lights, Hanukkah Nights.* New York: HarperCollins, 1992. A family celebrates Hanukkah. Playful illustrations capture the warmth of the holiday. Good use of ordinal numbers.

Krahn, F. *How Santa Claus Had a Long and Difficult Journey Delivering His Presents.* New York: Delacorte Press, 1970. A marvelously humorous, wordless tale about the problems Santa has one Christmas Eve. Ask children to notice the author's use of red and green.

Medearis, A. S. *Seven Spools of Thread: A Kwanzaa Story.* Morton Grove, IL: Albert Whitman & Co, 2000. Magnificent woodcuts of African life compliment the story of seven Ashanti brothers who must turn thread into gold. The brothers' cooperation embodies the seven principles of Kwanzaa.

Pinkney, A. D. and B. Pinkney. *Seven Candles for Kwanzaa.* New York: Dial, 1993 Beautiful illustrations and child-appropriate text describe the origins and practices of Kwanzaa.

Prelutsky, J. *It's Christmas.* New York: Mulberry Books, 1995. Twelve funny rhymes about Christmas situations that kids can relate to.

Siebold, O. and V. Walsh. *Olive, the Other Reindeer.* San Francisco: Chronicle, 1997. Olive the dog thinks he's a reindeer and goes to the North Pole to help Santa.

Soto, G. *Too Many Tamales.* New York: Putnam, 1993. On Christmas Eve, how do you find something lost in a tamale?

Spier, P. *People.* New York: Doubleday. 1980. A wordless book about people all over the world. Use this book as a picture reference when you discuss holiday customs in other countries.

Van Allsburg, C. *Polar Express.* New York: Houghton Mifflin, 1985. A favorite Christmas story about a magical train ride to the North Pole.

January Curriculum

Life in Winter

Imaginary Friends and Monsters

Life in Winter

CONCEPTS

- Winter is the season that comes after fall and before spring.
- The weather is often very cold in winter, but in some areas it stays warm.
- Sometimes the temperature drops below freezing (32° F, 0° C). Then, water freezes and ice and icicles may form.
- It snows in some places in winter. Other areas get little or no snow.
- Some animals, such as bears and turtles, hibernate (sleep for several weeks) in the winter, when it is too cold to find food.
- Some birds migrate (fly to warmer areas) to find food and live during the winter.

CONTINUING CONCEPTS

- **Colors** White is the color of snow. Have children explore how other colors change when mixed with white.
- **Geometric Shapes** Focus on the circle as the shape used to construct most snow people. Compare ice cubes to geometric shapes.
  Review circle, triangle, square, and rectangle through the Snowflake Shapes bulletin board. Introduce the hexagon to interested children.
- **Health and Nutrition** Talk about why we need to wear mittens and warm clothing in the winter.
  Discuss which fruits and vegetables are in season during the winter. Explain that we buy fruits and vegetables from other countries, so more of them are available to us all year.
- **Senses** Have children close their eyes and identify sandpaper geometric shapes.
  Discuss things we can see, hear, and touch outside that tell us it is winter.
- **Traditional Rhymes and Tales** Recite "Three Little Kittens" with the children, and read or tell the children the stories "Cinderella" and "Hansel and Gretel."

PORTFOLIO PRODUCTS

At this midpoint of the school year, an effective way to demonstrate children's growth and readiness levels is to have children make products they have made at the beginning of the school year and then analyze the changes in the products to evaluate how children's competencies have changed.

- Have each child repeat the Look What I Can Do book activity (p. 8). and use both booklets the child has made to assess his or her growth over time. During family conferences, use the two booklets to document each child's progress.

ART

✳ Easel or Tabletop Painting: White

Materials: white tempera paint; blue or black construction paper; brushes

1. Provide children with white paint, and encourage free exploration using white paint on dark paper. Discuss why white is a winter color.

Materials: white tempera paint; red, blue, and yellow tempera paints; teaspoons; paper; paper plates or plastic foam food trays; brushes

2. Provide tempera paints in the three primary colors and white paint. Invite children to mix one teaspoon of a primary color with a teaspoon of white on a paper plate or food tray. Discuss what happens. Ask, "What do you think would happen to another color if you added white?" Encourage children to paint using the colors they mixed.

✳ Sponge-Paint Snow Pictures

Materials: sponge scraps; clothespins with springs; white tempera paint; paper plate or plastic foam food tray; light blue construction paper; crayons or markers

1. **Snowy Day** – Have children draw a picture of any outdoor scene or object on blue paper. Then show them how to clip a clothes pin on a piece of sponge to make a handle, dip the sponge in the white paint, and lightly touch the sponge to the paper to create a snowy scene.
2. **Snow People** – Provide sponges cut in circles of different sizes. Talk about the differences in size. Arrange the circles in sequence from smallest to largest. Have children choose three descending sizes that they can dip in white paint to make snow people. Some children may want to choose many different sizes to create an entire snow family. Children can use crayons or markers to add details after the paint dries.

✳ Sculptures

Material: plastic foam packing pieces; colored toothpicks; glue

Children create three-dimensional snow sculptures using packing pieces and toothpicks. They occasionally add a touch of glue as needed to hold a toothpick in place.

✳ Play-Dough Snow People

Materials: white play dough (see Appendix II, p. 275); colored play dough

Make play dough without adding color and small amounts of play dough in various colors. Children roll balls in different sizes to make snow people. Encourage them to add arms if they like. Provide colored play dough so that the children can add details, such as hats, hair, eyes, and brooms, to complete their snow people.

✳ Thumbprint Winter Scenes

Materials: white tempera paint and assorted colors of tempera on plastic foam food trays or paper plates; twigs; glue; blue construction paper; paintbrushes

Show photographs or pictures of snowy scenes and discuss visible signs of winter, such as snow, bare trees, and winter clothing. If it is snowy in your area, talk with the children about the snow-related things they have seen, such as people shoveling snow and snow plows.

Have children paint a white strip across the bottom of the construction paper to make the snowy ground. Invite them to use a variety of paint colors to add houses, people, and animals. When the paint is dry, they glue on one or more small twigs to make bare winter trees. Finally, they dip their thumbs in the paint and print falling snowflake thumbprints all over the paper.

✳ White Collage

Materials: cotton balls; cotton swabs; white construction-paper scraps; white buttons; popped corn; white plastic foam packing pieces; rice; other white collage materials you have available; glue; 9" × 12" construction or Manila paper

Talk about white being the color of winter because it is the color of snow. Have the children make a collage from a large variety of white materials. Have the children or an adult print *white* at the bottom of each child's picture.

✳ Chalk Drawings

Materials: white chalk; 9" × 12" construction paper in a dark color; paper cup; water; inexpensive hair spray

Children freely draw pictures or designs on the paper with the chalk. Encourage the children to produce a different effect by dipping the chalk into it before drawing. Spray each finished paper with hair spray to prevent the chalk from rubbing off.

✳ Winter Mural (A Whole-Class Project)

Materials: butcher paper 24" × 35" or larger; blue and white tempera paints; brushes; twigs; crayons or markers; Manila paper; scissors; fiberfill, cotton puffs, or paper doilies

Children take turns painting the top part of the butcher paper blue for the sky and the bottom part white for snow-covered hills and ground. When dry, children draw people, houses, sleds, pets, and other details on Manila paper, cut them out, and glue them on the mural. Children can glue on twigs to make bare trees and use fiberfill, cotton puffs, or doilies to make snow people. Discuss other details children may wish to add to complete their winter mural.

✳ Rice Snow Pictures

Materials: liquid starch; blue tempera powder; slick, white shelf paper or finger painting paper; raw white rice; small sponges in a small tub or bowl of water

Refer to Finger Paint (Appendix II, p. 274) for information on this painting technique. Cover the work area with newspaper. Have children use their fingertips to stir the tempera powder into the starch and then use the mixture to finger paint all over the paper. Squeeze a few drops of water on the painting if it becomes too dry.

When the children are done finger painting, have them wash their hands and quickly sprinkle rice all over their painting before it dries. The rice will stick to the starch if the painting is dried flat. Children will enjoy feeling the different textures within the dry painting.

✳ Sparkly Snowflakes Mobiles

Materials: 6-inch circle stencil to trace around; white paper (not construction paper, as it does not cut easily); scissors; brushes; sparkle paint (see Appendix II, p. 276)

Children trace around the circle stencil and cut out their own circles. They follow the procedure below to make their own snowflakes.

1. Fold the circle in half.
2. Cut out shapes along the fold.
3. Open the circle and fold it in half another way to make a new fold line.
4. Cut out shapes along the second fold.
5. Continue opening and refolding as long as children wish or until the snowflake design is complete.

Lay the snowflakes on newspapers on a tabletop. Have children brush the sparkle paint on one side of the snowflake. When the first side is dry, they paint the second side. Tie strings on the snowflakes when they are completely dry and hang them from the ceiling so that they dance and sparkle in the light.

BLOCKS

Display pictures of ice castles and igloos in the block area. Show the children some standard ice cubes. Help them decide which kind of block is shaped like an ice cube. Tell them the name of that solid shape. Encourage the children to build ice castles using the blocks that are most like ice cubes. Children can add other blocks as needed.

BULLETIN BOARD

✳ Snowflake Shapes

Cover the board with blue or black butcher paper and pin up the caption *Snowflake Shapes*. Use white paper to make cutout circles, triangles, rectangles, squares, and hexagons in different sizes. Then, use each geometric shape to make a snowflake by repeatedly folding the shape in half and cutting along the fold line until a snowflake effect is achieved. Randomly attach these snowflake shapes all over the board. Staple a length of yarn to each snowflake shape. Along the bottom of the board, attach large sandpaper cutouts of the same geometric shapes you used to make the snowflakes. Have children use the yarn to match each snowflake to the appropriate sandpaper shape at the bottom. Then undo the matches so that the bulletin board is ready for another child.

1. During circle time, talk about the shape of real snowflakes. Show pictures from books such as *Snowflake Bentley* by Jacqueline B. Martin. Count the number of sides on several snowflakes. Ask children what they learned. If children are interested, tell them that a six-sided figure is called a hexagon.

2. Play a game in which children take turns trying to identify the geometric figure by feeling one of the sandpaper shapes without looking at it.

COOKING

✳ Popcorn Snowstorm

Wash hands. Create a popcorn snowstorm by popping popcorn without putting the lid on the popper. Place the popper on a clean, open sheet so that the popcorn stays clean. (Some popcorn poppers get hot on the bottom. For safety's sake, set the popper on a cookie sheet or large cutting board before placing it on the sheet.) Have the children sit on the outer edge of the sheet. Talk about how the popping corn looks like falling snow. When all the kernels have popped, have the children collect the popcorn to share and eat.

✳ Meringue Snow Piles

4 egg whites at room temperature
1 cup sugar

$\frac{1}{2}$ *teaspoon lemon juice*
$\frac{1}{2}$ *teaspoon vanilla*

If you live in an area that has snow, talk about piles of snow along roadways and driveways. Ask, "What makes the snow pile up like that? Why is it important to remove snow from roadways and walkways?"

Wash hands and involve the children as much as possible in the mixing process. Grease cookie sheets and line them with wax paper or baking parchment. Take turns beating egg whites until they are foamy. Add lemon juice and beat until soft peaks form. Add sugar to the egg whites, one tablespoon at a time, while beating at high speed. Stiff glossy peaks will form. Beat in the vanilla.

Have the children use a tablespoon to mound some of the meringue mixture onto a cookie sheet. Bake the cookies at 200° F for an hour to an hour and a half until dry. Remove to a flat surface to cool. The recipe makes approximately 25 meringue snow piles.

Talk about the tools and the sequence of actions involved in making the snow piles. Role play the use of each tool.

LANGUAGE ARTS

✳ Fingerplay - Snowflakes

Snowflakes, snowflakes spinning all around.
  (Flutter fingers high above head, in the air, slowly falling to ground.)
Snowflakes, snowflakes falling to the ground.
Snowflakes, snowflakes so cold and white.
Snowflakes, snowflakes, will you stay all night?

✳ Signs of Winter

Discuss the things we can see, hear, and touch outside that tell us it is winter. If weather permits, go for a short walk and look for frost, dead leaves, bare trees, evergreens, snow, ice, icicles, warm clothing on people, water vapor from noses and mouths, and winter birds. When you return, complete a copy of the Senses Chart (Activity Master 14, p. 291). For each sense, list and draw the signs of winter the children experienced.

✳ Word Wall

Add the word *winter* to the word wall. Add other topic-related words that children suggest. Place a piece of colored plastic (cut from a plastic report cover) over cards with words you wish to highlight and encourage children to incorporate in their writing.

✳ Winter Begins With W (A Whole-Class Project)

On a piece of chart paper, draw or attach small winter scenes. Write *Winter Begins With W* at the top of the paper. Have children cut pictures from magazines and draw pictures of things that begin with the letter *w*. Discuss each picture and the word that describes it, and then have children glue each picture on the paper. Print the word beside each picture. Children can continue the activity at center and free time until the chart paper is filled with pictures.

✳ Unique: Snowflakes and Children

Talk about how both snowflakes and children are unique. Explain that everyone is a little bit different and everyone is special and that the same thing is true for snowflakes. Tell children that while all snowflakes have six sides, they all have different designs. Also help children realize that while all children have heads, mouths, noses, and other similar features, each child is special and different from everyone else. Tell children, "Nobody is exactly like you!"

Introduce the book *Snowflake Bentley* by Jacqueline B. Martin. Tell the story in your own words and share the pictures, or read the book aloud to those children who are ready for it.

If possible, go outside to catch snowflakes on hands and paper and examine them closely. Try to count the six sides.

✳ Memory Game

Put some winter-related objects on a tray or tabletop. Possible winter objects include paper snowflakes, paper snow person, mitten, scarf, dead leaf, and birdseed. You may also use the topic pictures on page 111.

Cover the objects and then secretly remove or add one item. Uncover the objects and ask the children what is missing or has been added. Just before you remove the cover, you may recite:

Remember, remember what you see.
Now something is different; what can it be?

Vary the number of objects from three to six or more, depending on the age and experience of the children.

To extend the activity, try removing or adding more than one item at a time and have the children identify the missing or added objects. Consider ending the activity by removing all of the items and having children recall them.

✳ The Changing Moon

Eve Bunting's *Moonstick* tells of a Dakota Indian boy who marks a stick to record changes in life and nature that arrive with each new moon. Make a classroom moonstick to record time and events as the year progresses. Provide a stick that is a few feet long and one to two inches in diameter. Use permanent ink markers in different colors to mark wide rings on the stick to represent different months and special events. Use the moonstick to recall events the children have experienced together.

✳ Winter Fairy Tales

Read or tell the stories "Cinderella" and "Hansel and Gretel." Invite children to tell the parts they know. Discuss in which season these stories probably took place. Talk about how the stories would be different or how parts of the stories would be affected if they took place in the winter. For example, there would not have been a pumpkin growing outside that could be turned into Cinderella's coach; Hansel and Gretel could have left footprints in the snow instead of a trail of crumbs.

✳ Matched Pairs

Read aloud the story *The Mitten* by Jan Brett. Retell the story. Each time another animal enters the mitten, have the children chant the repeating list of animals.

Bring in several pairs of mittens or, if possible, use the children's mittens. You may also use cutouts of differently colored pairs of mittens. Mix up the pairs and have the children find the matches. Repeat the activity, using the term *pair* as appropriate. You can vary the activity in the following ways:

1. Provide flannel-board figures of all the animals and the boy. Attach a real white mitten to the board and have the children choose the animal to put in the mitten as you read the story.
2. Have children sit in a circle. Pass the mitten around as the story progresses and have the children insert the animals.

✳ The Inuit

Read aloud *Mama, Do You Love Me?* by Barbara M. Joosse. Discuss the fact that although native Arctic people call themselves Inuits, they are often referred to as Eskimos. Share the glossary at the end of the book with children who are interested. Talk about how the Arctic region is cold and has snow and ice. Find the Arctic region on a map (Greenland, northern Canada, parts of Russia, and Alaska) and compare it to the region in which the children live.

✳ Winter Riddles

Make up two or three riddles about winter things and have the children guess the solutions. For example, tell the children, "Children have fun sitting on me and riding down a snowy hill. What am I?" When the children catch on, have them make up riddles for one another.

MATH

✳ Calendar

Provide the children who can write numerals with their own copy of a blank calendar (Activity Master 3, p. 280). Help them write the name of the month and fill in the dates in the appropriate spaces. Ask them to compare the calendar they made last month with this month's calendar. Invite children to draw ten winter things in the margin to decorate their personal calendar. Count together by tens each day at calendar time. Ask children who are ready to skip-count by tens to use a yellow crayon to circle or color the numerals 10, 20, and 30. Have children mark holidays and other special days, including children's birthdays, on the calendar.

✳ Snowballs

Provide a ball of white play dough (see Appendix II, p. 275) for each child. Write a numeral that the children recognize on the board or a chart. Have the children make as many play-dough snowballs as the numeral indicates. Repeat as time permits. You can use the snowballs to create more challenging math problems for children who are ready for them. For example, say, "You have 3 snow balls. How many more do you need to make to have 4?"

For children who are ready, write an equation such as 3 + 1 = ____. Have the children make each group of snowballs, combine them, and complete the equation. You can also use the same process with subtraction.

✳ Shapes: Circles

Talk about how a snow person is usually made by rolling round shapes.

1. Use the Circle Snow Person pattern (Activity Master 15, p. 292) at the end of this unit to make circles for a felt snow person. Have the children take turns building a snow person by putting felt circles on a flannel board and showing the total number of circles used. Discuss the sizes of the circles and how to arrange them in order by size.

2. Let the children take turns matching the felt circles to the circles of the Circle Snow Person pattern.

3. Older children can cut out the circles on the pattern themselves and glue them together to make a snow person.

✳ Ordinal Numbers

Put three shoeboxes on the floor in a corner of the room. Label the boxes *first, second,* and *third.* Give one child a white beanbag or a white plastic foam ball of the kind used to make tree ornaments. Have the children take turns throwing the "snowball" into a box that you identify. For example, say, "Toss the snowball into the third box."

✳ Measurement: One Cup, One Half Cup, and Time

Crush enough ice cubes to fill one cup and one half cup. (Measuring cups for cooking work best.) Note what time it is when you put the ice in the cups. Ask, "Which do you think will melt faster, the cup of ice or the half cup of ice?" Keep track of how many minutes each takes to melt at room temperature. Measure the water after the ice has melted. Ask, "Does the water fill the cup and the half cup? Which takes up more space, ice or water?"

MOVEMENT

✳ Winter Movements

Have the children perform the following movements:
1. Lie down inside the classroom and pretend to make angels in the snow.
2. Pretend to melt like snow people. Sink as slowly as you can to the floor.
3. Pretend to go ice-skating or skiing. Slide smoothly and carefully in your stocking feet.
4. Stretch down and up to lift large snowballs and place them one on top of another to make a snow person. Stretch very tall to put a hat "way up on top" of the highest ball.
5. Pretend to make snowballs and throw them with overhand and underhand motions.

✳ Footprints in the Snow

Make footprint cutouts. Tape them to the carpet or floor so that they won't slide when stepped on. Have the children walk in the footprints.

Vary the pattern of the prints. Make it curve or zigzag. Vary the length between steps so that the children have to stretch or tip toe.

✳ An Action Poem – Playing in the Snow

Five little children playing in the snow,
    (Wave five fingers over head.)
Jumping up and down in a straight row.
    (Children jump up and down.)
One fell down and hurt his toe,
    (Fall down.)
Ooooooh!
    (Hold foot and rock back and forth.)
Four little children playing in the snow . . .
    (Repeat actions above.)
Three little children playing . . .
    (Repeat actions above.)
Two little children playing . . .
    (Repeat actions above.)
One little child playing . . .
    (Repeat actions above.)
No little children playing in the snow,
    (Shake heads sadly.)
In to see mother they must go.
    (Walk in place.)
Mother smiles sweetly and fixes the toe.
    (Clap hands.)
Five little children playing in the snow.
    (Wave five fingers over head.)

MUSIC

✳ Frosty the Snowman

Play a tape of the song "Frosty the Snowman." Sing the song with the children several times.

✳ Skater's Waltz

Play a recording of "Skater's Waltz" or another selection of instrumental music that suggests smooth, gliding movement. The children take off their shoes and pretend to skate by sliding smoothly in rhythm to the music.

✳ Hibernation Song

(Tune: "Are You Sleeping?")
Are you sleeping? Are you sleeping?
Little bears, little bears.
Wintertime has come now, food is hard to find now.
Hibernate. Hibernate.

The children stretch arms as the song begins and end the song by curling up on the floor as if hibernating like little bear cubs. Substitute other hibernating animals that the children identified when they researched hibernation.

ROLE PLAY

✳ Winter Clothes

Provide winter clothing in several sizes for the children to try on and use for role-play activities. Some suggested articles of clothing include mittens, winter coats of different styles, scarves, and boots.

Place *The Jacket I Wear in the Snow* by Shirley Neitzel and a full-length mirror in the role-play area. Provide children's clothes that are described in the story and invite children to try on the clothes in the order in which they are mentioned. If possible, take a picture of each child in a complete winter outfit and post the photos in the role-play area.

✳ Snow Shoveling

Provide cardboard cutouts of snow shovels. Have children pretend to shovel the snow off driveways so that cars and trucks can be moved. You may wish to provide a box of small white packing pieces so that children can shovel the pieces from one box into another.

SCIENCE

✳ Hibernation

Read J. Arnosky's *Every Autumn Comes the Bear* to the class. This excellent book shows how a bear prepares for hibernation. Discuss how some living creatures, such as bears and turtles, sleep for several weeks in the winter when it is too cold to find food. Challenge children to do research to learn about hibernation. They can ask adult family members for information, consult books, or visit an appropriate Web site on the Internet to identify other examples of hibernating animals During circle time, have children who found information share it with the group.

Note: Be sure to tell children to ask an adult family member for permission and assistance before using the Internet.

✳ Migration

Talk about how some birds migrate to warmer areas where they can more easily find food and live during the winter. Read the poem "Something Told the Wild Geese" in Barbara Rogasky's *Winter Poems*. Challenge children to watch for birds this week to find out which birds are in your area during the winter. If possible, provide a picture of birds from an encyclopedia or a guidebook to help children identify the birds they see. Talk about what birds like to eat and discuss why it is harder for birds to find food in the winter.

✳ Bird Feeder

Make a bird feeder to hang outside a window or wherever the children can maintain it and see birds using it. Remember to keep the feeders cared for and full of seed once the birds have come to rely on them.

1. **Pinecone Feeders** – Tie a long string around a pinecone. Spread a small amount of peanut butter mixed with lots of birdseed on the pinecone. (Be sure to mix the seeds and the peanut butter together well, as peanut butter by itself may cause birds' beaks to stick together.) Hang the feeder on a tree branch.

2. **Milk Carton Feeder** – Clean out a small milk carton. Attach a long string firmly to the top. Cut an opening large enough for a bird to fit through. Attach a small dowel rod beneath it for a bird perch. Fill the bottom of the feeder with birdseed and hang it securely outside.

3. **Pretzel String** – String small pretzels on a length of fat yarn. Tie the yarn outside.

✳ Window Fog

Have children breathe on classroom windows or glass doors and draw pictures with their fingers in the "window fog." Talk about how water vapor forms on the glass as their warm breath contacts the cold glass.

✳ Ice Melts, Snow Melts

Bring in a piece of ice or an icicle from outside (or from the freezer if outside temperatures are above freezing). Talk about how the ice looks and feels. Remind the children of the terms *solid, melted,* and *liquid* that were introduced in the Holiday Season unit. Ask, "What will happen when this ice gets warm?" Have some children hold a piece of ice in their hands for a few seconds. Ask them, "How does it feel?" Point out any water on their hands. Ask, "How did your hands get wet?"

If possible, repeat the same experiment using snow. Read the Shel Silverstein poem "Snowman." Discuss whether or not a snowman could last until July.

✳ Providing Food for Outside Animals

Talk about the fact that most outdoor plants do not grow in places where it is cold and icy in winter. Explain that this is the reason why farmers and other people provide food for animals that live outside most of the time, such as cattle, sheep, and horses. Try to find pictures of outside animals being fed and show them to the children.

TRANSITION ACTIVITY

1. Have the children perform the action poem "Playing in the Snow," p. 120.
2. Have children play "Icicles." Play an instrumental recording with a gentle rhythm that suggests slowly moving water. Stop the music periodically and have children freeze in an icicle pose.
3. Say to the children, "When I call your name, tell me your favorite thing about winter." Call a child's name, pause for his or her response, and then go on to the next child. Keep the activity moving quickly to maintain children's interest.

CHILDREN'S BOOKS

Brett, J. *The Mitten.* New York: Scholastic, 1989. A boy loses his mitten in the snow, and several woodland animals try to make it their home. Involves sequence skills.

Briggs, Raymond. *The Snowman.* New York: Random House, 1978. A wordless book about a boy interacting with a snowman who comes to life. Good language and writing opportunities.

Bunting, E. *Moonstick.* New York: HarperCollins, 1997. Dakota Indian boy discovers changes in life and nature with each new moon. Use in the classroom to explore the passage of time.

Ehlert, L. *Snowballs.* New York: Trumpet, 1995. Brightly colored pictures and simple text tell of making a snow person family. Children can use the collage of items at the end of the book to determine which snow person used each item.

Fleming, D. *Time to Sleep.* New York: Henry Holt, 1997. Bear can tell winter is coming. Bear tells snail, snail tells skunk, and the sequence builds.

George, L. *In the Snow: Who's Been Here?* New York: Mulberry, 1999. Children who are out sledding find clues that an animal has been there. The next page shows which animal.

Gershator, P. *When It Starts to Snow.* New York: Henry Holt, 1998. Find out what different animals do when winter comes.

Joose, B. M. and Lavallee, B. *Mama, Do You Love Me?*. San Francisco: Chronicle Books, 1991. A beautiful and timeless story about an Inuit daughter's attempt to find the limit of her mother's love.

Keats, E. J. *The Snowy Day*. New York: Viking, 1962. The classic story of a child's adventure on a snowy day.

Martin, B. *Polar Bear, Polar Bear, What Do You See?* New York: Holt, 1991. A very predictable pattern book that children "read" after just one read-aloud exposure. Have the children rewrite the story using the pattern.

Martin, J. B. *Snowflake Bentley*. Boston: Houghton Mifflin, 1998. Persistence and family support are modeled in this picture biography of Wilson "Snowflake" Bentley, a self-taught photographer and scientist who studied the uniqueness of snowflakes.

Mendez, P. *Black Snowman*. New York: Scholastic, 1991. A magical snowman helps an impoverished black youth take pride in his heritage.

Miller, N. *Emmett's Snowball*. New York: Henry Holt, 1997. The whole town joins in the efforts of a small boy to build a snowball. Guess the ending!

Munsch, R. *Thomas' Snowsuit*. Toronto, Canada: Annick Press Ltd, 1985. All kinds of silly problems occur because Thomas does not want to put on his snowsuit.

Neitzel, S. *The Jacket I Wear in the Snow*. New York: Mulberry, 1989. A young girl goes through the sequence of all the clothes she must put on in winter. This is a cumulative tale that could be used when dressing weather dolls or for a flannel-board sequencing activity.

Rogasky, B. *Winter Poems*. New York: Scholastic, 1994. Excellent vocabulary and content supported by glorious illustrations.

Shaw, Charles. *It Looked Like Spilt Milk*. New York: Harper & Row, 1947. A pattern book using cloud images. You may wish use the pattern for a writing activity about snow.

Shulevitz, U. *Snow*. New York: Farrar Straus Giroux, 1998. An award-winning tale of the optimism of a boy and his dog who are wishing for snow.

Sierra, J. *Antarctic Antics: A Book of Penguin Poems*. San Diego: Gulliver Books, 1998. The life of baby Emperor penguins depicted in rhyme.

Silverstein, S. "Snowman," *Where the Sidewalk Ends*. New York: Harper & Row, 1974. This silly rhyme tells about a snowman that wants to see July.

Stewart, P. *A Little Bit of Winter*. New York: HarperCollins, 1998. Rabbit saves a bit of winter for his friend the hedgehog, who knows nothing about winter because he hibernates.

Imaginary Friends and Monsters

CONCEPTS

- Sometimes people feel afraid of monsters and the dark.
- Some things that scare us may also be scared of us. What is scary depends on one's point of view.
- Monsters can be funny rather than scary.
- Some children invent imaginary friends.
- Children need opportunities to use their creative imaginations.
- Children need to explore in order to begin to distinguish fantasy from reality.

CONTINUING CONCEPTS

- **Colors** Encourage children to identify the colors they see in pictures and use in their art.
- **Geometric Shapes** Have children identify the shapes used in monster faces. Have them look for circles, triangles, squares, and rectangles in pictures and monster figures.
- **Health and Nutrition** Discuss the value of vegetables in a healthy diet.
- **Senses** Talk about the different ways monsters look in picture books.
    Have children listen to the sound effects they created on their tape of monster sounds.
    Have children make goo and talk about how it feels.
    Listen to fiction books for enjoyment.
    When appropriate, play recorded music quietly to provide background sound during learning experiences.
- **Traditional Rhymes and Tales** Tell the children the story "Jack and the Beanstalk."

PORTFOLIO PRODUCTS

The teacher or children can consider the following suggestion as they select at least one product from this unit to place in each portfolio.

On copies of the Monster Chart (Activity Master 16, p. 293), write *Scary* at the top of one column and *Funny* at the top of the other. Then have each child draw examples of scary and funny things in the appropriate column of the chart.

✳ Easel or Tabletop Painting: Easel Monsters

Materials: easel; tempera paints; brushes; large paper

This activity guarantees a successful experience for each child because any painted shape can be a monster. You may wish to encourage children to paint large figures by reading or telling them the story "Jack and the Beanstalk." Talk about how giants and monsters are similar and different. Then invite children to paint a giant monster. Brainstorm with the children which colors they want to use to paint monsters and which features they want their monster to have. Ask, "How many eyes might your monster have? How many feet?"

✳ Monster Puppets

Materials: paper plates; glue; stapler; construction-paper scraps; yarn; buttons; miscellaneous collage materials; crayons or markers

Have children cut enough paper plates in half to produce one half plate for each child. To make a hand puppet, glue or staple each half plate to the front of one whole plate. Children's hands will easily fit inside the pocket that is formed.

Children make a monster face on the back of the whole plate. They can draw or glue on big eyes, ears, and other facial features. They may wish to add horns, hair, and fur as well. Encourage each child to think of a way to make his or her puppet unique. Use the monster puppets in role play and music activities.

✳ Hanging Out with a Monster

Materials: butcher paper; stapler; paints and markers

Talk about how monsters can be silly looking or funny instead of scary. Show several children's books about monsters to the class and talk about what the authors and illustrators did to make the monsters look funny rather than scary.

Make a class list of the unusual funny features a monster could have. As the children share their ideas, draw their funny monster on a sheet of $8\frac{1}{2}"\times11"$ paper. Then use butcher paper to make a larger version of the drawing that is about 36 inches long and 36 inches wide. Cut out two monster shapes, one for the front and one for the back of the monster. Throughout the day, have the children take turns coloring and making designs on the monster's front and back.

When the both sides of the monster are dry, have the children help staple the two sides together, leaving an opening at the top. Throughout the day, whenever there is paper trash, have children crumple it into a tight ball and gently stuff it into the monster. Allow them to continue doing this until the monster is well stuffed. Staple the monster closed and hang it in a reading area or corner that contains lots of monster books. Hang a sign that reads *Hanging Out With a Funny Monster.*

✳ Monster Goo

Materials: goo (see Appendix II, p. 274); food coloring (optional)

Have each child prepare a ball of the goo mixture. Talk about how the goo feels. Then have them stretch and mold the goo to explore what shapes it can make. Encourage the children to see how many different monster shapes they can create with the goo. Ask them to talk about their monster shapes as they work and, if possible, take photographs to record their creations.

To vary the activity, add a drop of food coloring to each ball of goo. Have children knead the color into the goo and talk about how the color gradually spreads and changes the color of the goo.

✳ Scribble Monsters

Materials: 9" × 12" Manila paper; crayons

Have children use a dark-colored crayon to scribble a design on a piece of paper. Encourage them to draw all over the page using whole-arm movements. Look at the scribbles and talk about the different shapes. Ask, "Who can find a circle scribble? a triangle? a zigzag? a wiggly line?"

Then have children look for monsters in the scribbles. Ask, "Which scribble could be a monster's head? …a monster's body?" Have the children use bright colors to color in parts of the scribbles to complete their monster. Encourage them to add facial features, extra legs, horns, and so forth.

✳ Friendly Monster (A Small-Group Project)

Materials: household and school objects; masking tape

Read the book *Franklin Stein* by Ellen Raskin. In the story, Franklin makes a friendly monster out of household objects. Have the children work in pairs or small groups to plan the simple household objects and recycled materials they might use to make a friendly monster. Have them ask a parent's permission to bring in those objects from home the next day. On the following day, give each group masking tape and have the children complete a monster. They will need quite a lot of time for this activity.

If possible, videotape or take photographs of each group at work. You can display photographs alongside the completed monsters. Allow the children to take turns taking the photographs or video home to share with their families. When interest lessens, the monsters may be disassembled and the objects returned.

Note: Avoid providing the materials the children need. They have more ownership of the activity and a greater sense of responsibility for the outcome if they select and obtain the materials. The completed monsters tend to be more varied as well.

BLOCKS

✳ Monster Blocks

Transform the block center into a monster blocks area by switching from floor blocks to box blocks. Provide a variety of cardboard boxes in a variety of sizes. Encourage the children to build with the boxes. Talk about the shapes and sizes of the boxes and encourage children to stack or arrange the boxes by size.

BULLETIN BOARD

✳ Monsters in a Row

Put four to six large monster figures in a row across the board. Under the monsters, use pushpins to pin up several pictures or drawings of child-oriented objects, such as a ball, bicycle, book, doll, truck, pail, and shovel. Each day, review ordinal numbers by having the children pin pictures next to the monster figures. Ask questions such as the following:

- The first monster likes to play with dolls. What do you need to pin up next to it?
- The second monster wants something to read. What do you need to pin up next to it?
- The third monster needs something fun to play with at the beach. What do you need to pin up next to it?
- The fourth monster wants to take a ride. What do you need to pin up next to it?

You could also use prepositions to help the children become familiar with position words. For example, say:

- "Put the ball beside the first monster."
- "Put the truck under the second monster."

Vary the questions or directions and have the children reorganize the board several times. When the children are familiar with the activity, have them make up directions or questions for one another.

COOKING

✳ Vegetable Creatures

Fresh vegetables that the children enjoy   *Plastic knives*
Low-fat cream cheese   *Round toothpicks*

Wash hands. Cut up very hard vegetables, like carrots, but have the children help you wash, clean, and cut up the other vegetables. Help individual children create vegetable creatures by selecting vegetable pieces and using toothpicks and cream cheese to stick the pieces together.

Invite children to use their imaginations to name the creatures. Ask if these monsters are scary. As the children eat their vegetable creatures, read aloud Ruth Brown's *If at First You Do Not See.* Have the children compare their vegetable creatures to the surprising vegetable creatures in the book.

✳ Bread Blobs

Loaf of bread
Peanut butter and jelly or cream cheese
Plastic knives

Wash hands. Each child carefully tears crusts from one slice of bread to suggest a monster shape. Children then use plastic knives to spread peanut butter and jelly or cream cheese on the shapes. Talk about the differences in shapes, and identify the largest and the smallest. Let the children roll small pieces of the crust and leftover bread to make eyes and other details. Read a fun monster book to the group as they enjoy their bread blobs.

LANGUAGE ARTS

✳ Action Play –Silly Monster

I'm a silly monster, rather small and sweet.
(Crouch down small.)
I have big toes and sixteen feet!
(Wiggle toes and stomp feet.)
I'm a silly monster of gigantic size.
(Stand on tiptoes.)
I have long arms that can reach to the skies.
(Stretch arms high overhead.)
I'm a silly monster with teeth like a crocodile.
(Open mouth and show teeth.)
But don't be afraid, I only use my teeth to smile.
(Give a huge smile.)
I'm a silly monster as sleepy as can be.
(Yawn widely.)
Sit down on the floor and rest with me.
(Sit down; hold head in hands as if asleep.)

✳ Word Wall

Add the words *imaginary* and *monster* to the word wall. Add other topic-related words that children suggest. Add a high-frequency word you want children to use. Place a piece of colored plastic (cut from plastic report cover) over cards with words you wish to highlight and encourage children to incorporate in their writing.

✳ Lacing Monsters

Lacing shapes is a left-to-right sequencing activity that appeals to children. Refer to the Lacing Cards procedure (Appendix I, p. 271). Duplicate the Monster Pattern (Activity Master 17, p. 294) or use any simple monster shape to make the lacing cards.

✳ Monster Match

Glue matching pairs of monster pictures on small index cards. Make the number of pairs that is most appropriate for the children. Have the children use the cards to play a matching or concentration game.

✳ Real or Imaginary

Discuss what is real and what is imaginary. Reread a favorite monster book and ask the children to decide which parts are real and which are imaginary. Duplicate the Monster Chart (Activity Master 16, p. 293). Write *Real* in the left-hand column and *Imaginary* in the right-hand column, and record each of the children's ideas on the appropriate side.

Discuss imaginary friends with older children who are able to distinguish reality and fantasy. Some children may want to talk about an imaginary friend they had when they were younger.

✳ Scary or Funny

Draw two large monster shapes on chart paper or poster board. Write *Scary* on one paper and *Funny* on the other. Brainstorm with the children to develop a list of scary and funny words about monsters and write the words on the appropriate chart. Encourage children to use some of these words in their writing.

✳ Making Predictions

Use *There's a Nightmare in My Closet* by Mercer Mayer with each of the following activities.
1. **Prediction –** Show the cover of the book. Ask the children to predict what the story is about. Write their responses on the chalkboard or on chart paper. After you have read the book, have the children compare their predictions to what happened in the story. Put a check next to the predictions that were accurate.
2. **New Adventure –** Take one of the predictions made during the discussion about the cover. Work with the children to write a new story based on that prediction.

✳ Wild Things

Use *Where the Wild Things Are* by Maurice Sendak to complete the following activities:
1. **Monster Sounds –** Read the story aloud. Ask, "How do you think these monsters would sound if we could actually hear them?" Tape record the children making monster sounds. As you read the story aloud, play the children's recording for sound effects during the wild rumpus part of the story.
2. **Feelings and Actions –** Discuss the fact that Max was sent to bed without supper. Ask, "Why did he send the wild things to bed without supper?" Talk about how the way we feel and act influences how others feel and act toward us.
3. **Favorite Wild Thing –** Reread the story, and have the children vote on their favorite wild thing.
4. **Acrostic –** Use the term *wild things* as an acrostic to organize and retell events in the story. Emphasize the sequence of the most significant events. The letter *N* has been left blank in the following acrostic so that you can fill it in with your students.

W	Went to bed without supper
I	Imagined going to where the wild things are
L	Liked telling the wild things what to do
D	Danced a wild rumpus together
T	Told the wild things to stop
H	Held his scepter high in the air
I	Imagined he was with people who loved him
N	
G	Got into his boat
S	Sailed back to his room

❋ Monster Begins With M (A Whole-Class Project)

Point out that monster begins with *m*. Help the children list and count the number of *m* words they can think of to describe a monster, such as *mud* monster, *marshmallow* monster, and *moon* monster. Have children use breakfast cereal to form the letter *m* on a large index card, count the pieces of cereal they used, and then glue the cereal in the *m* shape. Write on each card: *I used _____ pieces of cereal to make this m.*

With your help, children can combine the *m* words to create monster tongue twisters, such as, *The mud monster munched many marshmallows.*

❋ Monster Story Frame

Write the following story frame on a large piece of chart paper. Laminate the paper if possible, so it can be reused. Brainstorm with the children and write a list of words to fit each of the following categories. Encourage children to think of two to four words for each category so that they have choices later. Then work with the children as they create a story using the list of words. Alternatively, you may wish to write the children's brainstormed words on small cards that can be taped in the appropriate place in the story as they are used.

1. Monster names
2. Places to live
3. Things to be afraid of
4. Scary words
5. Funny things to do
6. More monster names
7. More funny things to do

Once upon a time there was a monster named __1__ who lived in a spooky __2__. The monster was so unhappy because it was afraid of __3__. It had tried saying scary words like __4__ and __4__, and it had tried doing funny things like __5__ and __5__, but it was still afraid.

One day it met another monster named __6__ who told the monster that it would never have to be afraid again. They would be friends and help each other. So after that, they were always friends and did funny things like __7__ together.

The End

✳ Numeral Recognition: Monster Feet

Make a set of 5 or 9 monster-sized feet and write a numeral from 1 through 5 or from 1 through 9 on each foot. Laminate the feet so that they can be reused. Tape the feet on the floor in consecutive number order; later, tape them in random order. Children say the numeral as they step on each foot. To vary the activity, call out a numeral and ask a child to find the monster foot that shows the numeral and stand on or beside the foot.

✳ Counting Bean Monsters

Get an inexpensive shoe-storage pocket hanger, available in discount stores. On each pocket, staple or tape a card with a numeral printed on it. Provide a box of lima bean monsters, beans with eyes drawn on them using a permanent ink marker. Have the children count the appropriate number of bean monsters for each numbered pocket and place the beans inside.

✳ Make a Monster

Make a flannel-board monster by enlarging the Monster Pattern (Activity Master 17, p. 294) and using the enlargement as a stencil. Make flannel or felt monster cutout features, such as claws, spots, ears, eyes, fangs, and horns. Have children take turns adding features to the monster. For example, have a child add two claws at the end of a monster hand and have another child add four spots on the tummy. After each addition, touch and count the parts to review the number.

Model this activity several times until the children are familiar with it. Then give each child a copy of Activity Master 17. Have children take turns describing how many claws, spots, ears, eyes, fangs, and horns each child should draw on his or her monster. When all the children have completed their monsters, have each child choose a name for his or her monster. Write the monsters' names on the activity masters.

Place the felt monster and the felt features in the math center for children to use independently. As they work, ask questions such as, "How many eyes did you add?" Consider taking photographs of the felt monsters.

✳ Monster Measurement

Provide several books with pictures of monsters. Have each child use a ruler to measure the height of one monster in each book to the nearest inch and compare the height with measurements that other children found. Discuss which monster is the tallest and which the shortest.

✳ Long and Short

Make two felt monster cutouts, one that is rather tall and the other short. You may wish to enlarge Activity Master 17 (p. 294), and use the actual size and the enlargement as stencils for the cutouts. Also make a variety of long and short felt parts to add to the monsters, such as tails, horns, hair, arms, teeth, and claws. Show the children the tall and short monster and the monster parts. Discuss the terms *tall, short,* and *long.* Then select an item and ask the children to decide if it is long or short. Place the long felt parts on the tall monster shape and the short parts on the short monster. Mix up the pieces, and repeat the activity by having the children select monster parts and then place them on the appropriate monster. Put all the felt pieces in the math center so that children can continue to classify the parts on their own.

✳ Ordinals

Review the order of the monsters on the bulletin board. Point to each monster and have the children chant the terms *first, second, third,* and so forth. You could continue to review ordinals whenever the children line up by asking questions such as, "Who is first? Who is second? Who is last"? To help children realize that order depends on one's point of view, have a line of children turn around so that the first child becomes the last in line. Repeat this many times.

MOVEMENT

✳ Monster Feet

Use the monster feet you made earlier (see p. 132). Tape the feet on the floor in consecutive number order but in a curving path, leaving a yard or so between each foot. Instruct each child to take a different kind of step each time he or she steps from one foot to another. For example, have children take giant steps, tiptoe, or hop from one foot to the next. You could also have the children walk backward, slide, crawl on their hands and knees, and lie on their tummies and pull themselves forward using just their arms.

✳ Monster Chant

Say the chant together as you and the children act out the movements. Encourage children to help you create additional rhyming couplets to add to the chant.

Monster, monster, turn around;
Monster, monster, jump up and down.
Monster, monster, touch your toes;
Monster, monster, squeeze your nose.
Monster, monster, bend your knee;
Monster, monster, climb a tree.
Monster, monster, hold one leg out;
Monster, monster, hop about.
Monster, monster, wave your hand;
Monster, monster, march in the band.
Monster, monster, you've done your best;
Monster, monster, sit down and rest.

✳ Monster Pass

Stand in a circle. Have one child make a monster face at the next child in the circle. That child tries to imitate the face and passes it to the next child, and so on until the monster face has been passed around the entire circle. Vary the activity by having children pass a monster pose around the circle.

✳ Going for a Monster Walk

Invite the children to pretend to be Max in *Where the Wild Things Are* and go on a monster hunt. Give each direction below in sequence and have the children follow the directions. Point out to children that they are acting out events in the story.

1. Go upstairs to your room.
2. Row your boat across the ocean.
3. Take a giant step up on the land.
4. Move your arms as if walking through tall grass.
5. Use large, exaggerated, tree-climbing movements.
6. Rest in a cave.
7. March with the monsters.
9. Do a monster dance.
10. Let the wild rumpus begin!
11. Now stop! (Have everyone freeze in position. Repeat steps 10 and 11 several times for fun.)
12. Wave good-bye to all your monster friends.
    Use large, exaggerated, tree-climbing movements.
    Move your arms as if walking through tall grass.
    Take a giant step down to the water.
    Get back into bed.
13. Eat your supper and go to sleep.

MUSIC

✳ I Know an Old Monster

(Tune: "Old Lady Who Swallowed a Fly")

Have children make up adaptations of this popular old song in response to the start: *I know an old monster who swallowed a* _____. Write their adaptations on a piece of chart paper. Then have them sing their new song again and again. Encourage them to sing the song in a silly way.

You can vary the activity in the following ways:

1. As children learn the sequence of their song, have them sit in a line and hold either the object or a picture of the object swallowed by the monster. As the song progresses, have each child stand up and sit down at the appropriate time.
2. Have the children accompany each line of the song with a different instrument, for example, bells, triangle, drums, rhythm sticks, autoharp, and hand clapping. Tape-record a performance. Then replay it and have the children guess which instrument was played for each line. Also talk about which instrument is played first, second, third, or last.

✳ Monster Mash

Play a tape or CD of instrumental music. Have the children do the monster mash by assuming a monster-like pose as they dance, sway, or march to the rhythm. Next, call out certain emotions, such as happy, scared, silly, angry, and sad, and have the children act the emotions as they do the monster mash. To vary the activity, play another instrumental song, and invite the children hold the monster puppets (see p. 126) they made previously as they move in rhythm to the music.

✳ Hairy, Scary Monster

(Tune: "Itsy, Bitsy Spider")

The hairy, scary monster went to the school to play,
But when the children saw him, they all were scared away.
The teacher told the children to come right back again.
"If we're kind and smile and play with him he'll learn to be our friend."

ROLE PLAY

✳ Monster Family

Add the monster puppets (see p. 126) made previously to the role-play center. Suggest that the children pretend to be a monster family that is doing family things in the house. You could place a blanket or sheet over a table to create a cave for the monsters to live in. To control the noise and activity level, you could name the family the Gentle Monster Family or the Friendly Monster Family.

✳ Creative Dramatics

Encourage children to act out one of their favorite monster books. If you wish to provide props, keep them simple in order to encourage children to use their imaginations.

✳ Monster Wraps

Provide an old sheet or a long piece of butcher paper to make a monster wrap costume. Wrap the sheet or paper around a child of average size to determine where the front of the costume will be. If the costume is intended to cover the head, determine where to cut small holes for the eyes and arms. Have children use markers, crayons, or paints, and yarn pieces to decorate the monster costume. Loosely wrap the decorated sheet or paper around a child and pin, staple, or tape it together.

Put the monster wrap costume in the role-play area. If you have a full-length mirror, place it in the area. Children delight in looking at themselves in costume.

SCIENCE

✳ Scary/Happy Sounds

Explain that people who work on radio and television programs and in the movies make special sounds to go along with the stories. Tell children that these special sounds are called "sound effects." Some things are used to make scary, spooky sounds, while other things are used to make happy sounds, like the sound of a bubbly brook. Allow the children to search the room for things that make scary, spooky sounds and things that make happy sounds.

1. Duplicate the Monster Chart (Activity Master 16, p. 293). Write *Scary* or *Spooky* on the left side and *Happy* on the right side. Record the results of the children's search by listing words and/or drawing pictures of the objects they used to make each kind of sound.

2. Have the children help you tape record all the scary, spooky sounds they produced. Play the children's tape to produce sound effects when you read a monster book.

✳ What Is Sound?

Following the experiments with sound effects, talk with the children about what they think sound is. Accept all of their ideas and encourage them to think about it.

Ask the children to lightly touch their hands to their throats as they hum, laugh, and talk. Ask the children, "What do you feel?" Extend a ruler or thin piece of wood or plastic halfway over the edge of a table. As you hold one end down on the table, flick/spring the extended end with your finger. Ask, "What do you see? What do you hear?" Then have the children take turns flicking the end. Ask, "What do you feel?" Use the word *vibration* if children discuss the movement that makes the sound.

TRANSITION ACTIVITIES

✳ Monster Eyes

Cut the plastic six-pack holders of soda containers apart into three pairs of rings until you have a pair for each child. Have the children hold these "monster eyes" up to their faces and follow directions such as those listed below.

Look way up high.
Look to the right.
Look to the left.
Look at the floor.
Look at a friend and smile.

Also have the children use the plastic rings to follow directions that include prepositions and parts of the body.

Put the eyes on your head.
Put the eyes in your hand.
Put the eyes beside your ear.
Put the eyes under your knee.

✳ Scary Eyes

Have the children use the monster eyes from the previous activity as they say this rhyme.

See my big, round scary eyes,
    (Hold monster eyes close to eyes.)
Watch out, here's my big surprise—Boo!
    (Lean forward before saying "boo.")

CHILDREN'S BOOKS

Brown, R. *If at First You Do Not See.* New York: Holt, 1982. Turn each page all around to see the surprising changes.

Drescher, H. *Simon's Book.* New York: Scholastic, 1983. A young boy falls asleep as he begins to draw a story about a scary monster. Encourages the imagination.

Emberley, E. *Go Away, Big Green Monster!* New York: Little, Brown, 1992. Heavy die-cut pages and vivid colors allow this monster to grow and then disappear as the book is read. Good sequencing applications.

Emberley, E. and A. Miranda. *Glad Monster, Sad Monster: A Book about Feelings.* New York: Scholastic, 1997. Each monster character experiences different emotions. Children try on a mask to see how they look when they express that emotion.

Gerstein, M. *The Absolutely Awful Alphabet.* San Diego: Harcourt Brace, 1999. A monster for each letter has awful plans for the next letter.

Graves, K. *Frank Was a Monster Who Wanted to Dance.* San Francisco: Chronicle, 1999. The wacky illustrations and laugh-out-loud text make children ask for multiple readings.

Hoban, R. *Monsters.* New York: Scholastic, 1990. A boy draws monsters that he thinks are real.

Howe, J. *There's a Dragon in My Sleeping Bag.* New York: Aladdin, 1994. Two brothers try to out do each other in inventing imaginary friends.

Mayer, M. *There's a Nightmare in My Closet.* New York: Dial, 1968.
There's an Alligator Under My Bed. New York: Dial, 1987.
There's Something in My Attic. New York: Dial, 1988.
A series that deals appropriately with the fears experienced by many children.

McNaughton, C. *Guess Who's Just Moved in Next Door?* New York: Trumpet, 1991. A rhyming story with a good introduction to the concept that what is scary depends on your perspective.

Munsch, R. *David's Father.* Toronto, Canada: Annick Press, 1993. A humorous tale about an unusual family who seems scary until you get to know them.

Prelutsky, J., ed. *Imagine That! Poems of Never-Was.* New York: Knopf. 1998. A collection of poems about imaginary creatures and machines created by award-winning authors.

Raskin, E. *Franklin Stein.* New York: Atheneum, 1972. A boy uses household objects to make a friendly monster. Encourages creative thinking.

Sendak, M. *Where the Wild Things Are.* New York: Harper & Row, 1963. In this award-winning children's classic, a boy's imagination takes over when he is sent to his room.

Stone, J. *The Monster at the End of This Book*. New York: Western Publishing Co, 1980. A Sesame Street book in which Grover worries on page after page about meeting a monster at the end of the book.

Viorst, J. *My Mama Says There Aren't Any Zombies, Ghosts, Vampires, Creatures, Demons, Monsters, Fiends, Goblins, or Things*. New York: Atheneum, 1976. This book is especially helpful when read aloud to children who are afraid of monsters at bedtime or in the dark.

February Curriculum

Valentines and Friendship

Dinosaurs

Valentines and Friendship

CONCEPTS

- The tradition of sharing valentines is fun for children.
- Traditional valentine colors are red, pink, and white.
- Friendship, sharing, and love are important aspects of the holiday.
- Friends help each other and care about each other.
- Our heart is an important muscle inside our body; it does not look like a valentine.
- Eating a balanced diet and getting plenty of exercise and rest help keep our hearts healthy.

CONTINUING CONCEPTS

- **Colors** Have children mix red and white to create pink tempera.
  Help children identify red, pink, and white as valentine colors and talk about why those colors are associated with valentines.
- **Geometric Shapes** Understand that a heart-shaped figure can be symmetrical.
  Identify geometric shapes, including circles, triangles, rectangles, and squares, in different sizes and positions.
- **Health and Nutrition** Discuss the importance of a balanced diet, exercise, and rest.
  Learn about the human heart and what it does.
- **Senses** Have the children feel the beating of their own hearts.
  Have children use a stethoscope to listen to their hearts and compare the sound of the heart when standing still with the sound after running in place for 30 seconds.
  Post topic-related pictures for children to see and discuss.
- **Traditional Rhymes and Tales** Recite "The Queen of Hearts" with the children.

PORTFOLIO PRODUCTS

Select or have the children select at least one product from this unit to place in each portfolio. One suggestion follows.
- Using a child's completed art project, ask the child to tell you about the project and write what the child dictates. This product provides a celebration of the child's art and indicates oral-language development, fluency, and concept mastery.

ART

✳ Easel or Tabletop Painting

1. The Colors of Valentines

Materials: tempera paints in red and white; paper; paper plates; brushes

Provide children with red and white paint. Have each child put a spoonful of red paint and a spoonful of white on a small paper plate. Ask the children what they think will happen to the color if they stir the colors with a brush. Have the children stir the colors to make pink paint. Talk about how the white changes the color. Ask, "What would you do if you wanted a lighter pink color?" Encourage children to paint using the pink paint they created.

2. Heart-Shaped Holes

Materials: paper; scissors; tempera paints; brushes

For each child, cut out three heart-shaped holes from a sheet of paper. Cut out one small, one medium, and one large hole and position the holes randomly on the sheet. Have the children paint on the paper. Use the terms *small, medium,* and *large* as you discuss the heart shapes with the children. Talk about what happens when they are painting and come to a hole.

✳ Valentine Bags

The following activities are listed in order from easiest to slightly more difficult.

1. Heart Collage Bags

Materials: white paper bags; small, precut, pink and red paper hearts or heart stickers of various sizes; glue; cotton swabs; glitter; spoons

Children glue the precut pink and red hearts all over the bag. The child or an adult prints the child's name in large letters on the bag. Children use cotton swabs to paint glue over the letters of their names and then spoon glitter on the glue. Tap the excess glitter off on a paper and recycle it.

2. Laced Plates Bags

Materials: white paper plates; hole punch; red yarn; markers; construction paper; stickers; scissors; markers

Provide one whole paper plate and one half paper plate for each child. Children punch holes around the edges of the plates. Then they use red yarn to lace the plates together to form a pocket. The child or an adult prints each child's name in large letters on the bag. Decorate as desired with paper cutouts, stickers, and markers.

3. Folded-Hearts Bags

Materials: 9-inch red, white, and pink construction paper squares; glue; cotton swabs; pink, red, or silver glitter; plastic spoons; scissors

Each child uses one white or pink square and one red square. Show children how to fold each square in half and cut as large a heart as possible from each paper. Next, they overlap the folded halves and glue them together to form a bag. Staple on a strip of red or pink construction paper to make a handle. The child or an adult prints the child's name in large letters on the bag. Children then decorate their bags by applying glue with a cotton swab and spooning on glitter.

❋ Friendship Tree

Materials: candy hearts with messages; white paper; scissors; markers or crayons; hole punch; yarn

Recycle the Friendship tree made earlier in the year (see p. 3) or create a new one with the caption *Friendship Tree.*

Show the children some candy hearts that show messages. If appropriate, let each child eat one candy as you share some of the messages. Then have children cut heart shapes out of white paper and write a message on the heart to another child in the class. Have them decorate the heart with markers or crayons. Then they use a hole punch to make a hole in their heart message, thread an 8-inch piece of yarn through the hole, and hang the message on the tree.

Be sure all children receive messages. If you notice that a child does not have a message, you can write one or ask a child to help. Use the friendship tree to display the heart messages.

❋ Heart Creatures

Materials: white, pink, and red construction paper; glue; crayons or markers; scissors

Show children how to fold and cut hearts in several sizes. Have them make white, pink, and red hearts. As a class, arrange the hearts on a piece of paper so that they form heart creatures such as butterflies, puppets, people, and animals. Talk about the various sizes and encourage children to try different arrangements.

When children finish arranging the hearts, they glue one heart creature to a piece of colored paper and use crayons and markers to add details, such as faces, hair, antenna, and clothes.

❋ Heart Fold-overs

Materials: 9-inch white construction paper squares; red and pink tempera paint; spoons or brushes; scissors

Show children how to fold paper and cut a heart shape. Talk about *whole* and *half* as you work. Children then cut a heart shape, open the folded heart, and use spoons or brushes to put dots of white, red, or pink paint on one side of the heart. They fold the heart over and rub the back gently to spread the paint. Before the children open the folded heart, ask them what they think may have happened. Have them open the hearts and talk about the patterns. Some children may want to put additional dots of paint on the heart and repeat the process.

✳ Symmetry

Materials: construction-paper heart shapes cut in half; white paper; valentine cards cut in half; glue; markers or crayons

1. Make a heart shape by folding and cutting a piece of paper. Open the heart and explain that both sides match because they are exactly the same. Explain that the line in the middle is called a *line of symmetry.*
2. Give each child a paper heart shape cut in half vertically. Have the children glue the half on paper. Hold a mirror vertically at the edge of the half heart to show children that the heart looks whole when viewed in the mirror. Explain that both sides match. Then have children draw the missing half of the heart on their paper.

BLOCKS

Encourage children to practice friendship and sharing at the block area. Compliment them as they use kind statements and share with one another. Post examples of things friends do when they build with blocks. Examples may include Friends share; Friends work together; and Friends help each other.

BULLETIN BOARD

✳ The Faces of Friendship

1. Border

Materials: 8-inch circles of construction paper in several facial colors; yarn; buttons; construction-paper scraps; macaroni; glue

Talk about how heads and faces are shaped like circles. Have children make facial features by gluing materials on a circle. Encourage them to think about their own features and try to show their own hair color and facial features. Suggest that children use yarn or construction-paper strips for hair, buttons or construction-paper shapes for eyes and a nose, and construction-paper shapes or macaroni to form mouths, eyebrows, and ears. Show them how to make three-dimensional faces by gluing construction-paper loops behind features, such as eyes, to make them stand out from the rest of the face.

Print each child's name on a tag and staple the tag under the child's face creation. Use the faces to make a bulletin-board border.

2. Interior

Prepare multiple heart shapes and randomly arrange them all over the board. Use pink and red tissue paper and cut the hearts with pinking shears for an attractive look. Cut smaller white hearts that will fit inside the colored tissue-paper hearts.

Discuss with the children friendly things they could do and say. Write each idea on one white heart and make a matching copy on a second white heart. Staple one white heart message on each colored heart on the board. Leave the white hearts slightly folded so that they can stand out and create a three-dimensional effect.

Put the matching white hearts in a valentine bag (see pp. 141–142) or a basket. Have children use Velcro® or pushpins to attach the hearts to the matching hearts on the bulletin board.

You can use the board during circle, center, or free time in the following ways.

1. Have the children search the heart messages to find each letter of the alphabet.

2. Have the children count the number of hearts of each color. Depending on the children's readiness, you may wish to help them find the total number of hearts on the board. You could write a number sentence that shows the addition.

    7 red hearts + 8 pink hearts = 15 hearts

COOKING

✳ Rice Krispies® Hearts

3 tablespoons margarine
10-oz. package marshmallows
Red food coloring

6 cups Rice Krispies® cereal
Wax paper
Craft sticks

Wash hands. Heat the margarine and marshmallows together in a microwave on high for two minutes. Stir to combine. Microwave the mixture on high for one more minute. Stir until smooth. Stir in a few drops of red food coloring and the cereal. Cool the mixture slightly. Give a small amount to each child on a piece of wax paper. Have children use their fingers and a craft stick to make a heart shape.

Give each child more of the mixture. Have children mold an extra heart and wrap it in plastic wrap to share with someone or serve at a Valentine celebration with friends.

✳ Valentine Cookies

Baked sugar cookies in heart shapes
Canned frosting
Red hot cinnamon candy or
candy conversation hearts

Plastic knives
Wax paper

Wash hands. Discuss how children feel when they get less of something than someone else does. Show them the candy. Ask them what they should do with it. Stress that friends know how to share. Have children count candy pieces together so that each child gets an equal share. Then have children work on pieces of wax paper to spread frosting on the baked cookies and then decorate them with the candy.

LANGUAGE ARTS

✳ Fingerplay – Valentine Hearts

Three little hearts, happy all day;
   (Hold up three fingers.)
One got a job and moved away.
Two little hearts, looking so neat!
   (Two fingers.)
One got hungry and went home to eat.
One little heart, lonely and blue.
   (One finger.)
I made him happy; I gave him to you!
   (Point to a child.)

To enhance the activity, make finger-puppet hearts to use with this fingerplay. Sew together the top and sides of two, small, red felt hearts. Leave the bottom tip of the heart open for a finger. As an alternative, have children make finger puppets using construction paper hearts glued together as described.

✳ Word Wall

Add the words *valentines* and *friends* to the word wall. Add other topic-related words that children suggest and any high-frequency words you want the children to use. Place a piece of colored plastic (cut from a plastic report cover) over a word card to highlight a word you want children to incorporate in their writing.

✳ Valentine Begins With V (A Whole-Class Project)

On a large piece of butcher paper, draw a large valentine. Write *Valentine Begins With V* at the top of the paper. Children cut out pictures from magazines and draw pictures of things that begin with *v.* Discuss each picture and then have children glue the pictures on the butcher paper. Print the word beside each picture. You may wish to have children continue the activity at center and free time until the paper is covered with pictures.

✳ Valentine Rhymes

Recite for the children the valentine rhyme *Roses are red, violets are blue; I made a valentine and gave it to you.* Have the children think of as many words as they can that rhyme with *blue.* Invite children to rewrite the valentine rhyme by using different rhyming words in place of *you* and changing the second line when necessary to suit the new words. Tell them silly rhymes are welcome because they add to the rhyming fun.

Copy the rhymes on a large piece of chart paper. Ask children to draw pictures on the chart to illustrate the rhymes.

Roses are red, violets are blue,
I made a silly valentine that looks like a shoe.
Roses are red, violets are blue,
I gave you a valentine and some candy hearts too.

✳ Field Trip

Visit a post office. You may want to have children bring stamps from home and mail a valentine they have made to a friend or family member.

✳ What Friends Do

Read "The Letter" from A. Lobel's *Frog and Toad Are Friends*. The entire book makes a profound statement on friendship and what friends do for each other. Ask the children to share their responses to the story.

✳ Visit From a Mail Carrier

Ask the mail carrier who delivers the school's mail to show the children his or her uniform and bag. Ask the mail carrier to discuss the sequence of events in the mail delivery process by answering the question "How does a letter get from the mailbox or post office to our house?" After the visit, write a class letter thanking the mail carrier for teaching the class about how mail is delivered.

✳ The Jolly Postman

Read aloud the Ahlbergs' *The Jolly Postman*. Children delight in the letters that may be taken out of each envelope and read. Talk about the nursery rhymes and folk tales used in the book. Give the children white hearts. Together, write new valentines to deliver to some of the characters in the book. An example could be: *Be my valentine, Little Bear. I will fix your chair.* Fold the valentines in half and place them in each envelope instead of the original letter. Place this valentine version of *The Jolly Postman* in the reading center for children to enjoy.

✳ Love Mobile

Use a dowel rod or coat hanger as the base. Use brightly colored construction paper to make 9-inch-high letters that spell *LOVE*. Use thread to hang the letters from the dowel or coat hanger. Attach 4-inch hearts of white, pink, and red to each letter. On the hearts, write messages similar to those on the valentine candy hearts; for example, *I love you* and *My friend*. Read the messages to the class. Discuss why a heart shape means love.

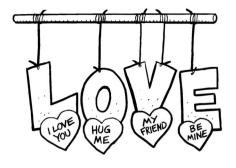

✳ Friends

Read Rebecca Jones' *Matthew and Tilly*. Talk about whether the children have ever had an argument with someone they care about. Encourage them to share their ideas about the best things to do to resolve arguments. Then, write the word *friend* as an acrostic. Together write words and ideas about friendship next to each letter.

✳ Pop-Out Friendly Cards

Materials: 9" x 12" Manila paper; markers or crayons; construction-paper scraps; glue

Children help each other trace around both hands and cut out the hand shapes. They glue the hands together as if the hands are shaking each other. Fold a 9" × 12" piece of paper in half. Show the children how to glue just the edges of the wrists on each side of the paper so that the paper hands pop out when the card is opened.

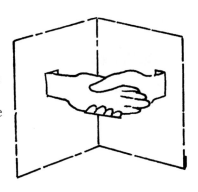

Write or have the children copy *Be My Friend* on the outside of each card. Then have each child write or dictate to an adult the message he or she wants to add to the inside of the card. Children can use markers, crayons, and construction paper to decorate their cards. Invite children to read their card to the class. Suggest they give the card to someone they would like to have for a friend.

✳ Loving, Caring, Sharing Collage

Put a 24" × 36" piece of paper on the wall at children's eye level with the caption *Loving, Caring, and Sharing.* Have children find magazine and newspaper pictures that show people loving, caring, or sharing, and then glue the pictures on the paper. To increase the children's interest, add some snapshots of children in the classroom helping and sharing with each other.

✳ A Valentine Celebration With Friends

Plan a Valentine celebration with a friendship theme. During center or free time, help a few children at a time to put valentine greetings they have made or purchased in their valentine bags (see pp. 141–142). Ensure that all children receive a supply of valentines by having extras on hand that you can add to bags as needed. Serve the Rice Krispies® hearts or valentine cookies the children made (see p. 144). You may also wish to serve candy hearts with messages.

As the bags and snacks are served, help the children practice making courteous responses. As children eat their snacks, ask them what they do to show others they are a friend.

✳ Valentine Lollipops

Provide a class-sized set of laminated, heart-shaped, red construction-paper cutouts stapled on craft sticks to resemble lollipops. (See Appendix I, p. 271.) Print letters of the alphabet on some lollipops and tape pictures of objects beginning with each letter on other lollipops. Have children identify the letters, tell the sounds they make, and match the letter sounds to the names of objects.

Then, give each child a lollipop that shows an object and have the child try to sell the lollipop by quietly searching for another child who can correctly identify the object. When the second child names the object, he or she is given the lollipop to try to sell to someone else. Children can repeat the following chant as they play: *Lollipop, lollipop. Who will buy my lollipop?*

To develop more advanced literacy skills, use only the lollipops with alphabet letters on them. Have the children show a letter to another child who must name something that begins with the sound of that letter.

You could also wipe off the letters and print high-frequency words the children have been introduced to. Children can "sell" these lollipops to other children who can identify the words.

MATH

✳ Calendar

Give children who can write numerals a copy of the blank calendar (Activity Master 3, p. 280). Help them to write the name of the month and the days of the week and fill in the dates in the appropriate spaces. Ask children what they notice when they compare their calendar from last month with this month's calendar. Ask children to skip count by twos and use red to circle or color the numerals they count (2, 4, 6, and so on). Count together by twos each day at calendar time. Invite children to draw pairs of items along the margins of their calendar. Have children mark Valentine's Day and other special days, including children's birthdays, on the calendar.

✳ Mail Carrier

Materials: shoe boxes; envelopes; heart-shaped stickers; marker

Provide several shoe boxes or small boxes. Write a numeral on each one. Provide a set of envelopes that show matching numerals or matching sets of heart stickers. Have the children deliver the envelopes by identifying the numeral or number on each and placing the envelope in the box with the same numeral.

For children who show a higher level of math readiness, write incomplete number sentences on each envelope, such as 3 – 1 or 2 + 2, and have the children match each to a numbered box.

✳ Valentine Jump

Give each child a valentine with a numeral on it. Then hold up a numeral and have the child holding that numeral jump that number of times. Other responses may be substituted, such as clapping, nodding the head, or turning around.

✳ Felt Hearts

1. Make a set of red felt hearts. Add one at a time to a flannel board as children count. Older children may be able to count backwards, as you take away one at a time.
2. Add a set of pink and white hearts. Create simple addition or subtraction number sentences and have children use the hearts to show the number sentences.
3. Create repeating patterns with the different colors for the children to identify and replicate. Then, have children extend the patterns or create their own patterns.

✳ The Weight of a Heart

Almost everyone's heart is about the same size and weighs less than one pound. Use a scale and a ball of play dough that weighs about one pound to show the children about how much one pound is. Have children take turns holding the ball. Then challenge them to find objects in the classroom that weigh about one pound.

✳ Size Relationships

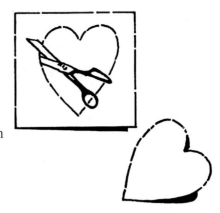

Provide positive and negative stencils of hearts in four sizes. Have the children match each positive stencil to the negative stencil of the same size. Explain that this is like finding two puzzle pieces that fit together.

Have children arrange the positive stencils in order from smallest to largest. Invite the children to trace them on a piece of paper in the same order. Also have them arrange the negative stencils in order from largest to smallest. Ask children to compare and discuss the two arrangements.

✳ Whole and Half

Fold hearts in half. Compare the whole and the half. Put two halves together and help children to recognize that two halves make one whole. At snack time, break graham crackers in half. Count the pieces and discuss them, using the terms *whole* and *half.*

✳ Geometric-Figure Lollipops

Use the lollipops you made previously (see p. 147). Draw a circle, rectangle, square, triangle, or heart in different sizes and positions on each lollipop. Show the lollipops one at a time to the children and have them identify the shape on each. Discuss how a geometric shape is still that shape even when it is large, small, or placed in different positions. Then, give each child a lollipop and have the child try to sell the lollipop, as described on p. 147.

MOVEMENT

✳ Shadow Play

After reading aloud K. Narahashi's *I Have a Friend,* discuss how shadows follow us like a friend. Provide a flashlight and challenge children to follow the beam's direction as you move it slowly. Then, have children take turns controlling the flashlight's beam.

✳ Beanbag Toss

Cut out a large valentine shape and tape it on the floor in a corner or low-traffic area of the room. Have children take turns tossing two or three beanbags into the valentine.

You may wish to make heart-shaped bean bags by cutting out two heart-shaped pieces of red felt, sewing the edges together around three-quarters of the outside, filling the bags with rice or dried beans, and sewing the remaining edges together.

✳ Valentine Hop

Tape several large valentine cutouts randomly on the floor. Have the children hop from one to another. Vary the activity by having them walk, slide, or crawl.

MUSIC

✳ Musical Hearts

Play recorded music. The children stop on hearts arranged in a circle on the floor each time the music stops. Eliminate competition by using one heart for each child. The focus is on having fun by listening to the music and stopping on a heart shape, rather than on eliminating children one at a time.

✳ Ten Happy Valentines

(Tune: "Ten Little Indians")

One happy, two happy, three happy valentines.
Four happy, five happy, six happy valentines.
Seven happy, eight happy, nine happy valentines.
Ten valentines to send.

Ten happy, nine happy, eight happy valentines.
Seven happy, six happy, five happy valentines.
Four happy, three happy, two happy valentines.
One valentine, that's the end!

Have children stand in a row, each holding a valentine with a numeral from 1–10 on it. You could use each number more than once if more than ten children are involved. Have the children stand up as they sing their number in the first verse and sit down as they sing their number in the second verse

ROLE PLAY

✳ Post Office

Involve children in setting up a post office in the role-play area. A post office is an excellent role-play activity that allows children to practice communication, classification, and organizational skills. You may wish to write parents a letter asking them to lend or donate items for the post office. Include a list of suggested items and invite them to add others.

Use some or all of the following suggestions for gathering and setting up materials for the post office.

1. Go to a post office and get a small supply of their free materials for consumers, such as stickers and priority mail packets.
2. Use an old, large purse or canvas bag as a mailbag.
3. Ask parents to provide throwaway junk mail from home to enhance sorting and delivery tasks.
4. Gather a collection of stamps, for example, those used in advertisements for ordering magazines.
5. Ask card shops for cards and envelopes they would otherwise throw away.
6. Wrap a few boxes in plain brown paper.
7. Use rubber stamps to make stamps on letters or packages. Children particularly enjoy stamping *fragile* and *airmail* on items.

8. Make a postal delivery truck using a large cardboard box with a chair and steering wheel inside. Put the post office logo on the outside.

9. Use play money and a cash register so that children can pretend to buy stamps and pay for mailing packages.

Suggest tasks that you want the children to role play in order to practice the skills you want them to develop. For example, you may want children to match envelopes that show their names, colors, numbers, shapes, high-frequency words, or letters of the alphabet to boxes that display the same words, colors, numbers, and so forth.

✳ Giving and Receiving Courteously

Help children learn courteous behavior by having them role play giving and receiving a valentine or sharing pieces of candy. Explain that what we say can make people feel good. Ask children to share examples of good things to say. Expand their repertoire of responses beyond a simple "thank you" and "you're welcome." Ask, "What else could we say when someone gives us something?"

SCIENCE

✳ Does a Real Heart Look Like a Valentine?

Show a pictures or drawings of a real human heart. (You can find pictures in reference books or contact the American Heart Association for information that is suitable for young children.) Compare the heart to the shape of a valentine heart. Talk about the ways the heart looks different from a valentine.

Make a two-column chart. Draw a human heart shape at the top of one column and a valentine heart shape at the top of the other column. List on the chart all the differences stated by the children.

✳ Learning About Our Hearts

1. Have children feel their hearts beating by sitting quietly and placing their open hands against the left sides of their chests.

2. Talk about a stethoscope and how it helps doctors hear heartbeats more clearly. Discuss how the beating is the sound the heart makes as it pumps our blood all through our bodies.

3. Provide stethoscopes so that children can listen to each other's hearts beating.

4. Have children use a stethoscope to listen to a child's heart. Then have the child hop as the group counts to 30. The children immediately listen to the child's heart again and compare what they hear with what they heard before the child hopped. Explain that the heart beats faster to supply more blood when our bodies work harder. Discuss how exercise helps build a strong heart.

✳ Good for Our Hearts

Make a class poster that shows foods that are good for our hearts. Write the caption *Good Food for Our Hearts* on a piece of poster board, and have children cut out or draw pictures of healthy foods and glue them on the poster board.

TRANSITION ACTIVITY

✳ Valentine Lollipops

Use the Valentine Lollipops activity (p. 147) again to continue to give children an opportunity to practice the skills involved.

CHILDREN'S BOOKS

Ahlberg, J. and Ahlberg, A. *The Jolly Postman*. Boston: Little, Brown, 1986. With rhyming verse, the postman delivers letters to fairy-tale characters.

Blos, J. *One Very Best Valentine's Day*. New York: Aladdin, 1998. Barbara's bracelet of tiny hearts breaks. She saves the hearts and gives one to each member of her family on Valentine's Day.

Bourgeois, P. *Franklin's Valentines*. New York: Scholastic, 1998. When Franklin's valentines fall in the mud, he learns a lesson about the value of friends who give him cards even though he had none to give to them.

Gibbons, G. *The Post Office Book: Mail and How It Moves*. New York: HarperCollins, 1987. Simple text and good illustrations explain the postal process.

Jones, R. C. *Matthew and Tilly*. New York: Penguin, 1991. Two best friends have a fight and learn it is not much fun to play without a friend.

Lobel, A. *Frog and Toad Are Friends*. New York: Harper & Row, 1970. Five wonderful short stories about Frog and Toad and their friendship.

McPhail, D. *A Bug, A Bear, and A Boy*. New York: Scholastic, 1998. Concepts include Big and Little; Small and Large; Friendship and Love. One of a series. Reminiscent of the Frog and Toad series by A. Lobel. Good opportunity to compare and contrast two series.

Narahashi, K. *I Have a Friend*. New York: Macmillan, 1987. A small boy has a shadow for his friend.

Raschka, C. *Yo! Yes?*. New York: Orchard, 1993. The beginning of friendship is largely told in pictures. Children can "read" this book.

Sharmat, M. *Nate the Great and the Mushy Valentine*. New York: Bantam Doubleday Dell, 1999. Another boy detective and his trusty dog story. Nate searches for who is responsible for putting a valentine on Sludge's doghouse at the same time he tries to find a missing valentine for his friend Annie.

Smith, M. *Dear Daisy, Get Well Soon*. New York: Crown Publishers, Inc., 2000. A gentle story that promotes the value of friendship. Also concerns the days of the week and counting.

Tafuri, N. *Will You Be My Friend?* New York: Scholastic Press, 2000. Shy Bird and Bunny become friends as Bunny helps Bird after a tragedy. Bird is not so shy after that.

Viorst, J. "Since Hanna Moved Away," *If I Were in Charge of the World and Other Worries*. New York: Aladdin, 1981. A child is saddened by a friend's moving.

Dinosaurs

CONCEPTS

- The word *dinosaur* means "terrible lizard."
  Dinosaurs were animals that lived long ago; they do not exist today.
- Human beings did not live on Earth when dinosaurs were alive, so no one has ever seen a living dinosaur.
- Some dinosaurs were herbivores and ate only plants; others were carnivores and ate meat. Omnivores eat both plants and meat.
- Most dinosaurs were very large, but some were small.
- Scientists study dinosaur fossils, such as footprints, bones, and teeth, to learn about dinosaurs and how they lived.
- Scientists who study dinosaurs are called paleontologists.
- No one knows for sure why the dinosaurs became extinct.
- There are other kinds of animals that are extinct or endangered.

CONTINUING CONCEPTS

- **Colors** Encourage children to identify the colors that they think dinosaurs might have had.
- **Geometric Shapes** Relate basic geometric shapes to the shapes of dinosaurs.
- **Health and Nutrition** Discuss the value of vegetables in a healthy diet.
  Discuss the importance of having strong teeth to eat with.
  Compare the shape of the teeth of herbivores and carnivores.
- **Senses** Talk about the different ways dinosaurs look in picture books.
  Have children examine the layers of sedimentary dirt (p. 156).
  Have children feel chicken bones and discuss the size of each bone and where it is located within a chicken's skeleton.
- **Traditional Rhymes and Tales**: not applicable

PORTFOLIO PRODUCTS

Select or have the children select at least one product from this unit to place in each portfolio. One suggestion follows.

- Have each child record another entry on his or her audiotape. You can use the tape to assess oral-language development, fluency, and mastery of certain concepts. Be sure to state the child's name and the date at the beginning of the tape entry.

To evaluate the child's ability to tell a story, tape record the child telling a story about what might happen if a dinosaur came to school. To evaluate the child's understanding of number concepts, record the child telling an original math story problem as he or she manipulates small dinosaur figures.

ART

✳ Easel or Tabletop Painting

Materials: tempera paints; brushes; large sheets of paper

1. **Dinosaur Colors** – Encourage children to paint a large dinosaur that almost fills the sheet of paper. Discuss with the children which colors they want to use. Explain that they can use their imaginations because we do not know the actual colors of dinosaurs.
2. **Dinosaur-Shaped Paper** – Use easel paper to make large dinosaur cutouts. Have each child use brushes and tempera paints to paint one dinosaur.

✳ Chalk Sketches

Materials: brown or gray construction paper; chalk; hair spray

Study pictures of dinosaurs and discuss their attributes. Encourage children to look carefully at the sizes and shapes of the dinosaurs. Point out the shapes of bodies, heads, legs, feet, and tails. Talk about the location of bonelike plates on some dinosaurs. Then point out interesting size relationships, such as a tiny head on a huge body.

Give children paper and chalk. Remind them that we do not know the actual color of dinosaurs. Have them sketch one of the dinosaurs or make their own version of a dinosaur. Use hair spray as a fixative on completed sketches. Display the sketches with the caption *We study dinosaurs*. Invite children to write or dictate a sentence about the kind of dinosaur they drew.

✳ Stuffed Dinosaurs (A Whole-Class Activity)

Materials: butcher paper; stapler; tempera paints; newspapers; strings

Cut two matching dinosaur shapes from two pieces of 24" × 36" (or larger) paper. Have children use tempera paint to paint each shape on an area covered with newspapers.

Staple the shapes together, leaving an opening at the top of the dinosaur's back for stuffing. The children wad up pages of the newspaper and push them gently inside the stapled dinosaur until it is well stuffed. Staple the opening shut. Attach one or more strings and hang the stuffed dinosaur from the ceiling like a mobile.

If children are very interested in the activity, allow them to make more than one stuffed dinosaur. Use a variety of dinosaur shapes. Ask children to compare the stuffed dinosaurs.

✳ Play-Dough Dinosaurs

Materials: play dough (see Appendix II, p. 275); food coloring

Make two or more batches of colored play dough. Study pictures or picture books of dinosaurs with the children. Discuss the attributes of the dinosaurs in the pictures.

Have children roll ball and cylinder shapes for dinosaur bodies and heads. Children roll long, fat snake shapes for tails. They add small balls for spots, eyes, and other details. Use a shoe box as a cave for the dinosaurs if children want to display them.

Use small amounts of dough to make teeth in different shapes and sizes. Explain that herbivores had blunt teeth for chewing plants, whereas carnivores had sharp, pointed teeth for tearing and eating meat. Make a 6-inch roll of play dough that is pointed at one end and measure it with a ruler. Tell the children that Tyrannosaurus Rex had teeth that were that long.

Save the play-dough dinosaurs and teeth for the upcoming Museum activity (see p. 164).

✳ Kid-osuarus Tracks and Dinosaur Tracks

Materials: green tempera paint on plastic foam food trays; 3 long pieces of butcher paper; pan of soapy water; towels; sponges cut into dinosaur-track shapes

After discussing fossils and dinosaur tracks and studying pictures of tracks, give the children the sponge shapes and have them make paint tracks on the butcher paper. Display the sponge tracks with the caption *Dinosaur Tracks*.

Then have the children make kid-osaurus tracks by stepping barefoot into green tempera paint and walking on the second long paper. Provide a chair and a pan of soapy water so that children can sit down as soon as they are done and wash their feet. Display the feet print with a caption: *Kid-osaurus Tracks*.

On the third piece of paper, have a child walk slowly to make footprints. Then, have the same child run along the paper as an adult holds his or her hand to provide support. Talk about how the distance between the "walking" footprints is different from the distance between the "running" footprints.

✳ Dinosaur Macaroni Collage

Materials: macaroni; construction paper; dinosaur shapes (see Activity Master 18, p. 295); glue; poster board; scissors

Make dinosaur stencils by enlarging the dinosaur shapes on Activity Master 18, tracing them on poster board, and cutting them out. Children trace the stencils on construction paper and cut out a dinosaur shape. Give each child a handful of uncooked macaroni. Children add texture to the dinosaur shape by gluing macaroni all over it.

BLOCKS

Add plastic dinosaurs to the block area. Encourage children to build caves or other places for dinosaurs to live or hide in.

BULLETIN BOARD
✳ Construct a Dinosaur

Cut out large, simple parts of dinosaurs from poster board. Make a typical dinosaur body shape. Make two or three head shapes in different sizes. Cut out different sets of legs, like those of a Tyrannosaurus, a Stegosaurus, and an Apatosaurus. Then cut out additional features, such as tails, horns, teeth, and plates, in a variety of sizes.

Cover the board with dark butcher paper. Use lightly colored lettering to make the caption *Construct a Dinosaur*. Pull cotton apart so that it resembles clouds and staple it near the top of the board. Add a tree and hanging vines by twisting crepe paper. Add a patterned border of die-cut dinosaurs. Or make your own figures using the figures on Activity Master 18, p. 295, as stencils.

Demonstrate how to construct a dinosaur by using pushpins or temporary adhesive to assemble the dinosaur pieces on the bulletin board. Begin with the body shape. Have children suggest additional pieces until a dinosaur is complete. Discuss what kind of a dinosaur you constructed. Ask, "Is it an herbivore or carnivore? How do you know?"

Mix up the parts and have the children construct another complete dinosaur on the board. Ask, "What could we do to make this dinosaur different from the last one we constructed?"

If the bulletin board is too high for some children to use safely, have them put a dinosaur together on the floor. Then help them return the pieces to the bulletin board so that another child can use them.

COOKING

✳ Dino-Dough

2 cups peanut butter
1 cup dry milk powder
6 tablespoons honey
Vanilla wafers

Raisins
Pretzel sticks
Wax paper

Wash hands. Measure and mix the first three ingredients. Add small amounts of dry milk powder if the mixture is too sticky to handle. Give each child a piece of wax paper to work on and some of the mixture. Have the children use the mixture to form a dinosaur shape. Have children add raisins for eyes, vanilla wafers for plates of bone on the dinosaur's back, and pretzels for a spiked tail. Ask, "If we use all of these pieces, what kind of a dinosaur are we making?" *(Stegosaurus)*

✳ Sedimentary Dirt

2 cups Cheerios®
2 packages sugar-free instant chocolate
   pudding
2 cups cold skim milk
Chocolate wafers

Graham crackers
Clear plastic glasses, 1 per child
Spoons
Zippered plastic sandwich bags
Rolling pin (dowel rod or block)

Discuss what a paleontologist does. Explain that paleontologists examine layers of sediment to study dinosaur life. Show children how layers of sediment look by making sedimentary dirt with them.

Wash hands. Mix the pudding according to package directions and set aside. Have each child put two chocolate wafers and one graham cracker in separate plastic bags and crush them with a rolling pin. Each child makes an individual portion of sedimentary dirt by adding layers of ingredients to a clear plastic glass in the following order.

1. 1 tablespoon of cereal
2. 2 tablespoons of pudding
3. 2 crushed chocolate wafers
4. 1 crushed graham cracker

Examine and discuss the layers in the glasses. Use the term *sediment*. Discuss how each layer of sediment is a little different. Challenge children to use a spoon to scoop out one bite that has all four layers in it. Then have them to scoop out only one layer.

LANGUAGE ARTS

✳ Action Play – The Dinosaurs

The dinosaurs lived so long ago.
What happened to them we do not know!
Some were big and very tall,
    (Stretch hand up to show height.)
And some were really very small.
    (Crouch down low.)
They went in the water but lived on land
And left their footprints in the sand.
    (Stomp feet.)
The Stegosaurus had big plates of bone
    (Make a pointed shape with hands.)
Both on its tail and back.
The Apatosaurus had a long, long neck
    (Stretch neck up.)
And a tail that could give a WHACK!
    (Clap hands together sharply.)
But the meanest dinosaur of all, no doubt,
    (Shake finger warningly.)
Was the Tyrannosaurus Rex! Watch out!
    (Jump at each other and growl.)

✳ Word Wall

Add the word *dinosaur* to the word wall. Children may also want to add words for several kinds of dinosaurs. Add and emphasize any high-frequency words you want children to use. Count how many words are on the word wall. Write and display a sentence strip such as the following: *We have (the number) words on our word wall.* Place a piece of colored plastic (cut from a plastic report cover) over one of the word cards to highlight a word you want the children to incorporate in their writing.

✳ Vocabulary

Children readily learn specific vocabulary words when they are modeled and clearly integrated into discussions. Use scientific terms when appropriate. Many children will correctly use specific dinosaur names and terms such as *extinct, carnivore,* and *herbivore* if adults model them throughout this unit.

✳ Dinosaurs: Nonfiction Information

Children are really curious about dinosaurs! Read nonfiction books about dinosaurs to the children to increase their knowledge of different kinds of dinosaurs, what they ate, and how they lived. At times, you may prefer to show the best pictures in the books and simply explain the facts in your own words.

Explain to the children that scientists are still refining and clarifying what they know about dinosaurs. For example, scientists recently discovered that one dinosaur had been given two different names. For that reason, the Brontosaurus is now known as the Apatosaurus. Apatosaurus is now the correct species name because it was given first.

✳ Dinosaur Pronunciation Guide

Refer to nonfiction sources to check the pronunciation of dinosaur species. Many children want to use the correct pronunciation of dinosaur names. The following list includes the dinosaurs mentioned in this unit.

Apatosaurus	(ah-PAT-uh-saw-rus)
Brontosaurus	(BRON-tuh-saw-rus)
Saltopus	(SALT-oh-pus)
Stegosaurus	(STEG-uh-saw-rus)
Tyrannosaurus	(tie-RAN-uh-saw-rus)

✳ A Dinosaur KWL

Fold a large piece of butcher paper into thirds to form three columns. At the top of each column print one of each of the following captions: *What we KNOW about dinosaurs; What we WANT to learn; What we LEARNED.* Brainstorm with the children to elicit and record everything they know about dinosaurs. Make a mental note of any misinformation children have so that you can correct it later. Then record what they are interested in learning. Use that information as much as possible to guide your presentation of the unit content. As children learn new information, record it in the third column. Seeing the facts in the third column grow will help children realize how many new things they are learning.

✳ Dino-mite Learning

After children have spent several days working on this unit, provide a dinosaur shape with handwriting lines on it. Encourage children to say something they have learned about dinosaurs. Children or an adult helper writes each idea on a dinosaur shape. Post the dinosaur writings around the KWL chart described above. Later, have children take their writing home to share with family members.

✳ Dinosaur Begins With D (A Whole-Class Project)

On a large piece of butcher paper, draw a simple dinosaur shape. Write *Dinosaur Begins With D* at the top of the paper. Have children cut out magazine pictures or draw pictures of things that begin with *d.* Discuss each picture and then have children glue each one on the paper. Print the word beside each picture. Children can continue the activity at center and free time until the paper is filled with pictures.

✳ Helpful Dinosaurs

Read aloud Bernard Most's *If the Dinosaurs Came Back*. Review all the things the dinosaurs did to help people in that book. Work with children to generate a list of the attributes of several dinosaurs that children are familiar with. Ask children to figure out a way that a dinosaur could use each attribute to help others. Encourage children to illustrate their ideas and display them. The child or an adult writes a sentence on each picture that describes how the dinosaur could help others.

✳ Choral Speaking

Choral speaking is a dramatic form of recitation that involves taking turns. Most children have no experience with choral speaking, so begin slowly and progress to more complicated choral speaking after children gain experience.

Use the action play The Dinosaurs (p. 157). Encourage the children to add their own ideas for actions to the verse. You can divide the rhyme in many ways. For two groups, simply alternate lines of the rhyme. Group One says the first line, Group Two says the second line, Group One says the third line, and so on. Have everyone say "Watch out!" and jump and growl at the same time.

Have the class perform for another class or for visiting family members. You might want to tape record the children's performance for them to listen to later.

✳ Flannel-Board Dinosaurs

Make several dinosaurs from felt or nonwoven interfacing (see Activity Master 18, p. 295). During centers or free time, allow children to independently explore by putting the dinosaur figures on the board and taking them off. Encourage children to tell what kind of dinosaurs they are handling and what their dinosaurs are doing.

After the children have handled the pieces, work with them to create a class flannel-board story. Supply sentence stems and transition words to help children express their ideas more fluently. Write their story on chart paper as it develops. Read it several times together. Illustrate events in the story by adding the dinosaur figures to the flannel board at the appropriate times. Then tape record the class reading the story. Place the recording in the listening center with the flannel-board pieces so that the children can listen to and reenact the story many times.

✳ Dinosaur Tracks

Discuss how some of what is known about dinosaurs was learned by studying fossils of their footprints or tracks. For example, paleontologists can tell how tall dinosaurs were by examining the distance between their tracks. They can also tell how fast the dinosaurs were moving. Remind the children that they studied the distance between the tracks they made during the Kid-osuarus Tracks and Dinosaur Tracks activity (see p. 155). Ask children to decide which patterns were made by the child moving fast and by the child moving slowly.

☀ Imagination Time

Read Carol Carrick's imaginary tale *What Happened to Patrick's Dinosaurs?* Patrick creates an imaginative tale of dinosaurs flying away on a spaceship. Discuss other imaginative ideas with the children about what happened to the dinosaurs. Tape record individual children's ideas. Allow children to rewind the recording and listen again if they wish.

Encourage interested children to write sentences and make drawings to describe their own versions of how the dinosaurs became extinct. Collect children's sentences and drawings in a class book. Invite children to take turns pretending to be a visiting author and sharing their story by reading it to the class.

☀ Dinosaur Land Game

Create a simple class game by using the Candyland® game board as a model. Play the game using cutouts of dinosaurs or small plastic dinosaurs as game pieces. A pizza box makes a great game board and stores the pieces in one place. Ask the owner of a pizza shop for one or two unused boxes.

☀ Creative Analogies

Ask children to consider how they are like dinosaurs. Discuss their ideas. Then ask, "If you were a dinosaur, which one would you be?" Use copies of Activity Master 19, p. 296, to record the analogies children make between themselves and dinosaurs. Then have children illustrate their copies of the activity master. Display the children's work or use it to create a class book.

☀ Extinct Animals

Read together Ann Jonas' *Aardvarks Disembark!* As children ask questions or express interest, call their attention to the pictures of less-familiar or unfamiliar animals. Discuss what *extinct* means. Point out the animals that are extinct. Write *Extinct means . . .* at the top of a piece of chart paper and record accurate ideas that the children offer.

☀ Research

Encourage interested children to research theories of the extinction of dinosaurs. They can ask others for information or, with adult assistance, consult reference books. Some children may be able to write down some of the information they find, but tell children that they can draw pictures to show what they've found out or simply share their information orally. Allow them to share their information with the class at a convenient time.

Note: You may wish to send a letter to parents explaining that the objectives of having the children do research are to satisfy their curiosity and to motivate them to want to learn. Ask parents not to be concerned about the form the children's research takes and not to expect their child to copy lengthy data. Ask them to help you keep the learning experience comfortable and enjoyable for the child.

MATH

✳ Counting Dinosaurs

Use Activity Master 18, p. 295, to make several sets of dinosaurs. You can use nonwoven interfacing to make figures for the flannel board or construction paper to make figures for tabletop use. Guide the children as they count the dinosaurs by asking questions such as the following.

How many dinosaurs of each kind are there?

How many tall dinosaurs are there?

How many dinosaurs have long tails?

At first, have the children take turns manipulating the dinosaurs and counting each set. Then give each a child a set of dinosaurs so that everyone can make sets and count dinosaurs simultaneously.

✳ Addition/Subtraction

Supply small plastic dinosaurs. Show a set of two or three dinosaurs. Ask, "How many will there be if I add one more? How many will there be if I take one away?" Have the children help you make up simple story problems that they can act out and solve using the dinosaurs. When appropriate, write a number sentence for a problem and explain what it shows.

✳ Dinosaur Eggs

Tape or write a numeral on the outside of several plastic eggs (the type that come apart in halves). Provide small cutout or plastic dinosaurs. Have the children place the appropriate number of baby dinosaurs inside each egg.

✳ 350 Kinds of Dinosaurs

Explain that scientists have identified about 350 different kinds of dinosaurs and that new ones are still being found.

With children who are interested and mathematically ready, make a set of 350 objects. This activity can help children form a concrete sense of a large quantity. Select something children can help you collect and count to get them more interested and involved in the task. Consider, for example, having children cut one-inch squares of brightly colored paper. The children can line up the squares along the edge of a hallway. Number the squares before taping them in place so that a final count is always available. Post a sign that reads *There are 350 different kinds of dinosaurs!*

✳ Longer and Shorter Shapes

Hold up pictures or models of dinosaurs and have the children find dinosaurs with long necks or short legs and long tails or short tails. Show the children silhouettes of several kinds of dinosaur. Ask the children to classify the dinosaurs as longer or shorter. Ask children to explain why they categorized each dinosaur the way they did.

☀ Big, Bigger, Biggest

Copy and cut out three to eight dinosaurs of graduated sizes. Show children three of the dinosaurs. Talk about the size of each one. Have children place them in order from big to biggest. Mix them up and ask children to place them in order again.

If children express interest in continuing, repeat the seriation task using five and then eight dinosaurs. Say, "This dinosaur is big. Show me one that is bigger. Show me the one that is the biggest."

☀ The Biggest Plop

One big dinosaur standing on a rock,
Jumped into the water and made a big plop!
Two big dinosaurs standing on a rock.
Jumped into the water and made a bigger plop!
But the three big dinosaurs standing on a rock
Jumped into the water and made the biggest plop!

Have children help determine some appropriate movements such as holding up the appropriate number of fingers to show the number of dinosaurs and clapping their hands together for the plop.

☀ Tyrannosaurus Rex Teeth

Show the children the play dough teeth they made earlier (see pp. 154–155). Have the children use a ruler to measure the 6-inch roll of play dough that represents a Tyrannosaurus Rex's tooth. Ask children to find classroom objects that are about the same length. Provide rulers for measuring and comparing 6-inch lengths. Ask children what things they might find at home that are about the same length. Invite children to look for things at home and, on the following day, tell the class what they found. A toothbrush is an object children typically mention.

MOVEMENT

☀ Stilts

Provide one or two pairs of stilts. Make stilts using large empty cans with yarn strung through the top to make a rope to hold. Use tuna cans for younger children. Have the children walk around on the stilts and pretend they are dinosaurs. Ask children to tell how walking with stilts is like moving like a dinosaur.

✳ Dinosaur Tracks

Cut out large dinosaur footprints. Tape them to the floor. Have children follow the prints using long steps. Ask them to walk forward and then backward as they follow the footprints.

Tape baby dinosaur footprints to the floor beside the large prints. Children will discover that they need to use smaller steps to follow the baby prints forward and backward.

Talk about the fact that some of the dinosaurs were rather small. The Saltopus, for example, weighed only two pounds and was about the size of a cat. Have children walk as they think a Saltopus might have walked.

✳ Dinosaur Chant

Dinosaur, dinosaur, turn around.
Dinosaur, dinosaur, make your feet pound.
Dinosaur, dinosaur, stretch your neck toward the sky.
Dinosaur, dinosaur, blink and close one eye.
Dinosaur, dinosaur, wave your tail to the right.
Dinosaur, dinosaur, shake a leg with all your might.
Dinosaur, dinosaur, eating plants all day,
'Til Tyrannosaurus Rex comes to scare you away!

MUSIC

✳ Dinosaur Walk

Have children demonstrate how they think dinosaurs walked. Name different kinds of dinosaurs to encourage children to move in different ways. Then ask them to move like dinosaurs as music is played. Choose music that suggests the attributes of various dinosaurs. For example, play slow, solemn music to suggest the slow, giant steps of the Apatosaurus and dramatic instrumental music with a fast tempo to suggest a fierce Tyrannosaurus.

✳ Rhythmastics

To help children develop listening skills and a sense of rhythm, clap a rhythmic pattern. Have the children softly clap to repeat the pattern. Then ask a child to clap a different rhythmic pattern for the class to repeat.

Next, name a kind of dinosaur. Have the children softly clap to the rhythm of that word. Model a louder clap on the accented syllable. Also, model moving your hands forward for visual emphasis as you clap the accented syllable.

ROLE PLAY

✳ Museum

Read Aliki's *Dinosaurs Are Different*. The story is about a young child's visit to a museum to study dinosaur bones. Discuss the book with the children. Ask any children who have been to a museum to tell about what they saw and did there.

Have children create a dinosaur museum. The children can build shelves with blocks and arrange the dinosaur fossils (see p. 165) and the play-dough dinosaurs and the teeth they made (see pp. 154–155). Children can also display the dinosaur tracks (p. 155) and the stuffed dinosaurs (p. 154) they made.

Discuss the role of a museum curator and provide a hat or badge for the curator to wear. Have the children make entrance tickets. Provide magnifying glasses and other appropriate props. Supply appropriate pictures, such as the children's chalk sketches of dinosaurs (see p. 154). Provide index cards and let the children make cards with dinosaur names and sentences about dinosaurs to display beside dinosaur pictures or play-dough figures.

SCIENCE

✳ Excavations

To explain fossil excavation to the children, share the National Wildlife Federation's *Digging Into Dinosaurs* with the class. Discuss how paleontologists examine layers of sediment to study dinosaur life. Show children how the layers are deposited one upon another by having five or six children stack their hands, one child's hand over another's. Explain that each layer of sediment is a little different from the others.

Remind the children of the Sedimentary Dirt they made (p. 156). Relate the four layers from the bottom up to bones, mud, sand, and dirt that were deposited one on top of another.

✳ Cookie Excavations

Materials: chocolate-chip cookies; round toothpicks; napkins

Show children how to use the toothpick to excavate the chocolate chips. Let children work on a napkin with a cookie and toothpick. Count how many chips they excavate. Ask children to discuss how this is like the work of paleontologists.

✳ Bones and Skeletons

Discuss how scientists and paleontologists put together dinosaur bones to learn how dinosaurs looked. Post pictures of dinosaur skeletons and discuss them.

Bring the complete skeleton of a boiled chicken. Compare the skeleton to a photograph of a chicken. Have children feel the size of their own leg bone and compare it to the size of the chicken bone. Talk about how bones give our bodies' shape and strength.

Ask the children to look carefully at the chicken skeleton. Then have them close their eyes. Take one bone from the skeleton and let the children decide where it belongs. Supply a magnifying glass so that children may study the bones closely.

✳ Dinosaur Fossil Eggs

Let children help press a layer of play dough in the bottom of a small box or shoe box lid. Others then help place six to ten pebbles and leaves closely together and press them into the dough. Ask children to gently remove the pebbles and leaves so that their indentations remain.

As children watch, mix one cup of plaster of Paris with enough water so that the mixture pours easily. Pour the plaster over the indentations in the play dough. After it hardens, ask the children what they think will happen when you lift the plaster out of the box. Lift the plaster and show how the shapes look like fossils of dinosaur eggs. Explain that this is the process paleontologists follow to make forms to study dinosaur fossils.

To vary the activity, use chicken bones to make dinosaur fossils. Be sure to boil the bones to clean them.

TRANSITION ACTIVITY
✳ Dinosaur Bone Game

Provide a real bone or choose something to represent a bone. Have one child pretend to be a dinosaur and sit with his or her back to the class. Place the bone right behind the "dinosaur." Silently point to one child who then tries to tiptoe up behind to steal the bone without the dinosaur knowing.

If the dinosaur hears, she or he roars and the child must sit down. If the child is successful in stealing the bone, the group says, "Dinosaur, dinosaur, where's your bone?" The dinosaur tries to guess who is hiding the bone, and then the game begins again.

CHILDREN'S BOOKS

Aliki. *Dinosaurs Are Different.* New York: Crowell, 1985. This book describes a young child's visit to a museum to study dinosaur bones.

Carrick, C. *What Happened to Patrick's Dinosaurs?* New York: Clarion, 1986. An imaginary tale of what one boy thinks dinosaurs did and what happened to them.

Dodson, P. *An Alphabet of Dinosaurs.* New York: Bryon Press Visual Publications, Inc., 1995. Information is included on each dinosaur's physical features, habits, size, and diet, where it was found, and the meaning of its name. Line drawings of skeletons are also included.

Fleischman, P. *Time Train.* New York: Harper & Row, 1991. A train takes children back to the time of dinosaurs.

Jonas, A. *Aardvarks Disembark!* New York: Greenwillow, 1990. Numerous species of animals disembark from the ark in alphabetical order. Extinct or endangered species are included.

Most, B. *ABC T-Rex.* San Diego: Harcourt Brace, 2000. The letters of the alphabet are devoured by a young T-Rex.
How Big Were the Dinosaurs? San Diego: Harcourt Brace, 1994. Dinosaurs are compared in size to familiar objects.

If the Dinosaurs Came Back. San Diego: Harcourt Brace, 1991. Imagine if dinosaurs came back what they could do to help people.

National Wildlife Federation. *Digging Into Dinosaurs*. New York: McGraw-Hill, 1997. Non-fiction information and illustrations.

Pallotta, J. *The Dinosaur Alphabet Book*. Watertown, MA: Charlesbridge, 1991. An alphabet book with great illustrations and in-depth information about dinosaurs.
The Extinct Alphabet Book. Watertown, MA: Charlesbridge, 1993. An alphabet book with great illustrations and in-depth information about animals other than dinosaurs that are extinct.

Silverstein, S. "If I Had a Brontosaurus," *Where the Sidewalk Ends*. New York: Harper and Row, 1974. A humerous book of light verse that delights children.

Strickland, P. *Ten Terrible Dinosaurs*. New York: Dutton, 1997. A countdown dinosaur book for the numbers 10 to 1. A fun way to talk about subtraction.
Dinosaur Roar! New York: Dutton, 1994. Rhyming text. Concept of opposites with a dinosaur theme.

March Curriculum

The Animal Kingdom

Birds – Real and Imaginary

MARCH CURRICULUM

The Animal Kingdom

CONCEPTS

- Animals live in their natural habitats, on farms, in zoos, and in homes with people.
- Farms are places where people live and raise animals and crops. Farmland is usually distant from cities.
- A zoo is a place where wild animals are protected and may be safely observed by people.
- A pet is usually a tame animal that someone takes care of in a home and treats with love.
- Animals need food, water, care, and a safe environment to survive and be happy.
- Some animals hibernate and some migrate in the winter.
- Veterinarians are doctors who care for sick and well animals.
- There are animals that are extinct or endangered.

CONTINUING CONCEPTS

- **Colors** Identify the colors of different animals, including black and white animals.
  Discuss the colors and patterns that help camouflage animals.
- **Geometric Shapes** Relate basic geometric shapes to the shapes of animals.
- **Health and Nutrition** Discuss safety and supervision around animals.
  Discuss how animals need a healthy diet and a safe environment, just as humans do.
- **Senses** Talk about the sounds animals make.
  Discuss how animals use each of their senses to survive.
  Display realistic pictures and photographs of real animals around the room as well as whimsical pictures of animals and compare the two kinds of illustration.
  Compare the ways different animal coverings feel when touched.
  Use a feely box and determine which animal or how many animals are inside.
- **Traditional Rhymes and Tales** Recite "Hey, Diddle, Diddle," "Little Bo-Peep," "Mary Had a Little Lamb," and "Three Blind Mice" with the children.

PORTFOLIO PRODUCTS

Consider the following suggestion as you or the children select at least one product from this unit to place in each portfolio.
- Include the fun fact flaps book (see p. 176) that each child made to share the results of his or her research on animals. Look for evidence of the child's artistic and writing skills and evaluate the depth of the information provided.

BACKGROUND INFORMATION

One goal of this unit and the following unit, Birds – Real and Imaginary, is to help children understand the natural environments of animals, as well as artificial environments, such as zoos. The concepts of endangered species and wildlife conservation are important ideas but difficult for young children to understand. Nevertheless, introducing the idea that it is important to protect birds and animals is warranted if handled in a developmentally appropriate manner.

ART

✳ Easel or Tabletop Painting

1. Black and White

Materials: black and white tempera paints; paper; brushes

Display pictures of animals that are black and white, such as zebras, skunks, penguins, and orca whales. Discuss how their color patterns help them survive in their natural environments. Give children black and white paint and encourage them to create a new black and white animal. Take children's dictation as they talk about how the animal benefits from being black and white.

2. Colors and Markings

Materials: large pieces of paper; tempera paints; brushes in two or more sizes

Discuss the colors and markings of animals. Explain that animals often have colors and markings that help them blend into their environments. Have children paint animals and talk about where each animal might live given its coloring and markings. Encourage children to use brushes of different sizes to finish the markings on their animal.

✳ Animal Shapes

Materials: precut geometric shapes of many kinds, colors, and sizes; glue; Manila or construction paper; crayons and markers

Study pictures of a wide variety of animals with different habitats. List and discuss the animals' attributes. Encourage children to look carefully at the sizes and shapes of different animals. Point out the shapes of bodies, heads, ears, legs, feet, and tails, and the colors and patterns on some animals. Point out interesting size relationships, such as very long necks or tails, and talk about how those features may be useful.

Give children geometric shapes and have them explore by putting the shapes together in various ways to make animals. Encourage them to try different sizes for the body and different shapes for the head and legs. Ask questions such as, "How would it look if we put a triangle there? What could be used to make strips or spots?"

Later, supply glue and have children glue their shapes together to make an animal. Children can use crayons or markers to draw the animal's habitat.

✳ Grrrreat Cut Paper Animals

Materials: construction paper scraps; glue; scissors; children's writing from the Grrrreat Animal Writing activity, p. 175

Give the children construction paper scraps and have them cut out animal features, such as a head, facial details, mane, legs, tail, horns, stripes, and spots. They then use their Grrrreat Animal Writings paper as the body of the animal and glue the animal features to the edges of the paper. Display the completed works with the caption *Grrrreat Writing.*

✳ Camouflage Colors

Materials: tempera paints; paper; brushes; scissors; glue or tape

As a class, study Laura Godwin's *Little White Dog.* Notice how the animals disappear into the background color that matches their color. Discuss how an animal's environment can help hide the animal when its color is similar to color in the environment.

Have children paint an animal of their choice using mainly one color and then cut out the animal. Then they paint a background by covering an entire sheet of paper using the color of their animal. When dry, they tape or glue the animal cutout to the background paper. Talk about how the animals seem to disappear into the background.

✳ Camouflage Flap Pictures

Materials: Manila paper; scraps of construction paper; picture of a tropical animal; glue; cotton swabs; scissors; crayons or markers

Introduce the concept of camouflage by sharing J. Dewey's *Can You Find Me? A Book About Animal Camouflage.* Talk about what camouflage means and how it helps animals stay safe in their natural environments. Use construction paper to cut out large jungle leaf shapes. Lay the leaves on top of a picture of a tropical animal to show how the environment camouflages the animal.

Have children draw and color pictures of a favorite animal. Encourage them to add stripes, spots, and color as appropriate. Ask them to tell another child what they know about the animal. Discuss where each animal lives. Invite children to cut out large leaves, rocks, trees, and other natural objects that are native to their animal's environment. Show children how to glue just a single edge of each natural object on top of the animal as if it is camouflaged behind the natural objects. When the glue is dry, the children can fold open the natural objects to reveal the animal underneath.

Encourage the children to take turns showing their camouflage flap pictures and telling about the animal and its habitat.

✳ Shaving Cream Movements

Materials: shaving cream; recording of "Carnival of Animals" by Saint-Saen, "The Baby Elephant Walk" by Henry Mancini, or a similar recording

Squirt a two-inch blob of shaving cream on the tabletop space in front of each child. Start the music and have the children show the ways various animals move by moving the shaving cream with their hands in rhythm with the music. You can also suggest the following movements to the children.

Move your hands like a seal sliding down a rock into his pool.

Move like an elephant.

Make your fingers hop around like a kangaroo or wallaby.

When the activity is finished, have children help clean up by wiping the shaving cream off the table with paper towels and washing the table with water and a sponge.

✳ Animal Drawing Starts

Materials: copies of Drawing Starts (Activity Master 20, p. 297); crayons or markers

Show the children the sheet of drawing starts. Explain that the marks on the sheet are drawings that aren't finished yet and that each mark is really a part of an animal. To show children they can position the sheet in any way, hold it and turn it clockwise several times. As you turn the sheet, say, "You may draw with your paper like this, or this, or this, or this."

Encourage the children to use the drawing starts to draw a complete animal. As children finish their drawings, have them write about their pictures or dictate a description of their animals to you. Exhibit the completed drawings on the wall or in a class book. Make a sign or a cover for the book that says *These drawings started like this.* (Show the drawing starts.) *Now take a look at them!*

✳ Class-Pet Floor Pillow

Materials: large pieces of fake fur; packing pieces; two or three Ping-Pong balls; red felt scraps; black marker; sewing machine; large needle and thread; glue

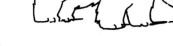

As a class, choose an animal to make as a class pet. On butcher paper, draw a large outline of the animal to use as a pattern. Use the outline to cut two pieces of fake fur. Sew the pieces together around the outside edges, leaving an opening for stuffing.

Let the children help stuff the animal with packing pieces. Sew the edges closed. (It is probably easiest to do this by hand, since the stuffed animal is harder to sew using a sewing machine.) If supervised, four- to six-year-olds can safely take turns helping to sew the opening closed with a large needle.

If the animal has a black nose, use the marker to color one ball black. Color large pupils on each of the other balls to make google eyes. Glue the eyes and nose on the animal. Add other details such as whiskers or horns if appropriate.

Together, name the class pet and place it where children may lie on it to enjoy a book or quiet moment. Talk about how the fur feels when touched.

BLOCKS

Add plastic animals or pictures of animals to the block area and encourage children to build a pet shop or zoo. They may want to write the name of each species of animal on small pieces of paper and add a label to the cages or zoo habitats. Also encourage the children to build shelters for pets that live in houses or to build fences and barns for farm animals.

BULLETIN BOARD
✳ Animal Textures

Create a bulletin board with texture and touch appeal. Cover simple geometric shapes with fabric and materials that suggest the skin, hair, fur, or hide of various animals. Suggested fabrics and materials for different animals include the following.

Canvas: elephant, rhinoceros, hippopotamus
Short fake furs: cats, dogs, hamsters, monkeys, camels, bears, zebras
Long fake furs: llamas, manes of all kinds
Smooth vinyl: seals
Textured vinyl in a reptile pattern: snakes, alligators
Fine sandpaper: tongues of lions and tigers; fish scales

Use yarn, pipe cleaners, construction paper, and buttons to add a few suggestive details, such as whiskers, eyes, noses, horns, and tails, to the geometric shapes. To increase the visual appeal of the board, add arrows with a word for a texture, such as *rough* or *soft,* on each, and position each one so that it points to a shape with that texture.

Use a colored marker to outline several 4" × 6" index cards. Staple one index card under each textured shape.

Introduce the board and discuss how the shapes represent animals, even though they do not look exactly like the animals. Use the term *symbol* if appropriate. Have children take turns gently feeling each animal. Talk about each shape and which animal might have the same texture as that shape. Write each possible animal on the card under the shape.

Talk with the children about how animals in their natural habitats or zoos are wild and can't be touched or petted. Explain that children need to judge how the animals might feel by looking at them.

The following activities could be completed during circle time.

1. Have children identify the geometric shapes and colors on the board.

2. Have the children compare and contrast the textures on the board. Encourage children to use descriptive language. Brainstorm with the children to develop a list of words that describe the various textures.

3. Discuss how a particular covering helps animals in their environments. Explain why members of the cat family have rough tongues and why some animals need long fur.

COOKING

✳ Animal Crackers

Packages of animal crackers *Plastic knives or craft sticks*
Canned frosting *Wax paper or paper plates*

Wash hands. Have each child count out a certain number of cookies and frost each cookie before eating it. Discuss the number of different kinds of animals. Graph the total number of each kind of animal in one package.

✳ Lion Cookies

Baked peanut butter cookies *Raisins*
Non-dairy whipped topping *Plastic knives*
Yellow food coloring *Wax paper*

Wash hands. Give a 12-inch piece of wax paper to each child. Then give each child a baked cookie and a knife. Put a dollop of whipped topping on the upper corner of each piece of wax paper and add one drop of food coloring to the topping. Children use the knife to mix in the coloring and then spread the topping around the outer edge of the cookie to make a lion's mane. They make facial features by dipping raisins in the topping and adding them to the cookie.

LANGUAGE ARTS

✳ Fingerplay – Skip to the Zoo

1-2-3
  (Put up 1-2-3 fingers.)
Skip to the zoo with me.
  (Point to self.)
1-2-3
  (Put up 1-2-3 fingers.)
What do you think we'll see?
  (Shade eyes with hand and look out.)
I spy a giraffe with a funny long neck,
  (Separate arms as far apart as possible.)
And a shiny seal swimming by the deck,
  (Move each arm like a flipper.)

And a baby kangaroo in a hop-a-long ride,
  (Hands together in hopping action.)
And a rhinoceros with his wrinkled-up hide.
  (Wrinkle up face and wiggle it.)
Those are a few of the things we'll see,
  (Shade eyes with hand.)
If you'll skip along to the zoo with me.
  (Beckoning motion with arm.)

✳ Word Wall

Add the word *animal* to the word wall. Add other topic-related words that children suggest. Count how many words are on the word wall. Write a sentence strip that says, for example, *We have 20 words on our word wall.* Place a piece of colored plastic (cut from a plastic report cover) over one or more of the word cards to highlight words you want children to use in their writing.

✳ Animal Mothers and Babies

Read aloud P. M. Ryan's *A Pinky Is a Baby Mouse: And Other Baby Animal Names.* Review the names of mother and baby animals, including chicken, chick; pig, piglet; cat, kitten; goose, gosling; horse, colt; cow, calf; sheep, lamb; dog, puppy; and duck, duckling.

Provide pictures of animal adults and babies. As you hold the pictures up for all to see, have the children find the baby that goes with each mother animal.

✳ Animal Attributes

Read David Small's *Imogene's Antlers* aloud to the class. Fold a large piece of chart paper in half to make two columns. Label one column *What you <u>cannot</u> do with antlers* and the second column *What you <u>can</u> do with antlers.* List the children's ideas in each column.

Discuss other attributes of animals. Select one and talk about what children would look like and what they could do and could not do if they had that attribute. Then, invite children to name another attribute of animals and draw a picture of what they would look like if they had that attribute. Suggest that children write a sentence on their paper about what they could or could not do with that attribute.

Collect their pictures and sentences and use them to make a class book.

✳ Animals Should Definitely Not . . . .

Read the humorous book *Animals Should Definitely Not Wear Clothing* by Judi Barrett. After one or two readings, children love to say the "because" part as each picture is shown. Older children may enjoy creating a new version of the story. Write the following open-ended sentence on chart paper or the chalkboard.

Animals should definitely not _____ because _____.

Have the children complete the sentences using humorous suggestions. Even fairly serious suggestions that require higher-level thinking, such as *Animals should definitely not be harmed by zoo visitors because . . .* can turn into funny sentences.

✳ Home Matching Game

Read aloud some or all of the book *A House Is a House for Me* by M. A. Hoberman. Display pictures of different animals and places where they live. Also display pictures of children and different kinds of houses. You may wish to laminate the pictures and use temporary adhesive to display them on a chalkboard. Have the children work together as a class to match each picture with an appropriate home. Begin by displaying four or five pictures and then add more pictures as children become more familiar with the game. With somewhat older children, discuss which animals can be matched to more than one picture. For example, the fish could live in an aquarium or the ocean.

✳ Nursery Rhymes

1. Record individual children reciting traditional rhymes that mention animals. Place the tape in a listening center for children to enjoy.

2. Recite "Little Bo Peep." Ask children to name all the different kinds of animals they can think of. Print each animal word on the chalkboard or on a piece of chart paper so that the children can see the words in print. Change the word *Peep* to a made-up word that rhymes with each of the animal words on the list. Say each made-up word rhyme and have children supply the animal word that rhymes. Some examples follow.

   Little Bo Pat has lost her _____ . (cat)
   Little Bo Pish has lost her _____ . (fish)

✳ Peek-A-Boo Spots

Materials: 4" × 6" index cards; crayons or markers; hole punch

Show pictures of animals with spots and discuss why these animals have spots. Explain that some animals have spots only when they are babies. Talk about how the spots on baby animals help protect them because they blend into their environment.

Brainstorm a list of all the animals with spots. Invite children to draw a picture of a spotted animal on an index card. Then, show children how to use a hole punch to punch holes all over the animal. Children hold their finished animal up to the light to view the peek-a-boo spots. Tape the finished animals to the windows so that light shows through.

✳ Animal Adjectives

Have children think of adjectives to describe animals. Explain that an adjective is a word that tells something about a person, animal, place, or thing. Give examples. Invite them to think of other adjectives and list the children's words. Encourage children to use the adjectives orally and in their writing.

Consider printing each adjective in a different color as children offer them. The color adds visual interest and helps children find specific words.

✳ What Am I?

Reread the list of adjectives together. Use the list to create riddles about animals you have discussed previously. For example, tell children, "I am small and soft. I purr when you pet me. What am I?" After presenting several riddles to the children, invite them to use adjectives to make up animal riddles for others to guess.

✳ Grrrreat Animal Writings

Have children discuss their favorite animal or the animal they find most interesting. Read together the words on the class animal adjectives list (see above).

Then name a certain animal and have the children think about it. Say a specific adjective and have children stand up if the adjective describes the animal. Continue with three or four more adjectives.

Write a sentence pattern on the board or paper, such as

The _____ , _____ , _____ lives _____ .
    adjective   adjective   animal   location or habitat

Use the adjectives children identified as being accurate to complete the sentence. Continue by working together to form a few more sentences. Some examples follow.

> *The long, green snake lives in a big tree.*
> *The huge, gray elephant lives in the forest.*

Help individual children match adjectives on the animal adjectives list to their favorite animal. Invite them to write one or more sentences about it. Many children can use the sentence pattern to complete a sentence. Others may be able to write their own sentences without a pattern. Encourage interested children to write a second sentence that includes different adjectives that describe the animal. Encourage children to begin a sentence with a capital letter and use a period, as you have modeled.

Use the completed sentences to create Grrrreat Cut Paper Animals (see p. 169).

✳ Endangered or Extinct

Read Ann Jonas' *Aardvarks Disembark!* to the class. Ask children what they think *endangered* means. Record their ideas, consult reference materials if they express an interest, and then give or help them formulate a definition that incorporates the idea that endangered animals are those having trouble staying alive in their natural environments. Use the same process to develop a definition of *extinct*. Compare the two definitions. Ask children to decide if dinosaurs are endangered or extinct.

✳ Letters to Save Endangered Animals

Help children write letters to a state or national agency sharing their concerns about an endangered species. Invite children to illustrate their letters. Encourage children who are ready to begin each sentence with a capital letter and to use a period at the end. Some children may have noticed your use of commas and want to add them also.

✳ Animal Classifications

Brainstorm a list of attributes to use as categories for classifying animals. Examples of possible attributes are given below. Provide pictures or models of a wide variety of animals, and have the children sort the pictures into the different categories. Discuss animals that can be included in multiple categories. Ask, "Which categories include most of the animals?"

Examples of attributes/categories include carnivore, herbivore, omnivore; walks on four legs, walks on two legs; flies, swims, walks; has tail, doesn't have tail; has horn, doesn't have horn; large, small; found in a home, on a farm, in a zoo, in a natural environment.

✳ Fun Fact Flaps

Invite children to choose an animal to research. Suggest that they talk to others and look up information with adult help. Their goal is to find four significant and perhaps less well-known facts about their animal. Show them how to make a flap strip. Fold a piece of paper in half from top to bottom. Then fold the paper in half again and then in half again. When you open the paper, there will be eight sections. Cut the three fold lines from the right edge to the centerfold to create flaps. Have each child cut the paper to make a flap strip. On each flap, have children draw a picture to show something about their animal and then lift the flap to write the fact in the space behind the flap.

✳ Veterinarian Visit

Invite a veterinarian to come to your class to share information about what a veterinarian does. The veterinarian may be able to bring a small animal to class to demonstrate the safe care and handling of certain kinds of animals.

MATH

✳ Calendar

Provide the children who can write numerals with their own copy of a blank calendar (Activity Master 3, p. 280). Help them write the name of the month and fill in the dates in the appropriate sections. Each day at calendar time, skip-count together by fives. When children are familiar with skip-counting by fives, have them do so on their own and use a blue crayon or marker to circle or color the numerals they count (5, 10, 15, 20, 25, and 30). Invite children to draw groups of five objects along the margins of their calendar. Have children mark holidays or other special days, including children's birthdays, on their calendar. Have children compare this month's calendar to the one they made last month.

✳ Silent Numbers

Show children a card with a numeral from 1 to 10 on it. Children hold up the correct number of fingers for that numeral. Do the activity in silence. Repeat the task by displaying pictures that show from one to ten animals.

✳ Matthew and His Pets

Use a cardboard box and add stuffed or plastic animals to the box, one by one, as you recite the poem below. Have children say the missing number each time. Say the last line of the poem by counting together as you remove the animals from the box.

Matthew had a little box. "I know what this can be.
I'll make this box a pet house and get some pets for me."
He put in one but said: "I'm just not done.
I know what to do; add another and make _____ .
But really it would be much nicer to have _____ .
There still is room for more. I'll add another and make _____ .
Another pet arrives, so altogether I have _____ .
This is a good mix. I'll add one more and I'll have _____ .
How many pets in all can there be? Can you count them all with me?"
One, two, three, four, five, six!

✳ Feely Box

Provide a set of small, plastic animals. Out of view of the children, put one or more plastic animals of one type inside the feely box. Have children take turns feeling what's inside the box to discover which animal and how many animals are inside. Repeat the game with a different type or number of animals.

✳ Animal Flannel-Board Cutouts

Use one of the unit topic cards that shows an animal to make several felt cutouts. Have the class select a number from 1 through 10. Then tell the children, "Quietly tell me to stop when I have put (a number from 1 through 10) animals on the flannel board." Slowly add one cutout at a time to the board until the children say "Stop." Repeat the activity, using a different number. You could also have children take turns adding the felt cutouts to the board.

✳ Masking-Tape Animals

Compare the sizes of several animals. Use masking tape to make a large, simple, scaled outline of a favorite dinosaur on an uncarpeted section of the floor. Then use tape to make simple outlines of some common animals or birds that are living today; for example, a pig, horse, or crow. Be sure to show each figure in correct size proportion to the others. Measure the height of each figure and compare the measurements. As you discuss the measurements with the children, model the use of measurement terms like *height, feet, inches, tall, tallest, short,* and *shortest*.

✳ Feed the Pets

Materials: $\frac{1}{4}$-, $\frac{1}{2}$-, and 1-cup measuring cups; pictures of a small, medium, and large pet; one small, one medium, and one large bowl; packing pieces

Tape a picture of one pet on each bowl. Tape a drawing of a $\frac{1}{4}$-cup measuring cup on the small pet bowl, a drawing of a $\frac{1}{2}$-cup measuring cup on the medium pet bowl, and a drawing of a 1-cup measuring cup on the large pet bowl. Have children take turns pretending to feed the animals by carefully measuring the appropriate amount of pretend pet food (packing pieces) into each bowl.

✳ Near and Far

Give half the children a laminated numeral. Have them position themselves randomly around the classroom. The other children follow directions you give, such as, "Chris, stand near the person holding the numeral three," or "Traci, stand far from the person holding the numeral five." When children are familiar with the activity, have them take turns giving the instructions.

MOVEMENT

✳ Animal Movements

Have the children do these animal movements in the gym or another large, open space.
Dog: Crawl on all fours, moving very slowly at first and then faster.
Cat: On all fours, stretch the body, keeping arms and legs straight. Move the back and bottom down, then stretch back up like a cat when it's afraid or angry.
Fish: Lie on the tummy on the floor. Pull forward using both arms as fins to swim across the floor. Wiggle the legs together slowly, like a waving fish tail.
Bird: Stand, arms stretched back, body bent slightly forward as if a bird gliding in flight. Run slowly and gently flap wings as if flying.

✳ Walk Your Dog

Have the children work in pairs, with one pretending to be a child walking a dog and the other pretending to be the dog. Ask the pairs to complete the following movements. Then have the children trade places and repeat the movements.

1. Walk forward.
2. Turn around two times.
3. Ask the dog to roll over.
4. Pretend to throw a ball, which the dog pretends to catch and bring back.
5. Have the dog lie down for a nap.

✳ Pet Ball

Use soft foam balls and challenge pairs of children to play ball without using their hands or feet. Explain that they can push the ball with their noses as pets do. (To avoid having the children spread germs, discourage them from picking up the ball with their teeth.)

MUSIC

✳ Familiar Songs About Animals

Sing familiar songs that involve animals, such as "Oh Where, Oh Where Has My Little Dog Gone," "Mary Had a Little Lamb," "Farmer in the Dell," "I Know an Old Lady Who Swallowed a Fly," "Old McDonald Had a Farm," and "Bingo."

✳ The Way of the Animals

(Tune: "Here We Go Round the Mulberry Bush")

1. *This is the way the elephant moves, elephant moves, elephant moves.*
   This is the way the elephant moves, early in the morning.
   (Arms form a trunk; sing while walking slowly.)
2. *This is the way the giraffe eats . . .*
   (Stretch neck, stretch out tongue.)
3. *This is the way the kangaroo hops . . .*
   (Hop around in rhythm.)
4. *This is the way the horse gallops . . .*
   (Gallop in rhythm.)
5. *This is the way the long snake slides . . .*
   (Lay down and wiggle whole body.)

Encourage children to suggest and act out additional verses.

ROLE PLAY

✳ Veterinarian's Office

Discuss the job of a veterinarian. Ask if any children have taken a pet to a veterinarian. Set up a veterinarian's office for children to role play examining and caring for pets. Send a note to parents one or two weeks in advance asking them to share appropriate items. Include a list of suggested items and invite them to add others. Props may include several large and small stuffed animals, waiting room chairs, examination table, stethoscope, doctor's white coat, doctor's kit, paper for signs and prescriptions, a small table, writing pad, and phone for a reception desk.

Display animal posters or pictures of animals the children have drawn. Place the materials in the role-play area and let children decide how to arrange and use them.

SCIENCE

✳ Live Classroom Pet

Having a classroom pet is especially important today because many children no longer have pets in their homes. If possible, keep a small animal (hamster, guinea pig, gerbil, lizard, bird) of some kind in the classroom for a time. Children benefit from caring for a living animal that depends on them. They can also learn to handle a pet gently.

✳ Hibernation

Review the books and discussions about animal hibernation that were introduced in the Life in Winter unit.

✳ Observation of Live Pets

Have children observe the behavior of a pet over several days. Provide a class science journal with the printed title *Observations*. Ask children to draw pictures and write about what they observe. Tell them that scientists learn by observing and making notes and drawings about their observations.

Discuss what the children have noticed about their pets. Prompt the discussion with questions such as, "How does the pet eat and drink? What does the pet do to sleep? Does the pet wash? What does it do if a person holds it or touches it?" If a child expresses a misconception about a pet, ask him or her to observe the animal some more to see if that is true. Discuss the point again after the child has had a chance to observe the pet again.

✳ Animal Fur or Synthetic Fur

Discuss why animals have fur. Provide some samples of synthetic fur and real animal fur. Provide a magnifying glass. Have the children feel, smell, and visually examine the furs. Discuss how the synthetic fur and the real fur are alike and how they are different. Have the children classify the fur samples as animal fur or not animal fur.

Give the children a piece of lamb's wool and have them feel it. Ask them to compare the wool to real fur. Ask, "How is the wool like the fur?"

TRANSITION ACTIVITIES
✳ Monkey See, Monkey Do

Monkey see and monkey do. A monkey does the same as you.

A leader acts out a movement, and the children copy it as they recite the verse above. Then a new leader acts out a different movement and the children copy it.

✳ Animal Questions

Have the children discuss any of the following subjects.
1. Things people do to take care of animals
2. Animals that are large and animals that are small
3. Animals that swim
4. Animals that eat vegetables, fruit, or meat
5. Animals found on farms
6. Animals found in zoos

CHILDREN'S BOOKS

Barrett, J. *Animals Should Definitely Not Wear Clothing.* New York: Atheneum, 1970. Humorous illustrations of the problems animals would have with clothes. Employs an effective writing pattern.

Cannon, J. *Verdi.* San Diego: Harcourt Brace, 1997. Verdi discovers he can grow up being green and still be himself.

Carle, E. *Does a Kangaroo Have a Mother, Too?* New York: HarperCollins, 2000. A variety of animal mothers and babies answer the question. Reminiscent of *Brown Bear, Brown Bear.*

Cherry, L. *The Great Kapok Tree*. San Diego: Harcourt Brace, 1990. A man falls asleep under a rain forest tree that he intends to cut down. Animals visit him in his sleep and convince him of the importance of the rain forest.

Dewey, J. *Can You Find Me? A Book About Animal Camouflage*. New York: Scholastic, 1996. Good information about how animals use camouflage.

Edwards, P. *Some Smug Slug*. New York: HarperCollins, 1996. Alliterative use of the letter *s*. Offers rich vocabulary and hidden visual elements that children can search for.

Ehlert, L. *Color Farm*. New York: Trumpet, 1990.
Color Zoo. New York: Scholastic, 1988. Layered, die cut illustrations of simple geometric figures change into something new with every turn of the page. Award-winning books. Good for encouraging color and shape recognition.

Elting, M. and M. Folsom. *Q is for Duck: An Alphabet Guessing Game*. New York: Clarion, 1980. *Q* is for duck because a duck quacks. This alphabet book requires children to figure out the relationship between a letter and a word.

Godwin, L. *Little White Dog*. New York: Hyperion, 1998. Solid-colored animals are camouflaged against the background. Promotes development of sequencing skills.

Hoberman, M. A. *A House Is a House for Me*. New York: Viking, 1978. In rhyming verse, many containers and coverings for animals are described as kinds of houses.

Jonas, A. *Aardvarks Disembark!* New York: Greenwillow, 1990. Numerous species of animals disembark from the ark in alphabetical order. Extinct or endangered species are indicated.

Martin, B. *Brown Bear, Brown Bear, What Do You See?* New York, Holt, 1983.
Polar Bear, Polar Bear, What Do You See? New York: Holt, 1991. These are very predictable pattern books that children "read" after just one read-aloud. Offers a pattern that you can use to have children rewrite the story.

Numeroff, L. J. *If You Give a Moose a Muffin*. New York: HarperCollins, 1989.
If You Give a Mouse a Cookie. New York: HarperCollins, 1985.
If You Give a Pig a Pancake. New York: HarperCollins, 1998. Children love these highly predictable circle stories. Provide effective prompts for many writing activities.

Ryan, P. M. *A Pinky Is a Baby Mouse: And Other Baby Animal Names*. New York: Hyperion, 1997. The different names of baby animals, *a* to *z*, are explained in rhyming verses.

Small, D. *Imogene's Antlers*. New York: Crown, 1985. A young girl wakes up with antlers. Good creative thinking and problem-solving opportunities.

Young, E. *Seven Blind Mice*. New York: Philomel, 1992. Seven mice have different views of what they encounter. Prediction skills, colors, days of the week, and ordinals are modeled.

Birds — Real and Imaginary

CONCEPTS

- Birds live in their natural habitats, on farms, in zoos, and in homes with people.
- Birds need food, water, care, and a safe environment to survive.
- Feathers protect birds and help them fly.
- Birds are different sizes and colors.
- Different kinds of birds lay eggs of different sizes and colors.
- Some birds migrate south in fall and winter and return north in the spring.
- Birds use many kinds of materials to weave a nest.
- Some birds that children may see include ducks, chickens, blue jays, cardinals, robins, woodpeckers, crows, seagulls, parakeets, parrots, and sparrows.
- Birds are not the only animals that lay eggs.

CONTINUING CONCEPTS

- **Colors** Identify the many different colors of birds.
  Discuss the colors and patterns that birds have. Talk about how colors and patterns may help camouflage birds and help them to attract mates.
- **Geometric Shapes** Relate basic geometric shapes to the shapes of birds.
  Introduce ovals and relate the shape of an oval to the shape of a bird's egg.
  Point out that a bird's beak has a shape like a triangle.
- **Health and Nutrition** Discuss the importance of safe behavior and supervision when children are around birds.
  Understand that birds need a healthy diet and a safe environment, just as humans do.
  Have children compare birds' joints to human joints.
- **Senses** Talk about the sounds birds make.
  Discuss birds' keen sense of sight.
  Have children describe and compare how different bird feathers feel when touched.
- **Traditional Rhymes and Tales** Recite "Sing a Song of Sixpence" with the children and tell them the fairy tale "The Golden Goose."

PORTFOLIO PRODUCTS

Select or have the children select at least one product from this unit to place in each portfolio. One suggestion follows.
- Copy a recent entry from each child's journal. This product celebrates the child's art, emergent literacy, and fine-motor skills.

ART

✳ Easel or Tabletop Painting

1. Birds of Many Colors

Materials: paper; tempera paints in several colors; brushes

Provide tempera paint to match the colors of birds observed in your area (see the Bird Graph activity, p. 191). Have children paint birds using those colors. Talk with each child about the colors of any birds he or she has seen. Ask, "Do you know the name of a bird that has that color?"

2. Colors and Markings

Materials: large pieces of paper; tempera paints in several bright colors; brushes in two or more sizes

Discuss the colors and markings of birds. Explain that birds in different environments have colors and markings that help them blend into the environment or attract other birds. Invite children to paint birds and to explore using brushes of different sizes.

3. Feather Painting

Materials: natural feathers with a sturdy shaft that will support the weight of paint; tempera paints, slightly thinned; paper

Dip a feather in paint and model for the children how to lightly stroke the feather on the paper. Have children explore how many different types of strokes a feather can produce by using the whole feather, the tip, or just the edge of the feather.

Note: As a health precaution, do not obtain feathers from a barnyard.

4. Feather Duster

Materials: large pieces of paper; thin tempera paints; inexpensive feather dusters; deep plastic foam food trays; large coat box or lid

Put the paper in the bottom of the box. Pour paint into deep food trays so that children can dip the ends of the feathers into the paint as if using a brush. Use a different duster for each color. At the end of the activity, have the children wash the duster by swishing it in a bucket with three inches of water. Gently shake the excess water from the feathers. Hang the dusters on a hook or store them in a can with the handle down.

Display several finished paintings. Discuss the differences in the paintings produced with a feather and those painted with a feather duster.

✳ Bird Sculpture

Materials: pipe cleaners or plastic-coated telephone or electric wire; construction paper scraps

Demonstrate how to make imaginary birds by twisting together colored pipe cleaners or wire. Discuss

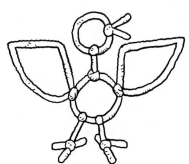

which geometric figures are like the different parts of birds. Show children how to bend the wire or pipe cleaner into a head and a body shape and how to twist them to make legs, wings, beaks, and other body parts. Demonstrate how one piece can be wrapped around other pieces to increase the size of the sculpture. Add details such as eyes with construction paper.

Ask children to think of a bird that they want to make. Talk about the features of each bird as they make their choices. Ask, "What can you tell me about the size of your bird? Do you want to make a real or an imaginary bird?" Provide the wire or pipe cleaners and have the children make their bird sculptures. Display the sculptures around the room with a small stand-up card on which the child's name is printed.

Note: Telephone repair workers and electricians usually have wire scraps to give away. Wires with different widths, colors, and lengths are all usable.

❋ Flying Crayons Mural

Materials: long pieces of butcher paper; boxes of crayons; a recording of Tchaikovsky's "Swan Lake" or some other flowing instrumental music

Spread the paper on the tabletop. Place boxes of crayons in the middle of the table so that several children can work together. Play the music for a brief time and discuss how the music suggests the graceful movements of birds flying in the air or swimming in the water. Have the children practice moving their hands and arms in rhythm to the music. Then play the music again and have the children color the paper. Consider stopping the music from time to time and having the children change colors each time the music stops.

❋ Egg Mosaics

Materials: Manila paper cut in egg shapes of several sizes; crepe paper or colored tissue paper; glue; brushes or cotton swabs

Thin the glue with water. Have the children tear the crepe paper or tissue in smaller pieces. Then have the children brush the glue on the egg and add the pieces of colored paper until the egg is covered with "mosaics." Encourage children to overlap colors and ask them to notice what happens to the colors. Talk about how bird's eggs are different sizes and different colors.

❋ Dough Bird Eggs and Nests

Materials: white play dough made without added color (see Appendix II, p. 275); food coloring in several colors

Make the play dough in the classroom with the children or prepare it in advance. Give each child a small amount of the white dough. Talk about the colors of birds that children have seen. Have each child name a color a bird has. Then have each child use a finger to make a hole in his or her ball of dough. Drop several drops of a food coloring in the hole. Have children knead the dough for a couple of minutes to mix the color thoroughly. Ask children to talk about the color changes they observe.

Encourage the children to mold a nest, eggs, and a bird shape. Invite children to trade colors of dough so that everyone can use different colors. Display the finished products on a table on individual pieces of cardboard clearly labeled with each artist's name.

✳ Animals That Lay Eggs

Materials: <u>Chickens Aren't the Only Ones</u> by Ruth Heller; crayons or markers; paper

Discuss with the children the fact that many animals lay eggs, just as birds do. Brainstorm with the children to generate a list of animals that lay eggs. Many children may know that dinosaurs, snakes, and turtles lay eggs. If a child names a bird such as a turkey or duck, accept the idea by saying, "Yes, that is another kind of bird that lays eggs."

Read *Chickens Aren't the Only Ones.* Then give the children paper and crayons or markers, and encourage them to draw a picture of an animal, other than a bird, that lays eggs.

BLOCKS

Add a yardstick or meter stick and a ruler to the block area. Provide the largest blocks available in your room plus smaller unit blocks. Encourage the children to build large and small birdhouses. Then use the measuring sticks to compare the sizes of the birdhouses. Ask, "Which is larger (or smaller)? What type of bird might live in a large birdhouse? What type of bird might live in a small birdhouse?"

BULLETIN BOARD

✳ Bird in the Nest (A Group Project)

Begin this project after children have had a chance to observe and discuss real birds' nests (see p. 195).

1. Background

Materials: butcher paper; blue finger paint; yellow tempera paint; brushes or sponges; brown paper grocery bags

Cut a piece of butcher paper to cover the top half of the bulletin board. Draw a large sun on the paper. Lay the paper on a tabletop and have some children paint the sun yellow with brushes or sponges. Have several children take turns making a blue sky by finger painting the rest of the paper. Have children help twist grocery bags to form a three-dimensional bare tree trunk and limb and attach them along the left side and across the bottom of the board.

2. Nest

Materials: butcher paper approximately 24" × 36"; brown tempera paint; sponges; glue; natural items for nest making that were collected outside

Cut a large nest shape from the paper. Have children use sponges to paint the nest brown. While the nest dries, take the children outside and encourage them to collect things a bird might use to make a nest; for example, twigs, grass, and weeds. Have the children glue the materials to the paper nest. As the children work, discuss how some birds use mud to construct a nest whereas other birds weave materials to hold a nest together. Display the nest on the tree limb on the bulletin board.

3. Bird

Materials: $1\frac{1}{2}" \times 9"$ construction paper strips in colors of some of the birds in your area; construction scraps in yellow and black

Have children make a paper-chain bird to place on the nest. Children work together to glue the strips into rings and combine them into long paper chains. Coil the chains around and around to make the bird's body in a size that will fit in the nest. Coil other chains around to make the bird's head. Make two large, yellow triangles to form a beak and two black circles to make eyes and add these features to the bird.

During circle time, name the kinds of birds that look like this one. With the class, write a step-by-step description of how the class made the bulletin-board display. Display the story beside the bulletin board and reread it from time to time with the children.

COOKING

✳ Birdseed Biscuits

Refrigerated biscuits
Sesame or poppy seeds
Soft margarine

Several pastry brushes
Wax paper
Plastic knives

Wash hands. Provide wax paper to work on. Each child cuts a biscuit in half as you talk about whole and half and one piece and two pieces. The children explore rolling and shaping each half. Then they use pastry brushes to brush the biscuits with margarine. Next, have them sprinkle sesame or poppy seeds on the biscuits. Put the biscuits on a baking sheet and place a small strip of foil with each child's initials next to his or her biscuit. Bake according to the directions on the package. As the biscuits bake, talk about birds that eat seeds. Ask the children to think about where birds would find seeds to eat.

✳ Eating Like a Bird

Several kinds of prepared cereals
Small paper cups
Small paper plates

Have the children try eating without using their hands. Ask them to sit at a table and have them mix several different cereals in a paper cup. Then have them try to eat the cereal from the cup without using their hands. Ask the children to talk about why it is hard. Then have them pour their cereal onto a paper plate and try to eat the cereal again.

Finally, have them use their fingers to nibble on the cereal while you show them pictures of different kinds of birds eating. Talk about how the shape and size of a bird's beak influence what the bird eats. Compare the size and shape of the beak of a bird that eats seeds and nuts with the beak of a bird that catches and eats fish. Talk about how birds take water into their beaks and then tilt their heads up so that the water slides down their throats.

LANGUAGE ARTS

✳ Fingerplay – Flying Birds

Tape one 4-inch long strip of crepe paper in blue, yellow, black, red, or white to each finger and the thumb of one hand. Flutter each finger like a wing during the appropriate part of the fingerplay. Provide strips for the children's fingers and repeat the activity.

Here is a little bluebird, flying by, flying by.
Here is a yellow canary, flying by, flying by.
Here is a big black crow, flying by, flying by.
Here is a red cardinal, flying by, flying by.
Here is a graceful white gull, flying by, flying by.
All the birds fly peacefully by, adding color to the sky.

✳ Word Wall

Add the word *bird* to the word wall. Add color words and other topic-related words that the children suggest. Count how many words are on the word wall. Write a sentence strip that says *We have (the number) words on our word wall* and display it. Place a piece of colored plastic (cut from a plastic report cover) over one or more of the word cards that you want children to incorporate in their writing.

✳ Bird Begins With B (A Whole-Class Project)

On a large piece of yellow butcher paper, draw a large bird shape. Write *Bird Begins With B* at the top of the paper. Have children cut pictures out of magazines and draw pictures of things that begin with *b*. Discuss each picture and then have children glue the pictures on the paper. Print the name of the object beside each picture. Children could continue the activity at center and free time until the paper is filled with pictures.

✳ Birds Color-Wheel Match

Materials: poster board; tempera paints or markers; clothespins with springs

Cut out a circle from poster board. Divide the circle into several sections as shown. Ask the children to watch for birds in the area and then tell you the color and the kind of birds they see. As the children begin to report on the birds, color one section of the circle to show each color the children have seen. You could also write the name of the color within each section.

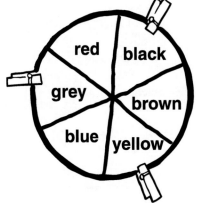

Use each color shown on the bird color wheel to paint three to four clothespins. Show children how each clothespin may be clipped to the matching colored section of the color wheel. Later, put the color wheel and clothespins in a center and have individual children match the clothespins to sections of the color wheel.

Explain to children that birds have color vision. They may use their color vision to locate food, identify a mate, and navigate during flight.

✳ Favorite Birds Book

Materials: magazines; scissors; glue; construction paper

Children cut out pictures of the birds they like. Each child glues the pictures on a piece of construction paper. The child or an adult prints a sentence the child composes about the birds on the paper and prints the child's name under the sentence.

Staple or bind the pages together to make a class book, with the title *Our Favorite Birds* on the front cover. Keep the book in the reading center where children may look at it.

✳ Real or Imaginary

Show pictures of real birds and illustrations of imaginary birds, such as Mayzie in *Horton Hatches the Egg* by Dr. Seuss. Discuss the differences between things that are real and things that are imaginary.

✳ Ten Reasons People Like Birds

Children use a tape recorder and take turns interviewing classmates and teachers in other classes about what people like about birds. Plan interview questions with the children in advance. Talk in advance about how to use the tape recorder.

After all the children have interviewed at least one person, compile the results. Write all of the different reasons people like birds on a piece of chart paper as the tape plays. Have the children listen carefully and tell when a reason is repeated. Make tally marks next to reasons that are given more than once. Try to develop a list of the ten reasons mentioned most often. Discuss the most important things the children learned in this interview activity.

✳ An Unusual Alphabet

Read aloud L. Tryon's *Albert's Alphabet,* a story in which Albert the duck uses surprising materials to create an unusual alphabet. Provide recycled materials, paper scraps, collage materials, twigs and other natural objects, and masking tape. Have children work together to see how many letters of the alphabet they can construct using the materials. Display their results. Place each letter in alphabetical order as it is finished, leaving spaces to add missing letters. Discuss which

letters still need to be made. Emphasize the terms *before* and *after*. For example, ask, "Which letter comes after *r?* Which letter comes before *d?*"

✳ Nesting Places

The Best Nest by P. D. Eastman is a great story that makes the point that the grass is not always greener on the other side. Pause as you read the book and have the children predict what will happen each time the characters try to move into a new place. Midway through the story, have the children try to locate places that would make good nests for birds.

✳ Where Is the Bird?

Use the realistic drawing of a bird on the topic card on p. 167 as a stencil. Cut out birds from construction paper in several different colors. Laminate the birds if you wish to reuse them.

Give each child a bird. Take a bird and hold it on or near your body. Describe where the bird is and have the children place their birds in the same position. For example, say, "My bluebird is on top of my head."

You may wish to have children give each other directions. Suggest prepositions if the children giving directions need help. Remind children to tell the color of their bird each time they give a direction. A child may say, for example, "My yellow bird is under my chin."

Vary the game with older children by first placing your bird and then asking the children to use appropriate prepositions to tell you where the bird is. You may ask, for example, "Where is my red bird?" Children might respond by saying, "It is on top of your hand."

✳ Red Bird, Red Bird Chant

Read *Brown Bear, Brown Bear, What Do You See?* by Bill Martin, Jr. several times to the class as a preliminary to the following activity. The children should become familiar with the predictable structure of the book. Then introduce them to the following adaptation, a chant called "Red Bird, Red Bird." Hold up a picture or sticker of each bird as you recite the lines and encourage the children to join in.

CHANTER	CHANT	PICTURE POSSIBILITIES
Children	Red bird, red bird, What do you see?	cardinal
Teacher	I see a blue bird, Looking at me.	
Children	Blue bird, blue bird, What do you see?	blue jay
Teacher	I see a yellow bird Looking at me.	
Children	Yellow bird, yellow bird, What do you see?	canary
Teacher	I see a green bird Looking at me.	
Children	Green bird, green bird, What do you see?	parrot
Teacher	I see a white bird Looking at me.	
Children	White bird, white bird, What do you see?	dove or gull
Teacher	I see a brown bird Looking at me.	
Children	Brown bird, brown bird, What do you see?	sparrow
Teacher	I see a black bird Looking at me.	
Children	Black bird, black bird, What do you see?	crow

Teacher	I see a smiling teacher Looking at me.	
Children	Teacher, teacher, What do you see?	photo of the teacher
Teacher	I see wonderful children Looking at me!	group photo of children

✳ Red Bird, Red Bird Book

Produce a class book about the Red Bird, Red Bird chant. Copy one couplet from the chant on each page. Have the children draw the bird for each couplet and color it appropriately. Use either photographs or a child's drawing for the last two couplets. Put the pages together with metal rings or in a plastic binder.

Tape record the children as they read the book with you. Place the book and tape in the listening center or an area where individual children may listen to it.

✳ To Fly or Not to Fly

Create a pocket folder game. On the inside pocket on the left print *Can Fly;* on the pocket on the right print *Cannot Fly.* Draw a picture clue for each side of the folder; for example, a bird and a truck. For each category, provide several stickers and small pictures from magazines. Store the pictures in an envelope kept inside the folder. Have children sort the pictures by placing them in the appropriate pocket. Introduce this activity to small groups of children before allowing the children to use it independently.

Some children may be ready to understand that all birds have feathers but all birds do not fly. Talk about how flightless birds have smaller wings and feathers that are too coarse to support flight. Tell the children that the penguin and the ostrich are two examples of birds that cannot fly. Display pictures of these two birds as you talk. Challenge children to do research to identify other flightless birds. Invite them to share what they learn with the class.

✳ Bird Communication

Take the children outdoors and have them sit quietly and listen to bird sounds. If it is not possible to go outside, play a tape of bird sounds or visit a pet store that sells birds.

Ask the children to try to make whistles and sounds like birds do. Tape record the sounds they make and play the tape for them. Ask them to close their eyes and listen. Ask, "Do you sound like real birds?" Accept any ideas the children share about the similarities and differences. Explain that birds have good hearing and that although they do not have ears, they do have ear openings in the sides of their heads. Talk about how birds use their whistles to communicate with each other, in much the same way we use words to communicate.

MATH

✳ Nests and Eggs Flannel Board Game

Draw and color nests on nonwoven interfacing. Cut them out individually and write a numeral on each nest. Cut oval egg shapes from light blue felt. Prepare as many as appropriate for your children's level of math readiness. Then invite children to put the correct number of eggs in each nest.

✳ Counting Birds

Count the birds in a variety of pictures in the children's books you have been using. Emphasize words for colors as you count and compare the birds. For example, say, "I see two red cardinals and one brown sparrow. How many birds are there altogether?"

✳ Bag-of-Birds

Use the realistic bird picture on the topic card on page 167 as a stencil and cut out five or more bird shapes for each child. Put a given number of dots on one side and a matching numeral on the other side of each bird shape. Give each child a resealable bag in which to store the birds. Children can play numerous games with their sets.

1. Add a twig to the bag-of-birds. Give children simple problems for them to act out with their sets. For example, say, "There are two birds on the branch. One flies away. How many are left on the branch?"

2. Cut out birdhouses from construction paper. Add a given number of dots on one side and the matching numeral on the other side of each birdhouse. Hold up a birdhouse and ask the children to hold up the bird that matches the number of dots or the numeral on that birdhouse.

3. Children arrange the sets of birds in numerical order from least to greatest and from greatest to least.

✳ Bird Graph

Use the Graphing Grid (Activity Master 21, p. 298) to graph the number of birds of each color that the children have seen during a school week. Write in a color word and color the square at the bottom of a column when children report seeing a bird or birds of a particular color. As children report their sightings, use a matching crayon to color a square in the column above for each bird of that color. (When birds are multicolored, graph the bird based on its predominant color.) Each day, graph the data children provide. At the end of the week, count the number of colored squares in each column. Talk about which color was seen the most, the least, or not at all. Also, discuss with the children where they saw each bird and what kind of bird they think it was.

✳ Four and Twenty Blackbirds

Recite the traditional rhyme "Sing a Song of Sixpence." Challenge older children to make a group of 4 and a group of 20, combine the groups, and count to determine how many birds there are all together.

✳ A Bird's Life Cycle

Have children put pictures of an egg, a baby bird, and an adult bird in the sequence that shows the life cycle of a bird. Use ordinals as you discuss the sequence. Ask, "In a bird's life, which comes first? Which comes second? Which comes third (or last)?"

✳ Size Them Up (or Down)

Enlarge the realistic bird picture on the topic card on page 167 to make bird stencils in several different sizes. Cut out one shape in each size from construction paper. You may wish to laminate the shapes so that they can be reused many times. Put a piece of temporary adhesive on the back of the shapes. Have the children take turns arranging the birds by placing them on a chalkboard or easel in order from smallest to largest or vice versa.

✳ Heavier and Lighter Eggs

Fill plastic eggs with different amounts of sand, pebbles, cornmeal, oatmeal, cotton balls, dried beans, rice, or feathers. Label two plastic foam food trays *Heavier* and *Lighter*. Glue a picture of something heavy and a picture of something light on the trays to provide a clue about the word label on each tray. Allow the children to take turns handling and classifying the eggs by placing each one on a tray. Provide a balance scale for children who want to weigh and compare the eggs in each category. During center or free time, invite children to repeat the activity individually.

✳ Triangles

Compare a bird's beak to the shape of a triangle and an egg to the shape of an oval. Have children search for naturally occurring examples of triangles and ovals in the room or school.

MOVEMENT

✳ Weaving a Nest

Use several very long pieces of string or yarn, each rolled into a small ball. Attach one end of each string to something in the room; for example, a table leg. Talk about how some birds weave nests from twigs, string, and other materials. Have children quietly weave each string all through the room — under, over, around, and through objects. When they finish weaving, the room should be covered with loosely woven yarn or string. Each child should then give the end of his or her string to another child who must then undo the weaving right up to the starting point. Have each child wind the string into a ball so that it can be reused.

Repeat the activity several times, varying it by suggesting different ways children should move as they weave or undo the weaving. Tiptoeing, crawling, hopping, and walking backward are some possible movements.

✳ Hatching

Children crouch down close to the floor. They pretend to be an egg in a nest. Keeping their arms at their sides, they move their noses like a bird's beak to peck several times at the imaginary shell, then slowly stretch out and hatch from the egg.

MUSIC

✳ The Golden Goose

Read the fairy tale "The Golden Goose," in which everyone who touches the goose becomes stuck to it. Play a recording of slow instrumental music. Have each child create a slow-motion dance in which the child moves like a bird in rhythm to the music. Tell children that when a child touches another child the two become stuck together at that spot and must continue slowly dancing together. Continue until everyone becomes attached to at least one other person. Stop the music and have children freeze in their positions. Quickly talk about the humorous human sculptures they have made. Name the parts of the children's bodies that are touching. Then start over from the beginning.

✳ Swans Go Swimming

(Tune: "Mulberry Bush")

Talk about the fact that birds can walk, fly, or swim. Encourage the children to name all the birds they can think of that move in each of these ways. Then substitute a type of bird suggested by the children for each verse of the song. As the children sing, have them act out each verse in pairs, trios, or quartets.

Swans go swimming two by two,
Two by two, two by two.
You swim with me,
I'll swim with you,
Two by two.
Chicks go walking three by three,
Three by three, three by three.
We'll walk in a line
As straight as can be,
Three by three.
Robins go flying four by four,
Four by four, four by four.
We'll fly to the south
As we've done before,
Four by four.

ROLE PLAY

✳ Feed the Chickens

Provide clothing and props, such as a basket and plastic eggs, for children to use as they pretend to be a farmer who is feeding the chickens. Demonstrate to the children how a farmer might lightly toss chicken feed on the ground for the chickens to eat. Demonstrate gathering eggs from imaginary nests and putting eggs in the basket. Then have children pretend to feed the chickens and gather eggs.

✳ Ornithologists

Set up an area where children can pretend to be scientists who study birds. Binoculars, books about birds, drawing paper, and small note pads will stimulate the children's imaginations.

SCIENCE

✳ Migration

Review some of the books from the Life in Winter unit that provide information on bird migration. Discuss why birds migrate and north-south migration patterns in the United States.

✳ Hatching Eggs

Most children have never seen eggs hatching. Read a children's book that tells about hatching chickens or ducks. Get fertile eggs from a farmer or hatchery. Use a commercial incubator, build your own incubator, or rent one from a hatchery.

Chicken eggs take approximately 21 days to hatch. Make a paper chain of 21 paper eggs glued together. Number the eggs so that the first egg is number 20 and the last egg is 1. Glue a baby chick at the end of the chain. Each day, have the children tear off one egg to help them anticipate when the chicks will hatch.

Discuss care of the eggs, including maintaining a constant temperature in the incubator and turning the eggs. Keep an observation chart near the eggs and add children's comments as they observe changes in the eggs. When the chicks have hatched, keep them in the room for a day or two. Allow children to handle them gently, when supervision is available.

Make arrangements with a local farmer to raise the chickens. If possible, include a field trip to the farm to deliver the baby chickens as a class. The children will enjoy seeing their baby chicks' new home and knowing they will be well cared for.

✳ Feathers

1. Help children understand how feathers help birds fly. Provide feathers with a stiff shaft. Pull a feather downward and have children examine it with a magnifying glass. "Zip" the feather back together by smoothing the shaft upward with your finger. Explain that this simulates the preening action of birds. Tell children that birds must preen their feathers to keep them zipped in order to eliminate holes that air can pass through, since holes make it difficult for them to fly.
2. Help the children understand how feathers protect birds. Provide feathers and an eyedropper of water. Have the children drop water on the feathers and notice what the water drops do when they hit the feathers. Talk about how birds are protected by the way the water drops form beads. Ask the children to observe real birds to learn how a bird holds its tail and wing feathers when it is raining hard.

✳ Bird Watchers

Provide binoculars and a class science journal in which children may make notes of what they observe. Throw some birdseed in an area where children can observe birds from a safe distance without startling them. Ask the children to try to answer the following questions.

1. How do birds take off when they start to fly? Can you hear takeoff sounds?
2. How do birds eat seed?
3. How are a bird's feet shaped?
4. Is the bird alone or in a group?
5. Does the bird walk or hop on the ground?

✳ Bird Nests

Provide an abandoned bird's nest that has been sprayed with a safe insecticide before the children handle it. Examine the nest with the children. List all the materials the bird used to make the nest. Allow the children to take the nest apart and then try to put it back together again. Discuss how difficult it is for a bird to build a nest. Ask, "Do you think the bird can do it quickly or does it take the bird a long time? How does the bird make all the materials stay together"? Have children carefully wash their hands when they have finished handling the nest.

TRANSITION ACTIVITY
✳ Light as a Feather

1. Ask children if they have ever heard the expression "light as a feather." Demonstrate how to blow on a feather to keep it aloft. Give each child a feather to blow on and keep up in the air. Emphasize having fun rather than competing to see who can keep a feather aloft for the longest amount of time. When a feather falls, have the child simply pick it up and continue.
2. Tell the children to try moving while they keep their feathers aloft by blowing on them. Or have children walk along a taped line or from one designated place to another while blowing on their feathers.

CHILDREN'S BOOKS

Bang, M. *Goose.* New York: Blue Sky Press, 1996. Goose feels different from his family of woodchucks until he finds his wings.

Cannon, J. *Stellaluna.* New York: Harcourt Brace, 1993. A baby bat accidentally lands in the nest of baby birds and begins a lesson in differences and friendship.

Duvoisin, R. *Petunia.* New York: Trumpet, 1950. Petunia the goose thinks she is wise because she holds a book under her wing.

Eastman, P. D. *The Best Nest.* New York: Random House, 1968. A great story illustrating that the grass is not always greener on the other side. Good for prediction skills.

Heller, R. *Chickens Aren't the Only Ones.* New York: Grosset & Dunlap, 1981. An appealing book that incorporates science, language arts, and art as it discusses all the animals that lay eggs. Good rhyme.

Kalman, B. *Birds That Don't Fly.* New York: Crabtree Publishers, 1997. Wonderful photographs. Flightless birds, their habitat and behavior. Helps children understand why some birds can't fly.

Martin, Jr., B. *Brown Bear, Brown Bear, What Do You See?* New York: Holt, 1983. Very predictable pattern book that children "read" after just one read-aloud exposure. Provides a good pattern for rewriting the story.

Neitzel, S. *The House I'll Build for the Wrens.* New York: Greenwillow, 1997. A cumulative rhyme, with a rebus, about building a house for wrens. Starts with a boy and his plans and ends with a proud mom looking at her son and his unique creation.

Pallotta, J. *The Bird Alphabet Book.* Watertown, MA: Charlesbridge, 1990. Birds from *a* to *z,* some familiar and some not. Plenty of factual information and great illustrations.

Parsons, A. *Amazing Birds.* New York: Alfred A. Knopf, 1990. Wonderful photographs and factual information. Great for browsing.

Ross, T. *Eggbert the Slightly Cracked Egg.* New York: Putnam's Sons, 1994. Eggbert has many adventures trying to fit in and be accepted.

Seuss, Dr. *Horton Hatches the Egg.* New York: Random House, 1940. The classic tale of Horton the elephant who replaces lazy Mayzie on her nest and finally hatches an elephant bird. Addictive rhyme and repeating lines.

Sill, J. *About Birds: A Guide for Children.* Atlanta: Peachtree Publishers, 1997. Reference for the child who wants more in-depth information.

Simmons, J. *Daisy and the Egg.* Boston: Little, Brown, 1998. Daisy the duck waits for the arrival of her new brother or sister. She helps by sitting on the egg and it hatches. Lovely imaginative art and color.

Tryon, L. *Albert's Alphabet.* New York: Aladdin, 1994. Albert the duck creates the alphabet in a clever way. Good problem-solving opportunities.

April
Curriculum

Spring and Growing Things
Insects and Spiders

Spring and Growing Things

CONCEPTS

- Spring is the season that comes after winter and before summer.
- Plants begin to grow in spring. The grass turns green; leaves grow on trees and bushes; and some flowers bloom.
- Some people grow fresh fruits and vegetables to eat by planting seeds in their gardens.
- The weather in the spring is warmer, and it rains more in some areas.
- Days become longer and nights become shorter.

CONTINUING CONCEPTS

- **Colors** Help children identify spring colors and talk about why those colors are associated with spring.
  Have children count and graph the colors of flowers they see around school and near their homes.
- **Geometric Shapes** Review circles, triangles, and rectangles. Prepare a large rectangular container and a large circular container with soil for planting. Consider planting rows of seeds to form a triangle and rectangle when they sprout.
  Have children compare an oval and a circle.
- **Health and Nutrition** Discuss the importance of eating fruits and vegetables.
  Graph children's favorite fruits and vegetables.
- **Senses** Talk about the way some things feel in spring, including a new leaf that is opening, a fully developed leaf, a blade of grass, pussy willows, and flower stems and petals.
  Discuss the taste of fresh spring fruits and vegetables, like strawberries and snap peas.
  Talk about the way things smell in spring, including freshly cut grass, soil that is moist and ready for planting, and different kinds of flowers.
  Listen to the sound of a spring shower.
- **Traditional Rhymes and Tales** Recite "Mary, Mary Quite Contrary" with the children and tell them the story of "Jack and the Beanstalk."

PORTFOLIO PRODUCTS

Consider the following suggestion as you select or have the children select at least one product from this unit to place in each portfolio.
- Children use the word *spring* that is displayed on the word wall, write about spring, and illustrate what they like about the season. This product celebrates the child's creative art, emergent literacy, and fine-motor skills.

ART

✳ Easel or Tabletop Painting: Spring Colors

Materials: tempera paints in white, red, blue, and yellow; plastic foam food trays; paper; brushes and sponges

Demonstrate how to mix white with the other colors to produce pastel shades. Then have children mix a pastel color in each corner of a food tray. Encourage children to freely explore as they mix colors and paint with them. Name each color and discuss where children might see it. Then have the children paint large flower shapes in spring colors using a brush or sponge.

✳ Monet's Impressionism

Materials: watercolors; tempera paints; brushes; brushes of various sizes

After reading *Linnea in Monet's Garden* by Christina Bjork, show the children other paintings by Monet of his flowers and garden. Explain that Monet painted the way he did because he wanted to share his impressions and feelings about his garden. Invite children to paint their impressions of a garden by using brushes of different sizes, tempera paints in pastel colors, and watercolors. Display their paintings with the caption *Impression Paintings*.

✳ Spring Butterflies

Materials: coffee filters; small, clean sponges; food coloring; eyedroppers; butterfly pattern from the topic card on p. 197

Enlarge the butterfly pattern on the topic card on page 197 and use the enlargements to make three or four stencils of butterflies in different sizes. Use the stencils to cut many different-sized butterflies from the coffee filter paper, or have the children help you cut them out. Then have each child use a sponge to dampen a butterfly and fold it in half. The children drop different colors of food coloring on the folded wings until the wings are covered with color. Ask children to unfold the butterflies, and put them aside to dry. Give the dried butterflies to the children and talk about how the technique resulted in each wing having the same pattern of colors.

✳ Sniff Art

1. Fragrance Garden

Materials: cupcake baking cups or nut cups; construction paper; glue; cotton balls; powdered tempera paints; plastic sandwich bags; nearly empty bottles of perfume; eyedroppers

Children glue cupcake baking cups or small nut cups on a piece of construction paper to represent the blossoms of flowers and then add construction-paper stems and leaves to each cup. They then color cotton balls by putting each one into a sandwich bag with a teaspoon of powdered tempera and shaking the bag gently. They glue each colored cotton ball in the center of a cupcake or nut cup and gently pull the cotton apart to fluff it slightly. Finally, they use an eyedropper to add a drop of perfume to each ball.

2. Lemon and Orange Groves

Materials: real twigs; tissue paper; construction paper; cotton balls; powdered tempera paints in yellow and orange; plastic sandwich bags; lemon and orange extract

Show children pictures of groves of lemon and orange trees. Provide a lemon and an orange and have the children compare them.

Have each child glue a twig to a piece of construction paper and then glue on several smaller twigs as if they are branching off the first twig. The children add tissue-paper leaves or blossoms to their tree, color cotton balls yellow for a lemon tree or orange for an orange tree, and glue several cotton balls on their tree. Finally, have them use an eyedropper to add a drop of lemon or orange extract to each cotton ball.

You could do either of these art activities as a group project by putting a large piece of butcher paper on the wall. Children can paint a sky, a sun, the ground, a pond, and houses. Then they can "plant" a scented grove of lemon or orange trees and a flower garden.

✳ Nature Collage

Take the class on a spring walk to observe signs of spring (see p. 208). Provide glue and construction paper and have each child make a collage of the items collected on the walk.

✳ Spring Vegetable Prints

Materials: plastic foam food trays; tempera paint; vegetables; Manila paper

Green peppers, onions, radishes, carrots, potatoes, celery, and squash make interesting shapes and prints. Cut the vegetables into slices or pieces that are easy to handle. Let them dry for a while or pat the cut ends of each vegetable so that the paint adheres better.

Put small amounts of paint on each tray. The children gently dip each vegetable slice into the paint and press it on paper again and again until it no longer prints. Encourage them to use a variety of vegetables and colors. Name each vegetable and color as the children work.

✳ Cereal Blooms

Materials: puffed wheat or circle-shaped cereal; glue; construction paper in pastel colors; construction paper scraps

Children make construction-paper stems and leaves and glue them on pastel sheets of paper. They then glue clusters of puffed wheat or circle-shaped cereal on the stems to make blossoms. Show children how to fringe strips of paper to look like grass. After children have finished making their flowers, have them glue the fringed strips along the bottom edge of their paper. Leave the fringe sticking out to create a three-dimensional effect.

☀ Leaf Prints

Materials: several sizes and types of leaves; Manila paper; thickened tempera paints in several shades of green; soap flakes or wheat paste; brushes

Add the soap flakes or wheat paste to the tempera paints to thicken them. Cover a work area with newspaper. Children paint the back of a leaf with tempera paint. Then they keep pressing the leaf on the paper until it no longer prints. Encourage the children to use different shades of green and leaves of different types and sizes for a more interesting effect. Discuss the different shades of green. Ask, "What can you do to make the paint lighter in color?"

☀ Kites

Materials: kite pattern (Activity Master 22, p. 299); crayons or markers; hole punch; 4-inch pieces of drinking straws; string or thread; long, narrow strips of paper

Read "The Kite" from *Days with Frog and Toad* by Arnold Lobel to the class. Discuss the problems the characters have flying a kite and the way they cope with the problems. Explain that it is windy in many areas in the spring, so people like to fly kites during this season.

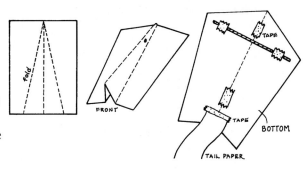

Show the children a completed kite made from the kite pattern. Point out the different parts of the kite. Inform them that this kite flies well and that everyone can make and fly a kite. Then, put the example out of sight so that the children do not think their kites need to look exactly like yours.

1. Duplicate Activity Master 22 to make one kite pattern for each child. Cut out the rectangular patterns. Have the children use crayons or markers to decorate the front of the pattern.
2. Demonstrate how to fold the kite pattern along the dashed line in the middle and punch a small hole as shown.
3. With the front of the kite faceup, fold the kite along the other two dashed lines so that the two sides are turned up. Turn the kite over. Tape the fold lines together to form a center seam. Tape a piece of a drinking straw on the back for support, as shown in the illustration.
4. Cut 2" × 18" strips of paper to make tails for the kites. (Adding machine tape makes a perfect tail. Ask storeowners or bookkeepers you know for donations or buy a roll of tape at an office-supply store.) Have children decorate the kite tail with crayons or markers. Tape the tail to the back as shown.
5. Tie a long string on the front of the kite by threading it through the punched hole. Tie a piece of a straw to the other end of the string to make it easier for the children to hold and wind up the string.

Children are usually excited by how easily they can make this kite fly!

☀ Ceramic Flowers

Materials: ceramic dough (see Appendix II, p. 273); small containers of water; baking rack or piece of screen; tempera paints; brushes

Give each child an equal amount of the dough. Show children how to roll thin stems and press small balls with their thumb or fist to make petals and leaves. Allow ample time for the children to explore using the dough. Then have each child make one or more flowers to keep. Suggest that they vary the size and shape of the petals. Model how to smooth dough pieces with a finger dipped in water.

Scratch the child's initials on the back of each flower. Dry the flowers on a rack or a screen to dry the underside. They dry in about 36 hours at room temperature. When the flowers are dry, have the children paint them with tempera paint.

BLOCKS

Fences – Add measurement tools such as a ruler and yardstick to the block area. Suggest that children build fences to surround a spring garden. Provide a ruler and a yardstick and assist in measuring the structures. Some children may not understand that the fence is, for example, 14 inches tall, but they can understand that it is taller than the ruler but not as tall as the yardstick. Encourage children to take turns measuring the structures.

Construction – Add plastic tools and a toolbox to the block area. Explain that many construction projects are started in the spring. Ask children why they think that is so.

Half and Whole – Demonstrate how two blocks of a certain size, laid end-to-end on top of a longer block, are the same length as the long block. Review the concepts of half and whole. Ask children to take turns selecting blocks to demonstrate half and whole.

BULLETIN BOARD

✳ Winter and Spring

Divide a bulletin board in half. Cover the left side of the board with dark-blue paper and the right side with light-blue. On the dark-blue side, prepare a twisted paper tree trunk from brown wrapping paper or brown grocery bags. Prepare a similar tree on the light-blue side, but add green leaves to it. Label the left side *Winter* and the right side *Spring.* Provide cutout pictures of winter and spring weather, clothes, and activities. Have the children take turns classifying the pictures by using

pushpins or temporary adhesive to attach each picture to the appropriate side of the board.

Talk about why one tree is bare and the other has leaves. Discuss the differences in the weather typical of each season. Talk about the different activities families do in each season. Identify some activities families do in both seasons. Invite children to draw additional pictures of winter or spring things to place on the board.

COOKING

✳ Yogurt Fruit Dip

One 8-ounce fruit yogurt
(Blueberry and peach work well.)

Round toothpicks
Plastic knives

2 bananas
2 apples
2 oranges

Small paper plates

Wash hands. Give each child a portion of each fruit to slice. Provide paper plates and let children measure one tablespoon of the yogurt onto their plates. Talk about how many pieces of fruit there are for each person. Pass the fruit and have each child take his or her share. Then have children spear the fruit slices with a toothpick and dip the fruit in the yogurt before eating.

❊ Vegetable Dip

Fresh vegetables
Plastic knives

Low-fat vegetable dip
Toothpicks

Wash hands. Provide fresh vegetables. Work together to wash the vegetables and cut them into pieces for dipping and snacking. Adults should cut the carrots, as they may be too hard for children to cut safely and comfortably.

Identify the vegetables and talk about their colors and shapes. Discuss which grew above the ground and which grew underground. Show children how to use a toothpick to pick up a piece of vegetable and dip it in the vegetable dip. Encourage children to taste different vegetables and talk about their taste and texture.

LANGUAGE ARTS

❊ Fingerplay – Plant a Seed

Plant a seed in the ground,
   (Plant a pretend seed in palm of one hand. Close fist.)
Water and sunshine all around.
   (Use other hand as a watering can and sprinkle water on seed.)
Little seed, in the ground so still,
Will you grow? Yes I will!
   (Slowly push index finger of one hand up through closed fist of the other hand.)

❊ Word Wall

Add the word *spring* to the word wall. Brainstorm and make a list of a few rhyming words for spring. To make the list visually appealing, write the words in a spring color on pastel paper. Add other topic-related words that children suggest. Add and review the high-frequency words you want children to use. Count how many words are on the word wall. Write a sentence strip that says *We have (the number) words on our word wall.* and display the strip. Place a piece of colored plastic, in a spring color if possible, over one or more of the word cards to highlight words you particularly want children to use in their writing.

❊ Spring Vocabulary

1. Use these topic-related words as naturally and frequently as possible: plant; soil or dirt; water; sun, sunlight, or sunshine; leaves; roots; primary root (the first root growth);

secondary roots (formed when the primary root begins to branch); sprout; and stem. Help children understand how these words relate to growing plants. Explain that secondary roots are formed when the primary root begins to branch and that a cutting in water needs secondary roots before it should be planted in dirt.

2. Recite "Mary, Mary Quite Contrary." Discuss the word *contrary*. Challenge the children to find contrary characters in books and stories you have read together. Read "Jack and the Beanstalk." Ask the children if they think Jack or the giant was contrary.

✳ Spring Begins With S (A Whole-Class Project)

On a large piece of yellow butcher paper, draw a large S. Write *Spring Begins With S* at the top of the paper. Have children cut pictures out of magazines and draw pictures of things that begin with *s*. Discuss each picture and let children glue each on the paper. Print a word that describes each picture beside it. You may wish to have children continue the activity at center and free time until the paper is filled with pictures.

✳ Feel Spring

Talk about the way some things feel in spring, such as a new leaf that is opening, a fully developed leaf, a blade of grass, pussy willows, a flower stem, and petals.

Provide a feely box (see Appendix I, p. 270). Out of sight of the children, put a spring-related object inside the box. Children put their hand gently inside the feely box and try to identify the object. Ask children to describe how it feels. Model descriptive words they could use.

✳ Smells of Spring

Talk about the way some things smell in spring; for example, freshly cut grass, moist soil, and two or three different kinds of flowers. Blindfold each child in turn (or ask the child to close his or her eyes) as you hold an object you've talked about and have the child smell and identify it.

✳ Jack's Beanstalk Display

Materials: green construction or butcher paper; crayons; markers; collage items

Retell or read "Jack and the Beanstalk." Review how the beanstalk grew from the beans thrown on the ground. Plant beans that have been soaked in water overnight. Plant them in a clear plastic container so that children can see the roots form (see Visible Roots, pp. 209–210).

Use pieces of green construction-paper pieces or twisted green butcher paper to make a large beanstalk that goes up one wall. (It is particularly fun if the stalk grows up to the ceiling.) Put a large paper leaf on the stalk for each child and print a child's name on the bottom edge of each leaf. To add a delightful element to the display, pin jeans pant legs with shoes attached to the ceiling, at the top of the beanstalk, to make it look as if the giant is climbing down.

Have children make pictures or write stories to display on their leaves. Change the leaves frequently as children create new products.

✳ Spring Storms

Many children fear storms. Read aloud Patricia Polacco's *Thunder Cake* and discuss how children feel about storms. Make a list together that compares the good things and the bad or scary things about storms. Invite the children to stand and act out one of the good things and then one of the scary or bad things about storms. Some children may be interested in making a thunder cake like the one in the story.

✳ I Spy a Spring Thing

Whether the class is outside or inside, have the children take turns finding and naming a sign of spring by saying each time, "I spy a spring thing. It's a _____." Examples of signs of spring include a new leaf, someone wearing a jacket instead of a coat, warmer sun, flowers, more insects or spiders, and greener grass.

✳ Spring Stories

Discuss the signs of spring observed as children played I Spy a Spring Thing. Talk about the items collected on the nature walk (see p. 208). Ask children to write a report or story about their spring walk. To help them organize their writing, discuss what they did first, second, and third on the spring walk. As children finish their stories, staple them to the nature collages they made in art (see p. 200).

✳ Look, Listen, and Say Boxes

Materials: two shoe boxes and lids, decorated if you wish; spring items

Use a marker to divide the inside of each lid into two equal sections. Number each section 1 or 2. Put three of the same spring objects into each box.

Have two children sit back-to-back. Give each child a Look, Listen, and Say Box and numbered lid. The children take turns putting one object in one section of the lid, describing that object without naming it, and telling the other child in which section of the lid to place the object. For example, for a blade of grass, a child might say, "Get the skinny green thing and put it in number 2." The second child figures out which object was described and puts it in the appropriate place. That child then describes objects for the first child to place.

After each child has had a turn, each numbered section should have an object in it and one object should be left in the box. The children then turn around to see if the Look, Listen, and Say Box lids match. Change the objects before a new pair of children begins to play the game.

After all the children are familiar with the activity, give a box and lid to each child. Have the entire class work in pairs to play Look, Listen, and Say at the same time.

Have older children play Look, Listen, and Say with a lid divided into four numbered sections and five spring objects in each box.

✳ Clothesline Classification

String a clothesline across a low-traffic area of the classroom. Have children cut out pictures of spring clothes from catalogs to hang on the line with pinch-type clothespins.

1. Discuss what is first, second, third, and last on the line.
2. Put all the cutout clothes in a pile or small basket. Have the children classify the clothing by type or by color. For example, say, "Hang up all the clothes with pink in them," or "Hang up all the clothes with zippers."

MATH

✳ Counting

1. Count leaves growing on classroom plants.
2. Count the natural objects found on the spring walk (see p. 208).
3. Ask parents to donate unneeded buttons. Count the buttons each child brings.
4. On a large plastic foam food tray, make four, six, or eight sections with a black marker. Print a numeral in each section. Supervise children as they push the appropriate number of pushpins into each section. Some children may also be able to count the total number of pushpins that were used.

✳ Classification

1. Classify buttons according to the number of holes, color, size, and the materials they are made from.
2. Save seeds from apples and oranges. Also use beans, acorns, and sunflower seeds. Put a mixture of these seeds into a small plastic bowl with a lid. Have the children sort the seeds by type into the sections of a four-egg or six-egg egg carton.

Challenge children with more advanced math skills to count the number of seeds of each kind and determine the total number of seeds.

✳ Number Bingo

Divide large index cards into fourths. Print one numeral, from 1 through 6, in each section. Make each card different. Use the number cube pattern (Activity Master 23, p. 300) to make a number cube. Cut out the pattern. Print a different numeral, from 1 through 6, on each side of the cube and fold and tape the cube together. Use small paper circles or buttons as game markers. Show children how to roll the number cube. Explain that if any player's card has the numeral showing on the top of the cube, he or she places a marker on the numeral on the card. Play the game until all players fill their cards. Have the children trade cards if they want to play again.

✳ Number Cube Numerals

Make several number cubes using the number cube pattern (Activity Master 23, p. 300). Write numerals appropriate to the children's readiness level on each number cube. Have the children take turns rolling the cube and naming the numeral on the top. You could also have children form a group of objects; for example, counters or pennies, to show the number on the top of the cube.

✳ Flower-pot Math

Purchase five or more small, plastic flower pots from a discount store or plant nursery. Glue small circles or dots on each pot to show each number from 1 through 5. Make flowers by using straws for stems and stapling on simple construction-paper petals and leaves. Have the children "plant" the flowers by putting the appropriate number in each pot.

You can extend the activity by using numbers greater than 5. You could also print numerals on the pots instead of dots.

☀ Graphs

1. Graph children's favorite fruits or vegetables. Have each child draw a small picture of her or his favorite fruit or vegetable. Assemble the graph by posting the children's pictures on a wall in columns according to the kind of fruit or vegetable. Discuss the results by counting each column and using the terms *more than* and *less than*.

2. Graph the number and colors of flowers children view in the area by having each child draw a small picture and using the pictures to make a graph like the fruits or vegetables graph described above.

☀ Circles, Rectangles, and Triangles

Count the number of each geometric shape the children can find in the room. Compare the totals. Use the terms *more than* and *less than* as you discuss the results.

☀ Ovals and Circles

Talk about how ovals and circles are similar and different. Have children search for naturally occurring examples of ovals and circles in the classroom.

MOVEMENT

☀ Beanbag Walk

Give each child a beanbag to balance on his or her head, shoulder, or outstretched arm while walking carefully around the room. Play soft or slow-paced music in the background.

☀ Beanbag Relay

Divide children into two or three groups. Have them line up, all facing in the same direction. The first child starts by passing the beanbag between his or her legs to the second child. That child passes the beanbag to the third child in the same manner. Continue to the end of the line. You can vary the activity by having the children do the following.

1. Pass the beanbag over their heads
2. Alternate between passing the beanbag between their legs and over their heads
3. Turn around one time before passing the beanbag to the next child

MUSIC

☀ Old McDonald Had a Garden

(Tune: "Old McDonald Had a Farm")

Old McDonald had a garden, E-I, E-I, oh.
In his garden he wanted to plant, E-I, E-I, oh.
With a plant-a-seed here and plant a-seed there,
    (Make bending and planting motion.)

Here a seed there a seed, everywhere a garden seed.
    (Point here and there.)
Old McDonald had a garden, E-I, E-I, oh.

Other verses:

1. *In his garden he had to water, E-I, E-I, oh.*
    With a sprinkle, sprinkle here...
2. *In his garden he had to hoe, E-I, E-I, oh.*
    With a chop, chop here...
3. *In his garden he had to pick, E-I, E-I, oh.*
    With a pick-a-carrot here and a pick-a-carrot there...

ROLE PLAY

✳ Gardening

Children stick the ends of artificial flowers into plastic foam pieces so that each flower stands by itself. Then they arrange the flowers as if in a garden and pretend to weed and water them. A toy hoe and other gardening tools can be added to the role-play area. The tools may be plastic or cut from heavy cardboard. A short piece of rope makes an effective watering hose. A watering can might also be included if available. Talk about the rows of plants and the geometric shapes being used. Say, for example, "Your garden is a large rectangle."

Provide plastic flowerpots in a variety of sizes, a tub of sand, and scoops. Invite children to carefully fill the pots with sand. Discuss how sand in the bottom of a pot provides drainage for the roots of a plant.

✳ Spring Cleaning

Discuss why people do spring cleaning. Provide aprons, clean rags, a dust mop, a broom, and dustpan. Children pretend to clean the home-living center or the room. Have the children use small amounts of spray window cleaner or vinegar and water to clean a window or mirror.

SCIENCE

✳ Spring Walk

Read "The Corner" from A. Lobel's *Frog and Toad All Year.* Then take the class on a walk to observe and listen to spring things as Frog and Toad did. Point out growing things as you walk. Talk about new leaves, green grass, sprouts, and blossoms.

Have each child carry a small paper sack to collect interesting things that are appropriate to pick up, such as a small stone, blade of grass, fallen blossom, or fallen twig. Back in class, have children look at their treasures with a magnifying glass. Have them count the objects they collected. Explore how many ways the group can classify the spring objects. Use the items to make a nature collage (see p. 200).

✳ Hairy Harry

Materials: plastic foam cups; markers; potting soil; grass seed; water; box

Decorate a large plastic foam cup to look like a face. Name the figure Harry. Fill it with potting soil and sow grass seed on the surface. Water the seed gently. In just two to three days, sprouts will grow and form Harry's hair. In a week, the sprouts should be two to fives inches tall. Let the children feel the sprouts. Have them gently run their fingers through the "hairy" growth.

Discuss how plants need soil, water, and light to grow. Plant seed in another cup but do not water it. Label it *No Water*. Contrast its growth with the growth of the plant that is watered.

Plant a third cup that you water but keep covered with a box. Label it *No Sunlight*. Compare the growth to the other Hairy Harrys. Ask children to explain the results.

✳ Eggshell Garden

Materials: eggshell halves; potting soil; flower seeds; craft sticks

Fill eggshell halves with potting soil. Store them in the egg cups of an egg carton so that they stand up. Plant several seeds in each shell. Have children lightly water the seeds with a teaspoon of water. Stick a craft stick with a child's name on it in each shell so that children can keep track of how their plants are growing. Marigold seeds grow well with this method.

When seedlings have several leaves, transplant them outside by showing children how to dig a narrow hole and gently crush the eggshells as the plant is placed in the ground. Place the plants in an area where children can continue to view and care for them.

✳ Tadpoles

Read Steven Kellogg's *The Mysterious Tadpole*. Discuss how tadpoles grow. Bring tadpoles into the classroom. Take photographs of the tadpoles as they change. Display the photos on a chart and write the date next to each photo to establish a record of the process of development. Discuss how the tadpoles change. Return the young frogs to their original pond.

✳ Container Garden

Put stones in the bottom of one to four large, deep plastic containers or tubs. Mix soil, some sand, and a little fertilizer and pour the mixture over the stones. Plant carrots, radishes, or cherry tomatoes. Plant only one variety of vegetable or fruit in each container and mark the container with the name and a picture of the vegetable or fruit. Let the children care for the plants. Keep a class chart or journal in which you record with the children what is done to care for the plants each day and what changes are observed. Encourage children to draw pictures of the growth process to display near the plants. Use the fruits and vegetables that are grown for snacks or for cooking activities.

✳ Visible Roots

Method 1 – Line the inside of a clear plastic glass with a paper towel. Stuff in more paper toweling or a sponge to hold the paper towel against the inside of the glass. Wet the toweling. Gently place lima beans which have been soaked in water overnight between the toweling and the glass so that they are easy to see through the outside of the glass.

Keep the toweling moist. In a few days, the children will see roots growing. Watch for the first (primary) roots and the branching (secondary) roots. Ask children to discuss what they see.

Method 2 – Use easy-to-root houseplants such as pathos, spider plants, philodendron, ivy, and coleus. Put cuttings in plastic glasses of water. Let the children watch as the roots begin to grow. Talk about primary roots and secondary roots and why roots are important to plants. Then place the plants in soil and watch them continue to grow. Save the plants to use as Mother's Day surprises in May.

TRANSITION ACTIVITIES

✳ Cotton-Ball Stretch

Each child balances a large, cosmetic cotton puff on the head, a shoulder, or an outstretched arm while carefully stretching the body, as if he or she is growing from a seed to a plant. Repeat the task several times.

✳ Beanbag Toss

Provide a beanbag. Ask each child to name something that grows in spring as they catch the gently tossed beanbag from one to another.

CHILDREN'S BOOKS

Bjork, C. *Linnea in Monet's Garden.* New York: Farrar, Straus & Giroux, 1987. A little girl wants to visit Monet's garden. Beautifully illustrated.

Bunting, E. *Sunflower House.* San Diego: Harcourt Brace, 1996. The story of the life cycle of sunflowers and the imagination of the young boy who plants them.
Flower Garden. San Diego: Harcourt Brace Jovanovich, 1994. A girl and her father create a flower garden for her mother.

Ehlert, L. *Planting a Rainbow.* San Diego: Harcourt Brace, 1988. A mother and child plant a rainbow of flowers every year in the family garden.

Gibbons, G. *From Seeds to Plant.* New York: Holiday House, 1991. Simple text that describes the plant cycle from seeds to plant and back to seeds. Great science connections.

Hall, Z. *The Surprise Garden.* New York: Blue Sky Press, 1998. Children plant vegetable seeds, track the growth of the plants, and eat the vegetables.
The Apple Pie Tree. New York: Blue Sky Press, 1996. Two sisters take us through a year in the life of the apple tree in their yard. Apple pie recipe included.

Heller, R. *The Reason for a Flower.* New York: Scholastic, 1983. Intriguing illustrations and nonfiction information given in rhyme.

Kellogg, S. *The Mysterious Tadpole.* New York: Dial, 1977. A tadpole grows in a surprising way.

Lobel, A. *Days With Frog and Toad.* New York: HarperCollins, 1979. Frog and Toad explore the meaning of friendship.
Frog and Toad All Year. New York: HarperCollins, 1976. Frog and Toad share funny adventures throughout the seasons.

McMillan, B. *Growing Colors*. New York: Mulberry, 1994. Vegetables that look good enough to eat. The colors in a garden are beautifully captured by McMillan's camera.

Polacco, P. *Thunder Cake*. New York: Philomel, 1990. A grandmother helps her granddaughter overcome her fear of thunderstorms.

Ray, M. *Mud*. San Diego: Harcourt Brace, Inc., 1996. On a spring night, the earth unfreezes and mud results. What happens next?
Red Rubber Boot Day. San Diego: Harcourt Brace, Inc., 2000. Sequel to *Mud*. Shows what is bound to happen on a spring day when it rains!

Rockwell, A. *First Comes Spring*. New York: Crowell, 1985. Seasonal changes, activities, and clothing are shown through the life of a young bear.

Schnur, S. *Spring: An Alphabet Acrostic*. New York: Clarion, 1999. Acrostic rhymes for seasonal words for each letter of the alphabet. Unique illustrations.

Welton, J. *Monet*. Chicago: The Art Institute of Chicago, 1992. Numerous colored prints provide an introduction to the art of Monet.

Insects and Spiders

CONCEPTS

- Insects have a body divided into three parts (head, thorax, and abdomen), three pairs of legs, and, if winged, two pair of wings.
- Insects we often see include ants, bees, beetles, butterflies, crickets, dragonflies, flies, fireflies, grasshoppers, ladybugs, mosquitoes, moths, and wasps.
- Spiders are not insects; spiders have eight legs and no wings.
- Most spiders spin webs to catch insects for food.
- Insects make sounds with parts of their bodies; they do not have voices like humans.
- Many insects are helpful; some insects are harmful.
- Insects and spiders hatch from eggs.
- Metamorphosis is the process by which an insect changes in form from an egg to a larvae to a pupa and finally to an adult.
- A cocoon is a silky covering that surrounds a pupa; a chrysalis is a hard-shelled covering that surrounds a pupa.
- Some insects and spiders live outside on the ground, under the ground, or around leaves and trees; some live inside.
- Some insects fly.

CONTINUING CONCEPTS

- **Colors** Have children use pictures and photographs to identify the full range of colors that insects display.
  Graph which colors occur most frequently in the insects recognized by the children.
- **Geometric Shapes** Review circle, square, rectangle, triangle, and oval.
  Identify parts of insects that have geometric shapes.
- **Health and Nutrition** Discuss the importance of not handling spiders.
- **Senses** Have children feel a sticky note and relate that to a spider's web.
  Have children look at *The Butterfly Alphabet* by Kjell Sandved and search the photographs to find each letter of the alphabet.
  Observe an ant colony.
  Observe the stages of the life cycle of silkworms.
  Have children use their bodies to feel and hear rhythmic sounds.
- **Traditional Rhymes and Tales** Recite "Little Miss Muffet" and "Itsy Bitsy Spider."

PORTFOLIO PRODUCTS

Select or have the children select at least one product from this unit to place in each portfolio. One suggestion follows.

- Have each child record another entry on his or her audiotape. You can use the tape to assess oral-language development, fluency, and mastery of certain concepts. Be sure to state the child's name and the date at the beginning of the tape entry.

To evaluate the child's ability to tell a story, tape record the child retelling one of the stories read aloud to the class. To evaluate the child's understanding of number concepts, record the child telling an original math story problem about a hungry caterpillar eating two different numbers of food items.

ART

✳ Easel or Tabletop Painting

Materials: tempera paints in black and in vivid colors; paper; brushes

Read G. McDermott's *Anansi the Spider*. Post some of the brightly-colored illustrations to inspire children. Provide similar colors and encourage children to paint insects using them.

✳ Tissue-Paper Collages

Materials: tissue paper in a variety of colors; scissors; crayons or markers

Eric Carle is known for his collage technique. Share and discuss several of the illustrations in his books, such as *The Very Busy Spider* and *The Very Hungry Caterpillar*. Study pictures of insects and talk about which parts of insects are shaped like geometric figures. Provide tissue paper for the children to cut or tear into insect shapes. Have them glue the tissue on construction paper and add details with paint or markers. Invite the children to overlap the tissue paper and discuss the color effects.

✳ Insects in the Grass

Materials: watercolors; brushes; green tissue paper in two or three shades of green; glue

After reading Denise Fleming's *In the Tall, Tall Grass,* have children paint scenes of insects and flowers. When the scenes are dry, have them cut strips of green tissue paper to glue across the bottom of the paper as tall grass. Encourage them to glue the grass on top of some insects as if they are partially hidden in the grass. Some children may be inspired by Fleming's art to try to develop their picture from the perspective of an insect in the grass.

✳ Rubber Band Spiders

Materials: black construction paper; rubber bands; crayons; $\frac{1}{4}$-inch elastic (found in fabric stores); glue

Talk about the shapes of spiders' bodies. Provide black construction paper for children to cut out one larger and one smaller circle to glue together to form a spider's body. Compare the sizes, using the terms *larger* and *smaller*. Study the patterns of colors found on spiders. Have children use crayons to add eyes and patterned designs to the cutout. Then have them cut rubber bands in half and glue or tape four rubber band pieces on each side of the spider's body to make wiggly legs. Recite "Little Miss Muffet" together as the children dangle their spiders. Suspend the spiders from the doorway and shelves with a length of elastic.

✳ Bees in Flight

Materials: finger paint (see Appendix II, p. 274); finger paint paper; recording of "Flight of the Bumblebee" by Rimsky-Korsakov

After the children have listened to "Flight of the Bumblebee" and moved like bees (see p. 222), let them finger paint while listening to the music playing softly. Talk about how bees often fly in swarms. Suggest they pretend their fingertips are bees flying around the paper.

✳ Cocoon (A Group Project)

Materials: long balloon; string; glue on a paper plate or plastic foam food tray

Blow up a long, cocoon-shaped balloon. Provide a ball of string. Talk about how silkworms spin cocoons in one continuous strand. Let children help dip sections of the string in glue. As you hold the balloon, have children wrap the string around and around the balloon until it is completely covered. Set the balloon aside to dry. Later, have children watch as you break the balloon and carefully pull out the pieces. Explain that what remains is the cocoon. Use the cocoon later as you talk about the stages in the life cycle of silkworms.

✳ Ladybug-on-a-Door (A Group Project)

Materials: butcher paper cut into a large oval and a smaller circle; tempera paints; construction paper; large black pipe cleaners; glue or tape

Show colored pictures of ladybugs. Ask if children have seen or handled ladybugs. Explain that most ladybugs are helpful in a garden because they eat harmful insects. Make the point that the children are like ladybugs because they also want to be helpful.

Have the children work together to create a large ladybug door decoration. Identify the oval and circle shapes. Have children take turns painting the large oval red and the smaller circle black. When the shapes are dry, tape or glue the black circle to the oval to form the head and body of the ladybug. Have children dip thumbs in black paint and paint thumb print dots all over the oval to make the ladybug's spots. Write children's names in small white letters beside their thumbprint spots. Use pipe cleaners to make antennae and legs. Place the completed ladybug on the door with the caption *We are helpful like ladybugs!*

✳ Bug-Dough Sculptures

Materials: ceramic dough (see Appendix II, p. 273); wire rack; tempera paints; cotton swabs

Give a golfball-sized portion of the dough to each child. Have children roll some dough into spheres and some into egg shapes. Identify and compare the shapes. Have the children mold the dough into insects and spiders. As the children work, talk about the different sizes and shapes of insects and spiders. Talk about how many legs a spider has compared with an insect. Talk about how some insects have wings and some do not. Model rolling out thin strips to make legs for insects and spiders. Model rolling small spheres for eyes or spots. Put the children's creations on a wire rack to air dry. When the insects and spiders are dry, have the children paint them. Suggest they use cotton swabs to paint details, like stripes and spots.

✳ Ant Trails

Materials: shallow boxes or lids; brown construction paper; white tempera paint; marbles; spoons

Talk with the children about the trails real ants make as you observe an ant farm in the classroom. Cut the paper to fit the bottom of each box. Put paint in small bowls and a marble in each bowl. Children use a spoon to remove each marble and place it in the box. They gently tip the box first one way, then the other, so that the marble rolls over the paper. Dip the marble back in the paint and repeat the process several times to make designs like ant trails underground.

✳ Feet Butterflies

Materials: construction paper; tissue-paper scraps or wallpaper scraps; glue; markers or crayons

Look at photographs and pictures of butterflies and discuss the symmetry of the wings and how they attach to the thorax of the insect. Help the children trace around their feet and cut them out. The children then glue tissue-paper or wallpaper scraps on the feet. Children cut out a butterfly body shape to glue between the feet, as shown. Children then add antennae to complete their multicolor feet butterflies.

You may wish to have children use a hole punch to make small holes all over their feet cutouts and then cover the holes with tissue-paper or wallpaper scraps. Using a hole punch helps to strengthen small hand muscles.

BLOCKS

✳ Insects

Add building kits with small parts, such as Tinkertoys®, to the block area and encourage the children to create insects. Ask them to explain which insect characteristics their insect exhibits. Encourage them to use blocks to make an environment in which insects might work and live. Invite them to construct tunnels for an ant colony.

BULLETIN BOARD

✳ Insects and Spiders

Connect the diagonal edges of the bulletin board and create a spider web in the center by stapling black yarn in place. Attach spiders and insects made by the children. Ensure that each creation has appropriate insect or spider attributes. Add the caption *Insects and Spiders* at the bottom of the board. Ask, "How do you know which are insects and which are spiders"?

During circle time, count the spiders and insects. Determine how many there are altogether. Let children use a pointer to find the spider or insect they made. Ask them to tell the group one attribute of real insects or spiders that their insect or spider also has.

Later, remove all of the insects and spiders and put them in a basket beside the board. Children take turns selecting one, telling if it is an insect or a spider, and then use a pushpin or temporary adhesive to place it on the board so that all of the spiders are on the web and all the insects are outside the web.

COOKING

✳ Ants on a Log

Celery	*Raisins*
Peanut butter	*Plastic serrated knives*

Wash hands. Show a whole celery and have the children help clean it. Have each child cut a stalk of celery with a plastic knife. Dry the celery with a paper towel. Then have children spread peanut butter in the celery sticks and add three or four raisins on top of the peanut butter. Talk about the different textures and flavors in the ants on a log treat.

✳ Butterfly Pretzels

Soft, low-fat cream cheese	*Plastic knives*
Pretzel bows and pretzel sticks	*Squares of wax paper*
Raisins	

Wash hands. Have each child spread a teaspoon of cream cheese in the shape of a butterfly's body on a square of wax paper. Then have them lay a stick pretzel for the body of the butterfly and a bow pretzel on each side of the body for a wing. Add raisin eyes if desired.

Suggest that the children eat the butterfly pretzels by dipping the pretzels in the cream cheese before taking each bite. As they eat the snack, talk with the children about the parts that aren't on their butterfly pretzels but would be on real butterflies, such as legs and antennae.

LANGUAGE ARTS

✳ Fingerplay – Ladybug

Ladybug so gentle,
    (Make circle with thumb and finger.)
Ladybug so light,
    (Move palm up and down slowly.)
Spread your tiny wings,
    (Wiggle spread fingers.)
And lift off in flight.
    (Raise hand up gently.)

✳ Fingerplay – Itsy Bitsy Spider

Have children perform this well-known fingerplay.

✳ Word Wall

Add the words *insect* and *spider* to the word wall. Add other topic-related words that children suggest. Add and emphasize the high-frequency words you want children to use. Count how many words are on the word wall. Write a sentence strip that says *We have (the number) words on our word wall* and display it. Place a piece of colored plastic, in a spring color if possible, over one or more of the word cards to highlight words you particularly want children to incorporate in their writing.

✳ Insect Begins With the Word In

On a piece of brown butcher paper, draw a large insect with attributes typical of many insects. At the top of the paper, write *Insect begins with the word in.* Brainstorm together other words that contain *in,* such as *pin* and *thin.* Write each word on the insect. Give small index cards to children who want to illustrate one of the words. When an illustration is complete, place it beside the word. Leave the paper up for several days. Invite children to continue thinking of other words to add to the list.

✳ Insect and Spider Web

Use a KWL chart to show what children **K**now about a spiders and insects, **W**ant to know about them, and what they have **L**earned.

As you begin the unit, find out what the children know about insects and spiders. Record what they know in the first column of a chart with three columns.

Ask the children what they would like to know about insects and spiders and add this information to the second column. As the unit progresses, add to the third column by showing what children have learned about insects and spiders. As children identify additional information they would like to have about the topic, you could also add it to the second column.

Use the chart to talk about what the children knew, what they have learned, and how much more they know now.

✳ Helpful Ladybugs

Remind children of the ladybug they made for the door. Develop the idea that the children are like ladybugs because they are helpful. As a class, brainstorm and list all the ways children help each other in the classroom. Place the list on the door with the ladybug display.

☀ Leaves for Food

1. Talk about the fact that some insects eat leaves. Try to show children some real leaves that have holes made by insects.

2. Provide one or more handheld paper hole punches and large leaf shapes cut from 4" × 6" index cards. Have children punch holes in the leaf shapes. Explain that these holes are like the holes that some insects make when they eat leaves. Compare the holes the children made to the size of holes produced by insects.

3. Provide several 12-inch pieces of yarn or rickrack. Children pretend the yarn or rickrack is a caterpillar that is eating. Have them weave the yarn or rickrack caterpillar in and out of the holes they punched in the paper leaves. Use the words *in* and *out* as the children are weaving.

4. Older children may enjoy following a series of oral directions as they weave, such as the following.

   Make the caterpillar go in and out of three holes.
   Move the caterpillar along the outside of the leaf.
   Make the caterpillar go halfway through a hole.
   Move the caterpillar two holes to the left.

☀ Bug Poetry

1. **I Like Bugs** – Read the poem "I Like Bugs" by Margaret Wise Brown. Use the structure of the poem to write the children's ideas about bugs, replacing the adjectives with ones they suggest. For example, let the children brainstorm several word possibilities for any of the following categories and then choose their three favorite words or phrases to complete the poem.

   1. Colors for bugs
   2. Places to find bugs
   3. Ways bugs move
   4. Sounds bugs make
   5. Kinds of bugs

2. **Little Black Bug** – Read the poem "Little Black Bug" by Margaret Wise Brown. As a class, create new verses for the poem. Write a verse about a little honeybee, a little firefly, or a little mosquito.

☀ Caterpillars and Butterflies

1. To encourage active listening, have children use their index finger to wiggle up their arm like a caterpillar each time the word *caterpillar* is read while you read aloud any book that has a caterpillar in it.

2. Make simple caterpillar finger puppets for children to use when reading or retelling a story. Cut the fingers from old gloves. Glue a pom-pom on each finger, then glue eyes, a mouth, and antennae on the pom-pom.

3. Read J. Kent's *The Caterpillar and the Polliwog.* Explain that polliwog is another term for tadpole. Compare the metamorphosis of the caterpillar with that of the caterpillar in E. Carle's *The Very Hungry Caterpillar.*

4. Read *The Very Busy Spider* by E. Carle. Give each child a long piece of yarn and a piece of felt or carpet sample. Reread the book. Have each child use the yarn to make a web on the felt or carpet as the spider in the story makes her web. Ask the children to notice whether the spider begins the web in the center or on an outside edge.

5. Use nonfabric interfacing to make sets of the foods eaten by the caterpillar in *The Very Hungry Caterpillar.* Children use a felt board and put the foods on the board in the order in which they are eaten by the caterpillar. Have them count the total number of food items used.

6. Discuss what real caterpillars eat. Use recommended nonfiction books to share factual information about caterpillars' needs and characteristics. Then, use the Comparing Caterpillars chart (Activity Master 24, p. 301). Work with the children to list and compare what the Very Hungry Caterpillar did and what he ate versus what real caterpillars do and eat. Invite children to find needed information by looking at books and asking others.

✳ Helpful or Harmful?

Recite together the nursery rhyme "Little Miss Muffet." Ask, "Why was Miss Muffet frightened by the spider?" Ask the children to talk about which, if any, spiders and insects frighten them. Explain that many spiders are helpful, but others bite, eat crops, or spread germs. Tell children that it is important to observe spiders rather than handle them.

Note: Since some spiders, such as the Recluse and Black Widow spiders, are dangerous, young children should be taught to treat spiders with caution.

Read or share A. Parsons' *Amazing Spiders* to share facts and information that will dispel myths about spiders. Discuss positive things about spiders. Ask the children to list which spiders or insects they like and what is interesting about them.

Discuss how fascinating it is to watch ants work, spiders weave webs, and insects move and eat. Emphasize the helpful things some insects do, such as pollinate fruits and flowers; provide food for birds, frogs, toads, and snakes; and provide us with honey.

✳ Attribute List

Challenge children to compare two of the insects they know well. First, have them observe live insects or study accurate pictures or photographs of the insects. Then ask children to determine three or more attributes of each insect that are similar and different. They could compare, for example, color, size, wing shapes, eyes, mouths, and sources of food. Record their ideas on a Venn Diagram.

✳ If I Were an Insect

1. Tape-record each child completing the sentence: *If I were an insect, I'd be_____* . Ask leading questions to encourage children to explain their choices. Have children listen to each other's interviews and identify who is speaking.

2. Invite children to draw a picture to illustrate their response. Write the completed sentences on the children's pictures.

3. If children are ready, challenge them to think about things from a different perspective. Ask, "If you were an insect, how would things around you look? How would a person look as you flew overhead?"

MATH

✳ The Anthill

Use the picture of an ant and construction paper to make several ants. Draw an anthill on poster board. Recite the counting rhyme that follows and place a number of ants on the anthill. Have the children count them. Repeat until the children are familiar with the activity. Vary the number of ants each time. Then have children take turns being the leader and placing the number of ants on the anthill.

Here's an anthill with no ants about.
So I called to them, "Little ants, come out."
Then how many ants did I get to see?
Let's find out. Count each one with me.
1-2-3-4. . .

✳ Insect and Spider Legs

1. Provide pictures of insects and spiders. Have children count the number of legs and classify each as an insect (six) or a spider (eight).

2. Get a plastic Cootie creature from a Cootie game box. Count the number of plastic legs provided as you put each on the creature. Ask the children if the game is correct. Ask, "Does the game use the right number of legs for an insect?"

3. Older children may enjoy using the Cootie creature to create number problems. Have children put some of the plastic legs on the creature and then ask the rest of the group to decide how many more legs are needed. Later, they can put some legs on the Cootie and then tell the group they intend to remove a certain number. The group figures out how many will be left.

✳ Insect Graph

On a table, tape a row of pictures of each kind of insect with which the children are familiar. Provide counters such as buttons or colored-paper squares. At the beginning of the unit, ask children to take one counter and lay it in a column above the picture of their favorite insect. When all have participated, discuss which column is the longest and count the number. Discuss what they know about that insect and why it is their favorite. Count and compare the number of counters in other columns. Take a photograph of the insect graph before removing the pictures and counters.

At the end of the unit, repeat the graphing process. Count and discuss the results. Share the photograph taken earlier and remind children of their earlier choices. Discuss why the results are or are not the same.

✳ Pairs

Discuss the term *pair*. Remind children that insects have three pairs of legs and some have two pairs of wings. Ask them to compare those numbers with their pairs of body parts, such as hands, feet, and legs.

Half and Whole

Show pictures of three insects the children can identify. Also provide copies of each picture in which the insect has been cut in half lengthwise (head to tail). Use the insect's name as you talk about whole and half. Challenge the children to find half and whole insects. Say, for example, "Find one half of the ant" and "Find the whole mosquito." Point out that each half of the insect has the same number of legs and wings.

Geoboard Spider Webs

Materials: commercially made geoboards and colored bands; or square wooden board (8" x 8"); 25 one-inch nails; hammer; black spray paint; colored rubber bands

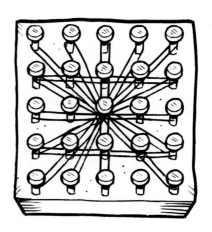

If a commercially made geoboard is not available, you can make a geoboard by hammering nails into a wooden square. Place the nails one-inch apart, in even rows over the entire board. Make five rows of five nails. To make a good background, spray paint the board black and allow it to dry.

Have children create spider webs by stretching the rubber bands on the pegs or nails. Ask, "How many different spider-web shapes can you make?" Have the children count how many nails are used to make each web.

Geometric Beehive

Draw a large beehive on poster board. On the hive, draw the geometric shapes children have studied, including rectangles, squares, circles, ovals, and triangles. Give children paper shapes that are the same as those shown on the poster board. Have children take turns pretending to be bees that are flying their shape to the matching shape on the hive. Ask children to name the shape each time. Later, place the beehive and set of shapes in a center so that children can match the shapes independently.

MOVEMENT

Becoming a Butterfly

A caterpillar crawls along, he creeps and creeps and creeps.
(Creep along on floor on tummies.)
He spins a hard-shelled chrysalis and then he goes to sleep.
(Roll over and over; stretch out and sleep.)
He changes inside that chrysalis and wakes up by and by.
(Move outstretched arms and legs in rhythm.)
He has new wings to spread and dry. Now he is a butterfly.
(Stretch out arms; flutter softly in place.)

✳ Grasshopper in the Grass

Give directions involving movements and have the children follow them. Vary the movements but repeat the same movement more than once so that children have to listen carefully in order to know what to do.

Grasshopper sits in the grass.
(Children squat down.)
Grasshopper hops on a leaf.
(Children jump up.)
Grasshopper sits and eats.
(Children squat down.)
Grasshopper hops to the ground.
(Children jump up.)

✳ Spider-Web Walk

Using several ropes or masking tape, make a simple spider web on the floor. Have children walk along the rope with their shoes on, with bare feet, backwards, with eyes open, and with eyes closed. Let children help create new webs and make suggestions of ways to walk on them.

MUSIC

✳ Bees in Flight

Play a recording of "The Flight of the Bumblebee" by Rimsky-Korsakov. Children use scarves or crepe-paper streamers and move with them in time to the music. At the end of the recording, have everyone drop to the floor and rest quietly.

✳ Old Lady Who Swallowed a Fly

Sing or play a recording of the folk song "The Old Lady Who Swallowed a Fly." Act out each part as you sing it with the children. For example, act out the line " . . . swallowed a spider, who wiggled and jiggled and tickled inside her." Help the children make up new verses about different insects, such as the following.

I know an old lady who swallowed a bee,
It went down inside her and stung her knee.
I know an old lady who swallowed a cricket
It jumped so much she had to kick it.

✳ Insect Sounds

Explain that insects do not have voices like humans, but they do make sounds with parts of their bodies. Some may hum or buzz by vibrating their wings. Others make sounds by rubbing one part of their body against another part, such as rubbing a part of one leg against part of another leg. Have children experiment making sounds with parts of their bodies. Help the children develop several movements that create sound and demonstrate them as a group. Play a soft recording while the children play the sounds they've created.

Insects

(Tune: "Are You Sleeping")

Ants and butterflies, beetles and fireflies,
See them working, see them eating,
On a leaf or in the ground,
Hopping, flying all around.
Bugs, bugs, bugs. I like bugs.

ROLE PLAY

Little Miss Muffet

Provide simple props for children to role play the nursery rhyme "Little Miss Muffet." Children can choose to be Miss Muffet or the spider and act out the part as all recite the verse.

Beekeeper

Provide pictures of beekeepers and beehives. Sew netting around the brim of a hat and add it to the dress-up clothes. Also, add a butterfly net to the role-play area. Children can use the hat and net to role play a beekeeper.

SCIENCE

Observing and Learning

Tell the children that scientists learn about things by watching carefully and thinking about what they see. Ask the children to look for and observe insects and spiders. During circle time each day, ask the children to tell what they have observed and learned. Ask, for example, "Did you find the insect outside or inside? What was it doing?" Record each observation and the name of the child who shared it on a class chart like the one below.

Observations	
Outside	**Inside**
Sarah: I saw black ants. They carried crumbs into an anthill.	Don: We found a little spider spinning a web in the corner.
David: A mosquito bit me.	Maria: We caught a cricket.

Share nonfiction books with children interested in knowing more about insects and spiders.

✳ Spider Webs

Find an abandoned spider web outside to observe with the children. Catch the web on a black piece of paper sprayed with clear varnish or spray glue. Let it dry. If the children find a broken or partial web, let them touch the strands. Discuss how the strands feel. Ask, "Why does the web stick to us? Why would a spider need a sticky web?"

Have the children continue to study the web inside. Provide a magnifying glass. Talk about how the spider constructs the outer sections in descending concentric patterns. Explain that the center of the web usually looks tangled.

✳ Bug Box

Catch and observe insects in a bug box. These boxes can be purchased or made. To make one, draw and cut out circles or flower shapes on the sides of an oatmeal box. Make several cutouts that will become the openings that children look through to observe the insects. Roll up some screening and fit it inside the box. Let it expand to touch the entire inside surface. Decorate the bug box by painting or gluing leaves, flowers, and insects on the outside.

Put some grass, leaves, and twigs in the box. Then, as insects are caught, put them in their new home, and put the lid on the box. After the children's observations are complete, release the insects in an appropriate place outdoors.

✳ Silkworms

Several school and science-supply companies sell silkworm eggs. If your area has mulberry trees, get some eggs and place them in a shoe box. As soon as the eggs hatch, keep a fresh supply of mulberry leaves in the box at all times. The worms grow quickly and spin cocoons that hang from the twigs and leaves in the box. When the moths emerge, they stay in the same area rather than fly away and soon lay eggs. Store some of the eggs in a small jar in the refrigerator so that you can bring them out to hatch next spring.

Provide pictures of the silkworms and cocoons. On a large calendar, note the day the eggs are placed in the shoe box and write what happens each day so that children learn the length of the silkworms' life cycle. Discuss how a cocoon is different from a chrysalis. Ask the children to observe how the worm gets out of the cocoon.

Use the string cocoon made in the Cocoon activity (see p. 214). As children describe the stages of the silkworm's life cycle, put a picture of a silkworm into the cocoon and, at the appropriate time, pull out a picture of a moth. Use the term *metamorphosis* when appropriate.

✳ An Ant Farm

Purchase an ant farm from a school, science-supply company, or toy store. Plan ahead and allow two to three weeks for the ants to arrive. Follow the directions for care and feeding of the ant colony. Several activities are possible as the ant colony develops.

1. Measure the length of the tunnels.
2. Count the number of dens the ants build.

3. Observe if the ants sleep or rest, eat in a specific place, travel alone or in groups, or cooperate in digging or eating. Have the children work together to keep an observation journal that records the ants' activities or the children's questions and the answers they find through observation.

4. Older children might enjoy using a stopwatch to time a solitary ant as it travels through a tunnel.

TRANSITION ACTIVITY
✳ Becoming a Butterfly

Have the children role play the stages of becoming a butterfly. Use the term *metamorphosis* when appropriate.

1. Egg: Make themselves into as small a ball as possible.
2. Caterpillar: Wiggle around the room.
3. Chrysalis: Roll up, cover head with arms and hands. Stay still in the chrysalis as long as appropriate.
4. Butterfly: Emerge from chrysalis by slowly opening up, standing up, spreading wings (arms) slowly to allow them to dry, and then gently flying away.

CHILDREN'S BOOKS

Allen, J. and T. Humphries. *Are You a Butterfly?* New York: Kingfisher, 2000. A unique approach to the life cycle of a butterfly. Offers a twist at the end.
Are You a Spider? New York: Kingfisher, 2000. A fresh approach to spider information.

Barner, B. *Bugs! Bugs! Bugs!* San Francisco: Chronicle, 1999. Colorful introduction to common bugs. Has a bug-o-meter at the end of the book for graphing.

Berger, M. *Chirping Crickets.* New York: HarperCollins, 1998. Life cycle and habitat of crickets. Explains why they chirp. Easy projects included.

Berger, M. and Berger, G. *Do All Spiders Spin Webs? Questions and Answers About Spiders.* New York: Scholastic, 2000. This book answers many questions asked by children and adults alike.

Bunting, E. *The Butterfly House.* New York: Scholastic, 1999. A young girl and her grandfather rescue a butterfly larva, build a house for it, and watch its metamorphosis.

Carle, E. *The Very Busy Spider.* New York: Philomel, 1984. Children can feel the pictures as the story is told of a spider and her web.
The Very Hungry Caterpillar. New York: Philomel, 1979. A children's favorite. A caterpillar eats his way through the book and becomes a butterfly.

Ferris, H., ed. *Favorite Poems Old and New.* New York: Doubleday, 1957. This book contains the poem "Little Black Bug" by Margaret Wise Brown, as well as other poems by Elizabeth Barrett Browning, Langston Hughes, and Kate Greenaway.

Florian, D. "The Ants," "The Caterpillar," and "The Firefly" in *Beast Feast.* San Diego: Harcourt Brace, 1994. Three clever poems and watercolor illustrations.

Kent, J. *The Caterpillar and the Polliwog.* Englewood Cliffs, NJ: Prentice- Hall, 1982. A polliwog watches a caterpillar to find out how the caterpillar changes to a butterfly.

McDermott, G. *Anansi the Spider.* New York: Scholastic, 1972. This award-winning tale describes one of the adventures of Anansi, a spider and folk hero to the Ashanti people.

Pallotta, J. *The Icky Bug Alphabet Book.* Watertown, MA: Charlesbridge, 1999. Stunning illustrations and a wealth of information on 26 bugs.

Parsons, A. *Amazing Spiders.* New York: Alfred A. Knopf, 1990. Interesting and full of facts and information that help to dispel myths about spiders.

Peet, B. *The Ant and the Elelphant.* New York: Scholastic, 1972. Who will save the elephant when he runs into trouble? Compare it to Aesop's fable of the mouse and the lion.

Rockwell, A. *Bumblebee, Bumblebee, Do You Know Me?* New York: HarperCollins, 1999. Riddle format that introduces children to common insects, both flying and crawling.

Sandved, K. B. *The Butterfly Alphabet.* New York: Scholastic, 1996. Stunning photographs and rhyming couplets reveal letters of the alphabet that occur naturally in butterflies and moths.

May Curriculum

People Work

Water and Rainbows

People Work

- There are many kinds of work that people do.
- People work at home, at school, and at a workplace away from home.
- People work to complete tasks and to earn money to buy things they need to live.
- It is important to work hard and keep trying when a task becomes difficult.
- People use different kinds of tools or machines to perform their jobs.
- Some people wear uniforms or special clothing to do their jobs.
- Different jobs require different skills and training.
- Every worker and every job is important.
- Either a woman or a man can do most jobs as long as he or she wants to do the work and has the training to do it.

CONTINUING CONCEPTS

- **Colors** Identify and discuss the colors of uniforms or special clothing that are part of some jobs, such as the white coats worn by health-care workers and the blue uniforms worn by many postal workers and police officers.
- **Geometric Shapes** Review circle, triangle, square, rectangle, and oval. Have children find examples of each shape in work environments, such as signs found outside offices.
- **Health and Nutrition** People need energy to work. Talk about how carbohydrates provide energy and are a necessary part of a healthy diet.
  Discuss the jobs people have that help others stay healthy, such as jobs in medical facilities and sports and fitness centers.
- **Senses** Have children close their eyes and identify longer and shorter pieces of yarn.
  Have children feel and shape play dough.
  Read books to children about workers and their jobs.
  Identify the sounds associated with certain jobs; for example, sounds made by workers on a construction site.
- **Traditional Rhymes and Tales** Recite "The Itsy Bitsy Spider" with the children and tell them the story "The Little Red Hen."

PORTFOLIO PRODUCTS

As the end of the school year nears, an effective way to demonstrate children's growth and readiness levels is to have children make products they made at the beginning and middle of the year and then analyze the changes in the products to evaluate how children's competencies have changed.

- Have each child do the "Look What I Can Do Book" activity (p. 8) again. Use the three booklets the child has made to assess his or her growth over time. During family conferences, use the three booklets to document each child's progress. Also, share the three booklets with each child so that the child realizes that he or she has learned a great deal and can do much more now than was possible at the beginning of the school year.

ART

✳ Easel or Tabletop Painting: People

Materials: large paper; tempera paints; brushes

Post pictures of people of all ages doing many different jobs. Then encourage children to paint people working. Ask children to tell about their pictures and write a brief description of them or dictate descriptions to an adult.

✳ Play Dough

Materials: play dough (see Appendix II, p. 275)

Give children play dough and allow time for them to explore. Encourage them to roll and combine shapes to create designs and objects. Explain that a sculptor works with clay to create art for others to enjoy.

✳ Pressed-Flower Arrangements

Materials: wild flowers; wax paper; iron

Talk about people who make flower arrangements or sell flower arrangements at florist shops or florist areas of grocery stores. Have the children pick and arrange small bunches of wild flowers or weeds. Talk about colors and shapes. Encourage children to try different ways to arrange the plants. Next, place each arrangement between two equal-sized pieces of wax paper and put something heavy on the arrangement to press it overnight. Then, use a warm iron to seal the edges.

Provide a precut paper frame for each child to glue over his or her arrangement. Ask children to identify the shape of the frame. As a variation, have children make narrow arrangements of flowers. Use the arrangements to make bookmarks.

✳ Stitching Designs

Materials: blunt needles; yarn in many bright colors; paper plates or burlap; marker

Discuss how tailors, seamstresses, and clothing designers work with fabrics to create clothes and other items we need and enjoy. Demonstrate how to make stitching designs by drawing a design or pattern on a paper plate or burlap. Show children how to sew over those designs with the needle and yarn. Sit with them as they draw designs or patterns and then stitch with the needle and yarn. Encourage children to use yarn in several colors.

✳ People-Work Collage

Materials: 9" × 12" paper; magazines and newspapers; scissors; glue; tissue paper

Discuss different occupations and jobs. Include the jobs that the parents of the children in the class and the children themselves do. Avoid male and/or female stereotypes when describing each occupation. For example, use the word *firefighter* instead of *fireman*.

Have children cut out pictures of people at work to glue on a collage. They could also cut out and glue on pictures of the things that are used by workers each day. When the children are finished gluing on the pictures, invite them to cut up small scraps of tissue paper to create confetti and then glue it all over the collage to add color and visual interest.

✳ Fire Finger Painting

Materials: red and yellow finger paint (see Appendix II, p. 274); paper

Have children finger paint with red and yellow paint to create pictures of a fire. Display the pictures on a wall beside a picture of a firefighter with a hose in hand. Add the caption *Firefighters help control fires.*

✳ Wood-Shaving Collage

Materials: wood shavings (collected from construction sites or woodworking shops); glue; 9" × 12" construction paper; construction-paper strips

Discuss construction jobs, woodworking shops, and how wood is used in building furniture and structures. If possible, show a real wood plane. Use the wood plane to smooth a piece of wood to show children how wood shavings are produced. Talk about who uses wood planes and why.

Have children create a collage by gluing the thin wood curls and other shavings on construction paper. Encourage them to glue one curl on top of another to produce a three-dimensional collage with more depth. Invite children to weave narrow strips of construction paper in and out of the wood curls to add color and visual interest.

✳ Yarn Prints (A Two-Day Project)

Materials: 4- to 6-inch squares of cardboard or poster board; yarn; cotton swabs; glue; construction-paper hats representing various jobs; tempera paints; brushes; 9" × 12" light-colored paper

Day 1 – Demonstrate how to make a large circle with the yarn on one of the poster-board squares and then use a cotton swab and glue to glue it in place. Cut smaller lengths of yarn and add facial features. If necessary, help children cut the yarn and create a face on a square. Encourage children to add

as many facial features and details to the faces and heads as they can. Some children may want to coil yarn to make hair. When the faces are complete, set them aside to dry.

Day 2 – Have the children lightly brush paint over the yarn outline and then press it on light-colored paper to make a print. Encourage them to repeat the process using different colors. Suggest that they overlap the prints for a more interesting effect. After the paint is dry, have children glue hats on several of the prints and talk about the kinds of workers who wear the various hats.

BLOCKS

✳ Construction Time

Post pictures of construction sites and provide some toy construction sets, such as Legos®, Lincoln Logs®, or Constructs®. Encourage children to work together to create a construction site. Talk about the jobs people have on real construction sites. Suggest that the children pretend they are construction workers of various kinds as they complete the block construction. Ask, "Why do workers at construction sites wear hard hats?"

BULLETIN BOARD

✳ People Work Outside and Inside

Divide a bulletin board in half by covering one side with light-blue paper and the other with any color that represents the inside of a building. Staple on wide yarn or a strip of ribbon to cover the middle line where the two colors meet. Make a border for the bulletin board of people's faces by giving the children circle shapes and having them use markers to add a face to each. Add the caption: *People Work Outside and Inside.*

On the blue half, add outside scenery, such as the sun, cotton clouds, a tree, and birds flying. On the other half, add details that suggest the inside of a building, such as windows, pictures on the walls, and furniture cut from advertisements. Provide several pictures of different workers doing inside and outside work. Have children classify each picture as one that shows inside work or outside work and then use a pushpin or temporary adhesive to attach the picture to the appropriate side of the board.

At circle time, show several tools workers use and ask children to identify people who work outside, inside, or both outside and inside as they use that tool.

COOKING

✳ Create-a-Pizza

English muffins or small hamburger bun halves
Pizza sauce
Grated cheese

Wash hands. Talk about workers in food stores and restaurants. Ask if anyone has ever been to a pizza shop. Name other places that prepare and sell food that children may be familiar with. Have the children put together their own pizza by spreading one or two teaspoons of sauce on a muffin or bun half. They can add a teaspoon of cheese if desired. Place the pizzas on a cookie sheet.

Write each child's name on a foil strip and place the strip beside his or her pizza. Bake the pizzas in a conventional or microwave oven until the cheese is melted.

Encourage the children to recall the steps in the pizza-making process as they eat the pizzas. Ask, "What did you do first?. . . second? . . . last?"

✳ Worker's Sack Lunch

Bread
Jelly and peanut butter
Apples
Carrot sticks

Small cookies or crackers (optional)
Plastic knives
Paper lunch bags

Talk about the fact that many workers carry their lunch to work. Provide paper lunch bags for the children to decorate. Put the child's name on his or her bag.

Wash hands. Have each child pack a bag lunch. Have the children cut one slice of bread in half, spread jelly and/or peanut butter on one half, and then cover it with other half. Supply apple slices, carrot sticks, and perhaps small cookies or crackers and have children select what they want to put in their lunch bag. Prepare the bag lunches early in the day and save them until later. Eat outside if the weather permits or in some unusual place that will add to the fun at lunchtime. Discuss why workers need breaks during their work time.

LANGUAGE ARTS

✳ Action Play – If I Were. . .

If I were a baker, what would I do?
Bake bread and cookies for me and you.
    (Put on hat and apron; mix up dough)
If I were a secretary, what would I do?
Work on a computer and other machines too.
    (Type on a computer.)

If I were a bus driver, what would I do?
Safely drive the people to work and school.
    (Drive a bus.)
If I were a police officer, what would I do?
Keep the city safe and protect all of you.
    (Hold up a hand to tell others to stop.)

Create other verses about the jobs of the family members of the children.

✳ Word Wall

Add the word *work* to the word wall. Add other topic-related words that children suggest. Emphasize the high-frequency words you want children to use. Have the children count how many words are on the word wall. Write a sentence strip that reads *We have (the number) words on our word wall.* Display the strip. Place a piece of colored plastic over one or more of the word cards to highlight words you particularly want children to read and incorporate in their writing.

✳ Tell Me About Your Work

Brainstorm a list of questions about work that the children want to ask people who work at school. Questions should focus on the tasks involved in each person's job and the tools they use. Have the children role play talking with workers and asking the questions.

Then take the children on a walk around the school and have them talk to people who work there. As the children ask questions, an adult writes down the answers they receive. Take a photograph of each worker. Later, put the photographs and information on sheets of paper and assemble the sheets to make a book entitled *People Work at School*. On the last page of the book, display photographs of the children working in class. Add a caption such as *We work at school to learn all we can.*

Finally, have the children draw pictures and write thank-you notes to each worker. Let the children deliver the notes and invite each worker to come to read the book made about the workers at school.

✳ Worker of the Day

Build upon children's experience interviewing workers at school by having them interview family members and friends about their jobs. Invite different workers to visit the class for a few minutes each day. Parents may be able to visit for ten minutes on their way to work or during their lunch hour. Have children interview the visitors about their jobs. Plan some questions for the children to ask, such as, "Where do you work? What do you do at work? How did you learn to do your job? What do you wear to work? What tools or things do you use to do your work?"

Together, make a worker-of-the-day collage. Take a photograph of each visitor to display on the collage and write a few words about that person and his or her job.

✳ The Little Red Hen

Read or retell the tale "The Little Red Hen." Invite children to join in on the repeating line *"Not I," said the ____*. Discuss why some of the animals did not want to help make the bread and why they all wanted to help eat it. Discuss the value of trying to help, doing one's best, and getting work done.

Use the story starter below to create a new version of the tale that involves working at school. Incorporate tasks that your class completes during the school day. Use the repeating line: *"I will, I will," said the _____.*

Ms. Cardova's class at Blackwell School had a big job to do. "We need to write letters to thank the _____ for visiting us and helping us learn about _____," she said. "Who will help me get the writing supplies?"

"I will, I will," said all of the children. And they quietly got the paper and pencils.

"Who will help me plan what to write?" said Ms. Cardova.

"I will, I will," said all of the children. And they made a list of the important things they wanted to say in the letters.

Continue the story pattern with the questions "Who will write a letter?" and "Who will help clean up?" End with the question "Who will have a snack with me to celebrate a job well done?"

✳ Itsy Bitsy Spider

Recite or sing together the popular rhyme "Itsy Bitsy Spider" as you do the fingerplay actions. Discuss the importance of working hard to complete tasks and not giving up quickly when tasks become difficult. Explain that the spider tried, ran into trouble, and had to try again. Emphasize that it didn't give up. Ask the children when they need to work hard and keep trying at school. Encourage them to discuss how they are like the itsy bitsy spider. Then have each child complete the sentence *I am like the Itsy Bitsy Spider when I. . .* and draw a picture to illustrate the sentence. Display the pictures with a copy of the "Itsy Bitsy Spider" rhyme.

✳ Riddle Time

Make up riddles about a job or worker for the children to guess. For example, tell the children, "I'm thinking of someone who wears a protective coat and boots and hat. Sometimes this person rides standing up on a big red or yellow truck. A large hose is one piece of equipment that this person uses on the job."

✳ Visit From a Firefighter

Ask firefighters to bring a fire engine or truck to the school and talk with the children about their work or take children on a field-trip to a fire station. Children could hold a hose to find out how heavy it is; try on a firefighter's coat or hat; stand on the truck; observe where the equipment is kept; and look inside the cab of the truck to see which controls make the light and siren work.

Ask a firefighter to explain the difference between a fire truck and a fire engine. Encourage children to count the number of wheels on the truck and ask the firefighter how many firefighters travel on this truck at one time.

Suggest that a firefighter put on a gas mask. Ask the firefighter to tell the children not to be afraid of or hide from a firefighter if they are ever in a fire.

✳ Helicopter Pilots

Materials: markers or crayons; scissors; tape

Show pictures of helicopters and talk about the work of a helicopter pilot. Duplicate the pattern below. Have the children decorate the patterns with markers or crayons and cut them out. Children can help each other fold and tape their patterns. The helicopters can then be flown inside or outside the room by simply holding them with the blades up and dropping them gently from a raised hand.

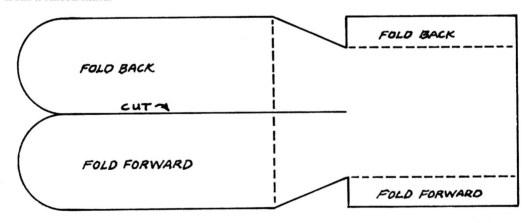

✳ Guess-a-Job

1. Hold up real objects or pictures of objects used in more than one type of job, such as a hammer, computer, stethoscope, scissors, and shovel. The children try to name as many occupations as they can that involve using that tool.

2. Show either an actual hat or a picture of a hat worn on different kinds of jobs. The children describe the kind of hat, the job, other equipment needed to perform that job, and whether it is an inside or outside job.

✳ Masks and Protective Glasses

Explain that some workers use a type of mask or protective glasses when they work. Display real masks such as a surgical mask, football helmet with face guard, oxygen mask, welder or sander goggles, safety glasses, and dark sunglasses. Let the children try on the masks or glasses and guess who wears them. Talk about why workers need to wear each kind of mask or glasses.

MATH

✳ Calendar

Provide the children who can write numerals with their own copy of a blank monthly calendar (Activity Master 3, p. 280). Help them to write the name of the month and fill the date in the appropriate place each day. Children can create patterns around the outside edges to complete their personal calendar. Invite them to mark any special days, including birthdays, on the calendar. Ask children what they notice when they compare their calendar from last month with this month's calendar.

✳ Number Up

Make cards with one numeral written on each. Hold up a numeral card and have the children tiptoe around the room to find that number of objects. For example, when you hold up the card that shows 2, children could tiptoe to two chairs, or point to two eyes, or hold up two crayons.

✳ Numeral Puzzles

Provide cardboard or poster-board cutouts of 6- to 8-inch numerals from 0 through 9. The children trace around the patterns to make their own set of numerals. Consider providing a paper in a variety of colors so that children can make each numeral a different color. They can then make numeral puzzles by cutting each numeral into the number of pieces that numeral represents; for example, three pieces for the numeral 3. Children should write their name or initials on each puzzle piece in case one is dropped. Store each puzzle in an envelope.

1. Have children assemble the puzzles several times and put the completed puzzles in numerical order.

2. Children who demonstrate higher math readiness can put numerals together to make two-digit numbers. For example, they could put the 1 and the 2 together to make 12. You could also ask, "What happens if you reverse the order of the numerals?"

Later, you could have children take their puzzles home to show family members.

✳ Six Boxes

Have children fold a piece of paper into six sections. Then hold up different numeral cards and have them write the numerals in sections of the paper. Then have children put small objects, such as counters, buttons, or beans, in each section to show the number. This activity is fun for children and provides a quick way for you to check their understanding of number concepts. Although the paper has only six sections, you can use numbers greater than 6 if the children know and are ready for these numbers.

✳ A Teacher at Work

Materials: magazine pictures; pieces of felt or Velcro; glue; 3-inch construction paper circles; markers

Cut out a picture of an adult to represent a teacher or use a photograph of yourself. Glue a piece of felt or Velcro® to the back of the picture or photo. Have children draw facial features on circles to represent the faces of children in the class. Glue felt or Velcro® on the back of each circle. Use the materials in the following ways.

1. Place the teacher figure on the felt board and have children count faces as they add them to the board.
2. Have the children use the circles to form a group that shows boys and a group that shows girls and count all the faces again. Similarly, have the children classify the faces by eye color and count the total number of faces.
3. Make up word problems that include children's names and have the class solve the problems by putting the appropriate number of faces on the board. For example, say, "Debra and May were reading with the teacher. Kevin and Ed came to join them. How many children were working with the teacher?"
4. Read Bill Martin's *Brown Bear, Brown Bear, What Do You See?* Ask children to count the children in the last picture.

✳ Sewing Strings of Buttons

Materials: blunt or plastic needles; thread; buttons

Give each child a needle and thread. Have children pretend to be tailors or seamstresses by stringing buttons and counting as each one is added. Call out different numbers of buttons for them to add to their threads each time.

To vary the activity, have the children create button patterns and then count the total number in the string of buttons.

✳ Graphing Future Jobs

Make a graph to show some of the jobs or occupations that children express interest in doing in the future. List and draw simple pictures of jobs and occupations across the bottom of a graph. Have each child write her or his name in the column that shows the job he or she selects. Discuss the results by counting each column and using the terms *more than* and *less than*.

✳ Longer and Shorter

1. Refer to things as being *longer* or *shorter* as often as possible in natural conversation throughout the day.
2. Cut longer and shorter lengths of yarn. Ask children to hold the yarn by both ends and pull it taut. Decide as a class which piece is longer or shorter. When the children become proficient at determining which piece is longer or shorter, have them close their eyes and determine by touch which of two pieces is longer or shorter.
3. Have the children fold a piece of Manila paper in half. With markers or red crayons, they draw a longer firefighter's ladder on one side and a shorter ladder on the other side. Print *longer* and *shorter* on the appropriate side.

✳ I Spy a Shape

Say "I spy" and name a geometric figure. Children search for naturally occurring examples of each shape in the room or school, point to each object, and name the shapes.

✳ Geoboards

Materials: geoboards (see p. 221); colored rubber bands

Children create geometric figures by stretching the rubber bands on the nails. Ask children to find out how many different squares they can make on the board. Have them count how many nails they use to make each square and count how many nails are on each side.

Provide pictures of other geometric figures for children to make on the geoboard. Ask children to keep a record of the shapes they are able to make. Have them write their name and draw each shape they make on a piece of paper. Have them count how many shapes in all they made and write the number at the bottom of the paper.

MOVEMENT

✳ Stop and Go

Make simple Stop and Go signs. Ask the children what they think the signs mean. Then have them tiptoe around the room and stop when you hold up the Stop sign and continue tiptoeing when you hold up the Go sign. Use each sign several times during the game.

Talk about traffic control and whose job it is to assist motorists and people who are walking.

✳ Worker Pantomime

Have the children stand in a circle and pretend to be workers doing different jobs. Children can take turns suggesting occupations such as a secretary working at a computer, a construction worker building a house, a chef preparing a cake, a teacher helping children learn, a janitor cleaning the school, and a doctor examining a patient.

✳ Clap Rhythms

Clap the syllables of children's names, such as *Ra-ul* or *Mis-sy.* Then clap the syllables of several kinds of jobs that the children suggest, such as *pi-lot* or *gar-den-er.* After clapping several different words, some children may be able to name words that have the same number of syllables as words you've clapped. You could ask, for example, "Can you think of another kind of work that has the same rhythm as sales-per-son?"

✳ Jogging

Use a timer to time children jogging in one place to music for one minute. Talk about workers who need to run, be strong, or have stamina, such as police, firefighters, lifeguards, and some kinds of construction workers.

MUSIC

✳ Workers Work

(Tune: "Mulberry Bush")
Children suggest different jobs and occupations. As the song is sung, have them decide how to act out each one.

This is the way the baker bakes . . .
This is the way the doctor helps us . . .
This is the way the teacher teaches . . .
This is the way the bus driver drives . . .
This is the way the children work . . .

✳ Teacher

(Tune: "Mary Had a Little Lamb")

Our teacher works at school each day,
School each day, school each day.
Our teacher works at school each day,
To help us learn and grow.
She smiles and helps us learn all day,
Learn all day, learn all day.
She smiles and helps us learn all day.
There's so much we want to know!

ROLE PLAY

✳ People Who Work

Change the props in the role-play area from time to time to suggest different occupations. As mentioned in connection with activities involving class stores, collecting materials and props is easier if you write a note to parents asking them to share needed items. Include a list of suggested items and invite them to add others. The list of possible items below is categorized by job type.

Involve children in setting up each area to encourage the development of their communication, classification, and organization skills. Encourage them to problem solve as they organize the materials. Children may arrange and use materials differently from the way you envisioned, but those differences usually add to the experience.

1. Doctor – stethoscope, bathroom scale, cotton balls, splint, Band-Aids®, bandages, white coat, pad of paper for prescriptions, doctor's bag

2. Librarian – books, magazines, ink pad, date stamp, index cards or paper rectangles to use as check-out cards, table and chairs to create reading area

3. Farmer – play barn, straw hat, neckerchief, garden tools, toy farm animals, fences, tractor, truck

4. Firefighter – firefighter's hat, child's rubber raincoat and boots, flashlight, small bucket, hose, rope, toy fire truck, homemade fire extinguisher made from a potato-chip can covered in foil, with a small, plastic hose attached to side

5. Dentist – toothbrushes, cardboard teeth, white coat, mirror, appointment book

6. Teacher – books, paper, ruler, crayons, chalkboard, eraser, chalk, pencils, desk or table, chairs

SCIENCE

✳ Machines

Walk around the school with the class searching for as many different kinds of machines as you can find. Talk about a computer, typewriter, video player, pencil sharpener, copy machine, vacuum cleaner, and other machines used in the school.

Discuss simple machines such as a hole punch, scissors, and tweezers. Let the children show you how these simple machines work.

Provide a pair of kitchen tongs, a pincher-type clothespin, and some tweezers. Have the children try to use these simple tools to pick up paper, crayons, paper clips, and small blocks. Ask, "Which works best for each object? How are these tools the same and how are they different"? Discuss which tools people would use as they do different jobs. For example, a parent cooking dinner or a chef could use the tongs. A person doing clock repairs or a nurse helping to remove a child's splinter could use tweezers.

✳ Repair Discovery

Discuss the important jobs done by people who repair broken or damaged items. Talk about repair work that children may have seen at school or at home. Provide an unusable clock, hair dryer, watch, or radio. Talk with the children about how these items are unusable and ready to be thrown away. Explain that since the items are unusable, the class may experiment with them. Provide simple, safe tools, such as small screwdrivers, and let the children help take each item apart. Observe and talk about what is inside. Remind the children that they always need adult permission to use tools and to take things apart.

TRANSITION ACTIVITY

✳ Good Morning Worker

One child is the worker and stands with his or her back to the rest of the class. A second child is chosen to tiptoe up to the first child and say, for example, "Good morning, Doctor." The first child tries to guess the name of the child behind him.

Vary the activity by suggesting different types of workers, such as salesperson, dentist, teacher, bus driver, food server, judge, teacher, doctor, cook, and nurse.

CHILDREN'S BOOKS

Deedy, C. *The Library Dragon*. Atlanta: Peachtree, 1994. The new librarian is a real dragon. Story hour stops and children aren't allowed to touch the books. Good problem-solving opportunities. Appealing illustrations.

Harper, C. M. *When I Grow Up*. San Francisco: Chronicle, 2001. Celebrates some of the qualities most admired in people.

Henkes, K. *Good-bye, Curtis*. New York: Greenwillow, 1995. The mail carrier retires after 42 years. People give him a party at the last house on his route.

Hennessy, B. G. *Road Builders*. New York: Puffin Books, 1994. Build a road with this book. It shows the step-by-step process and different machines involved.

Hoban, T. *Construction Zone*. New York: Greenwillow, 1997. Shows 13 kinds of large construction equipment. There is no text, but a glossary is provided at the end. Children love Hoban's photographs!

Maass, R. *Tugboats*. New York: Henry Holt and Company, 1997. Photographs document the important jobs that tugboats do in harbors. Depicts the crew keeping a tug working. Clear and understandable text.

Martin, B. *Brown Bear, Brown Bear, What Do You See?* New York: Holt, 1983.
Polar Bear, Polar Bear, What Do You See? New York: Holt, 1991. Very predictable pattern books that children "read" after hearing just once. Provides a good pattern for rewriting the story.

Mott, E. *Steam Train Ride*. New York: Walker & Company, 1991. Actual photographs of people running a steam train, complete with the water tower and stations.

Polacco, P. *Welcome Comfort*. New York: Philomel, 1999. A warm Christmas story in which the school custodian helps a lonely foster child learn to celebrate life.

Royston, A. *Big Machines*. Canada: Little, Brown, 1994. Bold photographs of machines that help people work.

Royston, A. *Truck Trouble*. New York: DK Publishing, Inc., 1998. Bold photographs of work trucks.

Sturges, P. *I Love Trucks*. New York: HarperCollins, 1999. Attractive illustrations that are multicultural and nonsexist, coupled with simple rhyming text.

Walter, V. *Hi, Pizza Man!* New York: Orchard Paperbacks, 1995. What to do while waiting for the pizza to come. Think up other possible delivery persons or even animals. Interactive good fun.

Zimmerman, A. and D. Clemesha. *Trashy Town*. New York: HarperCollins, 1999. Mr. Gill is the trash man and he loves to clean up his town.

Water and Rainbows

CONCEPTS

- All living things need water. People, animals, and plants must have water to live.
- Some things float in water. Some things dissolve in water.
- Water can be a liquid, a solid (ice), or a gas (steam). Water changes to ice when it is frozen. It changes to steam when it is boiled.
- The water cycle includes evaporation and condensation.
- Water cleans people, plants, animals, and the air.
- Water helps control fires.
- Water has recreational uses that many people enjoy, such as boating, fishing, and swimming.
- A rainbow is an arc of prismatic colors caused by the sun's rays reflecting in drops of water.
- The sequence of colors in a rainbow is red, orange, yellow, green, blue, indigo, and violet.

CONTINUING CONCEPTS

- **Colors** Have children compare the different colors of water by looking at photographs.
  Help children identify the colors of a rainbow.
- **Geometric Shapes** Review circle, triangle, square, rectangle, and oval.
  Have children find examples of geometric shapes in boats and fish.
  Explain that an arc is half of a circle.
- **Health and Nutrition** Discuss why animals and people need clean water.
  Explain how much water people need to drink every day to stay healthy.
  Discuss the importance of washing fruits and vegetables before eating them.
- **Senses** Talk about the look and smell of the Fragrant Watercolors, p. 242.
  Have children listen to the variations in pitch produced by different amounts of water in glasses.
  Have the children brainstorm words for the sounds water makes.
  Have the children feel and compare two forms of water—ice and liquid water.
- **Traditional Rhymes and Tales** Recite "Jack and Jill" with the children.

PORTFOLIO PRODUCTS

Consider the following suggestions as you or the children select at least one product from this unit to place in each portfolio.
- Place each child's completed monthly calendar in the portfolio as an indication of his or her ability to write and organize numerals. Include a language assessment by asking children to write or dictate what they notice when they compare their calendar from last month with this month's calendar. Also ask them to explain the patterns they created around the outside edges of the calendar.
- To assess fine-motor coordination and knowledge of geometric figures, have each child fold a large sheet of paper into four boxes, number each box, and then draw a different shape; for example, a circle, square, triangle, or diamond. Compare this product with the similar one

completed earlier (see Portfolio Products, pp. 30–31) and look for refinements in angle and shape. Add a language assessment by having each child explain in writing or through dictation which figure is his or her favorite and why.

ART

✳ Easel or Tabletop Painting

1. The Colors of Water

Materials: large paper; tempera paints in three or four shades of blue; large brushes

Provide pictures that show the different colors water might appear to be in ponds, lakes, or oceans. Tell interested children that the depth of the water and the impurities in the water make the water appear to be different shades of color, especially blues or greens. Let the children explore at the easel by creating pictures using the various shades of blue.

2. Rainbows

Materials: tempera paints in the colors of the rainbow; paper; brushes

Display pictures of rainbows. Ask if anyone has seen a rainbow and, if yes, when. Identify the colors of a rainbow and the shape of a rainbow.

Have children paint rainbows and encourage them to use the colors of the rainbow in their paintings. Talk with each child about the colors he or she is using. Name each color in the painting. Accept any rainbow a child creates, but note which children talk about or use the colors in the sequence in which they appear in a real rainbow.

✳ Watercolor Waves

Materials: Manila paper; watercolors; cup of water for each painter; brushes

Encourage children to cover a whole piece of paper with watercolor waves. The lighter hues make a pleasing picture. Discuss how watercolors look compared to tempera paint colors. Talk about how the rinsing water changes colors as the brushes are swished in it.

✳ Fragrant Watercolors

Materials: boxes of flavored gelatin in several different flavors; warm water; paintbrushes; paper

Help the children mix some gelatins with warm water. Gelatin mixtures should have the consistency of watercolor paints. Name and discuss the color of each. Smell each and discuss its fragrance. Ask children to close their eyes and have them try to identify a flavor by its smell. Then have the children paint pictures with the gelatin mixtures.

✳ The Rainbow Fish

Materials: watercolors; Manila paper; foil; yarn; glue; cotton swabs; circle-shaped cereal

Read *The Rainbow Fish* by Marcus Pfister. Discuss the colors and shapes of fish in the book. See if children can find all the colors of a rainbow in the book. Have children identify geometric shapes such as oval-shaped or circular bodies and triangular fins.

Encourage children to paint a large fish on a sheet of paper. Suggest that they add details, such as large eyes, fins and stripes, to each fish. Have children show water surrounding the fish. When the paintings are dry, give children yarn and glue. Show children how to use a cotton swab to put glue around the outer edge of their fish's body and cover the glue with yarn. Then have them make shiny fish scales by cutting small pieces of foil and gluing them on their fish.

Children can glue on round cereal pieces to make air bubbles coming from the fish. They can also draw and color underwater plants or outline them with yarn.

✳ Dry-Wet Ones

Materials: construction paper; sponge; cotton swabs; dry tempera paint powder in small paper cups or bowls

1. Children wet a piece of construction paper with a sponge and use a cotton swab to make designs with the dry tempera paint on the wet paper.
2. Alternatively, have children draw designs using a cotton swab and dry tempera colors on dry paper. Then have them lay a wet sheet of paper on top of their painting and pat the paper to transfer color onto the wet sheet. This method produces an unusual and interesting printing effect.

Have children compare the results of the dry and the wet method. Ask children which method and result they like more.

✳ Water Painting

Materials: buckets; house paintbrushes

Provide buckets of water and paintbrushes. Children use plain water to paint a fence, sidewalk, or the side of a building. It is great fun because the effect soon disappears. Ask children why they think the water disappears.

✳ Floatables

Materials: plastic foam scraps cut into approximately 3" × 5" pieces; small pieces of yarn, rickrack, construction paper, and buttons; toothpicks; plastic foam packing pieces

Children glue the pieces of yarn and packing pieces to the larger plastic foam blocks to create individually designed floatables.

They can use toothpicks to add more shapes to the constructions. Then the children have a float party. Provide a child's wading pool with three or four inches of water in it. Tie or tack a string to one end of each floatable. Show children how to blow on the floatables so that they move in the water and then pull on the string to bring them back.

✳ Ocean Waves

Materials: blue and green tempera paints; light-colored construction paper, folded in half; 12-inch pieces of string; plastic foam trays or paper plates

Children dip a piece of string in a small amount of paint poured on a paper plate or food tray. They place the string inside the folded paper and pull it up, down, and around, and then open the paper to see the design. Allow one child to hold down the paper as another child pulls the string. Talk about how the designs look like ocean waves. Let children dip the string again and pull it to make overlapping designs on the same sheet of folded paper. Have the children alternate between blue and green paint to make interesting color blends. Compare their designs with pictures of the different colors of water in oceans, lakes, and ponds.

✳ Shaving-Cream Prints

Materials: large sheets of paper; cans of shaving cream; dry tempera paint powder

Have the children stand around a table and work directly on the tabletop. Supply each child with a small amount of shaving cream. Talk about the shaving cream foam and the foam of the sea. Encourage the children to explore by spreading the cream. Talk about the waves in the ocean. Ask, "How can we use our hands and fingers to make waves in this cream?"

After children have made waves using their fingers, hands, and the sides of their hands, talk about the color of the ocean or large bodies of water. Supply dry tempera powder in the colors the children mention. Sprinkle a little tempera powder on the cream and let the children blend it into the shaving cream to create colored designs and waves.

Wash hands. Have children make a print of each design by laying a piece of paper on the design and pressing gently all over it. Tell them to lift the paper and set it aside to dry. Supply a bucket with a little water and sponges so that children can clean off the table.

BLOCKS

✳ At the Lake

Add small toy people to the block area. Let children bring boats if they wish. Encourage them to build swimming pools and lakes in which the toy people can swim. Suggest that they build boat ramps to back the boats into the lake.

BULLETIN BOARD

✳ Rainbows

Cover the board with a light blue or white paper. Divide it into seven strips using wide yarn or ribbon that begins at the top of the board and extends four feet below the bottom of the board. Display the caption *Rainbows* at the top of the board. In each strip, put a card on which you have printed a word for one of the colors of the rainbow. Arrange the cards in a rainbow-shaped arc in the sequence of colors in a rainbow. Add a border of raindrop cutouts along each side and across the top. Do not continue the border across the bottom of the board.

In each strip on the board, put up children's drawings, photographs, pictures, and a collage of items in different shades of that color. Position a long table along the bottom edge of the board. Extend the yarn or ribbon strips across the table and tape them to the table. Encourage children to find objects in each color and place them on the table beside the appropriate color strip.

During circle time, talk about the colors and chant them in sequence. Count and compare the number of objects of each color. Talk about the little words within the word *rainbow (rain, bow, a,* and *in)* and print these words on index cards.

COOKING

✳ Sailwiches

Bread slices	*Jelly*
Plastic knives	*Honey*
Softened low-fat cream cheese	*Margarine*

Wash hands. Tell children that they are creating "sailwiches" instead of sandwiches because of the shape of the bread. Help children cut their bread in half on the diagonal to make a triangular shape like a sail on a boat. Children spread one or more of the toppings on it and enjoy their sailwich as you share pictures or a book about sailboats. Discuss why sailboats float and move on the water.

Note: The children can eat the leftover bread scraps or use them to feed the birds or the ducks and geese at a nearby pond.

✳ Floats

1 cup of lemon-lime drink for each child	*Paper cups*
1 small scoop of sherbet for each child	*Straws*

Wash hands. Help children pour a cup of lemon-lime drink, leaving about a 2-inch space at the top of their glasses. They then carefully add a small scoop of sherbet. Ask children to notice what happens to the scoop of sherbet. Talk about why these drinks are called floats. Give children straws and have them sit down together to enjoy their floats.

✳ Apple Time

2–3 apples	*Cups*
Plastic knives	*Spoons*
Small paper plates or wax paper squares	*Large pitcher*
2 cans of apple juice concentrate	*Small plastic pitcher*
Water as needed, according to directions on	
the juice can	

This is an excellent task to do in conjunction with the Great Disappearing Act activity (see p. 253). Explain that water is in many of the things we eat and drink, so children's bodies get water by drinking and eating other foods and liquids besides water. Explain that you are going to conduct tasting experiments with apple products. Wash hands. Have children watch as you cut apples in halves, then in quarters, and finally in eighths. Talk about the fractions of the apple and show the children that the eight pieces can be put together to make a whole apple. Give each child an eighth of an apple to cut into smaller slices or pieces on a plate or piece of wax paper.

Set aside $\frac{1}{2}$ can of the concentrate. Let children help measure and mix the ingredients for $1\frac{1}{2}$ cans of juice to make a large pitcher of apple juice. Use the term *dissolve*. Pour some of the contents into a small plastic pitcher so that children can pour their own juice. Ask children to describe how the juice looks different from the way it did as a concentrate.

Have children use spoons to taste a small amount of the concentrate. Then have them taste their cup of juice. Talk about how the juice tastes. Help children realize that the juice is the apple-juice concentrate dissolved in water. Finally, let children eat a piece of the apple and compare the taste and texture to the taste and texture of apple juice and apple juice concentrate. Have some children try to identify an apple, the concentrate, or the apple juice with their eyes closed. Ask children to explain to others how they identified each food. Talk about *solid* and *liquid*. Finally, have children finish their apples and juice. Talk about other drinks that are made by dissolving something in water.

LANGUAGE ARTS

✳ Fingerplay – Drip, Drip, Drop

Drip, drop, drip, drop.
   (Use both index fingers to tap on a table, alternating from one finger to the other.)
Rain is falling all around,
   (Wiggle fingers of both hands, moving them from high in the air to the floor.)
Making puddles on the ground,
   (Circle arms to show large puddles.)
So feet can make a splish-splash sound.
   (Shuffle feet.)
Drip, drip, drop.
   (Hold arms over head and then lower arms and body to floor.)
   Use other words from the Sounds of Water list (see below) to substitute for the words *drip, drop* in the verse.

✳ Word Wall

Add the word *water* to the word wall. Add other topic-related words that children suggest. Emphasize the high-frequency words you want children to use. Have the children count how many words are on the word wall. Write a sentence strip that reads *We have (the number) words on our word wall.* Display the strip. Place a piece of blue plastic over one or more of the word cards to highlight words you particularly want children to read and incorporate in their writing.

✳ Water Begins With W (A Whole-Class Project)

On a large piece of blue butcher paper, draw a large drop of water. Write *Water Begins With W* at the top of the paper. Have children cut pictures out of magazines and draw pictures of things that begin with *w.* Discuss each picture and then have children glue each on the paper. Print the word that describes each object beside the picture. You may wish to have children continue the activity at center and free time until the paper is filled with pictures.

✳ The Sounds of Water

Brainstorm and list together words for the sounds of water. Display the words on or beside a large cutout of an ear. Add the caption *We hear water.* Words could include *drip, drop, run, splash, trickle, hiss,* and *gurgle.* Have children use the words to construct interesting sentences, such as, The water trickled from the hose.

✳ Fishing

Make fishing poles by tying one end of a 3-foot length of string to a dowel rod and a small magnet to the other end of the string. Cut several small and large fish from construction paper. Put a paper clip through the mouth of each fish and toss the fish on the floor. Have children sit on a chair near the "pond" and try to catch fish.

Discuss why fish must live in water. As each child catches a fish, ask her or him if it is a large or small fish. Ask children why the paper clip is attracted to the magnet.

Use the following suggestions to vary the activity.

1. Cut out fish in different colors. Have the children name the color of each fish they catch.

2. Glue a shape or letter on each fish. Have the children identify the shape or letter or tell something that is that shape or begins with that letter.

3. Use an opened paper clip to add a hook to the fishing pole. Make fish from plastic foam blocks and attach a large paper clip to the mouth of each fish. Then have children try to hook a fish that is swimming in a dishpan or tub of water.

✳ Uses for Water

1. Explore the idea that water keeps plants, animals, and people alive. Talk about how you must water plants for them to live. Ask if any children have pets. Ask, "Do pets need water? How do you know? Do you need water? When have you felt really thirsty?" Be sure children understand that water is in many of the things we eat and drink, so drinking a glass of water is not the only way we get water.

2. Explore the idea that water cleans people, plants, animals, and the air. Discuss how people use water for washing hands and faces, taking baths, washing food, washing dishes and clothes, and cleaning homes and buildings. Explain that rain washes our air and all plant life. Demonstrate with a dusty plant. Have children feel the dust. Spray the plant gently with water and have children feel the leaves again.

3. Explore the idea that water helps put out fires. Show a picture of a fire hydrant and explain to children what it is. Walk to a nearby hydrant so that they may see and touch one. Ask children to notice how many fire hydrants are around their neighborhood and where they are located. Later, talk about why fire hydrants are located in those places.

4. Explore the idea that water has recreational uses, such as boating, fishing, swimming, and playing in a sprinkler. Brainstorm and list the things children like to do to have fun in the water. Talk about bath time as a time when some children play in the water.

✳ Water From a Well

Recite "Jack and Jill" together. Explain that many people used to go to an outside well to get water for drinking, cooking, and washing. Show a picture of a well and ask if any of the children have ever seen one. Talk about how most people get water today. Discuss the pipes and faucets that are in most buildings.

✳ Water is . . .

Provide a 6 to 8-inch raindrop pattern. Have children use it as a stencil to cut out two raindrops. Have them write *Water is . . .* on one raindrop and then finish the sentence by writing and illustrating their ideas on the other raindrop. They may complete the sentence by writing or illustrating ideas such as *fun to swim in, where fish live,* or *my favorite drink.* Staple the two drops together, one on top of the other, so that someone has to lift the *Water is . . .* raindrop to see the child's response. Post the completed raindrops where children can repeatedly see and read them.

✳ Blue Day

Ask everyone to dress in something that is the color of water in the ocean. Talk about the different shades of blue that the children wear. Ask each child to name a favorite thing that is blue, such as water, the sky, or a favorite shirt.

✳ Rebus Sentences

Rebus sentences use pictures to substitute for some words. Show pictures of water activities to make a class rebus story. Glue a picture of a water activity in each sentence instead of writing the word for the activity. Also use pictures of things that need water.

Have the class work together to make up sentences about water that include the activities or things shown in the pictures. Provide simple sentence patterns, like the ones below. Some children may be able to use these sentence patterns to write rebus sentences independently.

We can _____ in the water.
_____ needs water to grow.

✳ Bubbles

Materials: Bubble Solution (see Appendix II, p. 273); plastic-coated wire, available at hardware stores; straws; paper cups

Blow a bubble into the air toward the sunlight. Ask, "What shape do you see? What colors can you see?" Relate a bubble to a rainbow and a sphere or round ball.

Give children straws to blow bubbles by blowing through the straw into a small amount of the solution in a paper cup. Point out that the bubbles grow and cluster together high above the top of the cup. Have children try to gently stick a straw through a bubble without breaking it.

Have children explain the process of blowing bubbles. Ask, "What do I need to do to blow bubbles?" Follow their directions and let them discover how to change their directions as needed. Ask sequence questions, such as, "What should I do first? What do I do next?"

Finally, let the children create a wide assortment of loops for blowing bubbles by bending wire into small loops, double loops, giant loops, and oval loops. Have them dip the loops into the mixture and blow bubbles. Talk about the shapes of the loops and the different bubble shapes they make.

Note: This bubble activity works best outside to avoid creating slippery spots on floors.

✳ Bubble Analogies

After completing the Bubbles activity, ask the children to complete the following open-ended sentence: *If I were a bubble, I would _____.* Have children write the sentence, or duplicate the sentence on the bottom of a sheet of Manila paper for them. Children then draw a picture to illustrate the bubble analogies. Combine the pictures into a class book titled *Our Bubble Book* so that children can read their analogies again and again. Consider tape recording an adult reading the book with the class. Children can listen to the tape independently and read along with *Our Bubble Book.* As the tape is made, say each child's name as his or her page is read.

✳ Water Play at School

Set up a water exploration activity for children inside. Put a small amount of water in a large plastic pan or sink. Provide sponges. As you put one corner of a dry sponge in the water, have the children watch the sponge gradually absorb water.

Provide plastic cups and glasses, plastic tubing, funnels, and measuring cups and spoons. Have big towels nearby for children to wipe up any spills that occur. You may wish to place all the water-play materials on a plastic drop cloth to protect the floor from spills.

Challenge children to use sponges, cups, funnels, and tubing to figure out the fastest way to move the water from one bucket to another without pouring it. Some children may enjoy timing the process.

MATH

✳ Sailboats

Make a set of sailboats using the sailboat picture on the topic card on page 227. Write numerals from 5 through 10 on each boat (or other numerals as appropriate for the children). Have children take turns putting the boats in numerical order.

✳ All Aboard

Use the set of boats made in the preceding activity. Appoint one person as the captain. He or she passes out the boats to other children. The captain then tells each child to "get aboard" in numerical order by saying, for example, "All aboard for number 5," or "All aboard for number 6." As children hear their number called, they "sail over" and stand by the captain.

✳ Seashell Scoop

Provide a sand bucket and shovel. Fill the bucket with small shells. (Shells can be purchased from a craft store.)

1. Children gently scoop out a shovelful of shells and count how many shells are in the shovelful.
2. Provide cards with a numeral on each, from 5 to 10 or more. Children scoop out shells and count out the appropriate number of shells to place on each card.
3. Ask children to find the biggest shell and the smallest shell.

If multiple examples of similar shells are available, create a repeating shell pattern and challenge children to replicate or extend it. Have children use the shells to create their own repeating shell patterns. Children can try to replicate or extend each other's patterns.

✳ Story Problems: How Many Fish?

Provide several zippered sandwich-sized plastic bags with ten or more goldfish crackers inside each. Create story problems for the children to solve and use the crackers as math manipulatives. Include the children's names in the problems. An example follows.

Austin feeds Jenny, the seal, two fish.
Josh feeds her one fish.
How many fish does Jenny get to eat?

Vary the difficulty of the problems according to the readiness of the children. Some children in the class may be ready to make up their own original problems for others to act out.

✳ Longer and Shorter Walk

Take the children outside and have them determine a longer distance and a shorter distance. Mark the beginning and the end of each distance with a rock. Children take turns carrying a cup or ladle full of water for both a longer distance and a shorter distance without spilling the water. Vary the method of walking to add to the fun.

✳ Whole and Half

Cut a circle in half. Show the half vertically and then horizontally. Ask children how the half is like a rainbow. Explain that the arc of a rainbow is like a half circle.

✳ Barefoot Prints

Take the children outside. Provide a dishpan or bucket of water. Have the children take off their shoes, wet their feet, and make footprints on the sidewalk. Use a 12-inch ruler to measure the footprints. Ask, "Whose feet are closest to twelve inches?" Have children walk heel-to-toe to make several footprints in a row. Use a yardstick to measure the footprints. Ask, "How many footprints make a yard?" Make footprints yourself or have another adult make footprints so that the children can compare the lengths of adult-sized and child-sized footprints.

✳ A Pattern of Boats

Make cutouts of sailboats and other boats in different colors. Create a repeating pattern along a wall. Make the pattern simple or more complex, as appropriate for the children. Discuss the pattern with the children. Help them to identify the sequence or part that repeats. Have children help measure the length of the border and count the number of boats. Add the caption *Our pattern is _____ feet long. It has _____ boats in it.*

When the children are not in the room, remove one boat from the pattern and have the children figure out what is missing. Then remove three or four boats, show them to the children, and have them figure out where to place each.

✳ Shape Painting

Invite children to use black to paint the outline of an oval and then use a different color to make thumbprints inside the shape. Challenge them to count the number of thumbprints inside the figure. Talk about inside and outside.

Encourage children to repeat the process using other geometric figures.

MOVEMENT

✳ Water-Squeeze Fun

Fill old liquid detergent bottles with water. Have children wear swim suits. Take the children outside, give each a squirt bottle, and let the fun begin!

✳ Swimming Left and Right

Have children lay down and stretch out on the floor. Have them act out the rhyme by making appropriate motions for each line.

We swim with our left arm, we swim with our right.
We roll over and over and kick with all of our might.
We swim on our side, we swim on our back.
We're getting lots of exercise, and that's a healthy fact!

✳ Dolphin Over the Water Game

The children form a circle. One to three children are dolphins and stand inside the circle. The group chants:

Dolphin over the water, dolphin over the sea,
Dolphin caught a fish, but can't catch me!

On the word *me,* the children on the edge of the circle sit down quickly while the children inside the circle try to touch someone before he or she sits down. Then children who are touched go to the middle and the game is repeated.

MUSIC

✳ Water Instruments

Pour different amounts of water into three glasses. Tap each gently with a stick or spoon. Ask children to talk about what they hear and what they notice happens to the sound when there is more water in the glass. Let the children help arrange the glasses in order from lowest to highest pitch.

Have children try to produce three ascending musical tones by pouring water into three glasses. Sing together a simple song such as "Are You Sleeping" and have children take turns tapping the glasses to accompany the song.

✳ Ocean in a Bottle

Use small, clear plastic bottles with tightly fitting lids. Fill the bottles with the following: $\frac{1}{2}$ cup baby oil, $\frac{1}{2}$ cup water, and 3 to 4 drops of blue food coloring. Replace the lid tightly. Turn the bottle on its side and gently rock it back and forth. The mixture inside rolls and moves like ocean waves.

Play a recording of slow, calming music and let children take turns moving the "ocean in a bottle" so that the waves move in time to the music.

✳ W-A-T-E-R

(Tune: "Bingo")

There's one thing everyone needs to live,
And water is that thing-o.
W-A-T-E-R, W-A-T-E-R, W-A-T-E-R,
And water is that thing-o.

✳ Row Your Boat

Sing "Row, Row, Row, Your Boat" while the children sit on the floor and pretend to be rowing. Children can also row in pairs. They sit facing each other, legs stretched out straight, and feet touching. Holding hands, they rock back and forth as they sing, gently pulling each other forward and backward in rhythm to the music.

ROLE PLAY

✳ Boat

Make a pretend boat by pushing two chairs together, seat to seat, or by providing a large box. Add a real oar or make oar shapes from heavy cardboard. Provide fishing poles without hooks so that children can pretend to fish. Talk with the children about recreational uses of water and lakes.

✳ Clothesline

Have the children wash and rinse out doll clothes. String a clothesline outside, provide spring-type clothespins, and have the children hang out the laundry to dry. Talk with the children about how water helps to clean clothes. Ask children what people put in water when they clean clothes and other things.

SCIENCE

✳ Water Cycle

Ask children where they think rain comes from. Draw and discuss the water cycle. Explain evaporation and condensation in simple terms.

✳ Making a Cloud

A simple experiment can help children understand how warm air rises into the atmosphere, meets colder air, and forms clouds. Carefully pour one cup of very hot water into a quart-sized, heat-proof glass jar. Darken the room. Set a metal pie pan of ice cubes on top of the opening of the jar. Shine a flashlight toward the middle of the jar and watch the cloud form. Explain to the children how these clouds gather more and more moisture until the drops get too heavy and fall back to Earth as raindrops.

✳ Water as Steam

Use a small electric teakettle to boil water and create steam. Brainstorm with the children where they might have seen steam. Possible situations include steam from a cooking pot, steam in a bathtub, or steam from a teakettle. Hold an aluminum pie pan in the path of the steam and watch for condensation.

Note: In the interest of safety, the children should not be allowed to hold their hands in the path of the steam to determine that it is hot. Explain that steam can produce bad burns.

✳ Forms of Water: Ice and Liquid

This two-day lesson shows how water changes from a liquid to ice and back to liquid.
Day One – Children put water in three or four different sizes and kinds of containers, such as a small juice can and a small plastic bowl. Children watch as you place the containers in a freezer. Ask children to predict what will happen to the water when you leave it in the freezer overnight.
Day Two – Children watch as you take the containers from the freezer. Talk about how the

containers feel. Remove the ice from the containers. Mix up the containers and the ice shapes and let children match each piece to the container from which it came. Talk about the size of the ice in each container and explain that water expands when it freezes.

Put the ice in a pan. Ask children to predict which piece will melt first and which will melt last. Record their predictions. Ask them why they think so. Then observe what happens over a period of time. Graph how long it takes each piece to melt. Discuss how temperature affects the form water takes.

Some children may want to draw pictures and write about the experiment. Remind them that scientists often record their observations in a notebook as they work.

✳ Floats-Sinks Experiment

Cut apart the Floats and Sinks cards (Activity Master 25, p. 302). Laminate them or put them in a clear plastic folder. Show the cards to the children and explain what each indicates.

Provide a pan with a small amount of water. Put together a collection of several small objects, some of which float (bottle lids, corks, plastic foam pieces) and some of which do not float (spoon, pencil, nail, and small car). Spread the objects on a towel. Have children take turns placing each object in the water and determining if it floats or does not float. They place objects that float next to the Floats card and those that sink next to the Sinks card.

After children have experimented with the objects, provide older children or those with advanced skills with a collection of different objects. Ask them to predict which objects will sink or float by placing each object by the Floats or Sinks card. Then they test their predictions by placing each object in the pan of water. Repeat the process with a third collection of objects if the children are interested.

Ask children to tell you why they think an object sinks or floats. Ask children who seem to understand the concept to find a different object in the room that they think will float.

✳ The Great Disappearing Act

Provide the children with several plastic glasses, half full of water. Supply craft sticks and a variety of ingredients that children can add to water to determine if they dissolve. Possible ingredients include sugar, salt, pepper, cornmeal, cornstarch, chili powder, dirt, sand, cooking oil, lemon juice, and food coloring.

Introduce the activity by asking what happens when a spoonful of sugar is mixed into water. Explain that this process is called *dissolving* and that some things dissolve in water but others do not.

Prepare a list of the ingredients, and have children predict whether each ingredient will dissolve. Record the predictions of the class under the categories *Dissolves* or *Does Not Dissolve*. Discuss the procedure for the experiment and then have children test each ingredient as you record the outcomes.

✳ Rainbows

Demonstrate how rainbows are made from water acting like a prism in the sunlight. Fill a clear plastic glass or bowl half full of water. Place it in direct sunlight. Put a mirror in the glass and hold it at an angle so that the sunlight strikes it. Have a child hold a piece of white poster board about two feet from the glass. Adjust the mirror's angle so that the sunlight reflects on the poster board and a rainbow forms on it.

Discuss the colors the children see in the rainbow. Together, name the colors from top to bottom. Tell the children that the colors always appear in the same order: red, orange, yellow, green, blue, indigo, and violet. Talk about the first letters in each color word. Tell children that a fun way to remember the order of the colors is by using the first letter of each color to make a name: ROY G. BIV. Write the letters and point to each one as children repeat the color sequence.

TRANSITION ACTIVITY
✳ Stand Up–Sit Down

Call out different activities for the children to do. If the activity involves water, the children stand up; if it does not, they sit down. Examples could include swimming, sleeping, fishing, wading, eating a hamburger, and showering. Vary the activity by calling out different colors. If it is a color in a rainbow, the children stand up; if not, they sit down.

CHILDREN'S BOOKS

Aliki. *My Visit to the Aquarium.* New York: HarperCollins, 1993. Colorful, multicultural illustrations. An abundance of factual information.

Cole, J. *The Magic School Bus at the Waterworks.* New York: Scholastic, 1986. Marvelous factual information in a fiction story about a class of children and their spirited teacher learning how water is supplied to homes.

Cowan, C. and M. Burhner. *My Life With the Wave.* New York: Lothrop, Lee & Shepard, 1997. A boy brings home a "stray" wave from his trip to the ocean. Havoc results.

Gibbon, G. *Exploring the Deep, Dark Sea.* Boston: Little, Brown, 1999. An informative book that invites children to join oceanographers as they explore the depths of ocean life.

Hess, K. *Come On, Rain!* New York: Scholastic, 1999. Examines the concept of drought before and after the rain. Multicultural connections.

Isadora, R. *Caribbean Dream.* New York: G. P. Putnam's Sons, 1998. Follow the activities of island children living on an island.

Jonas, A. *Splash.* New York: Greenwillow, 1995. Life around the pond.

Kalman, B. *A B Sea.* New York: Crabtree Publishing, 1995. An ABC book from the ocean. Brilliant photography and rich vocabulary.

Lionni. L. *Swimmy.* New York: Pantheon, 1963. A little fish learns about the power of working together. Award-winning book.

Pallotta, J. *The Underwater Alphabet Book.* Watertown, MA: Charlesbridge, 1991. An ABC information book with great illustrations.

Pfister, M. *The Rainbow Fish.* New York: North-South Books, 1995. A fish is too impressed with his own appearance until he learns the joy of sharing.

Sheldon, D. *The Whales' Song.* New York: Dial, 1990. Lilly's grandmother tells her the story of the whales she loved as a child, and Lilly wants to watch for the whales.

Stojic, M. *Rain.* New York: Crown Publishers, 2000. Repetitive, predictable story of the rain cycle in Africa. The animals enjoy the effects of the rain in their own unique ways.

Van Dusen, C. *Down to the Sea with Mr. Magee.* San Francisco: Chronicle, 1999. A playful whale changes Mr. Magee's outing at the sea.

June
Curriculum

Summertime and the Sun

Summertime and the Sun

CONCEPTS

- Summer is one season of the year. It comes after spring and before fall.
- The temperature is usually warm or hot in summer because our part of the Earth is tilted more toward the sun.
- The sun is a star that provides us light and heat.
- People wear lighter clothing in summer to help them stay cooler.
- Many people enjoy being outdoors in summer. They like to picnic, swim, and play outside.
- Some special fruits, such as berries, strawberries, watermelons, honeydew melons, and cantaloupes, are available in the summer.
- Some children do not go to school in the summer.
- Some people take trips or vacations to relax during the summer.

CONTINUING CONCEPTS

- **Colors** Discuss why bright colors are associated with summer.
    Have children identify the colors of summer fruits.
- **Geometric Shapes** Review circle, triangle, square, rectangle, and oval.
    Help children compare watermelons and cantaloupes to egg shapes and spheres.
- **Health and Nutrition** Discuss why it is important to protect your skin from the sun.
    Discuss the value of fruits in a healthy diet.
- **Senses** Talk about the color, texture, shape, and smell of summer fruits.
    Have children identify summer melons and berries by taste only.
    Have children feel the texture of sand.
    Discuss how it feels to get hot outside in the sun.
    Have children listen for summertime insects such as crickets and locusts.
- **Traditional Rhymes and Tales** Recite "Twinkle, Twinkle, Little Star," "Hey, Diddle, Diddle," and "Humpty Dumpty" with the children.

PORTFOLIO PRODUCTS

- Have each child complete his or her audiotape for the portfolio by recording summer plans. State the child's name and the date at the beginning of the tape.
- Select a few products from each child's portfolio to pass on to next year's teacher. The rest of the products can be put together and bound in a book to take home as a keepsake for the family. The audiotape can be stored in a zippered plastic bag and the edge of the bag inserted in the binding of the portfolio book.

✳ Easel or Tabletop Painting

1. Summer Colors

Materials: tempera paints in bright summer colors; paper; brushes

Provide children with paint in bright colors and encourage them to freely explore using and blending colors. Talk together about where children might see each color.

2. The Sun

Materials: tempera paints in bright shades of yellow; paper; brushes

Let children paint their interpretation of the sun. Ask, "How do you think the sun looks?"

✳ Mixing Summer Colors

Materials: summer fruits and vegetables; paper; different colors of tempera paints; brushes

Display a variety of summer fruits and vegetables for children to handle and smell. Talk about the color of each fruit. Work with the children to arrange a few fruits or vegetables by color, from darkest to lightest. Provide tempera paints in a variety of colors. Encourage the children to mix paints so that they match the colors of the fruits and vegetables. Have them use the colors they mixed to paint a fruit and vegetable arrangement or any picture they wish.

✳ Body Painting

Materials: body paint (see Appendix II, p. 273); brushes

Do this activity outside. Have the children measure and mix the ingredients for body paint in several colors. This paint won't harm skin or leave a stain. Have children wear shorts or swimsuits and paint their bodies using cotton swabs or clean paintbrushes. Encourage them to make lots of designs and patterns. You may wish to have children paint each other's arms, legs, or backs, if they feel comfortable doing so. Then have everyone help each other rinse off with a garden hose, or have the children get in a wading pool to wash off. Take lots of photographs!

✳ Summertime Artists

Materials: easels; tempera paints in bright colors; brushes; large sheets of newsprint paper

Move the painting easels outside. Identify the colors, and have children take turns painting at the easels. Use clothespins or tape to hang the paintings to dry on a fence or the side of the building. The display makes a lovely art show!

☀ Sidewalk Art

Materials: white or colored chalk

Children use chalk to draw on sidewalk sections. Each section becomes one child's personal drawing area. If necessary, the children can end the project by wiping off the chalk using water and a rag or sponge.

☀ Rock Painting

Materials: rocks; old newspaper; tempera paints and brushes; google eyes; shellac (optional)

Go on a walk and collect smooth rocks with the children. Then provide each child with tempera paint mixed with one tablespoon of soap flakes or soap powder so that the paint adheres well to the rock surface.

Brush off any dirt from the rocks and let the children wash the rocks as a water-play activity.

Cover the work area with newspaper. Have children paint a rock with bright colors and designs. Have them add google eyes to make pet rocks. When the rocks are dry, you could spray them with shellac.

The painted rocks can be used as paperweights, but children enjoy them without assigning them a useful purpose. Compare the children's painted rocks to rocks with natural color variations. Explain that the different minerals in natural rocks provide their color.

☀ Picture Postcards

Materials: 4" × 6" index cards; markers or crayons

Discuss how and why people send postcards to others during the summer. Have children fold a large index card in half. On one half, have them draw summer scenes or any picture they want. On the other half, have them write or dictate a message they want to send to someone.

☀ Sand Prints

Materials: fine sand; construction paper in bright summer colors; powdered tempera paints; glue; cotton swabs

Explain that water forms the sand that is found on beaches by grinding down rocks into smaller and smaller pieces.

Put $\frac{1}{2}$-inch of fine sand in the bottom of a large box lid. Invite children to feel the sand and use words to describe how it feels. You may wish to make colored sand by mixing the sand with tempera paint powder.

Cover the work area. Have children use cotton swabs to paint a glue design on a piece of construction paper. Then have them turn their designs over, gently press them into the sand, and lift the papers. Carefully shake off excess sand and set the prints aside to dry completely.

✳ Summer Clouds

Materials: white paint; spoons; blue construction paper; crayon or markers; glue

Read the book *It Looked Like Spilt Milk* by Charles Shaw to the children. Hold up a free-form white paper shape and say, "What could this be? Let's turn it around. Now what does it look like? What could we add to it to make it look like an animal or person or creature?" Encourage the children to think of something no one else has thought of.

Demonstrate how to fold a sheet of construction paper in half, put a spoonful of paint inside, close the paper, and gently rub the paper to spread the paint inside. Open the paper to show the result. Use the term *symmetry* as you discuss the design on the paper. Discuss with the children what the shape might be.

Have children make their own designs in the same way. If they aren't satisfied with the first result, let them add a little more paint to the same paper and close and rub again. Talk about what each design could be. Then have the children add details to complete the pictures. Have an adult or the children write a brief description, using the sentence pattern *Sometimes it looks like a _____, but it is a _____.*

Display the children's pictures with the original book or compile the pictures into a class book.

If children like this book and art activity, read David Wiesner's *Sector 7* to them. Challenge them to figure out how to make fish-shaped clouds.

BLOCKS

✳ Vacation Trips

Encourage the children to use blocks to build summer vacation places and the roads that lead to them. Provide small cars and suggest they use them to take summer vacation trips.

✳ Teeter-Totter or Seesaw

Discuss the fun of playing in the park on warm summer days. Encourage children to construct a small teeter-totter or seesaw by using a small block as the fulcrum and then balancing a longer flat board on top of it. Have them add blocks on top of the longer board to see what happens to the balance and add blocks to one side at a time or both sides at once. Finally, suggest that they use a heavier block on one side and determine what to do to balance the seesaw.

BULLETIN BOARD

✳ The Sun

Cover the board with bright orange or red paper. Display the caption *The Sun* in large letters at the top of the board. Make a summer border all around the board by outlining the board with simple flowers made by the children.

Provide a very large cutout of a circle for a sun and several elongated triangles for the sun's rays. Have children work together to completely cover the circle with a collage of yellow and orange tissue-paper squares. They can use cotton swabs to paint a touch of glue and then stick tissue squares in place. Other children can use the glue and tissue squares to cover the cutouts for the rays. When the rays are covered with tissue paper, have them use glitter or sequins and glue to trim the edges of the rays. Assemble the sun and the rays on the center of the board.

As children learn important facts about the sun, print each fact on a strip of paper or large index card and pin it on the board. Use glue and glitter to trim the edges of each fact card. During circle time, review the facts and compliment the child or children who shared each one.

COOKING

✳ Melon Party

Paper plates	*Melons*
Toothpicks	*Plastic knives*

Wash hands. Provide different kinds of melon, such as cantaloupe, honeydew, and watermelon. Cut open the melons. Have the children compare the seeds, the color, the smell, and finally, the taste. Then have the children close their eyes and give them small pieces of melon. Graph how many children could tell and could not tell what kind of melon they ate by simply tasting it. Give children slices of melon they want to eat. Have them cut each slice into smaller pieces and eat each piece with a toothpick. Have children who ask for a slice of watermelon count the seeds in their slice.

You may wish to repeat the activity using different kinds of berries, such as strawberries, blueberries, blackberries, and raspberries.

✳ Picnic Time

Plan a picnic outside for snack time. Invite one or two other classes. Each class makes some food item to share with the other classes. Talk about sharing and thanking others for what they share. Discuss the summer weather and why it is a good time for picnics.

✳ Homemade Ice Cream

Wash hands. Make homemade ice cream in the classroom using your favorite recipe. Discuss the purpose of the rock salt and the ice as you prepare the ice cream. Ask, "Why do you think people call it ice cream?' Serve the ice cream in small paper cups.

✳ Dripless Freeze Pops

1–2 packages of fruit-flavored gelatin	*Craft sticks*
Small paper cups	

Wash hands. Children help measure and mix fruit-flavored gelatin according to the directions on the package. Have the children compare its look and smell with the same kind of fresh fruit. For example, ask, "How is a strawberry like our strawberry gelatin?" Pour the gelatin into small paper cups, place a craft stick in each, and freeze. Tear off the paper cup for a delicious and dripless treat. Ask the children to compare its taste with the taste of fresh fruit.

LANGUAGE ARTS

✳ Fingerplay – Bright Sun

Hello bright sun! I'm glad you're here today.
   (Gently move arms in a circle overhead to make a shining sun.)
Please help me make a shadow so we can run and play.
   (Look over shoulder as if looking for a shadow; run fingers up arm.)

✳ Fingerplay – Summertime

Summertime has bright, hot days; we play outdoors in lots of ways.
   (Arms circle overhead to make a sun.)
Let's dive into a swimming pool. Oooh! It feels so wet and cool!
   (Hands in diving position, give a little jump, and swim in place.)
Let's all give a happy cheer 'cause summertime is here. Hurrah!
   (Jump in place; clap and cheer.)

✳ Word Wall

Add the words *summer* and *sun* to the word wall. Add other topic-related words that children suggest. Emphasize the high-frequency words you want children to use. Have the children count how many words are on the word wall. Write a sentence strip that reads *We have (the number) words on our word wall.* Display the strip. Place a piece of yellow plastic over one or more of the word cards to highlight words you want children to read and incorporate in their writing.

✳ Sunny Words

Brainstorm together all the words children can think of that have *sun* in them, such as *Sunday, sunflower, sunlight, sunburn, sunglasses,* and *sunrise.* Use a bright yellow marker to print the words on a large chart as children suggest them. Encourage children to continue the list by asking family members at home for additional words. During circle time, invite children to share additional words to print on the list. Count and record the number of words listed. Let interested children decorate the chart by coloring suns all around the borders of the chart and drawing illustrations for each word.

✳ Body-Painting Experience Chart

Display the photographs from the body-painting activity (see p. 257) and encourage the children to describe the photographs in detail. Say, for example, "Tell me what you were doing in this picture. What happened before this picture was taken? What happened after this picture was taken?" Help the children recall the activity in as much detail as possible.

Next, structure those details into a sequenced retelling of the activity. Fold a piece of chart paper horizontally into six rows to organize the chart story. Talk about the first thing the children did in the body-painting activity (measured and mixed the paint) and write about that in the top row. Go to the last row and talk about the last thing they did (washed themselves). Then add that to the chart story. As children discuss the other tasks or parts of the activity, help them decide in which row to write them. Ask, "Did that happen next or later?" When the story has been fully organized, encourage the children to add adjectives that make it more interesting. Then recopy it. Help the children agree upon a title and add it to the story. Invite children to draw pictures of the body painting to display around the completed story.

Reread the story together several times. Let children use a pointer to find specific letters or words. Ask them to find how many times a certain word, such as *paint,* is repeated in the story.

✳ Cloud Watching

Have the children lay on their backs outside and watch the clouds. They could also watch clouds from the inside by finding a comfortable position near a large window.

Guide the children's observations and thinking with open-ended questions such as the following:

Do clouds look soft or hard? . . . smooth or rough?
Do they have any pointed, sharp edges?
What words could we use to describe them?
How do clouds move?
Where are the clouds at night?
Why are some clouds gigantic and some very small?
If we could do imaginary things, how could we make the clouds move?

✳ Barefoot Walk

Walk barefoot outside with the children. Talk about how different surfaces feel. Encourage children to use words like *rough, smooth, hard,* and *soft.* Ask, "Which feels cooler—the grass, shady cement, or cement in the sun?

✳ Folk Tales and Nursery Rhymes in the Summer

Recite "Twinkle, Twinkle Little Star" with the children. Discuss how bright the stars can appear on clear summer nights. Encourage children to watch the stars tonight and recite the rhyme with a family member.

Review several folk tales you have shared with the children. Invite children to tell the parts they know. Discuss in which season these stories probably happened. Identify events or clues that suggest a story took place in summer. Talk about how a story might be different or what parts might be affected if the story happened in another season.

✳ Choral-Speaking Nursery Rhymes

Recite many of the nursery rhymes children know. Ask children to name their favorite nursery rhymes. Then divide the rhymes into parts for a choral-speaking activity. The following are two examples of ways to arrange a rhyme for choral speaking. Encourage the children to suggest actions that could be added as the rhyme is performed.

For two groups:

Group 1: Hey, Diddle, Diddle, the cat and the fiddle,
Group 2: The cow jumped over the moon.
Group 1: The little dog laughed to see such sport,
Group 2: And the dish ran away with the spoon.

For three groups:

Group 1: Humpty Dumpty sat on a wall.
Group 2: Humpty Dumpty had a great fall.
Group 3: All the king's horses and all the king's men
All: Couldn't put Humpty Dumpty together again!

✳ Suitcase Memory Game

1. Put three or four items related to summertime travel in a small suitcase. Show the children what you've packed. Close the suitcase and ask children to tell what is inside.
2. Place the suitcase where the children cannot see it and remove one item. Ask children to look in the suitcase and identify the missing item.
3. Provide several small items. Have children take turns choosing a few items to pack and quizzing the other children about what is inside.

✳ Travel Game

Say, "I'm going on a trip." Then share a riddle to describe something you are taking with you. Say, for example, "It is small. I need it to fix my hair. What am I taking?" Children guess the item and then take turns making up riddles of their own.

✳ Weather Dolls

Draw a boy and a girl outline on poster board. Glue felt underwear or a felt slip to the figures. Make several pieces of clothing from felt or nonwoven interfacing colored with markers. Items should include shorts, tops, coats, umbrella, swim suits, dress, jeans, hats, shoes, socks, and sandals.

During circle time, have children choose the most appropriate outfit to match the weather each day. Talk about how the temperature influences what we wear each day. Post the temperature beside the weather dolls. During free time or centers, let individual children dress the weather dolls.

✳ Postcard Puzzles

Talk about sending and receiving postcards. Show several summertime postcards and discuss what the pictures show about summer. Cut interesting postcards in several puzzle pieces. Choose a number that suits the readiness of the children. Have the children put the puzzles together.

Store the pieces of each puzzle in a separate zippered plastic bag to keep pieces from getting lost or mixed up. Put a dot of color on the back of each piece of a puzzle and a dot of the same color on the plastic bag. Use different color dots for each puzzle so that the pieces can be easily sorted if the puzzles get mixed up.

✳ Unfinished Sentences

Read each incomplete sentence and have the children complete them orally.

In the summer, I like to eat _____.
When it's hot, I want to _____.
I like to play _____.
After school, I am going to _____.
I like summer because _____.

MATH

✳ Calendar

Provide the children who can write numerals with their own copy of a blank calendar (Activity Master 3, p. 280). Help them write the name of the month and fill in the date in the appropriate place each day. Suggest that children mark special days, including the first day of summer and children's birthdays, on the calendar. Ask children to role play explaining a calendar to a younger child.

Give blank calendars to children who would like to complete July and August calendars at home during the summer.

✳ Counting

Sing the song "This Old Man" with the class and hold up the appropriate number of fingers for each verse as the children sing and act out the song.

✳ Sunny Days

Use the picture of the sun on the topic card on page 255 as a stencil and make several yellow felt suns. Cut out felt numerals that are appropriate for the children. Then have one child put several felt suns on the flannel board and a second child put up the correct numeral to tell how many suns are in that group. Have children continue to take turns creating other groups and matching numerals to them.

✳ Watermelon Match

Use construction paper to make a watermelon and color in the sections and seeds as shown. Also make a set of watermelon sections and write numerals on them, as shown. Have the children count the seeds in a section and then place the corresponding numeral on top.

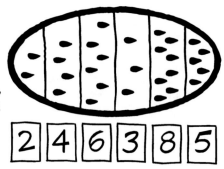

✳ Summer Flowers

Repeat variations of the Flower-pot Math activity (see p. 206). Make summer flowers with straw stems and construction-paper petals and leaves to place in small flowerpots with numerals on them. You can vary the activity in the following ways.

1. Increase the difficulty level by using larger numbers.
2. Have children find the flower that has the most petals and the least petals.
3. Have children find a flower that has one less petal than a particular flower.
4. Have children find a flower that has two more petals than a particular flower.

✳ Punched Numbers

Materials: plastic foam food trays; golf tees; markers

Use carpet scraps to protect tabletops. Have children write a numeral on a food tray and then use the tee to punch that number of holes in the tray. Children can work together to arrange the numerals in sequence from least to greatest and hang them with a string from the ceiling. As the pictures turn and the sunlight shows through the holes, talk about the patterns made by the light on the surfaces in the room. Compare these to the patterns made by the sun shining through the leaves of trees.

✳ Field-Day Measurements

Use a yardstick or meter stick to measure the width of the creek in the field-day Creek Jump activity (see p. 206) each time the width is changed.

✳ Summer Half and Summer Whole

Provide enough whole bananas for half the class. (Include yourself if there is an odd number of children.) Help the children count the number of children in the whole class. Divide the children into two groups and count each group. Discuss the total number in the whole class and the number in each of the two halves. Then have children count the number of bananas you brought. Ask children to figure out how everyone can share the bananas. If necessary, point out that the bananas can be cut in half. Have the children help you cut and serve the bananas.

✳ Searching for Shapes

Have children search the room for naturally occurring examples of all of the basic shapes.

✳ Geoboards

Materials: geoboards (see p. 221); colored rubber bands

Have children create geometric figures by stretching the rubber bands on the nails. Ask them to try to make as many different shapes as they can and count how many nails they used to make each shape. Have children draw each shape they make. At the bottom of their paper, ask them to write the numeral that shows how many shapes they made. Have children write their names on their sheet of drawings.

Ask them which shapes were the hardest to make on a geoboard (circles and ovals).

MOVEMENT

✳ Field Day

Hold a field day with several planned outdoor activities, such as races and hunts, in which everyone can participate. Minimize the element of competition and place the emphasis on having fun.

1. **Obstacle Course** – Set up an obstacle course and play Follow the Leader. Possible obstacles include chairs to climb over, tires or a ladder laying on the ground to walk through, boards to tiptoe on, and ropes to crawl under. The more variety the better. Let the children reorganize the obstacle course and then play Follow the Leader again.

2. **Creek Jump** – Create a creek by laying two pieces of rope on the ground so that they are parallel and close together. Have children take turns jumping the creek. Move the ropes a little further apart and let the children jump again. Continue spreading out the width of the creek as children continue to jump over it. Have them try jumping from a standing position and then from a running start.

3. **The Great Feather Blowup** – Provide a feather for each child. Their task is to keep the feather up in the air by blowing on it until you blow a whistle for time's up.

4. **Entanglement** – Have everyone hold hands. A leader begins weaving the line of people in and out between each other to entangle the line. Then the task is to get untangled and back into a straight line without letting go of each other's hands.

5. **Candy Hunt** – End the field day with a candy hunt. Hide 100 pieces of wrapped candy for the children to find. As children find the candy, have them line up the pieces in sets of fives or tens so that everyone can keep track of how many more pieces there are to search for. Have them share the candy equally when it is all found.

✳ Shadows

On a sunny day, have the children play shadow tag outside by running and trying to jump on someone else's shadow before he or she runs away. Discuss where the sun is and where children see shadows.

✳ Outside Tic-Tac-Toe

Use a stick to draw tic-tac-toe grids on the ground or use chalk on a sidewalk. Show children how to play tic-tac-toe by dropping beanbags on the squares. You will need ten bags for each game. Mark five beanbags with a large *X* and five with an *O* or use beanbags in two different colors.

MUSIC

✳ Shadow March

Play a recording of marching music outside on a sunny day. Have the children march in time to the music and watch their shadows move and change.

✳ Shadow Dancing

Materials: overhead projector

Have the children stand in front of the projector's light and move in time to the music. Encourage children to watch the movement of the shadows on the wall. Have children move only their hands, fingers, legs, upper body, or lower body. Remind children to move each part of the body in time to the music.

✳ Summer Song Writing

Sing "This Old Man" together. Then create new verses to go with summertime things.

This old man, he had fun.
He had fun in the hot summer _____ . (sun)
This old man, he ran a race.
He ran so fast he fell on his _____ . (face)
This old man, he liked to play.
He played outside on a summer _____ . (day)
This old man, he sat by a tree.
But he jumped up when he saw a _____ . (bee)

ROLE PLAY

✳ Beach Day

Provide items to use in role playing a day at the beach. Possible items include buckets and shovels for pretending to dig in the sand; a box of shells; sandals or thongs; a blanket or large towel to spread out for a picnic or sunbathing; sunglasses; a bathing cap; and an empty bottle for pretend sunscreen lotion.

✳ Tent

Make a large tent by draping a blanket over a clothesline or table. The children pretend to camp out. Provide real sleeping bags if possible or blankets or large towels that can be rolled up like bedrolls. Also include pans for cooking over a campfire and a flashlight.

SCIENCE

✳ The Sun

Share information about the sun and how important it is to our lives. Explain that it gives us heat and light and helps plants grow. Explain that the sun is a star even though it does not look like a star. Challenge children to talk with others to figure out what happens to the sun at night. Have them share their information during circle time.

✳ Sunlight and Shadows

Talk about what makes a shadow and where the sun has to be in order for shadows to appear. Read aloud Tana Hoban's *Shadows and Reflections* and Frank Asch's *Bear Shadow.* Bring a photographer's light or a lamp into the classroom. Move objects around in front of the light to make shadows. Turn off the light. Ask the children why the shadows disappear. Discuss shadows and what happens on sunny days and cloudy days. Talk about and show pictures of sundials.

✳ Shell Collection

Display several different types of shells. Talk about the animals that live in shells in the water. Provide a shoe box with sand in it so that children can bury and find the shells. Have children use the shells in the following ways.

1. Match shells of the same type.
2. Classify shells as small, medium, or large.
3. Classify shells into two or more groups by sorting them into piles. Explain the categories used for classifying the shells.
4. Use a magnifying glass to examine shells.
5. Talk about different shapes of shells. Show some that are mostly round and some that are long and narrow.

✳ Temperature Watching

Provide a real thermometer for children to observe and record daily temperatures. If a real thermometer is not available, use poster board to make a classroom thermometer. Draw the thermometer shape and write numerals for the temperatures. Cut a slot at the top and bottom to pull a piece of elastic through. Color half of the elastic red. Leave the other half white. Put the elastic through the slots and staple the ends together at the back of the thermometer. Move it so that the top of the red section lines up with the temperature for the day.

Encourage children to find out the temperature each morning before they come to school and write it down on a small piece of paper. Adjust the classroom thermometer each day to show the temperature that the children report. Post the notes on which they've written the temperature beside the thermometer. Adjust the thermometer again later in the day to show what happens to the temperature as the sun gets higher in the sky.

TRANSITION ACTIVITIES

✳ Sun Sponge

Provide a round yellow sponge. Toss the sponge to one child at a time. Say, "When you catch the sponge, tell what you like to do outside in the summer sun."

✳ Sun Positions

Make one 3-inch yellow, construction-paper circle for each child or duplicate the picture of the sun on the topic card on page 255. Pass out the sun shapes and give the children directions such as the following.

Make the sun shine over your head.
Move the sun back and forth by your face.
Put the sun on your right knee.
Move the sun up your left arm.

CHILDREN'S BOOKS

Adoff, A. *Touch the Poem.* New York: Blue Sky Press, 2000. Children can explore their senses with kid-friendly poetry throughout the seasons.

Anno, M. *Anno's Counting Book.* New York: Harper & Row, 1977. A wonderful wordless counting book that illustrates how a town grows through the seasons of the year.

Asch, F. *Bear Shadow.* New York: Aladdin, 1985. When his shadow scares a fish away, Bear tries to get rid of it.

Faulkner, L. *The Wide-Mouthed Frog.* New York: Dial, 1996. A wide-mouthed frog is interested in what other animals eat until he meets an alligator. The pop-open illustrations are fun.

Gottlieb, D. *Watermelon Day.* New York: Henry Holt, 1996. Jesse picks out a watermelon in her family's patch. She waits patiently for it to grow and ripen for her family's annual Watermelon Day celebration.

Heller, R. *The Reason for a Flower.* New York: Scholastic, 1983. Intriguing illustrations and nonfiction information told in rhyme.

Hoban, T. *Shadows and Reflections.* New York: Greenwillow, 1990. Hoban's wonderful photographs show the power of lines in reflections.

Lionni, L. *A Busy Year.* New York: Scholastic, 1992. Willie and Winnie love their tree through all of the seasons.

Maass, R. *When Summer Comes.* New York: Henry Holt, 1993. Summer fun activities shown for children across the United States; multicultural photographs.

Pallotta, J. *The Flower Alphabet Book.* Watertown, MA: Charlesbridge, 1990. Flowers representing every letter. Find out which can be added to tea or fed to chickens! Colorful illustrations plus lots of facts.

Sendak, M. *Chicken Soup with Rice.* New York: Houghton Mifflin, 1962. A patterned rhyme helps children learn the seasons and months of the year. Great to chant together.

Shaw, C. *It Looked Like Spilt Milk.* New York: Harper & Row, 1947. A pattern book using images in clouds. Rewrite the patterns using children's art for the illustrations.

Wiesner, D. *Sector 7.* New York: Clarion, 1999. On a school trip to the Empire State Building, a cloud befriends a boy and takes him to Sector 7. The boy's creativity soon influences how clouds are shaped.

APPENDIX I
FREE, INEXPENSIVE, OR SIMPLE-TO-MAKE TEACHING AIDS

✳ Blindfolds

If you know someone taking a long flight, ask him or her to save the blindfolds airlines sometimes provide to help people sleep. These blindfolds are less obtrusive and more comfortable for young children than a scarf tied around their heads.

✳ Chunky Crayons

Small or broken crayons can be remolded into a crayon with a different shape. Peel the paper off and separate by color. Put some crayons in a paper baking cup that is intended for lining muffin tins. Use multiple paper cups inside one another for strength. Place the cup into a microwave and cook on high for three to five minutes or until the crayons are melted to the consistency you prefer. Remove the cup and let it cool. Slip off the excess cups and reuse them. Peel the paper off the crayon chunk.

Remove the crayons before they are melted to a smooth consistency if you want them to produce a textured effect. Melt more than one color together for a multicolor effect.

✳ Feely Box or Mystery Bag

A feely box or mystery bag is an excellent way of having children use only their sense of touch to analyze objects. These devices introduce an element of surprise or mystery that children enjoy. Make a feely box by cutting a hole large enough for small hands to fit inside one end of a shoe box. Cut the toe off of a large sock. Pull the sock through the hole, leaving the bulk of the sock outside the box. Tape or glue the sock around the inside of the hole. Alternately, make a mystery bag by cutting off the bottom third of a jean leg. Sew one end shut and put a drawstring in the other end.

Add small objects to the feely box or mystery bag. Vary the number of objects and the complexity of the objects according to the readiness of the children. Use the feely box or mystery bag in the following ways.

1. Have children reach in to locate an object that you name. Explain that they can't peek into the bag.
2. Have children reach in and describe an object for others to name.
3. Have children reach in, feel an object, and name a related item displayed beside the bag or box. For example, "I feel a hammer. It goes with that nail."

✳ Flannel or Felt-Board Figures

Creating felt-board pieces for storytelling or other activities can be easy and inexpensive. Purchase nonwoven interfacing at a fabric or discount store. A yard provides enough interfacing for several stories or topics of study. Draw or trace figures on the interfacing. Use crayons or markers to color the pieces before cutting them out. If using crayons, lay a single layer of brown paper over the figures and press with a warm iron to set the color. Store in a folder with the story script or other unit activities. These figures are durable and easily adhere to the flannel board because they are so lightweight.

✳ Gluing Without Messes

Glue bottles can be frustrating and difficult for many small children to squeeze and handle successfully. They are also more expensive to replace than buying glue in bulk sizes. An alternative to messy, clogged glue bottles is to pour a small amount of glue on a butter tub lid or paper plate and let children use cotton swabs or small brushes as applicators. The clean up is simple and less glue is wasted.

✳ Lacing Cards

To make lacing cards, duplicate or trace any simple, topic-related shape on a piece of poster board or cardboard. Many of the pictures on the opening pages of the monthly sections work well as lacing card shapes. Use a hole punch to make holes every inch or so along the entire outside edge. Glue or tape one end of a piece of yarn to the top left edge of the shape. Encourage children to work from top to bottom and left to right as they lace the yarn in and out of the holes around the shape. Later you might want to number the holes so that the children follow a particular number sequence or pattern.

Hint: Stiffen the end of the yarn by wrapping tape around it or by dipping it in glue and drying it overnight.

✳ Lollipops for Transitions and Skill Development

Make a class-sized set of small construction cutouts stapled on craft sticks to resemble lollipops. Draw or write letters, words, numbers, or shapes on each lollipop.

The following are examples of what you could show.

1. Capital and lower-case letters
2. Numerals and groups of objects that show the same numbers
3. Geometric figures in different sizes and positions
4. Letters and pictures of objects beginning with those letters sounds
5. Colors and words for colors

Hand out a lollipop to each child and play one of the following games.

1. Find another child who has the lollipop that matches. When a match is made, the two children stand together.
2. Try to "sell" the lollipop by searching for someone who can correctly identify what is on the lollipop. When the "buyer" names the item, he or she is given the lollipop to try to sell to someone else. Children continue buying and selling lollipops as long as interest or time allows. Children repeat the following chant as they play: "Lollipop, lollipop. Who will buy my lollipop?"

Laminated cutouts work best because you can reuse one set of laminated lollipops by wiping off whatever has been drawn or written on them.

❋ Marker Holders

Turn an egg carton upside down and cut a hole in the bottom of each egg section. Place one marker upright in each hole to make it easily accessible.

❋ Sock Wipes

When working with chalk or wipe-off marking pens on a laminated surface, an overhead transparency, or a chalkboard, wear a sock on one hand and use it as an eraser as you work. The socks can be easily washed as needed. Also, provide socks for children to wear on one hand as they complete wipe-off folder games or chalk art.

❋ Sponges

Compressed sponges are available at hobby stores. They can be easily cut into desired shapes or smaller pieces. When put in water, they expand and enlarge.

❋ Stencils – Positive and Negative

When you cut stencils, you create both positive and negative stencils. It's like getting two for one! The positive stencil is the cutout object that can be traced around on the outside perimeter. The negative stencil is the stencil created when the cutout is removed. It can be traced on the inside of the frame. When stencils are small, younger children have more control and greater success with simple negative stencils.

❋ Sticker Match

Topic-related stickers of various kinds are available at many discount stores and teacher supply stores. Use those stickers to quickly create a matching game, a concentration game, and/or a bingo game. Limit the number of pairs of matching stickers to a number appropriate to the ability of the children.

APPENDIX II

ART RECIPES AND CONCOCTIONS

✳ Body Paint

1 cup inexpensive baby lotion
1 tablespoon liquid dish detergent
1 teaspoon tempera paint powder

Mix the ingredients. Add a few drops of water if the mixture is too thick.

✳ Bubble Solution

4 cups water
¼ cup light corn syrup
½ cup liquid dish detergent

Plastic-coated craft wire
Wire cutter

Thoroughly blend together the water and syrup. Then gently stir in the detergent. (If using very inexpensive detergent, use less water.) Store the solution in an airtight container.

To make a bubble wand, cut the wire into 6-inch to 8-inch lengths, one for each child. Shape the wire into a hoop with a handle. The children may dip their wands into the bubble mixture and blow into or wave the wand.

Note: Avoid adding food coloring to the solution as it can stain when the bubbles burst.

✳ Ceramic Dough

2 cups salt
⅔ cup water

½ cup cold water
1 cup cornstarch

Mix the salt and ⅔ cup of water together in a pan. Stir over medium heat until mixture is thoroughly heated (3–4 minutes). Remove from heat. Mix the cornstarch and ½ cup cold water together. Stir quickly into the first mixture. The final dough mixture should be stiff. If it does not thicken, reheat and stir for one more minute. Store in a plastic bag. Objects made from the dough can be left out to air dry for one to two days, depending on the size, and then painted with tempera paints.

✳ Cotton Dough Creations

2 cups flour
1 to 1½ cups water
Cotton balls

In a bowl, mix the flour and water a little at a time until they form a smooth paste. Cover the workspace with newspaper. Have children coat the cotton balls in the paste and then combine several balls to form creatures, letters, or creations of any shape. As the children create shapes, encourage them to maintain the puffy appearance of the balls rather than flattening them out. Place the creations on a cookie sheet. Bake them at 300° F for 30–45 minutes or until lightly browned and hard. They may be painted if desired.

✳ Hard-boiled Eggs and Dye

1 cup warm water
1 cup warm vinegar
2–3 drops food coloring

Hard-boiled eggs
Egg cartons

Stir the water, vinegar, and food coloring together in a small bowl. Dip each hardboiled egg in the solution until it's colored and then place the egg in an egg carton to dry.

Mix solutions of the three primary colors of yellow, red, and blue. Have children dip eggs in multiple colors and discuss how the colors of the dyed eggs change.

✳ Finger Paint

Liquid starch
Dry tempera powder
Small, clean sponges

Large pieces of white shelf paper or finger-painting paper

If using shelf paper, wipe each piece with a wet sponge so that the paint can be spread more easily. Place a drop of starch, about 1 to 2 inches in diameter, on each piece of wet paper. Sprinkle on the dry tempera powder. Have each child use one hand to mix the tempera and the starch together. After the tempera is well-mixed, have the children spread the color over the entire paper. They are now ready to finger paint.

With young children it is most effective to have them finger paint with only one hand, keeping the other hand behind their back or on their lap. This keeps one hand clean to scratch noses, open doorknobs, and to hug the teacher without a mess!

✳ Goo

White glue (not school glue)
Liquid starch
Paper cup

Popsicle stick or spoon
Food coloring (optional)
Plastic zippered bag

Pour equal amounts of glue and starch in a paper cup for each child. (For best results pour the glue into the cup first.) Add a small amount of food coloring if desired. Stir until the mixture forms a cohesive ball, then knead thoroughly until smooth. If the mixture is stringy, add more glue, a little at a time. Continue to knead the goo. Store in a plastic zippered bag.

✳ Modeling Dough

1 cup salt
1 cup flour

$\frac{3}{4}$ cup water
Food coloring

Mix flour and salt in a large bowl. Add water and mix well. Add food coloring if desired, or leave the dough white and paint the objects made with the dough with tempera paints when they are completely dry.

Store the modeling dough in plastic bags. Objects made from the dough can be left out to air dry for one to two days, depending on the size. The mixture can be spread on heavy-duty cardboard, and relief scenes can be created by digging out areas for ponds and roads or by building mountains and walls.

✳ Papier-Mâché Shapes

Medium- and large-sized heavyweight
    balloons
Flour and water paste, wallpaper paste,
    or liquid starch

Newspaper
Scissors (optional)
Tempera paints

Teach papier-mâché shape making as a group project first, before children attempt to make the shapes on an individual basis. Inflate one to three balloons and tie them off. Tear or let the children cut the newspaper into strips approximately 2 inches by 6 inches.

In a large bowl or plastic tub, gradually stir water into a cup of flour until it forms a paste. Alternately, use wallpaper paste or liquid starch. Demonstrate how to dip one entire paper strip into the paste, wipe off the excess paste by gently pulling the strip between two fingers, smooth the strip out on a balloon, and pat down the edges. Encourage the children to apply the strips repeatedly until each balloon is covered with one layer. Have them leave the tied end exposed. Allow the balloons to dry overnight on a piece of plastic.

Repeat the procedure the next day. Continue adding layers of newspaper strips over four or five days. When completed and dry, pop each balloon and pull it out of the papier-mache shape. The shape can be painted and details added to create a ball, globe, or other object.

✳ Play Dough

1 cup flour
½ cup salt
1 cup water

1 tablespoon cooking oil
2 teaspoons cream of tartar
Food coloring or tempera powder (optional)

Mix together all of the ingredients in a cooking pot. Heat the mixture over medium heat until it forms a ball. Knead the mixture for a few minutes to increase its smoothness. Store it in a plastic bag or a tightly covered container.

Before cooking the mixture, you may wish to add food coloring or dry tempera powder.

✳ Sawdust Molding Compound

1 cup sawdust
½ cup wallpaper paste
Water

Mix the dry ingredients together in a small bowl. Add water a little at a time until the compound is the consistency of soft putty. Have children mold the compound into a shape. Place the shape on a cookie rack to dry. The shape can be painted. Each recipe makes enough to form one shape.

✳ Soap Creations

3 cups Ivory® soap flakes
4 tablespoons warm water
Electric mixer

Mix the soap powder with water, adding the water a little at a time until the mixture forms a thick, claylike consistency. Give some of the mixture to each child to knead, squeeze, and explore. Talk about how it looks, feels, and smells. Have children mold the mixture into balls of soap or other desired shapes. The recipe makes about four cups.

✳ Sparkle Paint

½ cup flour
½ cup salt
½ cup water
Plastic squeeze bottles (optional)

1 teaspoon dry tempera powder
Paintbrushes
Poster board

Combine the flour, salt, water, and tempera powder to make paint. Have the children brush the paint on poster board. When the poster board dries, the salt will produce a sparkling look. Alternately, pour the paint into recycled plastic squeeze bottles such as liquid detergent bottles or mustard bottles. Place poster board in the bottom of shirt or dress boxes to limit the mess. Have children squeeze the mixture onto the pieces of poster board. Provide several different paint colors so that children can experiment with color blending as they paint.

APPENDIX III

ACTIVITY MASTERS

Activity Master 1: Alphabet Time, A–M 278

Activity Master 2: Alphabet Time, N–Z 279

Activity Master 3: Calendar 280

Activity Master 4: Look What I Can Do! Book (A) 281

Activity Master 5: Look What I Can Do! Book (B) 282

Activity Master 6: Look What I Can Do! Book (C) 283

Activity Master 7: Scarecrow Match 284

Activity Master 8: Circle Map 1 285

Activity Master 9: Circle Map 2 286

Activity Master 10: Tool Patterns 287

Activity Master 11: What Is Similar? What Is Different? 288

Activity Master 12: Pictographs 289

Activity Master 13: Toy Parts 290

Activity Master 14: Senses Chart 291

Activity Master 15: Circle Snow Person 292

Activity Master 16: Monster Chart 293

Activity Master 17: Monster Pattern 294

Activity Master 18: Dinosaur Shapes 295

Activity Master 19: Dinosaur Analogy 296

Activity Master 20: Drawing Starts 297

Activity Master 21: Graphing Grid 298

Activity Master 22: Kite Pattern 299

Activity Master 23: Number Cube Pattern 300

Activity Master 24: Comparing Caterpillars Chart 301

Activity Master 25: Floats and Sinks Cards 302

Alphabet Time, A–M

Activity Master 1

Name ____________________ Topic ____________________

A ____

B ____

C ____

D ____

E ____

F ____

G ____

H ____

I ____

J ____

K ____

L ____

M ____

See Introduction, page xi.

Name ____________________ Topic ____________________

N ______________________________

O ______________________________

P ______________________________

Q ______________________________

R ______________________________

S ______________________________

T ______________________________

U ______________________________

V ______________________________

W ______________________________

X ______________________________

Y ______________________________

Z ______________________________

See Introduction, page xi.

Calendar

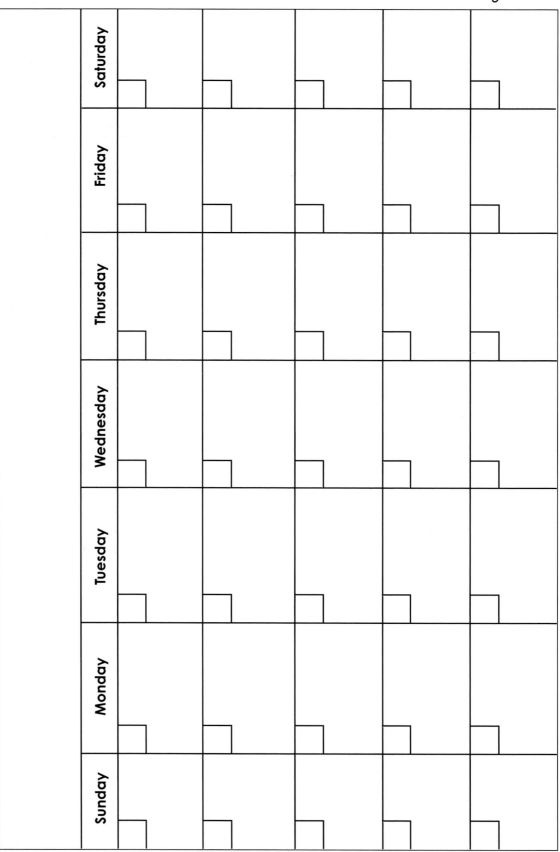

Sunday	Monday	Tuesday	Wednesday	Thursday	Friday	Saturday

Use to create a monthly calendar. See page xv.

Look What I Can Do!

by

_____

Date _____

✂

1. This is a picture of me.

2. I can write these numerals.

3. I can write these letters.

Look What I Can Do! Book (C)

4. I can draw these shapes.

5. This is what I like to do.

Scarecrow Match

Use with *Scarecrow Match*, page 37.

Circle Map 1

Rosie's Walk by Pat Hutchins

Rosie the hen went for a walk . . .

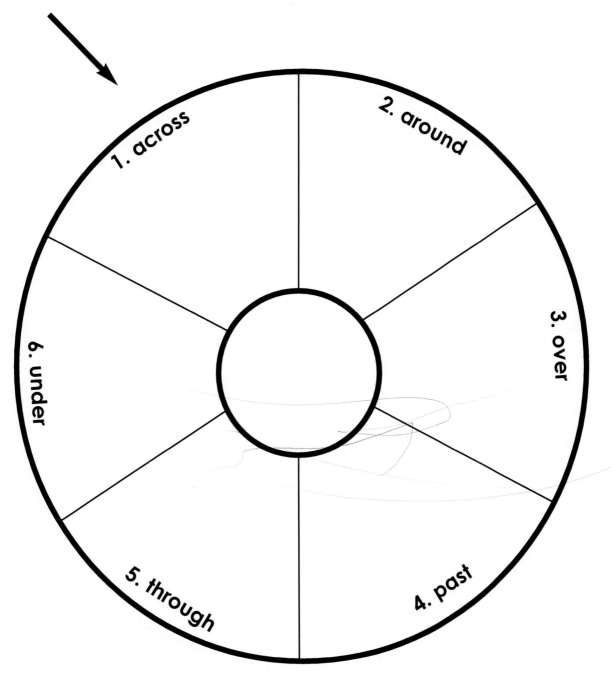

. . . and got back in time for dinner.

Use with *Going for a Walk*, page 49.

Circle Map 2

_____'s Walk

_____ went for a walk . . .

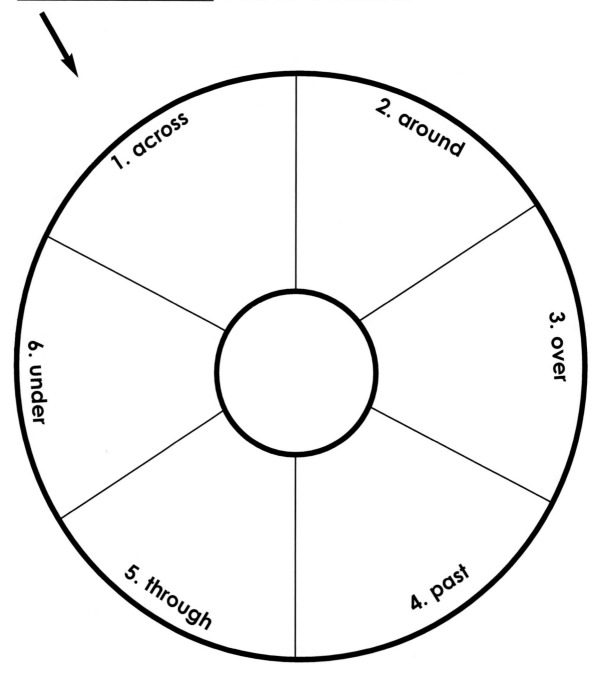

1. across
2. around
3. over
4. past
5. through
6. under

. . . and got back in time for _____ .

Use with *Going for a Walk*, page 49.

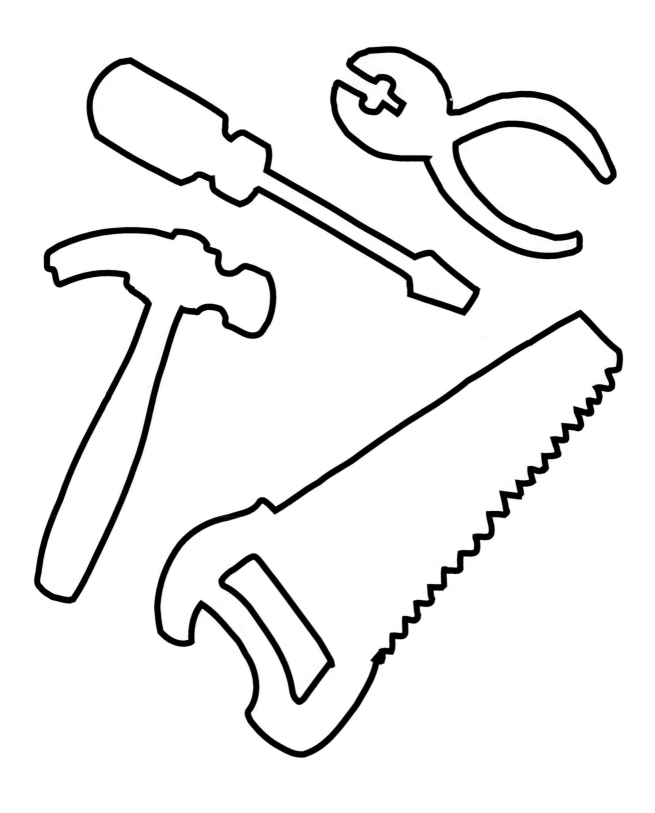

Use with *Splatter Painting*, page 58.

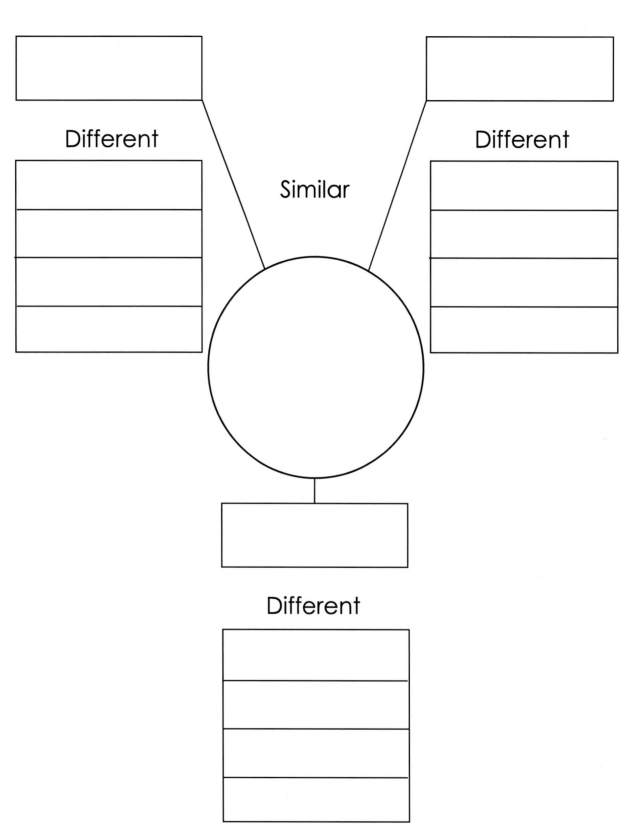

Different

Different

Similar

Different

Use with *Similar and Different*, page 62.

Pictographs

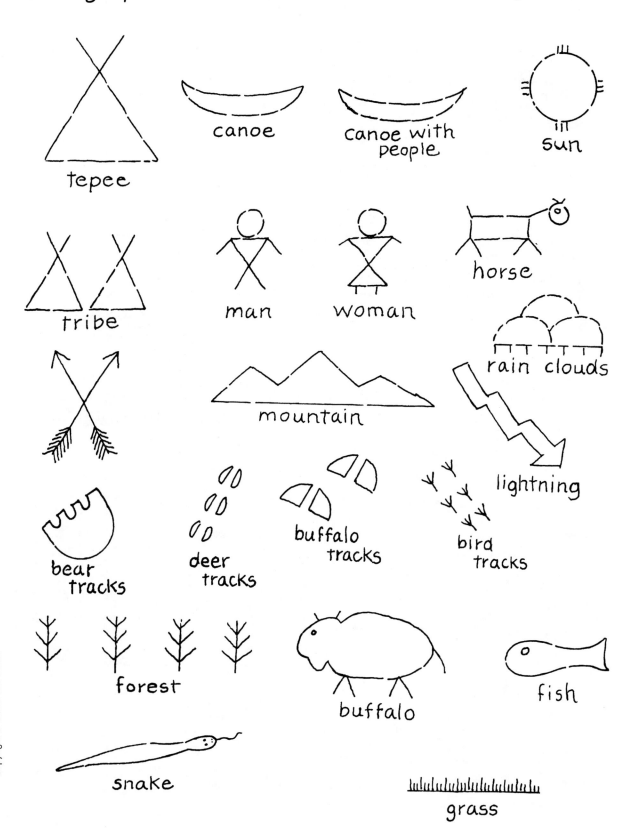

tepee

canoe

canoe with people

sun

tribe

man

woman

horse

mountain

rain clouds

lightning

bear tracks

deer tracks

buffalo tracks

bird tracks

forest

buffalo

fish

snake

grass

Toy Parts

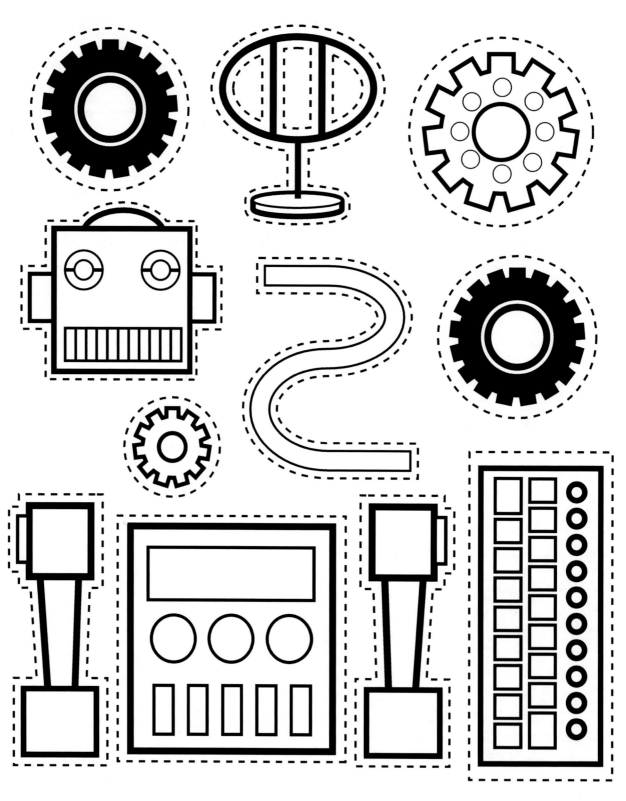

Use with *Create a Toy*, page 87.

Name _____

	I can see . . .
	I can hear . . .
	I can touch or feel . . .
	I can taste . . .
	I can smell . . .

Use with *Signs of Winter*, page 117.

Use with *Shapes: Circles*, page 119.

Monster Chart

Use with *Real or Imaginary*, page 130.

Monster Pattern

Use with *Make a Monster*, page 132.

Dinosaur Shapes

Use with *Dinosaur Macaroni Collage*, page 155.

Dinosaur Analogy

Name _____

If I were a dinosaur, I would

be a _____

because _____

_____

_____

_____.

Use with *Creative Analogies,* page 160.

Drawing Starts

Name _____

Use with *Animal Drawing Starts*, page 170.

Graphing Grid

Use with *Bird Graph*, page 191.

Kite Pattern

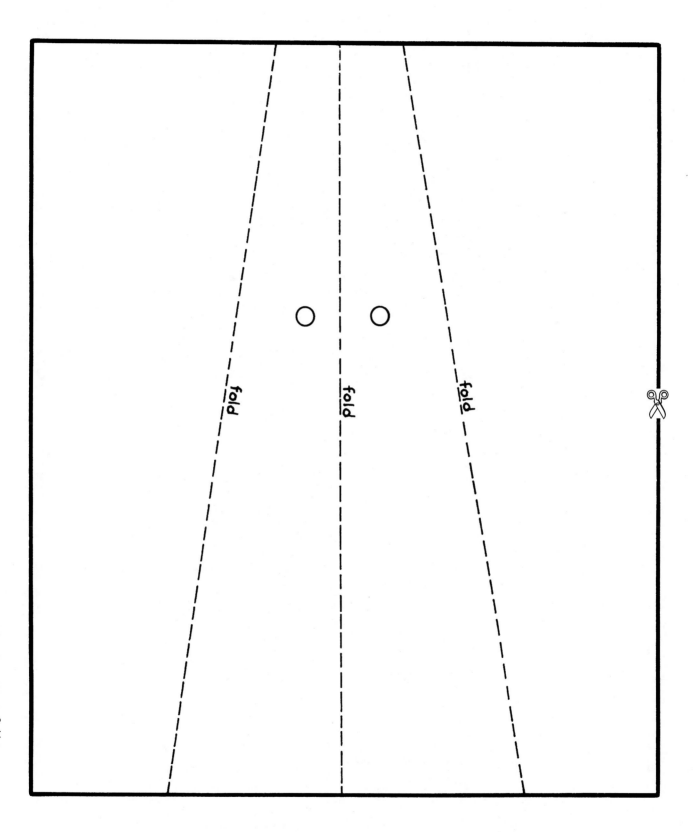

fold

fold

fold

Use with *Kites*, page 201.

Number Cube Pattern

Use with *Number Bingo*, page 206.

Comparing Caterpillars Chart

The Very Hungry Caterpillar

Real Caterpillars

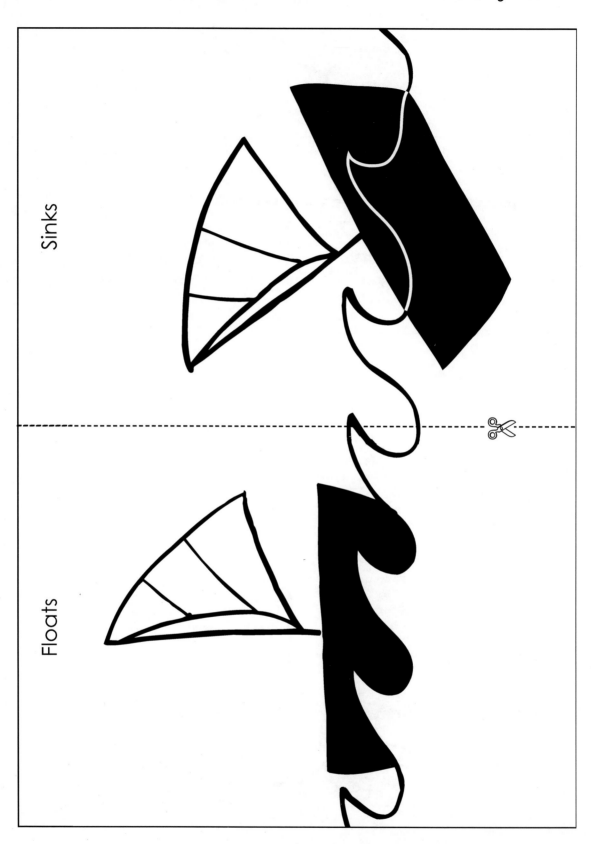

Sinks

Floats

Use with *Floats–Sinks Experiment*, page 253.